The Origin of Heresy

Routledge Studies in Religion

For Anne Beeson Royalty

Contents

Preface

This book has two points of origin in my graduate studies at Yale University: seminars on Justin Martyr and the second century with Bentley Layton; and extensive research on the Book of Revelation, guided by Susan Garrett and Wayne Meeks. I was fortunate to have these excellent teachers at Yale. As I finished my first book on Revelation, I became intrigued by how the harsh polemics of the Apocalypse were directed against other Christians, demonized as satanic enemies within the churches. In fact, the entire New Testament is full of such rhetoric—the rhetoric against intimate enemies that becomes heresy. Although Justin has been credited with creating the rhetoric of heresy, it was clear to me that this discourse began much earlier and developed throughout the first century. This book began as my attempt to connect the ragged edges of what became the New Testament texts, including Revelation, to the heresiological discourses of the second century, from Justin onwards.

A National Endowment for the Humanities Research Fellowship and a Stanford Humanities Center External (Visiting) Fellowship in 2005–2006 were essential for getting this project off the ground. I am very grateful for the support of the NEH and Stanford. We enjoyed a wonderful year at the Humanities Center, discussing ideas of all sorts, including my own, with a lively and stimulating group of fellows, including John Bender, Marcus Folch, Jehangir Malegam, Steven Justice, and Johannes Fabian; the Religious Studies Department at Stanford, including Arnold Eisen, Hester Gelber, and Brent Sockness; and the Empires and Cultures Workshop in the History Department. I would also like to thank Robert Gregg, Dale Martin, and William Placher (RIP 2008) for their early support of this project. In addition, I am thankful for a sabbatical and research support from Wabash College and the resources of Lilly Library, including the invaluable support of Susan Albrecht and Deborah Polley. And I am thankful to Laura Sterns and the editorial and production staff at Routledge for accepting this book and for their assistance in bringing it to publication expeditiously.

Several portions of this book have been presented at conferences of the European Association of Biblical Studies (Lisbon 2008 and Lincoln 2009, with special thanks to Moshe Lavee and Ronit Nikolsky), the Oxford

Patristics Conference (2007), and meetings of the Society of Biblical Literature in Boston (2008) and Rome (2009), as well as the Wabash College Humanities Colloquium. Conversations with colleagues including Denise Buell, Stephen Davis, Nicola Denzey Lewis, Rebecca Lyman, Outi Lehtipuu, Elaine Pagels, Gary Phillips, and Greg Snyder have been very helpful along the way. Colleagues kind enough to comment on earlier drafts include Christopher Frilingos, Susan Garrett, Michael Penn, William Placher, and James Watts. I am very thankful for their time and insights, as well as the comments of the anonymous readers of the manuscript. All mistakes remain my own.

Above all I am thankful for the support of my children, Nolen and Ginna, and my wife, Anne Beeson Royalty, during the years of hard work on this project. I dedicate this book to her with much love and affection.

PERMISSIONS

Quotations from the Bible are from the New Revised Standard Version Bible, copyright 1989, Division of Christian Education of the National Council of the Churches of Christ in the United States of America. Used by permission. All rights reserved.

Portions of Chapter 6 were originally published in "Dwelling on Visions: The Nature of the So-Called 'Colossians Heresy,'" *Biblica* 83 (2002): 329–57. Used by permission.

Abbreviations

Abbreviations are from *The SBL Handbook of Style for Ancient Near Eastern, Biblical, and Early Christian Studies*, ed. Patrick H. Alexander et al. (Peabody, MA: Hendrickson, 1999).

1Q, 2Q, 4Q, 5Q	Scrolls from Qumran Caves 1, 2, 4, 5
Ps.-Clem.	*Pseudo-Clementines*
Dio *Nicom.*	Dio Chrysostom, *To the Nicomedians*
Ep. Barn.	*Epistle of Barnabas*
Haer.	Irenaeus, *Adversus Haereses*
Ign.	Ignatius
Jos. *Ant., J.W.*	Josephus *Antiquities, Jewish War*
Jus. *Apol., Dial.*	Justin, *Apology, Dialogue with Trypho*
LSJ	Liddell, Scott and Jones, *A Greek-English Lexicon*
Luc.	Lucian
MT	Masoretic Text (of the Hebrew Bible)
OTP	Charlesworth, *Old Testament Pseudepigrapha*
Plat. *Apol.*	Plato, *Apology*
Pliny *Ep.*	Pliny the Younger, *Letters*
Suet. *Claud.*	Suetonius, *Claudius*
Wis. Sol.	*Wisdom of Solomon*
Xen.	Xenophon

Part I
Genealogy of a Discourse

1 The Origin of Heresy

There are so many ways to commit heresy these days as to suggest the old adage that it's getting hard to commit an original sin. One can commit heresy by serving the wrong wine at dinner, breaking with your political party on a policy, running on third-and-long, or changing a business plan. Every business, group, club, and organization seems to have its "heretics" who challenge the "reigning orthodoxy" of the system. One can still, of course, commit heresy the old-fashioned way—in a religious community.[1] Christians invented this concept still used so widely today. While shared among several religions, the idea of "heresy" is central to the history of Christianity, from the fourth-century ecumenical councils of Nicea and Chalcedon, to the Medieval Inquisition and Reformation, to recent clashes over sexual practice and critical church histories.

The word "heresy" comes from the ancient Greek word *hairesis*, meaning a choice, school of thought, sect, or party, which was itself derived from the verb *haireō*, which meant to choose or prefer one thing over another. The word *hairesis* had wide, fairly common, and non-pejorative meanings in the ancient Hellenistic world.[2] The meaning of the word changes, however, from the late first century CE, when it appears in writings of the Jewish historian Flavius Josephus and the Acts of the Apostles to designate what we might call denominations or sects of Judaism, to the middle of the second century, when Christian writers start to employ it with the technical sense of incorrect doctrine, religious deviance, or error.[3]

That significant ideological shift in the meaning of *hairesis* is the focus of this book: the origins of "heresy" in early Christianity and the development of heresiology, the Christian genre of polemical rhetoric against "heretics." The development of heresiology in orthodox Christianity from the second century CE onwards has been well studied by historians of the early Church; I will begin with a summary of that story. But going deeper into the origins, or genealogy, of the *idea* of heresy takes me to the rhetoric of difference and disagreement in the first-century texts of the New Testament and the writings of Second Temple Judaism. Here, I argue, we find the origin of what comes to be labeled "heresy" in the second century. In other words, there was such a thing as "heresy" in ancient Jewish and Christian discourse before it was called "heresy."

This discourse, the rhetoric of difference that becomes orthodox Christian heresiology, can be located in political conflicts between Christian groups of the first century. I argue that the orthodox project of political hegemony under the ideological banner of Christian unity begins, as with all the different aspects of Christianity, in the first century among Jesus' earliest followers. This book joins the larger historical project among scholars of early Christianity to recover lost and suppressed Christian voices. In addition to expressing my commitment to an ethic of theological diversity within Christianity, this book should call into question the demonizing, destructive heresiological patterns that continue to mark our religious and political rhetoric. Such correlations might be hard to break, since they are integral to the Christian notion of heresy. As a regime of knowledge and technology of power within early Christian social formations, the notion of heresy has had a political function, from its origins in apocalyptic Judaism and contested identities of "Israel" to its central polemical role in early Christian discourse. By the beginning of the second century, the notion of heresy was central to the political positioning of the early orthodox Christian party within the Roman Empire against a range of other Christian groups.

In this chapter, I introduce that claim by reconsidering traditional constructions of the origins of Christianity in a framework of truth preceding error, or "orthodoxy" before "heresy"; the thorny problems in constructing the history of earliest Christianity from the New Testament, which was assembled much later than the first century; and the methodological issues in reading these early texts as "Christian." I will describe my methodology of reading these texts by means of the rhetoric of difference and exclusion, with attention to Christian communities as colonial locations within the Roman Empire. I conclude with an outline of the book, my thesis, and the rhetoric of early Christian heresiology.

SPEAKING CHRISTIAN

The notion of heresy, I maintain, is integral to how people "speak Christian" and thus to Christian identity. This specifically Christian way of identifying and dealing with ideological difference has had long-lasting and profound effects on both Christian and later Islamic cultures. But it is important to clarify that I am using the word "Christian" as shorthand for one *type* of ancient Christianity, the party (a term I prefer because of its political connotations) that chose the term "orthodox" or "right-thinking" for themselves. Christian churches and denominations today, from Greek Orthodox (which retains the ancient name) and Roman Catholic to Baptist and Pentecostal churches, are theological descendants of the ancient orthodox Christians. As wide as the range of Christian beliefs and practices might appear today, it was even more diverse in the Roman Empire during the first few centuries. The range of people who took the name Christian—or who might be called "Christians" by historians today—was vast.

The orthodox party held that the ancient Hebrew Scriptures applied to Jesus of Nazareth and should be read as an "Old Testament"; that Jesus was both an actual man and the son of God; and that his death and resurrection were salvific acts of God in human history. That is an over-simplification but one intended to mark the similarities of modern Christian beliefs and the ancient orthodox Christians. Many if not most Christians today would find some point of agreement in these three dogmatic positions. But many, maybe even most people who followed Jesus of Nazareth in the first century had quite different ideas about who he was, where he came from, and what his death meant (if his death mattered to them at all). These other groups are often called Gnostic Christians, Marcionite Christians, Jewish Christians, and other inflected variations (inflections that retain the notion of "orthodox" origins). Scholars have even argued whether the word "Christian" should be used at all to describe these first- or second-century communities. I will, however, be more promiscuous in the use of the terms "orthodox" and "Christian" than many recent scholars. For the latter, I will include any text or group that focused their philosophy, belief, or practices on Jesus as a Christian text or community, regardless of whether they used the term. This would include Paul, the communities that produced the "Q source" found in Matthew and Luke, and the Gospel of Matthew itself. By so doing I do not mean to shoehorn the doctrine and ideology of fourth-century orthodox Christianity into these first-century texts and communities but rather to recognize some family resemblance within this wide diversity of belief and practices. And, as discussed ahead, I am *not* arguing for a common core of "true Christianity" in the first or second century. Furthermore, I will apply the term "orthodox," in lowercase, more freely than even the current favorite "proto-orthodox," not theologically but as a discursive and political label for leaders and communities in the generation after Paul, including some Gospel writers, disciples of Paul who wrote in his name, Ignatius of Antioch and Polycarp of Smyrna.[4] Within this wide variety of early Christianity, I will identify the ones who "spoke Christian" in ways that continue to mark Christian discourse today by employing the rhetoric of heresiology as the foundation of what came to be orthodox Christianity. Let us now turn to the acknowledged practitioners of this way of speaking Christian in the second century.

THE ORIGIN OF HERESY

The standard account for the origin of Christian heresiology begins with Justin of Flavia Neapolis about one hundred years after Paul founded churches in Asia and Greece.[5] Justin and the other second-century Christians discussed here might not be as familiar as Paul, Jesus, and his disciples. Justin was a teacher and apologist ("defender") of "Christians." He wrote two *Apologies* to the Emperor of Rome, who no doubt never received nor read them, as well as an intriguing *Dialogue* with a Jewish character of Justin's own literary creation named Trypho. An earlier contemporary of Justin by the name of Hegesippus was one of the first Christian historians. His writings are known only through Eusebius of Caesarea, whose fourth-century *Ecclesiastical History* (*E.H.*) provides an invaluable narrative of the development of Christianity—from his particular point of view and his strong advocacy of the Emperor Constantine. He quotes numerous texts at length, some of which would be otherwise lost. Irenaeus was a Christian bishop who wrote in Gaul (modern France) around 180 CE. He was a central figure in forming the New Testament canon as well as attacking a group of Christians he called "Gnostics."

These so-called Gnostics were part of a larger group of second-century Christian authors known mainly through the writings of their opponents, such as Justin and Irenaeus, until the Nag Hammadi texts were discovered in 1948 in Egypt. This was the greatest single trove of documents for non-orthodox ancient Christianities.[6] These Christian teachers were attacked and excluded by the orthodox as "heretics" from Justin and Irenaeus until late antiquity. The attacks could be bitter and harsh, and from our perspective often unfair, since orthodox writers distorted and misquoted their opponents' views. Not all orthodox Christians approached Gnostics the same way, of course. The philosopher Valentinus, while grouped among the "Gnostic" texts found at Nag Hammadi, was read and admired by orthodox writers such as Clement of Alexandria.

Around 150 CE, Justin faced a political problem. His church name, St. Justin Martyr, reveals the stakes at hand. And names were important for him, particularly the use of the name "Christian," which, as with the name and identity of "Jews," was in considerable flux at this time. In his *First Apology* addressed to the Emperor Antoninus Pius and his sons, the Senate, and the people of Rome, Justin argues that Jesus' followers have been condemned merely for the name "Christians" and that they deserve a fair hearing based on their deeds.[7] Yet in defending Christians from attack on this name alone, Justin does not mean *all* Christians. There are many who take this same name whom Justin does not defend (*1 Apol.* 7.3). An important part of his task in this *Apology* is to separate the "right-thinking" (*orthognōmoi*) Christians, including himself and his followers, from these others who also claim the name *Christianoi*. While his party of "right-thinking" Christians should not be condemned by the name alone, Justin offers no defense for these others. Rather, he attacks them.

In roughly the center of the speech, Justin turns directly against these other Christian teachers as part of his appeal to the Romans that his group "be accepted . . . because we are speaking the truth" (*1 Apol.* 23.1).[8] He claims that Simon, Menander, and Marcion, and their followers, all of whom are *called* Christians, really teach ideas put forth by demons.[9] These demons are central to the genealogical relationship Justin constructs for the other Christian teachers.[10] According to Justin, Simon Magus (the Simon of Acts 8:9–13) was a magician who traveled with a former prostitute, Helen, and was worshipped in Rome as a god.[11] Menander was a disciple of Simon's who, under demonic influence, deceived Christians at Antioch by magic arts. Finally Marcion, still active as a teacher in Justin's time, has "by the help of demons made many in every race of men to blaspheme and to deny God the Maker of the Universe." He insinuates that perhaps followers of *these* teachers have committed the "shameful deeds" (*ta dysphēma ekeina mythologoumena*, 26.7) fabled among the Romans. He calls the teachings of Simon and company "heresies" (*haireseis*, 26.8), and refers to a *Syntagma* or treatise "against all the *haireseis* that have arisen," the first Christian work of this kind.[12]

Justin's *Syntagma* has been lost, but this attack on other Christians in his *First Apology* has a parallel in his other major surviving text, the *Dialogue with Trypho*, written after the *Apology* but set in Ephesus during the 130s, close to the time of the Bar Kokhba war between the Romans and the Jews in Palestine.[13] The *Dialogue* begins with a stylized account of Justin's exploration of the four philosophical schools, his adoption of Platonism, and his conversion to Christianity.[14] An extensive dialogue follows between Justin and Trypho over the Christian interpretation of the Jewish scriptures.[15] In *Dial.* 35, responding to Justin's charges of Jewish "error" and "misinterpretation," the interlocutor Trypho presses him on why there are other teachers who take the name "Christian" but differ on practices such as eating meat purchased from the Greek temple. Justin argues that all who confess Jesus do not necessarily teach the doctrines of Jesus but rather the doctrines of various "false teachers." These blaspheming teachers utter "spirits of error" (*tēs planēs pneumatōn*) rather than truth (35.2).[16] As for those who follow these teachers, they should not be called "Christians" at all but rather Marcians, Valentinians, Basilidians, or Saturnilians after the teacher they follow.

Justin's task of defending the name "Christian" to the Romans is politically undermined by others claiming the same name but with different ideas; explaining Christianity to Trypho is ideologically complicated by the existence of other Christian teachers who hold different views. In both the *First Apology* and the *Dialogue with Trypho*, Justin employs heresiological constructions—that is, labeling a Christian opponent who has different ideas, beliefs, or practices as a "heretic"—when pressed on the issue of diversity among Christians. His heresiological rhetoric includes slandering their teaching, deeds, and moral character; and uniting these philosophers and groups genealogically under demonic influence in opposition to the "right-thinking" Christians, when in fact these other teachers were either legendary (in the case of Simon Magus) or unrelated to each other (in the case of Menander and Marcion). Justin employs the rhetoric of heresy as a discursive solution to the political problem of other Christian teachers with a diversity of different views that transgress the ideological boundaries of his own party.[17]

Orthodox writers follow Justin. In the last decades of the second century, Irenaeus combines Justin's heresiological rhetoric with the ideology of "apostolic tradition" to define the political and theological boundaries of orthodoxy.[18] The Latin writers Hippolytus and Tertullian also compose heresiological works, as do later authors such as Epiphanius and Augustine, and the genre becomes entrenched in orthodox Christianity.[19] Nevertheless, it has been argued that Justin was the first Christian writer to construct a unified description of differing and diverse Christian teachers and philosophers by construing these systems of thought as "*objets de connaissance*" (constructs) and labeling them as "heretics."[20] As a technical term in Christian texts, then, *hairesis* has been well known in Christian discourse since the second century.

Justin could be called the first Christian heresiologist. But he is by no means the first Christian writer to respond discursively to difference by marginalizing and demonizing Christian opponents. The negotiation with ideological differences in Justin's writings draws on patterns already established in early Christian discourse to identify "truth" and "error." Justin was adopting a cluster of rhetorical gestures inscribing political practices that have roots in Second Temple Jewish and early Christian discourse. The discursive practice of heresiology precedes Justin, even if the word *hairesis* is not used. Following Foucault, I am looking for the origin of the *idea* that someone could be a "heretic," a genealogy of heresiology.[21] Whereas Justin is generally recognized as marking the beginning of the "notion of heresy," to use Le Boulluec's phrase, he is the endpoint of my project. This discursive response to ideological difference was formed in the political contexts and conflicts of first-century Christian communities.

I situate this project in dialogue with recent scholarship on the formation of early Christian identity.[22] Three aspects distinguish my project. First, while there are multiple dimensions to the formation of group identity, my focus is the notion of heresy itself. I focus on the ideology of difference exclusively, rather than including broader questions about group socialization, practices, textual production, or other aspects of identity formation. The origin of heresiology as a political project is central. Second, my project differs from scholarship that focuses on polemical tropes in Christian discourse that function as part of heresiological rhetoric, such as sexual invective and slander, but do not analyze the notion of heresy itself.[23] My analysis will always move to the ideology of these rhetorical devices—the responses to difference theorized as "heresy" no matter the images employed.

Third, I will explore the idea of heresy in both the Second Temple Jewish and early Christian texts, including the texts in the canonical New Testament that have been excluded from the study of early Christian heresiology. While my project engages scholarship on Christian heresiology that, for the most part, begins the story with Justin and other second-century figures, the genealogy of heresy shifts focus from the second century CE to the last two centuries BCE and the first century CE and an earlier body of Jewish and Christian literature.[24] The notion of heresy can be identified before Justin's writings, in earlier Jewish and Christian texts, including those in the New Testament. The ideology of heresy precedes the technical use of the term. Opposition and disagreement among the followers of Jesus date to the controversies within the Pauline communities, the interactions between Paul and the Palestinian Jesus movement, and the activity of John the Baptist and Jesus themselves. And there were Jewish traditions of negotiating religious difference and disagreement that were hundreds of years old before John, Jesus, or Paul began to teach and preach. This genealogy looks for the origins of second-century heresiology in these texts and historical moments where the notion of heresy is first expressed.

Of course, historical study of the New Testament has a complex set of methodological problems. On the one hand, most of the first-century Christian texts still extant are New Testament texts. But the New Testament did not exist in the first century. What becomes the canon of the New Testament formed over hundreds of years, from the second to the fourth century and beyond, after which alternative texts and Christianities, non-orthodox Christianities, did not disappear. The methodological problem of the canon has divided critical scholarship on the New Testament from the history of early Christianity and the study of heresiology, which has focused almost exclusively on later or non-canonical Christian texts. The reasons the New Testament has taken a backseat in the history of heresiology has to do with the historiography of Christianity, a historiography that has often kept exegesis of the New Testament separate from the historical study of early Christianity by preserving an ideology of unity within the New Testament texts. How this came to be is a story worth re-examining.

THE HISTORIOGRAPHY OF HERESY: TRUTH BEFORE ERROR

In his attack on other Christian teachers, Justin employs the theme of an original truth and unity within the first followers of Jesus that is corrupted by teachers such as Simon under the influence of demons. The notion of truth preceding error implied in Justin's *Dialogue* is more fully expressed in the *Hypomnēmata* or "Memoirs" of Hegesippus. Written perhaps contemporaneously with Justin's *Apology*, it is here that we find the classic historiography of truth and error in early Christianity.

While no original copy of Hegesippus' *Hypomnēmata* survives, Eusebius includes an excerpt from it in his *Ecclesiastical History* that deals with the "beginning of the *haireseis* of his time" (*E.H.* 4.22).[25] The heresiology could be as much Eusebius' as Hegesippus' and should be read critically. Nonetheless, according to the excerpts we have, Hegesippus placed the beginning of heresies "after James the Just had suffered martyrdom." This James was the brother of Jesus, a man so holy his knees had grown "hard like a camel's because of his constant worship of God" (*E.H.* 2.23.6). He was a central figure in the Jerusalem Church (see Gal 1:18–20; 2:1–12).[26] His death would have been around 62 CE, some thirty years after the crucifixion of Jesus and close to time of the legendary date of Paul's death under Nero. At this point, Hegesippus writes, "they called the church virgin [*parthenon*], for it had not been corrupted by vain messages" (*E.H.* 4.22.4). But Thebouthis, who lost an election for bishop to a cousin of Jesus named Symeon, began the corruption of the church with "the seven heresies" at this point: "Simon, whence the Simonians, and Cleobius, whence the Cleobians, and Dositheus, whence the Dosithians," and so on (*E.H.* 4.22.6). [27] Each of the "vain messages" (*akoais mataiais*) or "heresies" that corrupt the "virgin church" had a founder and school, paralleling the genealogical web of opposition in Justin's writings. These commonalities suggest shared heresiological sources.[28] A second excerpt follows in Eusebius: "The same writer also described the sects which once existed among the Jews as follows: 'Now there were various opinions [*gnōmai diaphorai*] among the circumcision, among the children of Israel, against the tribe of Judah and the Messiah as follows: Essenes, Galileans, Hemerobaptists, Masbothei, Samaritans, Sadducees, and Pharisees'" (*E.H.* 4.22.7).[29] Eusebius ends the excerpt here, but the fourth-century historian adds a second dimension to the heresiology of the otherwise lost writings of Hegesippus. By pairing the quotations, Eusebius elides Hegesippus' description of the "corrupting" Christian *haireseis* with the teachings of Jewish *gnōmai diaphorai*, a heresiological move that could have been original to Hegesippus.

By placing this "corruption" after the death of James, Hegesippus significantly places the penetration of the so-called "virgin church" by "error" in the period after Jesus' immediate followers have died. According to Eusebius, there was some unity (*henosin*) in the church of the original apostles, who had, to this point, safeguarded the doctrine delivered by Jesus and kept the church "pure."[30] But it becomes "contaminated" by Theboutis' jealousy and association with Jewish *gnōmai diaphorai* in the next generation. This ancient idea that unity and doctrinal purity preceded divisions, that truth precedes error, has been a central tenet of Christian historiography. Ecclesiastical history becomes the story of the preservation of true doctrine despite heretical challenges that arise starting in the generation *after* the apostles, the so-called "post-apostolic" period. The church, under continuous assault from Satan, heretics, and persecutions, has preserved the essential truth of Christian orthodoxy ever since, according to this view.

But the study of early Christian origins has undergone a transformation in the past seventy-five years that has revised scholarly notions of orthodoxy, heresy, and the historiography of truth preceding error. While the roots of this sea-change are found in the origins of the historical-critical method and William Wrede's 1897 call for a thoroughly skeptical history of the early Christian religion, the methodological starting point for this project is Walter Bauer's seminal *Orthodoxy and Heresy in Earliest Christianity*.[31] Bauer critiqued the concept of "orthodoxy" as an original or majority position within early Christianity and the idea that heresy was a later, minority corruption of or reaction to orthodoxy. The Bauer thesis was that orthodoxy was a political movement, centered in Rome and a minority within the range of early Christianities, which over time gained control over various other schools of Christianity around the Mediterranean.[32] In 1971, at the same time *Orthodoxy and Heresy* was translated into English, the work of Robinson and Koester advanced the Bauer thesis for a new generation of scholars.[33] The significant work of Le Boulluec on "*la notion d'hérésie*" rather than heresy itself brought the critical historical methods of Michel Foucault to bear on the study of the construction of heresy in early Christianity.[34] Such new post-modern methodologies and an intense focus on noncanonical sources such as the Nag Hammadi texts have brought the study of what was previously called "heresy" to an intensity that Bauer might not have imagined. The literature is vast, but recent significant publications signal the importance of the Christian groups previously labeled "heretics," by historians as well as church councils, for our complete understanding of the development of Christian theology and social formations.[35]

Orthodoxy is no longer seen among historians as the original position of the so-called "apostolic church" but as a political, ecclesial, and theological ideology that formed from the second to fourth centuries, a view that is well anchored in the more extensive sources from that period. First-century Christian social formations did not have the unity imagined by church historians such as Hegesippus and Eusebius. Designations such as the "pure apostolic church" were constructed by the Orthodox party, which anchored its legitimacy in the ideology of an unbroken apostolic tradition from Jesus to Irenaeus and beyond.[36] So we return to the messy methodological problem of the New Testament canon as our source for earliest Christianity, which includes most of the earliest Christian writings. The canon gives the veneer of Christian unity to the New Testament period. But there was, of course, no "New Testament period" any more than there was a pure apostolic church. "New Testament Christianity" as read through the canon is a construct of Christian unity, uncritically preserving Hegesippus' historiography of error (i.e., non-canonical sources) creeping in *after* the death of the apostles and corrupting the unified Church. The montage that becomes the New Testament was formed according to notions of "apostolic tradition" from the late second to the fourth century.

It is in fact the inscribed rhetorics of difference and ideology of heresy in this variety of texts in the New Testament that I am interested in uncovering. But is it methodologically possible to write a history of discourse with these first-century texts that became, over the course of later centuries, the foundation of both Christian orthodoxy and Christian historiography? Bauer himself did not use the New Testament, deeming it "too unproductive" and "too disputed" as a source for understanding the history of heresy and orthodoxy.[37]

These methodological problems for the historical study of first-century Christian texts are aggravated by the canonical bent of New Testament studies, which tends towards exegesis of single books as opposed to the fields of patristic and early Christian studies, in which the canon as an object of study might be problematized but for which it is not a source in itself.[38] A methodological divide emerges among scholars according to whether they are studying the New Testament or later texts. If Justin or even Ignatius writes against an opponent, named or unnamed, most scholars now recognize that opponent as a "Docetic" or "Gnostic" *Christian*. If *Paul* writes against an opponent, for instance, his opposition in Galatia, that opposition is construed as "Jewish" or "Greek philosophers," or as "pre-Christian Gnostics," not as opposing Christians. Of course, that word itself further complicates the issue. While more traditional scholars, when writing about the first century, use the uninflected term "Christian" only for New Testament authors and groups, many scholars of the New Testament question the validity of that term for *any* first-century community, preferring instead variations of "the Jesus movement," "Pauline communities," and "Christ-centered communities."

The conflicting tendencies among New Testament scholars are to find theological unity across the New Testament canon (what Tina Pippin has called "the hermeneutics of acceptance") or to find completely localized, separate "Christianities" and "Jesus movements" in different sets of texts.[39] Let us consider the "unity" side of this divide first. Many scholars trace theological continuity from Jesus to his first followers through the orthodox theologians of the second and third centuries to the ecumenical councils of the fourth, even while acknowledging the critical challenges posed by the Bauer thesis and the re-discovery of non-canonical early Christian documents.[40] For instance, James Dunn accepts Bauer's rejection of first-century orthodoxy as well as the presence of diversity within the New Testament. He seeks instead a "unifying strand in earliest Christianity which identifies itself as Christianity."[41] His method is to survey the texts of New Testament, primarily Jesus in the Synoptic Gospels, Paul, Luke (identified as the theologian of Acts), and the Gospel of John, compare their differences (the "diversity" of his title), and then find the underlying unities to construct "New Testament Christianity." He finds this unity in Christian kerygma, confession, tradition, and Christology. But for Dunn, each apparent discovery of early Christian unity must include recognition of the contours of diversity as well. For instance, the distinctiveness of the *kerygmata* of the Acts sermons, Paul's letters, and John's Gospel respectively can be recognized only by acknowledging their differences.[42] He then goes beneath apparent differences to find unity in "the presupposition of proclamation," the theology implied by the public proclamation of the early church as he has recovered it.[43]

Dunn finds continuity between Jesus and the early Church and between Christianity and the Old Testament. But his choice of theological categories around which to organize Christian unity assumes the existence of some original orthodoxy. The unity he finds is an "abstraction" that could be found only from the perspective of the orthodox Christian church and its descendants.[44] Dunn thus plays down differences and shifts "radical diversity" to the second century, recapitulating Hegesippus' historiography of unity before diversity.[45] The unity of Christian kerygma, confession, tradition, and Christology is derived in part by limiting the sources and excluding Q and the *Gospel of Thomas* from being considered as "New Testament texts" (and thus challenging the unity of "New Testament Christianity"). Dunn's unity within diversity is constructed teleologically by his selection of New Testament texts and theological categories.

Burton L. Mack would seem to be at the opposite end of the spectrum from Dunn with regard to diversity in early Christian origins. His revision of the history of Christianity atomizes the religious movement at its moment of origin. Mack's argument is that there was no "big bang" of Christian origins, no actual movement led by Jesus of Nazareth from Galilee to the Temple in Jerusalem. Mack rejects the founding story of Jesus as a prophet who was killed, arguing rather for the "Q community" as the origin of the Jesus movement.[46] The original Jesus movements gathered around "a novel combination of three ideas that had been in the air since the breakdown of traditional cultures characteristic of the Greco-Roman age": the "vague" notion of a perfect society; the idea that any person was fit for this society or "kingdom"; and that a diverse mixture of people was not only acceptable but also essential to the nature of the kingdom.[47] Various Jesus movements then had independent lives around the eastern Mediterranean during the first century. Christianity as a religion formed later as the different movements coalesced. The Pauline "Christ Cult," independent from these Galilean Q communities, transformed the idea-centered movement into a religion about Jesus the God and the salvific, atoning effect of Jesus' death.[48] Mack claims the origins of the pronouncement stories in the Gospels originated in a Jewish group in Syria that did not fully understand the Q teachings, while the "preposterous" miracle stories in Mark originated in northern Palestine in a group that needed a myth of origin.[49] For Mack, different literary strands in the Gospels must have had social formations; each form or *Gattung* has an independent origin in a different group, before their collection into the Gospels.

While we might label Dunn the traditionalist and Mack the radical revisionist of Christian origins, both preserve the Hegesippian historiography of truth preceding error. Dunn sees the original unity of Christianity starting with the ministry and teaching of Jesus himself. He describes the building of an orthodox consensus within a Christian church that, for the most part, understood Jesus' actions and messages. For Dunn, the early Christian church "got it right" when they continued what Jesus had started.

Mack argues in contrast for the original purity of a "virgin" Q community (to borrow Hegesippus' term) that later becomes corrupted by association with Pharisaic Judaism; adoption of the mythology of miracles and apocalyptic ideologies; and the Pauline Christ cult. While Mack's revision of early Christian history appears to embrace radical diversity, especially in comparison with Dunn's more apologetic history of the church, he constructs the history of a movement from unity to diversity, from purity to corruption, following traditional Christian historiography, if not history.

Though ideologically separated, both sides approach the problem of difference similarly. Mack constructs an account for how different Jesus movements and Christ cults arose; Dunn carefully analyzes the different theologies and Christologies in the New Testament. But neither author tries to theorize the problem of difference itself. Dunn gives no account for how different views about Christ functioned socially or ideologically. Interestingly, when Dunn describes how early Christian writers countered or responded to alternative theologies and Christologies, he adopts the method of original Christian unity.[50] Mack stops short at noting polemic in the texts and does not probe the origins of difference. And scholars who do recognize difference within early Christianity nonetheless continue to seek deep underlying unity. For instance, Larry Hurtado argues that, despite the divisions between Paul and the Jerusalem church expressed in Galatians, there were no *Christological* differences between the Gentile and Palestinian (Aramaic-speaking) followers of Jesus; both groups worshipped Jesus as a God.[51] These scholars of early Christianity do not consider difference itself as an ideological strategy. This is where I start, at the *idea of difference itself.*

CHRISTIAN IDENTITY

Related to the problems associated with this historiography of unity before diversity in early Christianity is the question of Christian identity. When and how does that arise? And when—and for whom—can we use that term? Critical studies of Jewish identity in the first two centuries of the common era, before and after the wars with Rome, have cast doubts on theories of Christian history that employ developmental, evolutionary, or family models to isolate "Christian identity" or that mark "the parting of Judaism and Christianity" as a historical moment in the first century.[52] Some scholars warn against using the name Christian at all for the first century in order to avoid the teleology of orthodoxy and against essentializing first- and second-century Judaism as "not Christian." Several recent studies have placed these issues at the center of historical studies of the origins of early Christianity as part of its Second Temple Jewish context. The unifying strand in these studies is questioning the validity of essentializing labels of "Jewish" and "Christian" and examining the social and ideological processes of identity formation.

Two recent monographs by Daniel Boyarin and Denise Buell focus in particular on the relationship of Christian and Jewish identities in the second and later centuries. Boyarin's focus is on the "double function" of orthodox Christian heresiological discourse in constructing both "Jews and heretics—or rather Judaism and heresy."[53] Justin Martyr is for Boyarin an *early* example (my emphasis)

> of the discursive strategy that was to become fully elaborated by the end of the fourth century: that of distinguishing from the Christian side an orthodox Judaism as the true "other" of Christianity, such that two binary pairs are put into place, Judaism/Christianity and heresy/ orthodoxy, with Judaism, both supporting through semiotic opposition the notion of an autonomous Christianity, and being itself an ortho- doxy, also serving to mark the semantic distinction between orthodoxy and heresy.[54]

His project connects the production of regimes of knowledge within Chris- tian discourse as a construction not only of Christian identity as a universal religion but also of Jewishness as an alternate religion and orthodoxy over against heretics, construed as either Christian or Jewish.[55] So too Buell's project questions the construction of Christian "universality" over against Jewish "particularity" in both ancient and modern discourse. She works with ancient notions of race and ethnicity, notions ideologically juxtaposed against deconstructed nineteenth- and twentieth-century constructs of race and religion. Employing different models of ethnic reasoning, she examines the process of construction of Christian identities in the late antique world. Here, the "break" with Judaism (an idea fully problematized by Buell) as part of the formation of Christian identity in the ancient world is also a central issue.[56]

Buell does not work from New Testament or earlier texts beyond some introductory comments on 1 Peter and the Acts of the Apostles as well as various references to the biblical texts throughout.[57] Her study focuses on second-century and later texts and authors such as Justin, Clement, Tertul- lian, Origen, the *Gospel of Phillip* and *Acts of Andrew*, and the *Epistle to Diognetus*, a "tantalizing" document from about 200 CE that is central to the questions of formation of the Christian *genos*, or race, in her book.[58] Boyarin explicitly dismisses any first-century texts and communities from a study of heresiology, tracing the development of this discourse from Justin to Jerome and from the *Mishnah* to the *Babylonian Talmud*. While not- ing that some elements of later heresiological discourse were in place in texts such as the *Damascus Document* (which I treat in detail in the next chapter), Boyarin uses Troeltsch's conceptions of cult, sect, and church to buttress his claim that there was no notion of heresy in first-century texts. He marks the texts with which I begin my genealogy of heresiology, the Qumran scrolls and Paul's letters, sociologically as sects (for the Pauline communities) or actual cults (for Qumran) and as the originators of notions of supersessionism and "the New Israel."[59] The ideology of sectarian discourse, he argues, is distinct from the ideology of orthodoxy and heresy because these communities were not "churches" in the sociological sense. This dismissal raises methodological problems in an otherwise illuminating treatment. The sociological analysis of these communities is valuable, but *Border Lines* is not a sociological work. Therefore his relatively brief treatment employs sociological taxonomies for these first-century *communities* rather than reading for the discursive production of power/knowledge and the construction of identities in these *texts*, the artifacts of community discourse. In both cases he is looking at the relation of the social formations to "outsiders" rather than reading for heresy as a community discourse, a discourse central to the formation of identity.

While Boyarin and Buell concentrate on second-century and later texts, Judith Lieu focuses on the first and early second century in her study of Christian identity.[60] Lieu's set of questions overlaps and complements my own project, but hers is both broader in scope and more focused on the eventual separation of what came to be Christianity and Judaism. For her this is the central issue.[61] She studies in particular the relation of textual production and the construction of identities and how texts are related to the communities that produced them. Indeed, the spread of Christianity is intricately connected to the production of texts, and the production of texts inscribes acts of power, "of exclusion as well as inclusion."[62] Her conclusion highlights the production of identity through texts:

> It has been the constructions of identity by the texts with which we have been concerned, regardless of whether there were those whose self-understanding was produced or reproduced through them, yet also with the conviction that it was through its texts that early Christianity, as we know it, took shape.[63]

Her selection of sources from the New Testament implicates these first-century texts as central to questions of Christian identity and therefore intersects my project even more closely than Boyarin's or Buell's, in particular her chapter on "Boundaries." But her questions of "text and identity" and the separation of Judaism and Christianity are different from my focus on the genealogy of heresy.

I have more agreements than disagreements with Boyarin, Buell, and Lieu and this book should partner with these and other studies of the formation of early Christian identity and the discourse of heresiology in the second and subsequent centuries. The discourses of heresy and orthodoxy were central in the negotiation of the hybrid identities of "Christian" and "pagan." So too heresiology is central to the questions about the ongoing relationship and eventual sundering of Christian and Jew. But it was already central by the end of the first century in the variety of communities that remembered Jesus of Nazareth. Difference was inherent and Christians were arguing with each other from the beginning of Jesus' movement. One group responded to difference by adopting and transforming discourses of difference from Second Temple Judaism to construct a notion of heresy. Other Christians found alternative rhetorical responses to ideological difference. Comparing these discursive approaches brings us to the genealogy of heresy.

READING FOR DIFFERENCE

I locate this political discourse in New Testament texts. The methodological challenge in the critical study of the texts included in the New Testament (as opposed to the corpus of the New Testament itself) is to read inscribed enemies as alternative Christian groups rather than as "Jewish, Gnostic, or pagan."[64] To be sure, this is complicated by the paucity of alternative first-century Christian texts. But the canonical texts provide the best sources we have to study first-century Christianity from the inside, especially when so few of the non-canonical texts can be confidently dated to the first century. The focus on more recently discovered texts such as the Nag Hammadi corpus, as well as the extensive research on heresiology in Christian writers of the second century and subsequent periods, has left the heresiology of the New Testament texts unexamined. The New Testament is an unexploited source to connect first- and early second-century Christianity by means of the history of heresiology. It is in these earliest Christian texts adopted by the orthodox party that we find the origins of heresiology as the formative discourse of orthodox Christianity itself.

There are pitfalls in recovering this discourse of difference without recapitulating Hegesippus' historiography of "truth before error" or assuming the teleology of orthodoxy theology within the earliest Jesus movements by connecting dots in the map too soon. Reading for the history of discourse, rather than exclusively for the history of ideas or social history, will avoid them. I noted two approaches to early Christian origins earlier. The first, the more traditional historiography of early Christianity typified by James Dunn and Larry Hurtado, emphasizes unity. This approach starts by finding some original unity among the followers of Jesus, a unity that allows for diversity and difference but nevertheless has a Christian "core." The second, following the lead of Walter Bauer, focuses on diversity, as typified by Burton Mack. What became early Christianity was in fact a diverse set of unrelated groups. In this approach, one cannot talk about Christianity until there is some *political* unity, be that in the second or fourth century. My project offers a third way. The Jesus movements and Pauline communities were in fact very diverse but united in that they followed the words or deeds, or both, of Jesus (whether the significance was placed as during his earthly activity or after some spiritual resurrection). There was wide latitude in how these different groups understood Jesus of Nazareth. But by the end of the first century, some Christians highlighted *difference as a discursive move for group identity* ("we are the true Christians as opposed to those false Christians") and for political posturing of the *ekklēsia* (church) in the *oikoumenē* (Empire; "we the true Christians are good Romans"). I understand difference here as neither a theological position nor merely a social conflict, although to be sure there were different ideological positions and extensive conflicts between these groups. Rather, difference is a discursive move, an ideological strategy (in Foucault's parlance, a theory or theme). The methodology developed in this book is to theorize the construction of difference in early Christianity as a discursive move within the social and ideological context of competing Christianities, rather than as a departure from some original purity.

Such a project requires shifting our thinking about the "invention of Christianity" from the imperial theology of the fourth century or the anti-Gnostic ideologues of the second century back to the Second Temple Jewish and Hellenistic matrix of the first century. As noted, the abandonment of the notions of apostolic unity and the historical reliability of the canon has produced a picture of unrelated, localized Jesus movements, Pauline groups, Jewish Christians, Christian Jews, and other "Christianities" around the eastern and central Mediterranean in the first century. Various pastoral or ideological crises in the second century have been proposed as the formative event in moving these sectarian movements to some sort of social and discursive unity.[65] A prevailing view is that disciples of disciples, Paulinists, Jewish Christians, and "apostolic fathers" maintained variations of the Jesus movement in unrelated sectarian pockets until the shocks from "heretical" Christian teachers such as Marcion, Valentinus, or other Gnostics in the second century created a crisis that forced the formation of the nascent orthodox church.[66] These were important agents and struggles, but the move to the second century merely foregrounds a different set of figures while displacing up to one hundred years of source material and Christian history.[67] To be sure, each of the heresiologists had their own set of social and rhetorical exigencies; we have looked briefly at Justin's. But any second century "crisis of orthodoxy" relies on a historiography of the early Christian church that has not held up under critical scrutiny. If, reading against classic orthodox historiography, "truth" does not precede "error," then the Christian discourse of orthodoxy and heresy begins with the religious movements of John the Baptist, Jesus, and Paul.

The selection of Justin and Irenaeus as the inventors of heresy (and thus the originators of Christian orthodoxy) has teleological strength insofar as their party gained theological and political hegemony. Justin's rhetoric of "us" and "them," of *orthognōmoi* and *haireseis*, is seductive, but it elides the range of alternative Christianities in the binary categories of orthodox and heretical at the point of rhetorical clarity in the second century rather than at its discursive genesis in the first century. Christian communities had formed discursive responses to ideological difference well before Justin. In a genealogy of heresy, the texts of the New Testament are fully implicated as the starting point for this study. That raises further methodological problems, to which I now turn.

THE RHETORICS OF DIFFERENCE

The theoretical challenges are complex. I approach the genealogy of heresy by means of the rhetoric of difference.[68] The social-historical turn of the 1970s shifted the study of early Christianity from theological questions to the construction of social worlds and symbolic universes beneath the sacred canopy of religion.[69] The sociology of knowledge and interpretive cultural anthropology were the two pillars of this approach that emphasizes how religions form communities that cohere socially, culturally, and, by implication, ideologically.[70] But rather than reading for cohesion, I look instead at exclusion. Reading for difference within Christian social formations through inscribed internal polemics guides us to the origins of the notion of heresy. Difference can be mediated, highlighted, negotiated—or become the basis of group boundaries and ideological condemnation. The sociology of difference is as central here as the sociology of knowledge.[71]

The methodological problem of using the New Testament canon as a source of all first-century Christianities must always be in view. If we remove the canonical lens from our first-century sources, how do we read the snapshot of first-century Christianities without imposing the teleology of orthodox unity?[72] Polemics and the rhetoric of difference are signposts. The moments where theological, ideological, or moral differences are explicit become the lode-laden nuggets in the mine of Christian literature. I look for examples of "These people are wrong" that suggest latent Christian identities within the social formations inscribed in the texts. These clear instances of argument point to other narratives of conflict, often submerged, in early Christian discourse. I am, furthermore, looking at the argument not for the doctrinal decisions that become "orthodox" but rather the formation of patterns of discourse. This is central because my project defines orthodoxy as a political movement rather than by philosophical or theological content, and thus heresiology as a political discourse. For instance, the rhetoric of dogma and creed is more important here than what those creeds contain. Church historians might use New Testament texts such as Paul's letter to the Galatians in terms of records of "early Church controversies" where communities hashed out the issue of adherence to Jewish practices such as circumcision and interpretation of the scriptures.[73] For my project, Paul's position is less important than *how* his position constructs a notion of heresy and how that forms the discursive patterns of Christian heresiology.

Critical readings of difference reveal these competing ideologies within the earliest Christian texts. The construction of the "other" as "heretic" in

New Testament texts is a rhetorical performance. I look not only for difference socially performed but also for difference discursively inscribed.[74] But I do not pretend to read from text to context to see "what was really happening."[75] Rather, the discourse of difference inscribed in the New Testament foregrounds the ideologies of the communities that produced these texts. Nor do I read these opposing ideologies simplistically. To be sure, a notion of an "us" requires the existence of "them," real or imagined. But the discursive production of heresy involves more than interpreting group formation according to structural patterns of binary opposition. The notion of heresy, from its genesis in Second Temple Jewish sectarianism to its development in early Christian discourse, functioned politically. Christian orthodoxy employed the discourse of heresy not because every "us" has a "them" but because the politics of orthodoxy positioned both the Roman *oikoumenē*, and all other Christianities, as "them." The rhetoric of exclusion and the interpretation of ideological difference within Christian communities, difference theorized as "heresy," were political moves within early orthodox Christianity.

For the orthodox party, heresy was political in multiple senses of the term; the example of Justin earlier is revealing. The discourse of heresy functioned politically within the group itself to establish norms, boundaries, and social practices anchored ideologically in transcendent notions of the divine and the afterlife. It functioned politically in the marketplace of competing Christianities, an *agora* in which the nascent orthodox party actively sought *hēgemonia* (hegemony) over other Christians. And it was political in its mission within the Roman *oikoumenē* to create a Christian world. To be sure, the distinction between political and theological functions reflects a modern separation of religious and secular, "church" and "state." So too my reading for the politics of orthodoxy and heresy reveals a post-modern focus on ideology. These distinctions would not be evident in the ancient world, whether to an emperor presiding over a sacrifice in Rome; an Ephesian citizen in a procession to the Artemision; a priest in Jerusalem; or a Christian celebrating the Eucharist in Corinth. There was little or no separation of what we would call political and religious worldviews. But despite now hundreds of years of historical-critical study of the New Testament, theological or dogmatic interpretations of "orthodoxy" have dominated its interpretation. Therefore it is important to highlight the ways in which I read these texts socially and politically rather than theologically, by means of the history of ideas. I will keep this dual focus between ancient and post-modern perspectives in mind, avoiding double-vision as much as possible.

The problem of difference must also be theorized in the notion of heresy. Thus, heresiology includes a theory of origin, a "meta-language" about difference.[76] For instance, Hegesippus explains the origin of heresy by Theboutis' jealousy stemming from a power struggle within the church and contamination by Jewish *gnōmai diaphorai*. Somewhat earlier, Josephus explains differences among the Jews to the Romans with the model of the philosophical school, as discussed in Chapter 4. The same philosophical model is adopted by Justin in the *Dialogue with Trypho* for theorizing a range of people who "take the same name" of Christian. Justin's theories for the origin of difference are doxographic as well as demonic. Students corrupt their teachers' original teaching (*doxai*), resulting in multiple views within a philosophy and, by analogy, within Christianity (*Dial.* 1–8, 35). While Josephus and later Christian heresiologists adapt doxographic models, philosophy as a theoretical framework for difference is not found in first-century heresiology, although several texts include a doxography of opponents. In Second Temple Jewish and early Christian texts, we will find two related theories for the genesis of difference: the apocalyptic and the satanic. In the first, difference and division, personified in the appearance of "false Christs and false prophets," are a sign of the end times. In the second, different or opposing religious groups are explicitly satanic. Justin and subsequent orthodox Christians continue to employ these two theories of origin in heresiology as well. As demonstrated in this book, this apocalyptic, eschatological religious worldview was a central element in driving the discursive confrontations with opponents that produced the notion of heresy.

NEGOTIATING DIFFERENCE IN THE ROMAN EMPIRE

A further theoretical issue relates to the colonial locations of early Christian communities. The social conditions for the production of heresiological discourse are power struggles within a religious community. This discourse will be implicated in the dominant culture wherever located, classically expressing the problematic of "hybridity," as formulated by Homi Bhabha.[77] For instance, Justin's construction of heresy has been read as a hybrid negotiation with the dominant discourse of Hellenism.[78] The heresiologist is not necessarily, however, the subaltern voice. The rhetoric of difference internal to the community (the rhetoric of heresy) often precedes the appeal to the colonial cultural paradigm, although the discourse will be doubly implicated in imperial ideologies, inscribing polemics against the other colonial subject as well as entangling the community in the ideology of a suppressive empire. The place of *ekklēsia* within the Roman *oikoumenē* becomes then another point of ideological struggle within early Christian communities and in orthodox heresiological rhetoric.

Second-century orthodox Christianity embraced both Revelation and Rome. For both Justin and Irenaeus, respectively martyred and witness of martyrdoms, Roman violence against those who took the name "Christian" was a potent threat. For these orthodox leaders, chiliasm offered an ideology of passive resistance: a theodicy of displacement of retribution to a future world construed as an alternative Empire, "God's Kingdom."[79] The discourse of these second-century heresiologists inscribed both Christian apocalypticism against "Babylon" and a formative apologetics *pro imperium*. Here again I argue that, as with the notion of heresy itself, this rhetoric of empire develops from earlier Christian discourse. Paul and his imitators, John of Patmos, and Ignatius discursively negotiated their own places within the same Greco-Roman empire. In the colonial context of early Christianity, the orthodox party re-inscribes imperial ideologies against its Jewish and Christian opponents. These complex negotiations between ideological differences within Christian communities on the one hand and imperial power on the other will be explored more fully in this book.

The discourse of negotiating Jewish identities within various imperial contexts was hundreds of years old when John the Baptist, Jesus of Nazareth, and their disciples formed their original movements. Thus, the rhetorical patterns of resistance and accommodation in early Christian texts are fully contextualized only when read as part of Second Temple Jewish literature. We shall see time and again that ideological differences in early Christianity come from the *gnōmai diaphorai* of Second Temple Judaism, not via contagion as Hegesippus construed this but rather through their shared discursive traditions. [80]

THE CONTOURS OF FIRST-CENTURY CHRISTIANITY

Diversity marks the origins of the Jesus movements of the first century. This is not just a contemporary dictum but a methodological tool for digging into the genealogy of the notion of heresy. The re-discovery of lost Christian literature has confirmed that early Christianity was a rich and diverse movement, a diversity born of its Second Temple Jewish and Greco-Roman context. My thesis that the orthodox project of political hegemony under the banner of Christian ideological unity begins, as with all Christianities, in the first century among Jesus' earliest followers runs counter to some recent treatments of first-century Christianity. And yet while the publication and study of early Christian texts from Egypt have deepened our knowledge of the other Christianities hinted at in canonical and orthodox sources, they have also highlighted the distinctiveness of orthodox beliefs within the spectrum of first- and second-century Christianities. These recovered non-canonical texts represent developments of first-century traditions, just as orthodox texts continued to develop in turn. The extant first-century literature preserved in the New Testament was produced in a context marked not only by diversity but also by contentiousness over interpretations of the significance of Jesus and his teachings. Unfortunately we do not have any texts written by Paul's opponents in Corinth or Ephesus, but there is no reason to think such literature did not exist. It has been estimated that 85% of early Christian writings have been lost.[81] It follows to reason as well that there were a variety of ideological positions within the communities of Matthew, Mark, Luke, and John. Difference and division were constant. Fully recognizing this diversity in the first century reads against the Hegesippian construct of unity before diversity that has marked traditional Christian historiography.

My project, moreover, theorizes more contact between the various authors and communities represented in the New Testament texts than allowed by many scholars. The canonization process, to be sure, begins in the late second century. Accepting that Irenaeus and subsequent church leaders forged the canon from a diverse and significantly larger body of texts in no way means that 180 CE was the first point of contact for these various Christianities. In fact the evidence suggests that these communities, from the founding of the Pauline *ekklēsiai* to the interactions of second-century apologists, teachers, and philosophers such as Justin, Marcion, and Valentinus, had extensive contact with each other. The co-workers, associates, and various church members mentioned in the letters of Paul can be found moving from Ephesus to Rome and Alexandria to Corinth. Frequent contact and interaction were the norm rather than the exception.[82] The idea of frequent contact between various Christian communities has also been applied to the study of the Gospels.[83] The argument works better perhaps theoretically than in every particular application.[84] But the theory itself is critical for uncovering the notion of heresy in early Christian discourse.

Paul sought to construct a worldwide church, a united *ekklēsia* in the Roman Empire, a conscious project central to orthodox hegemony. Paul's rhetoric of the universal *ekklēsia*, an ideology supported by Matthew's Gospel, as shown in Chapter 5, would be as important for the orthodox project as his theology, which was in fact a point of great difference among Christian groups in the second century. Schism in Galatia with "Judaizers" and opposition from "super apostles" in Corinth, studied in Chapter 4, demonstrate the continuous interactions between Christian teachers, leaders, and communities. This pattern of travel between and contact among Christian communities in the first century has important ramifications for the interpretation of texts. First- and second-century Christian literature did not develop along completely independent lines until Irenaeus combined various texts under the ideology of apostolic traditions. Every non-narrative text from the first century mentions contact between Christian communities. Therefore we can assume contact as well among the authors and readers of narrative texts rather than pursue further the localization of early Christian texts and social formations. Bauckham's important questions about the production of Gospels for broader audiences beyond their immediate community should be considered, although it is not necessary to abandon the notion of such communities as historical constructs or heuristic devices.[85] This does not mean we should mimic the heresiology of the orthodox project by construing the teleological development of one true Christianity and false alternatives.[86] A genealogy of Christian heresy and orthodoxy in the first century need not imply a unified, univocal

"Christianity." Scholars have replicated the pattern of orthodox heresiological historiography in treatment of opponents in New Testament texts by assuming that these opponents could not be Christians. Positing this social movement around the Mediterranean, a movement in regular contact and conflict, does not imply the construction of one totalizing Christian discourse but rather the existence of one political movement, labeled here "orthodoxy," among alternative Christianities.[87] Indeed, the universality of the *ekklēsia* was one point of conflict with other Christian social formations and a node in the formation of the notion of heresy.

A brief look at orthodox dogma will help contextualize the historical approach I am following in subsequent chapters. These examples are by no means exhaustive but rather heuristic outlines to illustrate how to write a history of heresy in New Testament texts. Two central theological tenets of orthodox Christianity are the hypostatic Christology of Jesus Christ as Lord and God and the "physical" resurrection of Jesus and Christian followers.[88] The recent publications by Elaine Pagels and Karen King on the *Gospel of Thomas* and *Gospel of Mary* respectively have illuminated the different role of the resurrected Jesus in these texts and the communities that wrote and studied them. The contemporary Christian—mainstream liberal or evangelical Protestant, eastern Orthodox, or Roman Catholic—looking for redemptive sacrifice or some other atonement theory will no doubt be perplexed by the radically different Christologies in these Gospels. Christ here provides the example (or perhaps the *means* as the forerunner or pattern) for the Christian to explore the inner divine in her or his own soul. Christ opens up a new spiritual world for believers; in the *Gospel of Mary*, either Jesus describes to Mary Magdalene, or Mary herself describes to the apostles from her own inner spiritual illumination, the path of ascent for the soul past powers such as desire and ignorance to "heaven." The *Gospel of Thomas*, while in its final version a second-century text, preserves the outlines of a first-century alternative Christology that was later labeled heretical by the orthodox party. Pagels describes how Christ here does not "save" the believer so much as enable the believer to find his or her own salvation. The theme is familiar in the literature from Nag Hammadi; I will return to these Gospels in Chapters 5 and 6. The point, however, is not to systematize Gnostic Christology but to highlight the difference between these Christological formations and the theology of Paul, the followers of Paul, and the canonical gospels of Matthew, John, and Luke.[89] Nor were the theological issues settled quickly; Christians contested Christology for centuries. But the high hypostatic Christology adopted as creed at Nicaea and Chalcedon has roots in early texts such as the Christ Hymn in Phil 2:6–11, which is likely a pre-Pauline Christology, as well as the Fourth Gospel. Consistently applying the historiography of diversity in early Christianity allows us to locate the range of radically different Christologies in the first century.

Resurrection was a second defining dogma of orthodox Christianity and a point of difference among Jews well before the prophetic activity of John and Jesus. Traditionalist Jews, such as the upper-class Saddu-cees, did not accept the validity of resurrection while reforming move-ments and radical sects such as the Pharisees and Qumran community did. Early Christianity inherits this difference. What was controversial and divisive among Jewish groups of the Second Temple period would of course be controversial and divisive among the very first followers of Jesus and the interpretive communities that preserved and developed tra-ditions about Jesus. The range of understandings of belief in or denial of physical resurrection can be seen in first-century sources. For instance, Paul's struggles with the explanation of resurrection in 1 Corinthians 15 signals the contentiousness around this idea, an idea that would have been paired logically with the passion accounts and crucifixion of Jesus. The absorption of Q into Luke and Matthew suggests an early and continu-ing struggle between a Wisdom-oriented Christology that de-emphasized the passion story as central to understanding of the meaning of Jesus and the canonical Gospels' emphasis on passion and resurrection. Luke and John's extensive development of the resurrection appearances of Jesus demonstrates the contentiousness over the physical resurrection of Jesus within Christian communities at the turn of the centuries.[90] Docetic, Gnostic, "physical" or "literal" resurrection—the various doctrines all have first-century origins. Difference and division were integrally part of the range of first-century early Christian social formations.

As we shall see, some of these communities believed themselves to be in continuity with Judaism, others saw themselves breaking with and perfecting Judaism, and still other Christian communities would have considered themselves completely different from Judaism.[91] None of the original communities can be separated from the Jewish context, and yet the re-orientation of belief and practice around the executed Jesus of Nazareth entailed a new identity called "Christian." According to Luke this word is first used to describe followers of "the Way" in Antioch (Acts 11:26), but by that point in the first generation the movements were as diverse as they would be at the end of the first century. The word itself becomes highly contested in the second century, as Justin shows us, so Luke's description of the origin of the term is both politically tendentious as well as socially descriptive. There is no reason to see "Christianity" as a completely second-century invention any more than there is a reason to see the unity of the first generation of apostolic church corrupted by the jealousy of Thebouthis and the "heresies" of the Jews, as Hegesippus would have one think.

The unity of these early Christian orthodox social formations—formative and forming, Jewish and Gentile—will be demonstrated here by the rhetoric of exclusion, examination of difference, and polemics against other Christians. In short, the basket of rhetorical features that becomes central to orthodox Christian heresiology in the second century and following are clearly discern-ible in the first-century Christian texts included in the New Testament.

THE RHETORIC OF HERESY

Heresiology is a discourse that negotiates difference within religious communities by seeking ideological hegemony. It can be expressed in a variety of tropes and figures for political functions in communities socially connected by religious ideologies. In this genealogy of heresy in Christianity, I am tracing the development of a cluster of rhetorical forms.[92]

1   Membership (Salvation) Depends on Belief or Ideas

The notion of heresy inscribes by implication an ontology of belief. While religious identity in the ancient world was shaped primarily through custom and practice, Christian orthodoxy centered on belief; as Foucault writes, an "obligation to hold as true a set of propositions which constitutes a dogma."[93] I will trace the origins of doctrine or dogma (*doxa*) as determinative for inclusion in the soteriological community. The notion of dogmatic salvation has roots in sectarian writings of the Qumran community, in which *halakhic* positions define fissures between Second Temple Jewish groups. We will see how this rhetoric is employed and ideologically populated in first-century texts.

2   The Eschatological Idea That Disagreement Was Satanic or Demonic

The origins of religious difference must be theorized in the notion of heresy. The position on ideological difference that was systematized by the second century heresiologists has its origins in the dualistic worldview of Second Temple Jewish apocalypticism that explained religious difference via satanic tropes. This is the religious matrix for the Essenes at Qumran, the religious reform movements of John and Jesus in Galilee, and the formative religious and theological context for the early Christian communities that produced the first-century texts. This apocalyptic eschatological worldview drives confrontations with opponents.

3   The Importance of Received Tradition

The ideology of orthodoxy relies on tradition as a warrant. Received tradition, developed from Pharisaic as well as philosophical discourse, is related to the notion of dogma. As belief proper becomes the ideological center of first-century Christian orthodoxy, tradition gains power. Late first-century texts construct "tradition" as an ideological bulwark against opposing communities that embraced apocalyptic revelation and philosophical speculation. We will see this rhetorical-ideological move in the post-Pauline and Gospel texts.

4 The Doxography of Opposing Beliefs

As Christian orthodoxy centers increasingly on belief in received dogma to define its identity, classic heresiology of the second century and following includes a doxography of the views of the opposing teachers. I will trace this pattern from Qumran to late first-century texts. For philosophers, doxography functions to record and analyze different positions in order to transmit philosophical knowledge. Within early Christian heresiology, however, the function of heresiological doxography is ideological condemnation of different points of view by means of sarcasm, reduction, or other figures diminishing the intellectual quality of the opposing teachers.[94]

5 The Universalized Web of Opposition

The genealogy of heresy constructs a historiography of error, from its origins to contemporary opposing teachers or prophets, united against the true church. The origins of this familiar rhetoric of "us" and "them" in Christian orthodoxy are inscribed in theories of difference from Second Temple Jewish literature, most notably apocalyptic eschatology. The political function of this rhetoric, however, contextualizes the binary divisions as more than expressions of structuralist theories of identity. Within orthodox Christian discourse, all other religious groups and communities, whether Christian, Jewish, or Hellenistic, are elided within and with the *oikoumenē* as "other." And yet domination of this same *oikoumenē* is a political goal of orthodox Christians.

PLAN OF THE BOOK

In this introduction, I have outlined the problem at hand, the framework of the theoretical issues, and the scope of the investigation of the origins of Christian orthodoxy as read through the genealogy of heresiology. In the following chapters, I will examine Second Temple Jewish and early Christian texts to trace the developments of Christian heresiological rhetoric.

The multiple political functions of the ideology of heresy means that I will be alternating attention in this book between the internal politics of the early Christian communities; the social relationships between different communities; and political appeals to imperial outsiders. Heresiology always functioned at multiple levels; this alternation will both clarify the different functions as well as follow the nature of the sources available. Chapters 2, 3, and 4 read the rhetoric of difference in texts that have the strongest evidence for social-historical context of any first-century Jewish or Christian texts: Qumran, Jesus, and Paul. My attention will be on the internal and external political rhetoric of these communities, although since I return to Paul's appeal to empire in Chapter 7, I will focus in Chapter 4 more on the internal politics of the *ekklēsia*. Chapters 5 and 6, in contrast, focus on the more socially dislocated texts of the Gospel traditions and post-Pauline literature. My attention here is on the rhetorics of difference and formation of heresiology in the internal politics; the methodology for reading ideology is as much literary-rhetorical as social-historical. But the arc of political ideology from Qumran, Jesus, and Paul to the imperial politics analyzed in Chapter 7 guides the reading of this rhetoric.

Part I, "Genealogy of a Discourse," traces the development of the notion of heresy and the genre of heresiology. In Chapter 2, "The Rhetoric of Difference in Israel," I examine the discursive roots of early Christian heresiology in the rhetoric of difference in Second Temple Judaism, from Jeremiah to the sectarian texts from Qumran. In particular I highlight the apocalyptic dualism of the Qumran community; the role of *halakah* in defining community identities; the political struggles over the notion of "Israel" within the Qumran sectarian writings; the propaganda of the Hasmonean dynasty; and the book of Daniel.

In Chapter 3, "Reform and Revolution in the Roman Empire: John the Baptist and the Disciples of Jesus," I move from Qumran and other second-century Jewish groups to the apocalyptic reform movement of John the Baptist and his followers in Roman Judea, which included for at least a brief time Jesus of Nazareth. Both John's preaching and disciples were part of the earliest Jesus movements and connect them, socially and discursively, to the sectarian ideology of Qumran. I will also address some of the problems in the study of the historical Jesus here, which is not a focus of this book.

We turn next to the earliest available documents from the nascent Christian communities. In Chapter 4, "Paul and the Rhetoric of Difference," I will look at three key moments of difference and disagreement in Paul's letters to the Corinthians and Galatians. Here, I will show how Paul appropriates Roman imperial ideology in the discourse of the church community (the *ekklēsia*), via the tropes of *homonoia* (unity) and *stasis* (rebellion), and the ways Paul ideologically valorizes difference and disagreement by means of theological categories. Paul's apocalyptic eschatology is central to his confrontation with opponents.

Gospel traditions developed discursive traditions for the negotiation of difference and the rhetoric of disagreement concurrently with the Pauline communities. In Chapter 5, "The Christian Gospels as Narratives of Exclusion," I examine polemics and the rhetoric of difference in the Q document used by Matthew and Luke, the *Gospel of Thomas*; the Gospel of Matthew; and the *Didache*. The Gospels, both Sayings and Narrative texts, inscribe community divisions and strategies of exclusion in the words of Jesus himself. Here again, different eschatologies drive the responses to ideological difference.

Part II then turns to "The Politics of Heresy." In Chapter 6, "Policing the Boundaries: The Politics of Heresiology," I examine the political function within Christian communities of the rhetoric of difference in a set of later first- and second-century texts that incorporate the ideological notions of both "Christianity" and "heresy," including Colossians, Revelation, the epistles of John, Ignatius, Polycarp, and the Pastoral Epistles; and compare the heresiology in these texts to the rhetoric of difference in the *Gospel of Mary* and *Gospel of Judas*. These orthodox texts exhibit the full patterns of heresiological rhetoric.

In Chapter 7, "The Politics of Orthodoxy," I examine the ways in which imperial ideology functioned within orthodox Christian heresiology and the ways in which orthodox Christians appealed to Empire for hegemony within Christianities of the first and early second century. Here, I turn to imperialistic discourse in Romans, 1 Peter, Revelation, and Luke-Acts.

Chapter 8, "Conclusions," connects this study to the history of orthodox Christianity in the second century and the broader implications for the understanding of early Christianity and religious discourse.

The significance of this project for recovering the history of early Christianity is worth restating here. In the course of this book, I will describe how the notion of heresy was central to the formation of early Christian orthodoxy in the first as well as second century CE. The eventual political success of imperial, Nicene orthodoxy in the fourth century develops from the discursive formation of early, first-century orthodox Christianity, with its rhetorical and ideological constructions of heretical opposition. In tracing the development of these rhetorical constructions, I am also considering the origins of Christianity itself as a social formation within the Greco-Roman world.

2 The Rhetoric of Difference in Israel

*All those [who are ready] for battle shall march out and pitch their
camp before the king of the Kittim and before all the host of Satan
gathered about him for the Day [of Revenge] by the Sword of God.*

—The War Scroll[1]

INTRODUCTION

The search for the origins of the notion of heresy takes us first to the
Hebrew Scriptures. Early Christianity, both as a social movement and as a
discursive tradition, grows from Hebrew and Jewish prophetic traditions.
Jesus himself and leaders from Paul to Ignatius of Antioch were prophets
or spoke prophetically in the communities.[2] Prophets and prophecy were a
locus of struggle and difference in early Christian communities. Prophecy
was part of power struggles in ancient Israel as well. From its early origins to the Babylonian Exile and Restoration, prophecy was connected to
matters of kingship, foreign policy, control of the Temple, and rule of the
people.[3] The word of God, *děbar Yahweh*, was a discourse of political and
social power as well as theological power. Hebrew prophecy, moreover,
encompassed strong concerns for social justice for the poor, widows, and
orphans—the powerless in Israelite society.

I will focus in this chapter on one aspect of Israelite prophecy—the rhetoric of difference. Prophets who delivered the word of God to people or kings
frequently disagreed about what that word was or meant. The genealogy of
the notion of heresy begins with these discursive conflicts within ancient Israel
and Second Temple Judaism. I begin with some illustrative moments of conflict in pre-exilic biblical prophets that negotiate difference and disagreement
without heresiological rhetoric. In these examples, the response to difference
centers on Israelite unity. Then, I turn to the sectarian Covenant at Qumran, focusing on the rhetoric of separation; the dualistic eschatology; and the
polemical doxography in these Dead Sea Scroll texts. I contrast this rhetoric
of separation in the Qumran sectarian writings with the ideology of unity in
Daniel and the political propaganda of the Hasmoneans. The sectarian Dead
Sea Scrolls form the discursive origins of the Christian notion of heresy.

The discourse of difference in these texts incorporates struggles over the
political notion of Israel. Heresiological discourse functions politically at
multiple levels. Within the Second Temple period, the rhetoric of difference
involved political conflicts over the identity of "Israel" in addition to theological and ideological conflicts within Judaism.

PROPHETIC CONFLICT IN ANCIENT ISRAEL

Man of God and Old Prophet in Bethel (1 Kings 13:11–32)

My first example of prophetic conflict is from 1 Kings, part of the so-called Deuteronomic History.[4] The death of Solomon (ca. 922 BCE) and the subsequent struggle for succession, a struggle that rekindles divisions between Judah and the northern tribes of Israel, are the backdrop for one of the earliest stories about prophets in the Hebrew Bible.[5] This particular disagreement between prophets results in the death of one of them. Religious cult sites are at the center of this conflict. Solomon had centralized the cult in Jerusalem, along with other political and military functions. His taxation and labor policies aggravated tensions between Judah and the northern tribes; his son, Rehoboam, adopts an even harder-line policy (1 Kings 12:1–15).[6] Jeroboam, who was in political exile in Egypt, returned to lead the northern tribes against Rehoboam. But prophets had already acted as agents in these political conflicts. Ahijah, a prophet of the northern Israelite cult site of Shiloh, urged Jeroboam, then an official overseeing the *corvée* for Solomon's kingdom, to break off the northern tribes as punishment for Solomon's religious practices, which could be characterized as polytheistic or not exclusively Yahwistic (1 Kings 11:26–40). Jeroboam then re-established shrines in Bethel and Dan as part of separating the northern kingdom of Israel from the hegemony claimed by Judah (1 Kings 12:25–33).[7]

The conflict between north and south plays out in the narrative of 1 Kings 13 as conflict between northern and southern prophets. While Jeroboam was offering incense at the altar in Bethel, a "man of God" (*'îš 'ĕlōhîm*) from Judah proclaimed against the altar "by the word of YHWH" (*bidĕbar YHWH*).[8] Jeroboam answers the threat by trying to seize the Judean, but the king's hand is withered and the altar is destroyed. Jeroboam entreats the southerner's favor; the "man of God" heals the withered hand but has taken a vow not to eat or drink until he has returned to Judah and attempts to leave Bethel. This ironically foreshadows the next scene, in which an old prophet (*nābî' zāqēn*) in Bethel tricks the "man of God" into eating and drinking with him:

> Then the other said to him: "I also am a prophet as you are, and an angel spoke to me by the word of the LORD: Bring him back with you into your house so that he may eat food and drink water." But he was deceiving him. (1 Kings 13:18)

As soon as the "man of God" sits and eats at Bethel, the "word of the LORD" comes to the northern prophet again, who condemns the Judean to die away from his ancestral home. The Bethel prophet and his sons send the "man of God" back south on a donkey, where he is killed by a lion, confirming the prophecy of the northern prophet as well as the original commandment to the "man of God" not to honor the Bethel cult by eating or drinking outside of Judah.

Both prophets cite the "word of the LORD," the same Hebrew phrase in 1 Kings 13:9 and 13:18, to explain why the "man of God" should or should not eat in Bethel. The northern prophet utters what turns out to be false prophecy that ensnares the man from Judah to stay and eat, while the prophecy and vow of the man from Judah, a vow that kills him, turn out to be true. The division between the prophets is harsh; the old prophet of Bethel effectively assassinates the southern "man of God" by deceiving him with "the word of the LORD." But this conflict also shows the ideology of prophetic unity in Israel. While the old prophet of Bethel ostensibly supports the independence of the northern kingdom and the legitimacy of its cult, his deception of the "man of God" from Judah confirms the prophecy originally given to the Judean (1 Kings 13:9) and thus de-legitimates the Samarian cult site. The scene of reconciliation in 1 Kings 13:26–32 then subverts the division between the prophets as well as the authority of the northern prophet. He saddles his donkey to recover the body of the man of God, laments the death of his "brother," ('āḥî) and asks to be buried next to him, confirming that the "man of God" spoke the actual word of God against the shrine of Bethel and Jeroboam's kingdom. The two prophets were not enemies but brothers after all. The conflict ends in reconciliation.

The ideology of Judean hegemony over all Israel underlies this story. The conflict centers on the altar of Bethel, a cult site that challenged the power of Jerusalem, a power we might label both religious and political in contemporary terms but which was unified in ancient Israel. The theological question of where to worship, and *what* to worship—since Jeroboam had labeled the golden calves the "gods, O Israel, who brought you out of the land of Egypt" (1 Kings 12:28)—is a political conflict between north and south; "prophet" is a synecdoche for the kingdom. The story includes a second layer of political discourse. The "man of God" invokes the future king Josiah, inscribing the reforms of this later Davidic king onto these divisions between ancient Israel and Judah. Read at this level, the story of prophetic conflict and reconciliation expresses the ideology of a unified "Israel" under Judean control.

Yahweh, Israel, and the Nations

Heresiological conflict must involve adherents of the same god, in this case Yahweh. Conflict was common within Israelite prophecy, but a division between prophetic "brothers" that ends in death is infrequent. More frequently the rhetoric of difference is cast against worshippers of "other gods."[9] The conflict between Elijah and the prophets of Baal (1 Kings 18:20–40) is a typical example.[10] Here again, the ideology of the prophetic conflict centers on the political notion of "Israel." The prophets of Baal were clients of the Queen of Israel, Jezebel, the Phoenician wife of Ahab.

When Elijah responds to their attempt at fire, he prophetically re-enacts unified Israelite tribal identity by taking twelve stones for the altar. His victory is a victory of Israel, prophetically reconceived against the nations (the Gentiles or *goyîm*), represented by Phoenicia. The conflict ends with the slaughter of the Phoenician prophets (1 Kings 18:40).

Jeremiah

One of the most developed prophetic conflicts in the Hebrew Bible is between the Yahwistic prophet Jeremiah and the Jerusalem temple hierarchy in the final days of pre-exilic Jerusalem. Enmeshed in a situation of direct conflict with the priests, other prophets, and the royal authorities over the fate of the city, Jeremiah raises the problem of false prophecy more deeply than any other biblical prophet. The compositional issues of the Book of Jeremiah complicate our reading of these prophecies since they have been edited from a perspective in which the destruction of Jerusalem, the Exile, and perhaps the Restoration are all *fait accompli*.[11] Prophecy here is not predictive. But the discourse of truth and falsehood in Jeremiah draws our attention for its examination of true and false prophecy. The focus of this conflict is on the fate of Jerusalem. Jeremiah probes the nature and limits of false prophecy without condemning his prophetic and priestly opponents of heresy. Rather, Jeremiah's vision of restoration, a prophecy about the reunified land of Israel, casts the bitter disputes over false prophecy within an ideology of unity that eliminates conflict and divisions. As we shall see with the Qumran community and early Christianity, heresiological responses to difference do not include reunification with enemies.

Conflict in the Book of Jeremiah

The overwhelming threat in the Book of Jeremiah to Jerusalem is Babylon, the "destroyer of nations" (Jer 4:7).[12] The cause of Babylon's attack is Israel's abandonment of the covenant with God, featured in a *rîv* or covenant lawsuit in Jer 2:1–37 and 3:1–10. Israel is accused of adultery and "playing the whore" for worshipping other gods.[13] But the critique is more than an indictment of the people for breaking the covenant. Babylon is Yahweh's instrument, taking on the task of the "chosen nation" rather than Jerusalem itself.[14]

Babylon does God's will against Judah while the prophets and Temple priests, who oppose Jeremiah, undermine Yahweh's plan. An early word from Yahweh in the call narrative (1:4–19) pits Jeremiah against "the kings of Judah, its princes, its priests, and the people of the land. They will fight against you; but they shall not prevail" (1:18–19). Personal attacks and religious conflict run throughout the laments (or "confessions") and prose sermons in Jeremiah (see 12:6; 15:20–21; 17:18; 18:19–23; 20:10).[15] These conflicts are with the priests and prophets at the top of the social hierarchy (the "optimistic prophets"; 4:10; 5:12; 12:1; 15:17).[16] The priest Pashur, chief officer of the Temple, casts Jeremiah in stocks in order to stop his prophecies, eliciting a strong response from Jeremiah against Pashur and his household (20:3–6). This priestly conflict extends to the Judean priests already in Babylon, who attempt to encourage the Jerusalem authorities against Jeremiah (letter against Shemaiah, 29:24–32). Even the people of the northern village of Anatoth, Jeremiah's hometown, seek his life (11:18–23). Jeremiah links these attacks with the future of Israel, calling God's judgment on Jerusalem in 18:19–23.[17] For Jeremiah, the enemies of Jerusalem are *within* as much as without.

False Prophecy

The "Temple Sermon" centers on the prophecy of Jeremiah's opponents. The Book of Jeremiah contains two versions: a prose summary of the prophetic oracles in Jer 7:1–34 and a second summary of the speech and ensuing trial in 26:1–6.[18] Jeremiah directly confronts the people of Jerusalem who accept the ideology of the Royal Jerusalem prophecy and its eternal promise for Jerusalem and the "House of the LORD." The speech rings the changes with typical prophetic condemnation of the people's lack of attention to social justice (7:5–6), their immoral behavior (7:9), and the worship of Baal and other gods (7:9, 17–18). Most importantly, Jeremiah charges the people of Jerusalem with accepting a lie, "deceptive words" (7:4, *dibrê haššeqer*): "This is the temple of the LORD, the temple of the LORD, the temple of the LORD."[19] These "deceptive words" are in fact the words of other prophets and would be considered legitimate prophecy by many in Jerusalem. The prophecy of his Yahwistic co-religionists was based on Israelite scriptural traditions such as 2 Samuel 7 and Psalm 132.[20] Jeremiah's polemic elides false prophecy with immoral behavior and apostasy to Baal or Ishtar (7:8). The context of religious conflict between priests and prophets of the same god seems ripe for accusations of heresy. The conflict was, moreover, overtly political, as Jeremiah's pointed coupling of the future destruction of the Temple and the now-ancient destruction of Shiloh (7:14) highlights.

As with the clash between the "man of God" and the old prophet at Bethel earlier, the validity of prophecy depends on which side you are on. Jeremiah's charges against the Temple authorities are reversed when they bring Jeremiah to trial for sedition in a time of war. In context he was fortunate to be given a trial—Jeremiah's opponents, including King Jehoiakim, assassinated another prophet, Uriah, who had also prophesied the destruction of Jerusalem. He fled to Egypt but was captured there by royal agents and executed in Jerusalem. Jeremiah had political allies in Shaphan's family and escaped this fate (Jer 26:20–24).

Jeremiah's message against his opponents brings a charge of false prophecy: "This man deserves the sentence of death because he has prophesied against this city, as you have heard with your own ears" (26:11). In a time of war, Jeremiah's prophecy challenges Judah's "national security policy." Yet, paradoxically, while deeply divided by the politics of Jerusalem, the two sides are still ideologically united. As with the prophets of Judah and Bethel, both Jeremiah and his accusers function within the same ideological context, here the Deuteronomic law. The court is legitimate for Jeremiah (26:14) as well as for the establishment (26:16). It is a charge of blasphemy, invoking Yahweh's name in vain, not heresy, that the priests and prophets bring against him. The difference is critical, because blasphemy does not challenge the beliefs or ideology of the opponent, as heresy does.[21] Both sides, the Temple prophets and Jeremiah, accept the word of God as a legitimate warrant for prophecy. The Temple officials, however, cannot accept that such prophecy would be directed against the safety of Jerusalem promised to David. Jeremiah accepts the *framework* of the charges (i.e., there *is* such a thing as false prophecy) but then rejects the charge itself.[22] And in fact several officials accept Jeremiah's appeal to the word of Yahweh as defense against the charge of false prophecy, while others, "elders of the land," cite an older prophecy of Micah as precedent for Jeremiah's message (see Micah 3:12, cited in Jer 26:18).

The prophecy attacked by Jeremiah in his Temple Sermon, "This is the Temple of the LORD," has the same warrants as Jeremiah's prophecy *against* the Temple. Both sides accept the authority of "the word of the LORD." But Jeremiah explores the question of the origin of false prophecy and the genealogy of error more fully in Jer 14:13–16 and 23:9–40. He attacks his opponents' morality, their theology, and the source of their prophecy. The charges against these prophets include adultery, lying, and the evil of Sodom and Gomorrah (23:10, 14). Adultery was associated with religious practices that are not exclusively Yahwistic; Jeremiah recalls the Samarian prophets who led Israel astray prophesying by Baal. Jeremiah attacks the source of the prophecy even more than its content or the opposition's morality. The temple prophets do not speak the word of Yahweh; "I did not send them, nor did I command them or speak to them. They are prophesying a lying vision, worthless divination, and the deceit of their own minds" (14:14; cf. 23:16).[23] Jeremiah, who as a Northern prophetic emphasizes word over vision, is completely skeptical of the opposing prophets' ability to, as they claim, stand in Yahweh's council and see what will happen (23:18–22).[24] A legitimate prophet who had access to the council would convey Yahweh's words to the people rather than rely on dreams and visions: "Let the prophet who has a dream tell the dream (*ḥălôm*), but let the one who has my word (*děbarî*) speak my word faithfully" (Jer 23:28). The words spoken by these prophets are lies, stolen from each other rather than coming from Yahweh.

This conflict goes deeper than divisions over the content of prophecy and the future of the city of Jerusalem; it brings to light questions about the source of prophecy itself. The message of the Temple prophets is completely legitimate within the context of Royal Jerusalem theology, but for Jeremiah the visions of his opponents are not valid sources for prophecy. These divisions appear even deeper than the rift between Judah and Samaria explored via 1 Kings earlier. But the ideology of the unity of Israel under Yahweh again prevails.

Buying Land

The law in Deut 18:21–22 for judging prophets based on whether the prophecy comes to pass might have eventually adjudicated the conflict.[25] And yet, perhaps at the moment of Jerusalem's destruction, Jeremiah offers a consoling prophecy of hope and restoration in Jer 30–31, the so-called "Book of Consolation," and in the symbolic yet concrete act of purchasing land in Anatoth.[26] Jeremiah expresses a tradition in Hebrew prophecy of coupling judgment and promise. [27] This act of reconciliation between worshippers of Yahweh expresses the ideology of unity. Despite the rift with the priests and prophets of Jerusalem, Jeremiah prophesies a future in which all Israel will be restored. He neither demonizes nor condemns his opponents. The rhetoric of restoration invokes Israel and Judah, Ephraim and Jerusalem—it is an all-inclusive geography of hope for the people.

> Thus says the Lord:
> I am going to restore the fortunes of the tents of Jacob,
>   and have compassion on his dwellings;
> the city shall be rebuilt upon its mound,
>   and the citadel set on its rightful site
> . . . .
> At that time, says the Lord, I will be the God of all the families of
>   Israel, and they shall be my people.
>
> Jer 30:18, 31:1

Babylon will be destroyed as well (30:16). There is no intramural polemic in Jeremiah's consolation; indeed, there is no conflict, disagreement, or difference in the new covenant (31:31–34). The "law within them," written on their hearts, would eliminate the need for prophetic intercession or oracles. Jeremiah explores prophetic difference and disagreement more deeply than any other biblical prophet, but the ideology of reconciliation overcomes the rhetoric of difference.

THE HERESIOLOGICAL TURN AT QUMRAN

The story of prophetic conflict in the Hebrew Bible is much larger than these examples from 1 Kings and Jeremiah. The Babylonian Exile and post-exilic reconstitution of Jerusalem and Judea exposed deep ideological rifts within the Judean people, but these conflicts between various post-exilic prophets and prophetic groups are beyond my scope.[28] Most importantly for the formation of heresiological discourse, the Second Temple period also witnessed the development of Jewish apocalypticism.[29] We move then to the turbulent period of second-century Judaism and the rise of Jewish sectarianism after the Maccabean Revolt. This period of rapid social and religious change included the production of the most important non-biblical Jewish texts for the study of early Christianity—and therefore for the formation of heresiological discourse.[30]

Around 150 BCE, a priest or group of priests in Jerusalem wrote a tract outlining differences with an unnamed religious authority over the interpretation and practice of Jewish law, or *halakah*.[31] These differences, outlined in the Dead Sea Scroll 4QMMT, *Miqṣat Maʿaśē ha-Torah* or *A Halakhic Letter*, were at the center of the formation of a sectarian group that called itself the Covenant or Community (*yaḥad*) and that built a religious community at Qumran near the Dead Sea around 100 BCE.[32] The Dead Sea Scrolls mark a critical moment in the history of heresiological discourse. These sectarian documents contain significant discursive shifts from previous patterns of prophetic negotiation of difference to a sectarian, dualistic, and apocalyptic notion of a reconstructed "Israel" that excludes all other Jewish groups.[33] My earlier reading of Jeremiah provides a touchstone for these discursive changes in the sectarian scrolls; the upcoming comparison between another second-century political movement, the Hasmoneans, and another apocalyptic text, the Book of Daniel, further contextualizes this rhetorical fissure. Before turning to this analysis, there are two brief introductory matters.

Qumran and Christianity

First is the relationship of the Dead Sea Scrolls with what comes to be early Christianity. One can hardly overestimate the importance of the Dead Sea Scrolls for understanding the Second Temple Jewish context from which the movements of John the Baptist and Jesus emerged.[34] While elements of sectarian ideology have antecedents and parallels in other Second Temple texts, the complex of ideas in the scrolls as a whole does not.[35] Many of these ideas have parallels in early Christianity. The importance of the scrolls for Christianity as well as Second Temple Judaism was immediately evident on their discovery, and scholarship has increased exponentially since the release of all the scrolls in 1991.[36] For the most part, I will leave aside the exploration of the connections between the theology and social practices of Qumran and what becomes Christianity; this has been researched and debated extensively by experts in both fields. My focus is the rhetoric of difference in the Dead Sea Scrolls as the discursive origins of the Christian notion of heresy. I will examine here the functions of ideological difference in the formation of the identity of the community and the rhetorical construction of its opponents.

Problems in the Notion of the *Yaḥad*

Second, there are difficulties that arise in reconstructing a community from the scrolls themselves. The social and political contexts of this discourse are important for understanding the history of the community and identities of their opponents. The controversial history of the publication of the Qumran scrolls resulted in a wide range of preliminary theories; the formation of the consensus "Essene hypothesis," that the community that collected or produced this library was the Essene community of Jews described by Josephus (*J.W.* 2.119–61; *Ant.* 18.18–22) and other ancient writers; a variety of challenges to that consensus; and now a new series of revisions within that consensus.[37] According to Josephus, the Essenes "display an extraordinary interest in the writings of the ancients" (*palaiōn syntagmata*, *J.W.* 2.136). One of the central questions is, within the corpus of the Dead Sea Scrolls, what counts as a "sectarian" text, written by the Essene community, rather than one collected by the community. Biblical literature aside, the scrolls include large amounts of Enochic (i.e., *1 Enoch*) and other ancient apocryphal literature, such as the *Book of Jubilees*, recognized to have been central to but not written by the community. Although the origin of many of the scrolls as "sectarian" or not remains debated, there is a consensus that three texts, the *Halakhic Letter* (4QMMT), the *Damascus Document* (CD), and the *Community Rule* (1QS), are sectarian. These are central for reconstructing the history and identity of the community. They are central as well for sectarian rhetoric against its opponents.

The *Halakhic Letter* and *Damascus Document* inscribe the pre-history, origins, and foundation of the community while the *Community Rule* represents the post-100 CE period, when the community occupied Qumran.[38] These three formative sectarian texts suggest a progression of the community from a position within or close to the Jerusalem Temple hierarchy to an autonomous apocalyptic sect. The *Damascus Document* and the *Community Rule* indicate that this group broke off from some other group. The precise identity of the group in dialogue in 4QMMT is not critical to the development of the rhetoric of heresy; therefore, with acknowledgment of the alternatives, I will follow the consensus position that this community had priestly, Sadducean origins.

THE RHETORIC OF DIFFERENCE AT QUMRAN

These three documents from Qumran describe a community that constructed its identity around the ideology of difference, the rhetoric of separation, and the condemnation of the other. The Dead Sea Scrolls include extensive halakhic definition of their own and their opponents' positions, positions that determine eternal life or damnation as a "son of Belial" (Satan). While the Qumran community was geographically separated from the rest of Israel, the community constructed an ideological geography of the "true" Israel surrounded by the "sons of Belial" and the *Kittim*, foreigners or Romans. The social-political context for this development of a sectarian notion of "Israel" in the Qumran community was the Hasmonean state, which itself constructed a political ideology of Israel as a unified Hellenistic kingdom.

4QMMT, "Some Torah Precepts"[39]

I begin with a text that dates from the earliest stages of the movement that would become the Qumran covenant community. While there is little hint of communal organization here, this important document describes its ideological origins.[40] As noted earlier, most scholars locate the origins of the movement within the Sadducees. Again, the political context should be noted. As the Hasmoneans achieved military and then political success in Israel after 160 BCE, the Seleucid upstart Alexander Balas chose Jonathan, the brother of Judas Maccabee, as high priest.[41] The Hellenistic successors of Alexander the Great had elevated the religious aristocracy as the privileged leaders in Judea; the high priest was the political as well as religious leader in Jerusalem.[42] For the forerunners of the Qumran community, the Jerusalem priesthood was not Alexander's to give away, nor was it Jonathan's to take, since he was not a Zadokite.[43] The Hasmonean hold on the high priesthood continued with the accession of Simon (142 BCE) and then Simon's son John Hyrcanus (134–104 BCE). While a dispute with the Zadokite priesthood may be part of the pre-history of the sect, clearly the Hasmonean priesthood was unacceptable (4QMMT 82–85).[44]

The call for restoration of a "true" Zadokite priesthood is but part of the ideology of the Temple here. For the Covenanters, the Jerusalem temple was polluted and defiled. Furthermore, the Covenant held to a 364-day solar calendar, in contrast with the lunar calendar of the Hasmonean period (which was perhaps a Hellenistic innovation). This calendar is also attested in *1 Enoch* and *Jubilees*, which were important texts at Qumran.[45] The regularity of the solar calendar of exactly 52 weeks meant that each festival fell on the same day of the week every year. Major festivals for this group were work days for Jews who followed the Jerusalem calendar, and vice versa.[46]

In addition to the Temple and the calendar, 4QMMT highlights a range of halakhic issues that divided the authors from the Jerusalem priesthood: Sabbath observance, sacrifice, offerings, and, above, all purity. The "wheat of the Gentiles" should not be brought into the Temple (8). The priest in charge of the red heifer offering must be pure (18) while flowing liquids transfer impurity from vessel to vessel (60–61).[47] The letter implies that the geography of purity extends beyond the Temple itself to "the camp" (33) or "the holy camp" (63), the city of Jerusalem. The text highlights purity and uncleanness issues with regard to foreigners, "bastards," people with disabilities or deformities, animals, skin diseases, and corpses.

As I outlined in Chapter 1, the detailed, pejorative description of oppo-nents' beliefs is a central element of heresiology. The forebears of the Qumran community define themselves in opposition to another group by elucidating their halakhic positions and their opponents'. The *halakhot* (plural of halakah) in the *Temple Scroll* (11QT) offer a contrast that high-lights this doxographic feature in 4QMMT. The Temple Scroll, which is both longer and less fragmentary than 4QMMT, follows the biblical model of law in Leviticus or Deuteronomy.[48] Here is a passage on corpse impurity and liquids:

> If a man dies in your cities, the house in which the man has died shall be unclean for seven days. Whatever is in the house and whoever enters the house shall be unclean for seven days. Any food on which water has been poured shall be unclean, anything moistened shall be unclean. Earthenware vessels shall be unclean and whatever they contain shall be unclean for every clean man. The open (vessels) shall be unclean for every Israelite (with) whatever is moistened in them. (11QT 49)

4QMMT lists these same halakhic concerns in doxographic rather than legalistic form. "And concerning [the uncleanness of the corpse]: we say that (אנחו אומרים) every bone, [whether stripped of flesh] or complete is subject to the law concerning a dead or murdered person" (4QMMT 72–74). While the halakhic position is the same, the rhetorical function of the halakah here is to construct a community identity of "we" in contrast to "them." Similarly the view that liquids transmit impurity is found in ll. 58–61. The phrases "we say that" and "we think that" (אנחנו חושבים) are regular markers in 4QMMT. In both cases the phrase "we say that" qualifies this halakah as the ruling that distinguishes one community from another. All of these halakhic positions in 4QMMT construct an "us" and a "them." The rhetoric of difference is central to sectarian identity.

In addition to a doxography of difference, we find hints in 4QMMT of the sectarianism and eschatology that mark the Qumran community. These themes are latent rather than fully expressed and scholars have speculated that the authors of the letter held open the possibility of returning to the Jerusalem Temple.[49] "[And you know that] we have segregated ourselves from the rest of the peop[le (שפרשנו מרוב העם) and (that) we avoid] mingling in these affairs and associating with them in these things" (92–93). Further-more, in lines 99ff, there are several eschatological phrases such as "this is the end of days" (אחרית הימים). For the Qumran covenant community, ideo-logically at least, indeed it was.

The *Damascus Document*

The Dead Sea Scrolls include broader, and polemically sharper, notions of sectarianism, apocalyptic dualism, and eschatology within a literary framework of halakhic doxography. From 4QMMT we move to the fuller narrative in the *Damascus Document* (CD from its first discovery in Cairo).⁵⁰ The *Damascus Document* is the foundational text for the Qumran community.⁵¹ The rhetoric of difference here defines the communal and opponents' identities via a historiography of the *yaḥad* as the remnant of the true Israel; the ideology of biblical foundations for the community; cosmological dualism; and halakhic self-definition, with doxography of their opponents. This discourse is a prototype of Christian heresiology.

The historical elements of the *Damascus Document* have engaged the most scholarly speculation and analysis since the text seems to tell the story—or perhaps several versions of the story—of the origins of the Qumran community.⁵² Rather than focusing on the actual pre-history or origins of the community, I look at the rhetoric and ideology of this historiography. The *Damascus Document* constructs the history of the community in completely dualistic terms. Each historiographical passage in CD highlights a dualistic opposition between sets of contrasting "good guys" and "bad guys."⁵³ The community begins as "blind men groping for the way," 390 years after the Babylonian Exile, until God raised up the Teacher of Righteousness to lead them. Opposing the Teacher is "the Scoffer," the "man of mockery" who leads Israel astray with "the waters of falsehood." The charges against the "Scoffer" introduce a division between "all who know righteousness," the followers of the Teacher, and the "seekers after smooth things," the followers of the Scoffer. A second passage in CD II, 6–18 evokes the trope of the remnant raised by God, anointed by the Holy Spirit (II, 11–12), opposed by "those whom [God] hated."⁵⁴ The opposing group is attacked for its departure from the Way (2.6). CD III, 10–12 narrates a division between the first members of the Covenant who forsook "the Covenant of God" while the "remnant . . . held fast." And finally in V, 20–VI, 2, God raised up "men of discernment" in response to false prophecy (*wĕ-nab'ô seqer*) by "the tresspassers" (*hagabôl*).⁵⁵

More significantly, the text constructs a historiography of the *yaḥad* as the remnant of the true Israel. The *Damascus Document* prefigures these dualistic oppositions in biblical texts, thereby constructing the history of the community as the history of Israel. The Cave 4 fragments (in particular 4Q266 and 4Q270) suggest that the text was used in a covenant renewal ceremony patterned after Deuteronomy 29–30.⁵⁶ And other examples of biblical historiography from the Cairo text abound. The fall of the Watchers in heaven (Gen 6:1–4; *1 Enoch* 6–10) prefigures the divide in Israel between the Covenant and the sons of Belial (CD II, 18).⁵⁷ The "spouters," current enemies of the community, were prefigured in the prophetic conflict between Moses, Aaron, and the Egyptian magicians Jannes and Jambres (CD III, 19; cf. 4Q266, fr. 3 II, 6–7).⁵⁸ And the community itself is defined biblically by the "well rich in water" (III, 16), dug by the remnant or "penitents" (שבי) of Israel, that is identified as the Law (VI, 5).⁵⁹ The interpretation of law identifies this Qumran method (*pesher*) as a doctrinal marker of the men of

Holiness (CD IV, 8), while the quotation of Micah 7:2 in CD IV, 12 marks the separation of the Covenant from the "house of Judah" eschatologically:

> But when the age is completed, according to the number of those years, there shall be no more joining the house of Judah, but each man shall stand on his watch-tower: *The wall is built, the boundary far removed.*

The metaphors of wall, well, and boundary evoke the spatial identity of a community separated from the rest of Israel—actually no longer Israel at all, which is now solely defined ideologically in terms of the Covenant community, but rather "scoffers," "trespassers," "sons of Belial," and "removers of the boundary." So too the opponents are defined through biblical historiography against the True Israel. The *Damascus Document* presents a history of corruption by the evil inclination, *yeṣer ishmah*, from the Watchers of Gen 6:4 and *1 Enoch* through the patriarchs, the children of Israel in Egypt, and to the origins of the Covenant (II, 16–III, 12). The *Damascus Document* writes the community into the history of Israel and, just as significantly, writes other contemporaneous Jewish communities out of the sacred history.

The dualism of CD extends beyond this biblical historiography to ontological, social, and ideological dimensions within an apocalyptic, eschatological framework.[60] First, dualism is part of the nature of the universe itself. God has a dispute with all flesh (*rîb lô 'am kol basar*) and will condemn anyone who rejects him (CD I, 2). Scoffing or rejecting God is not a free choice; God "knew their deeds before ever they were created" and condemns the sinners to eternal wrath at the hand of the Angel of Destruction (II, 3–13).[61] Furthermore, the social world of the community is divided by the active agency of evil in the world. Belial is a present and future threat. While the "three nets of Belial"—fornication, riches, and the profanation of the Temple—ensnare Israel in the present (IV, 15), he will be unleashed against Israel at the completion of the age.[62] With the Temple, the "sons of the Pit" (VI, 15) are present and future threats. Just as the "apostates" or "backsliders" (VIII, 1) of the past were condemned, any member of the Covenant who departs from the precepts will be handed to Belial for destruction (VIII, 2; cf. XIX, 13–16). Only separation from apostates can avoid the coming wrath (VIII, 4–9).[63]

Finally, the dualistic historiography and eschatology in CD are grounded ideologically in halakah.[64] After the "scoffers" are attacked for their departure from the Way (II, 6), the Covenant is defined doctrinally as a revelation of Sabbaths, feasts, and the ways of truth (III, 14–15). The *Damascus Document* combines exhortation and polemical historiography with extensive halakhic instructions, primarily in the statutes (cols. IX–XVI) but also interspersed among the exhortation. The section opened by the exegesis of the Well (VI, 14–VII, 9) leads to a series of doctrinal precepts stemming from the correct interpretation of scripture: avoiding the Jerusalem Temple; separating from the "sons of the Pit" (VI, 15); not defrauding the poor; observing ritual purity; following the observances of Sabbath and Feast Days (the sectarian calendar) as derived in the New Covenant; and offering the correct sacrifices, offerings, and tithes ("holy things.").[65] The section furthermore delineates those who "live in camps" and take wives (CD VII, 6–7; cf. XII, 15 and *J.W.* 2.160–161).

The political context for the origins of the Qumran sectarian *yaḥad* comes to the fore at the conclusion of the Exhortation.[66] Before turning to the politics of the Covenant community, I will first examine the rigidly sectarian *Serekh ha-Yaḥad* or *Community Rule*.

The *Community Rule*

The formative ideology of the *Halakhic Letter* and biblical historiography of the *Damascus Document* was set in the sectarian stone of the *Community Rule* (1QS).[67] There is clearly some relationship between the statutes in CD and the rules of 1QS, despite some key differences.[68] The question of whether the praxis of the community followed one version or the other—or even the degree to which the *Community Rule* was an idealized or utopian document—is not a central issue. Sectarian discourse idealizes its social setting, in which boundaries are blurrier than might appear in the text. The rhetorical constructions of these boundaries between "us" and "them," here the "sons of Israel" and "sons of Belial," are my focus. We should assume more diversity within the community or communities that produced the Dead Sea Scrolls than implied by their rhetoric (for instance, the rules in CD for those who live in "camps" noted earlier, which suggests more porous boundaries).[69] Social and ideological diversity marked Second Temple Jewish movements. The first-century Jewish movements that inherited and modified Qumran ideology, such as the movements of John the Baptist and Jesus of Nazareth, exhibited this diversity as well.

The *Rule* describes a predetermined world in which the spirits of light and darkness, or truth and falsehood, wage war in each person, in whom God has planted an equal share of the warring spirits, until the final visitation of God and the purification of the world. A central section is the instruction on "The Sons of Light and Darkness" (1QS III, 12–IV, 25) that appears to have been an originally independent treatise.[70] This section includes a theory of dualism on which the ideology and *halakah* of the *Rule* stand.[71] It also provides an ontological theory for the *origin* of error in the community's ideological and social world. God has appointed "two spirits" (שתי רישם) for humankind (אנוש), the "spirits of truth and injustice" (והעול האמת). These two spirits correspond to a set of warring oppositions): the Prince of Light and Angel of Darkness who rule each group; the children of Israel and sons of Belial who compose each group; and an opposing set of moral qualities that mark each group (1QS IV, 4–11). Presiding over this is "the God of Israel," who created the spirits, loves the children of Israel, and hates the sons of Belial. The God of Israel rules over history as well as creation; the treatise ends with a strong eschatological condemnation of those controlled by the spirit of injustice:

> And the visitation of all who walk in this spirit shall be a multitude of plagues by the hand of all the destroying angels, everlasting damnation by the avenging wrath of the fury of God, eternal torment and endless disgrace together with shameful extinction in the fire of the dark regions. The times of all their generations shall be spent in sorrowful mourning and in bitter misery and in calamities of darkness until they are destroyed without remnant or survivor. (1QS IV, 12–14)

This passage recontextualizes the theory of the two spirits in the social setting of the community. The "sons of Belial" are the actual Judeans outside the community.

The threat of this evil spirit and damnation pervades the life of the community: "They shall separate from the congregation of the men of injustice" (1QS V, 2). Once there, all aspects of social life are controlled by the authorities within the community, the priests, Council, and Master. The hierarchy of the Community inscribed in 1QS epitomizes the rigid sectarian dualism of the document. The *Community Rule* constructs an evil opposition within the *yaḥad* itself that uses the dualism in the "Treatise of the Two Spirits" as an internal technology of control. There is a clear function for maintaining the edge, in light of the predestined outcome for each person according to this treatise. If the parts are equal, and each man struggles with it, then the authority of the Guardian or other authorities is increased by the ideology of eschatological damnation. Members of the Covenant could slip, thus suffering the punishments allotted to the sons of Belial. And there were plenty of opportunities to slip and be punished, even expelled. Expulsion from the community was the equivalent of death and eternal damnation.[72] The extensive rules for community life in cols. v–viii construct a community ruled by rigid *halakhot*.[73] While many rules for initiation, meals, study, and behavior are interesting in their own right for the construction of social life and community identity, the very comprehensiveness of the ideology of sectarian dualism is significant. No detail of social or religious life escapes the rule of the two spirits. But the *Rule* lacks the doxography of opposing views found in 4QMMT. In the dualistic ideology of 1QS, there is no need to explain or even acknowledge the beliefs of the sons of Belial.

Finally, we see in the *Rule* a fully reconstituted Israel as the Covenant community. All others are the "sons of Belial," no longer Jews or even humans. As in the *Damascus Document*, the identity of the community as "Israel" itself is constructed biblically. Here, however, it is not biblical historiography so much as the identity of the Covenant as the true Israel, surrounded by the sons of Belial, which marks the text. While there are relatively few biblical citations in 1QS compared to CD or 4QMMT, one central passage describes "the Everlasting Plantation, a House of Holiness for Israel, an Assembly of Supreme Holiness for Aaron" that is the properly constituted Council of the Community (VIII, 5–6). Two quotations from Isaiah identify the Council as "that precious corner-stone, whose foundations shall neither rock nor sway in their place" (VIII, 7–8; cf. Isa 28:16). Second, the true members of the "Community in Israel" must separate from "the habitation of unjust men and shall go into the wilderness to prepare the way of Him; as it is written, 'Prepare in the wilderness the way of. . . . , make straight in the desert a path for our God'" (VIII, 14; Isa 40:3). This Isaiah passage recurs as the identifying text for John the Baptist in the earliest Christian Gospels (see Chapter 3).

The rigid strictures on purity and separatism in the Covenant community can be read in the archaeology of Khirbet Qumran as well as the Dead Sea Scrolls. The community did not import ceramic vessels, to avoid impurity, but manufactured pottery on site, some with clay from Jerusalem.[74] The types of pottery found at Qumran, moreover, suggest the focus on purity in the Covenant.[75] The common storage jars found in Judea from first-century BCE to first-century CE sites had a "broad, bag-shaped body with sloping, rounded shoulders that widens toward the bottom" and relatively narrow necks that were easily sealed.[76] They had ring-handles on the shoulders that could be used to lift and empty these bag-shaped jars. At Qumran, numerous cylindrical and ovoid jars, with large bowl-shaped mouths, have been found. The lids were able to be opened on the Sabbath without violating the prohibition to break clay seals, while the contents could be dipped or scooped out more easily than the narrow-necked "bag jars," to avoid the impurity transferred when pouring a pure liquid into an impure container (4QMMT 55–58). The bowl-shaped lids also prevented moisture, with its attendant impurity, from coming into the jars since they overlapped the neck.[77] The purity concerns of the Covenant extended to toilet hygiene and dress, since the community viewed itself as a replacement for the temple and substitute for the sacrificial cult.[78] These various aspects of the material culture at Qumran underscore the rigid separatism of the sect from other Jews and Gentiles.[79]

THE HASMONEAN POLITICAL CONTEXT

What of these "unjust men" that the community separates from? Who actually were the "sons of Belial" in the second century BCE? The references to other Jewish leaders are obscure and debatable. It is not clear, nor essential to my argument, whether the founders were "Enochic" or "Sadducean," or who the Teacher of Righteousness actually was. The references to the political leaders, however, are more concrete. The political context for the development of a sectarian notion of "Israel" in the Dead Sea Scrolls was the Hasmonean state, which was in the process of constructing its own ideology of "Israel" as a Hellenistic kingdom.[80] The rhetoric of *separation* from Israel in the Dead Sea Scrolls can be read against the rhetoric of *unification* of Israel in Hasmonean propaganda.

We know from the Dead Sea Scrolls that the Seleucid and Hasmonean rulers were political targets of the community.[81] The Damascus Covenant interprets the "head of the asps" in Deut 32:33 as "the kings of Greece, who came to wreak vengeance upon them," where "them" refers to "the princes of Judah" or the "kings of the people" (CD B XIX, 22). This likely refers to the incursion by Antiochus IV and the Maccabean War. The Qumran *pesharîm* (biblical commentaries) de-historicize biblical texts and locate their meaning in the social world of the community.[82] In the *pesher* or Commentary on Hab 2:5–6, the "arrogant man" of the prophetic text is identified as the "Wicked Priest" who ruled over Israel, forsook God, and "betrayed the precepts for the sake of riches" (1QpHab VIII, 8–11). This *pesher* condemns this man for living in "the ways of abominations amidst every unclean defilement." This likely refers to Jonathan, who succeeded Judas Maccabeus as leader of the rebellion in 160 and accepted the high priesthood from Alexander Balas in 153. He was killed by Alexander's general Tryphon (1 Macc 13:23). The *Testimonia* (4Q175) applies Josh 6:26 to two "instruments of violence," perhaps father and son, who rule and rebuild Jerusalem as a "fortress of wickedness." The *pesher* on Nah 2:13 identifies a "furious young lion" who takes revenge against the "seekers of smooth things" by crucifying them (4Q169 frags. 3+4 I, 6–7), likely Alexander Jannaeus (ruled 103–76 BCE). Josephus writes that Jannaeus condemned eight hundred Pharisees to be crucified (*Ant.* 13.380–83; *J.W.* 1.96–8). The Nahum commentary also mentions two Greek kings, Antiochus and Demetrius. The 4QCalendrical Documents C^a and C^{d-e} (4Q322, 324a–b) contain references to Queen Salome Alexandra (ruled 76–66 BCE), the widow of Alexander Jannaeus, John Hyrcanus II (63–40 BCE), and M. Aemilius Scaurus, the first Roman governor of Syria from 65 to 62.

It is clear that the sectarian community at Qumran opposed the Hasmonean dynasty.[83] We have seen how the Temple, a central concern already in 4QMMT, became a focal point in the Damascus Covenant: "None of those brought into the Covenant shall enter the Temple to light his altar in vain" (CD VI, 12).[84] While at Qumran, social life created a substitute for Temple and sacrifice within the community.[85] From 153 to 37 BCE, the Jerusalem Temple was controlled by the Hasmoneans. They were the leaders of the "unjust men" from whom the Covenant must separate (1QS VIII, 14). The War Scroll describes the destruction of Belial's host with the Kittim (1QM I, 10–12; XIII, 4–6), which included the authorities in Jerusalem with the Romans. The community imagined a New Jerusalem, with a new Temple, after this final war.[86] Since the high priesthood was clearly a central point of ideological contention for the Qumran community, my focus turns to the Hasmonean political project as Hellenistic imperial dynasty after the succession of the priesthood from Jonathan to Simon in 142 BCE.[87]

A salient contrast between the Qumran *yaḥad* and the Hasmonean dynasty is not textual but archaeological. The still-unexplained cemetery at Qumran was unique within Judea.[88] The tombs at Qumran were individual inhumations from 1.5 to 2 meters in the marl, oriented north-south. The normal Judean practice was rock-cut caves shared by generations of families. These burial practices provide a sharp contrast between the separatist Qumran community and the Hasmoneans. Qumran burial was unique within Israel but the Hasmonean practices were typical among Hellenistic monarchs. 1 Macc 13:27–29 describes the tomb built by Simon in Modein for his fathers and brothers after the death of Jonathan:

> And Simon built a monument over the tomb of his father and his brothers; he made it high so that it might be seen, with polished stone at the front and the back. He also erected seven pyramids, opposite one another, for his father and mother and four brothers. For the pyramids he devised an elaborate setting, erecting about them great columns, and on the columns he put suits of armor for a permanent memorial, and beside the suits of armor he carved ships, so that they could be seen by all who sail the sea.

This ostentatious monument suggests the prototypical Hellenistic burial memorial, the eponymous Mausoleum of King Mausolos at Halicarnassus.[89] One of the seven wonders of the ancient world, it was described by Pliny the Elder as twenty-five cubits high, surrounded by columns, and with a pyramidal roof (*Natural History* 36.20). Another monument at Ephesus in Turkey, the Belevi Monument used by King Lysimachus as well as the Seleucid Antiochus III, had similar height (ten meters) and a pyramidal roof, and was encircled by columns.[90]

The pyramids and Doric columns of Simon's tomb at Modein projected the ideology of the Hasmonean dynasty as a powerful Hellenistic kingdom within the eastern Mediterranean world.[91] Where the Qumran community turned inward and redefined Israel as itself, the Hasmoneans turned outward and redefined Israel as a Hellenistic kingdom. Israel was hardly a naval power, but Simon directed the display of power so that it could be seen by "all who sail the sea" (*hypo pantōn tōn pleontōn tēn thalassan*), that is the Greco-Roman world, as well as his own people. Diplomacy was as important as military success for the Hasmoneans, and Jonathan had focused extensively on foreign policy. He and Simon had developed a network of embassies and treaties already with Rome and Sparta as well as extensive dealings with the Seleucids (1 Macc 12:1–23).[92] This tomb expressed the dynastic ambitions of the Hasmoneans in this Greco-Roman political context.[93] While building by the Hasmoneans pales in comparison to their successor Herod the Great, the luxurious palace and pool complex built at Jericho by the Hasmoneans included lavish decoration, colonnaded porches, frescoes, and mosaics.[94] According to Josephus, John Hyrcanus I also built a monumental tomb for himself in Jerusalem.[95]

These cultural practices are complemented by the political notion of "Israel" in the strongly pro-Hasmonean 1 Maccabees. [96] This important source for the history of the revolt and establishment of the Jewish monarchy likely obscures rather than reveals the social origins of the Hasmoneans in its biblical propaganda. [97] Political propaganda drapes authorities in the present with the perceived authority of their predecessors, and 1 Maccabees is a masterwork of that genre. Jonathan, Simon, and their successors had to forge political alliances in Judea as well as with foreign powers.[98] Trading on the history of Israel and biblical imagery was one part of sustaining the ideology of the Hasmonean dynasty. As with the Qumran sectarian narrative in the *Damascus Document*, 1 Maccabees constructs the history and ideology of the Hasmoneans as biblical history.[99] But in contrast with Qumran dualism, which divides the people into sons of light and darkness, 1 Maccabees constructs a unified Israel. The text proclaims for a Jewish audience the dynastic claims of Judas and Simon's successors as the rulers of Israel and the heirs of the mantles of biblical heroes such as the Judges, Moses, and most importantly David. The speech of Mattathias in 2:51–70 situates Judas and Simeon within the history of God's salvation of Israel by comparing them to the ancient heroes of the faith (see also 4:9–11). The text calls upon the biblical prototypes as positive models of piety (Judas in 1 Macc 3:19) and also by means of negative portrayals of the Jewish leaders who do not have God's favor in leading Israel (Joseph and Azariah, 5:55–62). When Jonathan succeeds Judas after his death, he is compared to a Judge (9:73) and consolidates his power as High Priest (10:21). 1 Maccabees supports the ideology that God's hand was at work in the Hasmoneans just as in the days of old.

Opposed to the Hasmoneans are the "evil Gentiles" (*ta ethnē*, 5:1–3), joined by some evil Jews (1:11, 43, 52–53).[100] The text refers to the Jews as an *ethnos*, *laos*, or above all "Israel," some sixty-three times, ten of which occur in the first chapter. [101] Thus Bickerman wrote that 1 Maccabees was "governed by a single idea, the opposition between Israel and the nations."[102] Given the involvement of the Hasmoneans with "the nations" as part of their diplomatic and political success, the rhetoric of 1 Maccabees is somewhat ironic.[103] But the unity of Israel under the Hasmoneans had strong ideological power within the contested, sectarian social world of Second Temple Judaism.[104] In the increasingly divided context of the second century, the Hasmonean political response is the construction through biblical tropes of the notion of a unified "Israel." While groups such as the "righteous" in 1 Macc 2:29 or the "Hasideans" in 2:42–44 could be the progenitors of Jewish sects, in 1 Maccabees they join the Hasmonean cause.[105]

The rhetoric of unified, God-ordained rule of Israel by the Hasmoneans, however, presents a potent contrast to the Qumran ideology of the Covenant as the true Israel. Politically, the two constructions of Israel were completely at odds with one another. By the time 1 Maccabees was written under John Hyrcanus I, the physical geography of Israel for the Qumran community was the settlement by the Dead Sea.[106] The political geography of the sectarian scrolls, however, was much larger, as we have seen. The strongly eschatological, apocalyptic worldview of the Covenant might suggest that this was a natural stance of the sect against the "world."[107] We see, however, that the rhetoric of "Israel" in the sectarian Dead Sea Scrolls had a particular political context, which was the projection of Hasmonean hegemony.

APOCALYPTIC DUALISM: THE CASE OF DANIEL

This last point raises an important question. Would an apocalyptic group such as the Qumran covenant naturally oppose the Maccabean authorities? That is one possible interpretation for the dualistic polemic against the Hasmoneans in the Dead Sea Scrolls. The sectarian discourse of apocalypticism can either reflect social dissonance, such as a social crisis within the community, or foster existing ideological differences with its divisive rhetoric.[108] But the politics in the sectarian Scrolls should not be dismissed as the inevitable consequence of an apocalyptic worldview. To be sure, apocalypticism, true to its roots in ancient Hebrew prophecy, expresses strong ideological disagreement between religious groups and concomitant polemical condemnation of opponents. But apocalyptic texts could also function as well to unify Israel in the face of invasion, destruction, and catastrophe.[109] Crisis and deprivation theories of millenarian movements do not fully account for the social and political functions of apocalyptic rhetoric for the group itself.[110] The politics of many apocalyptic texts, such as *1 Enoch* or the Book of Revelation, stand strongly against the authorities. But Jewish apocalypses could be strongly pro-Israel. This is the case for one salient example from this period.

The Book of Daniel, finalized during the early Maccabean revolt about one generation before 4QMMT, is part of the discursive context for both 1 Maccabees and the Qumran sectarian writings.[111] The social-political context for the apocalyptic visions in Daniel 7–12 is the invasion of Jerusalem in 167 BCE by Antiochus IV Epiphanes, represented symbolically as a horn on the "fourth beast" (Dan 7:8) or a conquering goat (8:9).[112] These visions describe how this "arrogant" and "exceedingly great" horn overthrows other "horns" or kings and attacks the holy city and people of God. In the complementary visions of the four beasts in Daniel 7 and the ram and goat in Daniel 8, God responds, limiting the desecration to three and a half years, overthrowing the arrogant king, and restoring an everlasting kingdom for the people of God (Dan 7:23–27; 8:23–27).[113] Daniel 9 is an extended prayer that contextualizes the current persecution of Jews by Antiochus with a reinterpretation of Jeremiah's prophecy of seventy years for the desolation of Jerusalem (Jer 25:11, 12; 29:10) as seventy *weeks* of years, a period that would extend Jeremiah's now-ancient prophecy about the Babylonian invasion of Jerusalem to the contemporary situation under Antiochus. This grounds the apocalyptic theology of Daniel in the now-classical prophecy of Jeremiah. Finally, in the extended vision of the Human One (*bar 'ĕnāš*, an angel or messiah) in Daniel 10–12, the "wise among the people," the *maśkîlîm*, offer instruction to the people, resist the persecution, and will be resurrected as martyrs (Dan 11:33–35; 12:1–3).[114] All five visions include overviews of the periods of history from the Persian to the Seleucid monarchs, with excessive detail on the events surrounding Antiochus IV and his immediate forebears.

This brief summary hardly does justice to the apocalyptic visions of this rich and complex text. The point here, however, is to consider Daniel's political stance within the range of apocalyptic Jewish responses to the invasion and persecution by Antiochus. Accepting the widely held view that the visions are the product of the "wise" or *maśkîlîm*, an elite scribal party, we see that they oppose Antiochus but do not fully embrace the Maccabees.[115] Their resistance to the Seleucids is less active than that of the warrior Maccabees, but it is resistance nonetheless, resulting in martyrdom for some of the group.[116] Here, we have an apocalyptic ideology that neither opposes the Hasmonean project, as the Qumran sectarians do, nor supports it whole-heartedly, as does the Animal Apocalypse in *1 Enoch* 85–91.[117] Nonetheless, Daniel 7–12 presents a politically unified, apocalyptic response. The restoration of Israel in 7:27 is for "the people of the holy ones of the Most High," not the "wise" alone. Gabriel responds to Daniel's prayer for "the sin of my people Israel" (9:20). This reinterpretation of Jeremiah's prophecy during the Babylonian conquest and exile is directed to "your people and your holy city" (9:24), not the in-group of "the wise." So too the human agent helps Daniel understand the future of "your people" (10:14). Daniel does not express a sectarian ideology that calls for withdrawing from the rest of Jewish society. In fact, the "wise among the people" offer guidance to the "many" (11:33).[118] To be sure, Daniel includes an element of apocalyptic dualism: "Many of those who sleep in the dust of the earth shall awake, some to everlasting life, and some to shame and everlasting contempt" (12:2). But this dualism has been displaced to the eschaton. Daniel is the first and only book of the Hebrew Bible to feature resurrection and judgment clearly in this way. But it is laconic in its description of how that process of reward and punishment affects its contemporary social world. The contrast to the sectarian Dead Sea Scrolls could not be greater, in both their dualistic rhetoric against Israel and political position against the Hasmoneans.

CONCLUSION

Prophetic, apocalyptic, and other renewal or reform movements take stands against the established religious authorities, for instance, the Jerusalem Temple, as well as other religious groups. Social conflict read through the rhetoric of difference is regularly, perhaps inevitably, the result. I have examined in this chapter a range of responses to ideological difference from ancient Israel and Second Temple Judaism. This range helps identify the nature of heresiological rhetoric at Qumran in comparison with the discursive responses in the other texts. The legends of 1 Kings show how prophetic conflict was narrated in the Deuteronomic History, while the story of Jeremiah shows how the deepest conflicts in pre-exilic Jerusalem were resolved under the ideology of Yahwistic unity. Jeremiah and Daniel are marked by the unified political notion of Israel in the context of deep ideological disagreements within Israel and invasion from without. Difference is negotiated and mediated by an ideology of unity within Israel.

The Dead Sea Scrolls, in contrast, reveal a community that constructed its very identity around the rhetoric of difference. The Qumran Covenant claimed the identity of the true Israel while all other Jews were, with the *Kittim*, designated as sons of Belial and destined for destruction. The Covenant formed a symbolic Temple community that awaited the New Temple from God; the Jerusalem Temple was also destined for destruction. Eschatological dualism functioned politically within the Covenant as an internal technology of control. Externally, the notion of Israel in the Dead Sea Scrolls opposed the hegemonic Hasmonean political ideology of Israel as a unified Hellenistic kingdom expressed in 1 Maccabees. Dualism is even part of the messages of hope and restoration; the sectarian writings claim the prophetic trope of restoration for all Israel expressed by both Jeremiah and Daniel as theirs alone. But comparison with Daniel showed that this dualistic, separatist rhetoric is not always part of an apocalyptic worldview.

This analysis of the rhetoric of difference in Second Temple Jewish texts is important for tracing the genealogy of the notion of heresy and the discourse of early Christian heresiology. I have identified a number of key rhetorical features in the scrolls that are part of early Christian heresiology. While some of these features are also exhibited in other Second Temple texts, the combination at Qumran is unique. These include the following:

The Doxography of Error

A central aspect of community identity is the elucidation of doctrinal differences to define "us" and "them." The *Halakhic Letter* focuses above all on doxography as a discursive marker of identity and ideological difference from their opponents.

Dualistic Eschatology

The ideology of the sectarian community included a radical bifurcation of the spiritual and material realms into good and evil. The dualism of the Covenant community extends from the cosmic and spiritual level to the social and political worldview as well as the anthropology of the members.

A Mechanism of Excommunication Based on Doctrine

In the *Damascus Document* and *Community Rule*, there is a doctrinal test for inclusion and exclusion in the salvific community. The ideological positions that define the community against its opponents become technologies of control within the community itself. This line cannot be crossed without completely losing one's identity as a member of the *yaḥad* and joining the sons of Belial. Expulsion equals eternal damnation.

Apocalyptic Condemnation of Opponents

What happens when that line is crossed? Qumran dualism is apocalyptic both in its ideology and eschatology. The eschatological fate of those outside the community (all other Jews and *Kittim*) is eternal damnation. The final triumph of Michael over Belial includes the ultimate punishment for the community's opponents.

Rejection of Alternative Points of View

The sectarian scrolls reject any alternative framework, whether that be the Sadducees, the Temple authorities, the Hasmoneans, or "seekers after smooth things," the Pharisees. No other notions of Temple, Priesthood, halakah, or Israel have any legitimacy. The example of the trial of Jeremiah after the Temple Sermon, in which both sides accepted the same ideological framework for true and false prophecy, shows the difference between the prophetic and heresiological frameworks of difference.

Reconstitution of the "True Israel"

The rhetoric of difference at Qumran represents a critical shift from prophetic discourse of difference found in Jeremiah or Daniel. The group no longer engages in a battle for the soul or destiny of Israel because it has reconstituted itself as the only true Israel. The political notion of "Israel" within the Qumran covenant develops during the period when the Hasmonean monarchy was establishing a competing, more inclusive notion of "Israel" as a Hellenistic empire.

The rhetoric of difference in the Qumran texts marks a nascent heresiological discourse. I will explore in subsequent chapters how this discourse was formative for the rhetoric and ideology of Christian heresiology. The next task is to examine the origins of Christianity itself in the reform and renewal movements of John the Baptist and Jesus of Nazareth, which ended in Judea under Roman rule.

3 Reform and Revolution in the Roman Empire

John the Baptist and the Disciples of Jesus

John said to the crowds that came out to be baptized by him, "You brood of vipers! Who warned you to flee from the wrath to come?"

Luke 3:7

INTRODUCTION

The study of the origins of heresy shifts to a different imperial context for Judea, from the Hasmonean kingdom in the second century before Christ to the Roman Empire in the first century of the Common Era. After the capture of Jerusalem by Pompey in 66 BCE, Roman rule in Palestine was exercised directly, in the persons of prefects and procurators with Roman troops under their command, and indirectly through clients such as Herod the Great, king of Israel from 37 to 4 BCE. The next generation of Roman clients included his sons and grandsons: Herod Antipas, the tetrarch of Galilee from his father's death to 39 CE; and the Herod Agrippas (I and II), who ruled various parts of Palestine in the 40s and 50s.[1] For most of the first century after Herod the Great's death, while Galilee was under the Herodians, Rome ruled Judea itself directly.

The first half of this century marks the origins of Christianity. What exactly these origins were, or how they can be measured, are extremely complicated, as I discussed in Chapter 1. I will mark the beginnings of what came to be Christianity, if not Christianity itself, in the apocalyptic movements within Judaism led by John the Baptist and Jesus of Nazareth. As we explore these two movements as the origins of Christianity and hence the Christian notion of heresy, I will emphasize several points. First, the rhetorical traditions I analyzed in the previous chapter were part of the milieu for these two men and their followers. As such the origins of Christianity were firmly planted in the discursive and ideological contexts of Second Temple Judaism. Second, these movements were intertwined from their origins through the mid-first century. Shared apocalyptic ideologies of religious renewal and reform brought Jesus to John and John's followers to the Jesus movement. Finally, the apocalyptic worldview of John and Jesus implicates their movements in an ideology of resistance to both the Jewish authorities in Galilee and Jerusalem and the Romans. As religious innovators, their movements forged new moments of religious conflict.

THE PROBLEM OF JESUS

There are enormous methodological problems with the "quest for the historical Jesus" and the Gospel sources. I do not plan to initiate such a quest here.[2] Nonetheless there are important issues to discuss at this point in order to introduce John the Baptist as a figure in the genealogy of the notion of heresy in early Christianity. The point of this inquiry on the historical Jesus is not "what did Jesus do or teach?" The question is, rather, what was the social milieu with respect to ideological differences in which Jesus taught and acted? For my purposes, it is more important to clarify the ideological contexts in which Jesus operated than to formalize the Jesus movement as a particular category within one taxonomy or another. This move is critical for the genealogy of heresy. To settle on one and only one "historical Jesus" suggests that the movement was unified and univocal. That is both methodologically unsound and historically improbable. As we have seen, various discursive patterns for negotiating difference were already part of the cultural history of Second Temple Judaism. Without recognizing this range of ideological differences within the earliest layers of the tradition—that is, around Jesus himself—as well as the variety of rhetorical responses to difference in Second Temple Judaism, then we fall back into the "error from truth" fallacy of orthodox historiography.

Jesus of Nazareth left no writings and, given the nature and transmission of the texts we have, it is difficult to prove what he did or did not do. All of the extant traditions about Jesus have been mediated through some community with their own particular, well-developed interpretations; I will analyze these traditions in more detail in Chapter 5. While scholars have tried to pinpoint the identity of "the historical Jesus," the variety of early Christian traditions *about* Jesus by the mid-first century points to a variety of traditions close to the *time* of Jesus. Thus I would argue that the main portraits of Jesus in our sources as constructed in recent scholarship—the apocalyptic Jesus, the Cynic Jesus, Jesus the Rabbi, the orthodox Jesus and Son of God—have touch points in the earliest traditions about Jesus. To be sure these "Jesus traditions" developed and changed within the first and second generations, but we can imagine that the variety of people who were disciples, followers, or supporters of Jesus had a variety of different views. Diversity was not only the hallmark of early Christianity; it was part of the Jesus movement itself. And with diversity comes difference and responses to difference.

To illustrate this theoretical claim, I turn to John the Baptist and his followers, a group that included Jesus at one point and which intersected the early Jesus movement for more than a generation. Study of John will give us insight into the social-rhetorical contexts in which the actions of Jesus would have been received, interpreted, and transmitted. Furthermore, John's rhetoric of difference links the Jesus movement to the discursive context of the Qumran sectarians.

JOHN THE BAPTIST AND THE FOLLOWERS OF JESUS

The source issues for John are less complex than for Jesus. There is no Gospel focusing exclusively on John, although he appears in several early Christian gospels. Furthermore, there is one independent first-century account of John's activity in Josephus' *Ant.* 18.116–19.[3] The sources on John do present some of the same methodological problems as the Gospel portraits of Jesus, since he too is presented in "biblical" terms by the Gospel writers and Josephus.[4] Josephus, however, indicates that a number of Jewish figures shaped their actions according to biblical themes as well.[5] Messianic leaders such as Judas, son of Hezekiah (ca. 4 BCE), Simon (ca. 4 BCE), and Athronges (4–2 BCE) and prophets such as the "Samaritan" (26–36 CE), Theudas (45 CE), and the "Egyptian" (ca. 56 CE) appropriated the symbols and sacred geography of ancient Israel.[6] The "Samaritan" led his followers to Mt. Gezirim, sacred to the Samaritans, while Theudas and "the Egyptian" went to the desert wilderness, crossed the Jordan River, and went to the Mount of Olives to signal the prophetic liberation of Israel. John was located in "the wilderness of Judea" (Matt 3:1) and baptized crowds in the Jordan River.[7] While the writers of the earliest Gospels interpreted the Hebrew prophetic texts so that their narratives take on these biblical themes, we must remember that these same Hebrew texts shaped the symbolic universes, worldviews, and actions of the agents themselves, including John and Jesus. John's activity at the Jordan, therefore, can be seen as prophetic in its own right, not merely a biblical trope by later Christian writers casting John as Elijah to Jesus the Messiah.[8]

These symbolic actions were, moreover, overtly political. We have already seen how the trope of symbolic geography was employed in 1 Maccabees to cast Judas and his brothers as biblical heroes in the mold of the judges or David. When Jonathan assumes leadership after the death of Judah, he escapes with a band of outlaws "into the wilderness of Tekoa," just as David had done.[9] For the Hasmoneans, this trope underscored their claims as leaders of Israel in the biblical model of old. Under the Romans, however, the message of liberation could be nothing but threatening to the authorities. Pontius Pilate responded quickly and brutally with armed forces to the "Samaritan," executing "the ringleaders as well as the most able among the fugitives" (Jos. *Ant.* 18.87). The Roman procurator Fadus beheaded Theudas and killed many of his followers (*Ant.* 20.98). John too was executed, by Herod Antipas, but whether his activity was seen as political as well as religious is debated by modern scholars.[10] According to both the Gospels and Josephus, John attracted crowds and some disciples. While he does not initiate a major prophetic movement, he continued to have some followers in the first century.[11] Josephus presents John as a different type of Jewish preacher, "a popular moral philosopher of Stoic hue, with a somewhat neo-Pythagorean rite of lustration."[12] Yet Josephus either overlooks or plays down John's strong eschatological message, and hence political opposition to the Roman and Jewish authorities.

The Gospels present John as clearly apocalyptic.[13] The central eschatological message is in the Q passage in Matt 3:7–10 (par. Luke 3:7–9) and the narrative description in Mark 1:1–8.[14] While there is not enough text to connect the quoted examples of John's preaching in the Gospels with a complete apocalyptic ideology such as we find in *1 Enoch* or Daniel, the eschatological message is forceful and violent. The metaphor of the axe cutting the roots and the trees being cast in the fire has parallels in Jewish apocalyptic literature.[15] This eschatological message of judgment, moreover, is polemically contextualized within a contested notion of Israel: "do not presume to say to yourselves, 'We have Abraham as our ancestor'" (Matt 3:9; Luke 3:8). Furthermore, the Jewish crowds coming to John from Jerusalem and around Judea were greeted by John with the cry of "brood of vipers" (reading Luke's "crowds," *ochloi*, instead of Matthew's "Pharisees and Sadducees").[16] The crowds could have included Pharisees and Sadducees as well as a broader swath of Judeans, and must have included Herodian informers who reported John's activity to the tetrarch.[17] These polemics place the identity of the people of Israel as a central theme in John's reform movement, recalling the contested identity of Israel in the sectarian Dead Sea Scrolls. For John, birth alone did not define the people of Israel. So too the Qumran Covenant community separated from the "sons of Belial," identifying themselves as the true Israel.

> And when these become members of the community in Israel according to all these rules, they shall separate from the habitation of unjust men [i.e., Jerusalem and the towns of Judea] and shall go into the wilderness to prepare the way of him; as it is written, *Prepare in the wilderness the way of . . ., make straight in the desert a path for our God.* (1QS VIII, 14–15)[18]

All four Gospels quote the same Isaiah passage for John (Mark 1:3; Matt 3:3; Luke 3:4; John 1:23). Clearly the association of John and Isa 40:3 was traditional in Christian communities by the end of the first century.[19] But that does not mean the tradition did not originate in John's immediate circle or his followers. The Qumran tradition itself could have suggested the association of John and the Isaiah passage within early Christian circles.

We cannot know whether John planned a political movement or revolt, but Herod Antipas had sound reasons for worrying about him.[20] The Q tradition (Luke 7:24–26; Matt 11:7–9) preserves the memory of John as a prophet in the wilderness whose symbolic attire evokes an identity against the authorities, those "in royal palaces."[21] Josephus writes that Herod feared "sedition" (*stasis*) from the growing crowd around John (*Ant.* 18.118). The Synoptic Gospels cite John's condemnation of Antipas' marriage to Herodias as the provocation for John's arrest and execution (Mark 6:17–29; Matt 14:3–12; Luke 3:19–20). The two accounts can be reconciled and provide further evidence not only that John was perceived as a threat by Herod but also that he attacked the ruler as well as other figures in the Jewish hierarchy as a "brood of vipers."[22]

John's eschatological preaching drew on strong traditions of resistance in a land that had been ruled by the Romans for almost one hundred years. In the second century BCE, the discursive landscape of apocalyptic ideology and Jewish messianism become more overtly political, as discussed in Chapter 2. For instance, we saw Daniel's tacit but passive support for the Maccabean revolt and the more active support for the Hasmoneans in the Animal Apocalypse of *1 Enoch* 85–91. Both of these early second-century apocalypses draw on the prominent tradition of the war between the Jews and Gentiles; the Animal Apocalypse ends with the slaughter of the nations (90:19). This theme appears in the Dead Sea Scrolls as well (CD VII, 20–21; 4Q161; 1QH XI, 35 [III, 35]).[23] Within the scrolls, the theme is most prominent in the War Scroll (1QM), which was composed after the Roman invasion of Jerusalem in 66 BCE.[24] This militant, dualistic text describes the future eschatological battle between God, Michael, the angels, and "Israel" against Belial and the *Kittim*, the Romans.[25] The text begins with an attack by the "sons of light" against the "sons of darkness," which include the army of Belial and the *Kittim*, that will "be a time of salvation for the people of God, an age of dominion for all the members of his company, and of everlasting destruction for the company of Belial" (1QM I, 1–5). The central section, cols. 2–9, describes elaborate regulations for warfare. The text concludes with a further description of "the time of distress for Israel to war against all the nations. There shall be eternal deliverance for the company of God, but destruction for all the nations of wickedness" (1QM XIV, 1–5).[26]

The ideology of Jewish messianism also takes on a stronger political slant in Judea under Roman domination. While the older, Christocentric view of church historians that all Jews in the first century were actively waiting for the same messiah has been discredited, Jewish messianism seems to have been widespread in the Second Temple period.[27] The primary models of messianic expectation included the dominant notion of a Davidic messiah; the messiah as Aaronic priest; the anointed Mosaic prophet; and the Danielic Son of Man.[28] These messianic ideologies were both eschatological and political. They were also extensions of an older theme found in the Hebrew prophets: the anticipation of the future age of the spirit, in which God or God's agents, such as the Messiah, will establish a kingdom and restore Israel's fortunes. This restoration included at various points a future ideal king and a peaceable kingdom; the rebuilding of the Temple;

agricultural bounty; social justice and equality; other nations serving Israel; and an intimate relationship with the God of Israel.[29] And when Israel no longer had its own king but a Gentile ruler, this theme also becomes one of political resistance.

This messianic political ideology occurs in a number of apocalyptic texts. The Qumran scrolls refer to two Messiahs, one Davidic and one Aaronic.[30] The "Rule of War" fragments (4Q285), related to the War Scroll, have the Davidic messiah in a more prominent role. The *locus classicus* of Davidic messianism is the *Psalms of Solomon* 17, which was written around the time of Pompey's capture of Jerusalem.[31] The Romans are hardly greeted as liberators: "See Lord, and raise up for [the people] their king, the son of David, to rule over your servant Israel . . . . Undergird him with the strength to destroy the unrighteous rulers, to purge Jerusalem from gentiles who trample her to destruction" (*Ps. Sol.* 17.21–22).[32] The *Targum Ps.-Jonathan* on Isaiah (2:13–16) directs the wrath of the "day of the Lord" against the Gentiles and tyrants.[33] In the Roman and Herodian periods, such statements could have been seen only as political positions against the *imperium* of Rome, however expressed. It is hardly surprising that John and other prophets were executed by Herod and Pilate.

John was an eschatological prophet whose activity challenged the power of Herod Antipas and the Jerusalem authorities. Was John also an Essene? Scholars line up on both sides of this question.[34] In mission, ideology, and scriptural associations with Isa 40:3, John has strong connections to the community at Qumran. The attack on the notion of "children of Abraham" aligns John's eschatological preaching at the Jordan with the ideology of Qumran by contesting the ideology of "Israel." As we saw in the previous chapter, the Covenant redefined "Israel" as the community itself, constituted of initiates who accepted the ideology and extensive rites of Qumran life. John's baptism for repentance, a "once-and-out" ritual that marked a significant transformation in the individual, contrasts with the elaborate and extended initiation for new members of the Covenant described in the *Community Rule*.

Perhaps the question itself is wrongly posed. The word "Essene" never appears in early Christian texts or rabbinic sources, neither for John or any of Jesus' followers, nor for anyone at all.[35] The identity of the Jewish religious group called "Essene" by Josephus seems in any case to have been broader than the community reconstructed from the sectarian texts of Qumran, which themselves are a subset of the large library recovered there of "the writings of the ancients" (*ta tōn palaiōn syntagmata*, *J.W.* 2.136). Josephus notes different types of Essenes in *J.W.* 2.160–61 that marry and have families.[36] He also writes that the Essenes live in many different places in Judea (*J.W.* 2.124). Their apocalyptic worldview was part of a broader religious culture in Judea that spread beyond Khirbet Qumran in the centuries around the turn of the era, as far as Egypt, according to Philo (*Contempl. Life*), including figures such as Bannus in the wilderness (Jos. *Life* 11). Rather than asking whether John the Baptist was an Essene, we should ask whether the historical context connects him—and therefore Jesus of Nazareth—to the eschatological and political ideology of Qumran. To this question, rather than the question of whether John the Baptist was actually at Qumran and went through Essene initiation, we can confidently answer "yes."[37]

The connection of Jesus himself and John, moreover, is one of the soundest historical findings about Jesus.[38] The earliest Gospels associate Jesus and John, including the *Gospel of Thomas* (46, 78). In Acts, Peter spells out the qualifications for a twelfth apostle to replace Judas as "one of the men who have accompanied us during all the time that the Lord Jesus went in and out among us, beginning from the baptism of John until the day when he was taken up from us" (Acts 1:21–22; cf. 10:37, 13:24). Calling Jesus a "disciple" of John need not limit our understanding of the relationship. At the very least, Jesus had some involvement (as a scholar, seeker, rabbi) with John, who had started an apocalyptic reform movement before Jesus initiated his own mission of eschatological renewal in Galilee. Of course, all of the New Testament evidence for these interactions is problematic because of the strong theological interest in diminishing John's role while elevating Jesus. That is to say we must read these passages carefully and critically—as with all the New Testament.

This connection of Jesus with John is significant for thinking about his followers even more than Jesus himself. While I will consider Jesus in more detail ahead, I focus on his followers to see the ways in which the earliest notions of Christian heresy, by way of its discursive roots at Qumran, developed. Early Christian texts, including the canonical Gospels, the *Gospel of Thomas*, and the Acts of the Apostles indicate not only contact between John and Jesus but also continued contact between their disciples. Apollos of Alexandria joined the Pauline *ekklēsia* in Ephesus "though he knew only the baptism of John" (Acts 18:24). Priscilla and Aquila, Paul's co-workers, quickly instruct Apollos in "the Way of God more accurately." Apollos goes to Corinth (see Chapter 4) and Paul arrives in Ephesus, where he also leads some disciples who had been baptized by John into the "holy spirit," "in the name of the Lord Jesus" (19:1–7). In each instance in Acts, John's baptism is both anterior and inferior to baptism into Christ. Attention to John's theological status in the new Christian economy was driven by the somewhat embarrassing fact that Jesus was, for some period of time, a follower of John. But this should not lead us to dismiss the evidence that some disciples of John became part of the Jesus movement. The messianic expectations underlying the questions from John about Jesus, "Are you the one who is to come, or are we to wait for another?" and Jesus' answers in Matt 11:2–4 suggest the shared ideology that would bring the disciples of the movements together.[39] My point is not whether Jesus was "the one who is to come," although that is clearly Matthew's.[40] Rather, this passage shows a shared interest in the coming of God's messiah that would attract people to both movements. Interestingly, Matthew places this Q story immediately after the discourse on discipleship in 10:1–11:1. Luke, in contrast, places the story after a narrative of Jesus' healing miracles, thereby supporting Jesus' answer to John (Luke 7:24–25). For Matthew, the issue of discipleship raises the problem of the relationship of the two men because disciples of both were part of the Christian community in Matthew's time. So too the concerns within various Christian traditions to "put John in his place" show that the movements were connected through the first century because John's followers were part of the early Christian communities.

Some followers of Jesus, perhaps even some of the twelve disciples, had been followers or disciples of John.[41] The apocalyptic ideology of John's movement was the connecting worldview for these people who subsequently joined Jesus, expecting the kingdom of God. The renewal movement of Jesus certainly attracted others with a worldview aligned with the dualistic, apocalyptic eschatology of Qumran or "Essene" Judaism. Jews in the first century explored new eschatological movements; otherwise there would have been no followers for John, Jesus, or the prophets and messiahs noted by Josephus. Josephus himself studied different types of Judaism, including the Essenes (*Life* 9–12) while Paul may have been similarly precocious and zealous in studies within the Pharisaic traditions (Gal 1:14, note *Ioudaïsmos*; Phil 3:4–6; Acts 22:3). By no means were *all* the followers of Jesus previously disciples of John, Essenes, nor even apocalyptic Jews. There must have been considerable diversity within the larger groups of followers.[42] The New Testament refers to disciples and "sympathizers" as council members, Zealots, Pharisees, Gentiles, and even a Roman soldier (Matt 8:5; Mark 15:43; 7:26; Luke 6:15; 7:36). The *Gospel of Thomas* and perhaps some elements of the Q tradition (see Chapter 5) testify to non-apocalyptic understandings of Jesus' teachings in the earliest generations of Christianity. But a significant apocalyptic ideology remained in the movement after the execution of Jesus well into the second century. Paul's letters and the Gospels illuminate this diversity, a diversity labeled "fragmentation" after Jesus in the orthodox tradition. The trope of breaking apart or falling away from the true teaching supports the orthodox ideology of original unity, but diversity and difference were original to the movement.

JESUS AFTER JOHN

While the sources have been shaped by followers of Jesus after his death, the historical reconstruction of Jesus as an eschatological apocalyptic prophet of renewal who challenged the Temple authorities and was executed for that remains sound.[43] It is clear that, regardless of whether we construe Jesus in this way, the ideology of apocalypticism was part of the earliest Jesus movement. This is important because apocalyptic dualism is central to early Christian notions of heresy. John, Jesus, and their followers were colonial subjects, which is a second condition for the production of heresy.

Finally, we seek intra-religious conflict. Jesus was executed by Roman officials with, possibly, the knowledge or even approval of Jewish authorities in Jerusalem who controlled the Temple precinct. That is evidence of conflict with the colonial power. What of conflict with other Jews?

While allowing for the layers of tradition added to the Gospels in the first and second centuries and the conflicts within the early Christian communities themselves, it is nonetheless clear that Jesus' activity also engendered conflict. The beginning of Jesus' activity was the arrest of John by Herod Antipas. There is a series of controversies with scribes, Pharisees, scribes of the Pharisees, and even John's disciples in Mark 2–3 over forgiving sins, company at meals ("commensality" or table fellowship), and Sabbath activities. These stories show evidence of retrojection of early church issues into the narrative of Jesus' ministry.[44] For instance, the charge of "blasphemy" in 2:7 and the conflicts over the Sabbath in 2:24 and 3:4 fit an early church context in which Jewish groups such as the Pharisees would more likely have leveled such accusations against the followers of Jesus. The stories also show redactional activity as a collection of increasing conflict between Jesus and the Jewish authorities, climaxing with the Herodians conspiring with the Pharisees to destroy Jesus (Mark 3:6). Individually, however, they suggest social conflict that likely arose from Jesus' activity.

A number of scholars of the historical Jesus have described aspects of Jesus' teaching and activity in Galilee that would have been controversial and could therefore have provoked conflict with other Jews. Interestingly enough scholars from quite different poles of the historical Jesus spectrum, E. P. Sanders and John Dominic Crossan, have marked similar activities of Jesus as both historically authentic and bound to cause disturbances.[45] Sanders' approach is minimalistic; he tries not to extend beyond the simplest explanations and the available evidence. His research focuses in particular on the Jewish law. Sanders rejects a number of potential causes for conflict, most notably any conflict over the status of the law such as the Sabbath or food laws that are featured in the Gospels but suggest later church controversies. He then settles on two primary areas of Jesus' teaching and activity that caused conflict before his execution. The first was Jesus' idea that his own mission took precedence over any other activity. Sanders bases this on analysis of one of the "hard sayings" in Matt 8:22 (= Luke 9:60), "let the dead bury the dead," a call to self-denial that would have forced the man to break the commandment to honor his parents. The second offence was that Jesus associated with *harmatōloi*, ordinarily translated "sinners" but which Sanders translates as "wicked," from the Hebrew *resha'im*. Sanders argues that this was a technical term for *habitual* sinners, who did not try to repent. He contends further that Jesus, as a preacher of the imminent kingdom of God, was not a preacher of repentance, as John arguably was, but rather of renewal.[46] This was, of course, an apocalyptic ideology.

In contrast to such minimalistic explanations, Crossan has used sociological theory and comparative anthropological studies to fill in gaps in the existing evidence about Jesus in his reconstruction of a "Cynic Jesus." Nonetheless, Crossan's notions of the centrality of "open commensality" and "radical egalitarianism" to Jesus' mission incorporate the same Gospel evidence as Sanders and offer parallel reasons for how Jesus would have caused conflict. Eating is at the center of Crossan's account. To be sure, his notion of "open commensality" incorporates a stronger political ideology in the notion of the kingdom of God than Sanders' reconstruction. But Crossan understands Jesus' eating with "the wicked," that is "those whom, in the opinion of the name callers, open and free association should be avoided," as a challenge to the contemporary society. In other words, Jesus associated with habitual sinners. Furthermore, Crossan also points to the family as a locus of conflict in the hard sayings in Mark 3:31–35; Luke 11:27–28 and 12:51–53; and *Gos. Thom. 55.* Crossan's interpretation of the import of these sayings is compatible with Sanders'. Normal family duties and relations are not as important as the kingdom of God (for Crossan, "Rule of God") that overthrows the current order and takes over the world like a mustard plant takes over a garden.

Both scholars, moreover, mark the symbolic destruction of the Jerusalem Temple (the cleansing or scourging of the Temple in Mark 11:15–19; John 2:14–17; and *Gos. Thom.* 71) as both historical and significant.[47] We could look further in the possible conflict caused by Jesus within Jewish Galilee.[48] I do not want to press the agreement of Sanders and Crossan too far, although when such alignments occur in the quest for the historical Jesus they are noteworthy. We can conclude that (1) there was some social conflict in the Jesus movement (2) Jesus' teaching and activity produced this conflict and (3) Jesus would have been aware of this conflict. These are related ideas. Religious conflict is necessary for the origin of heresy; it was violent disagreements over *halakah*, Temple, and the political identity of Israel that we saw at the heart of the Qumran's covenant's separatism and rhetoric of heresy. So too the rhetoric of John the Baptist combined apocalyptic ideology with strong political disagreement over the notions of Israel, directed at the authorities. Jesus' ministry ended with arrest and execution via crucifixion by the Romans as a political agitator, a ministry that began with an apocalyptic prophet at the Jordan River. These two points strongly support the historical reconstruction of Jesus as an apocalyptic prophet of renewal who challenged the authorities, both the Romans and their Jewish clients who controlled the Jerusalem Temple. Such challenges engendered conflicts within Galilee and Judea that became central to the Christian communities that formed after the crucifixion of Jesus.

CONCLUSION

In Chapter 1, I critiqued the classic historiography of an original pure doctrine delivered from Jesus to the apostles as an orthogenetic mythology of

Christian heresy. It is clear that no such purity ever existed. The Jesus movement, enmeshed in the apocalyptic renewal activity of John and the broader ideologies of eschatological Jewish groups such as the Essenes, originated in a highly diverse milieu. The disciples and followers of Jesus represented a range of apocalyptic and other Judaisms. The teaching and activity of Jesus engendered conflict with other Jewish leaders and teachers and ended with execution in Jerusalem after Jesus symbolically attacked the Temple itself. His followers fled the authorities and later regrouped.

We see that heresy was not a "post-apostolic corruption," as Hegesippus would have it, nor a second-century rhetorical formation of the "early Church." Rather it was an intrinsic part of the origins of what eventually came to be Christianity. The constellation of apocalyptic ideology and dualistic rhetoric from Second Temple Judaism that cohered around the early followers of John and Jesus marks the discursive beginnings of Christian notions of heresy. I have sketched the outlines of this hypothesis in the Gospel texts, recognizing the highly problematic nature of these sources. I will resume the history of these traditions in the rhetoric of the early Christian Gospels in Chapter 5. But we turn first to a more immediate source, Paul, an apocalyptic Jew who further shaped the heresiological tradition in the ideological context of building the *ekklēsia*. Conflict marked the ministry of Jesus; division immediately followed.

4 Paul and the Rhetoric of Difference

I urge Euodia and I urge Syntyche to be of the same mind in the Lord.

Phil 4:2

INTRODUCTION

In the previous chapter, I considered the methodological problems in reconstructing the "historical Jesus." Gaining a sense of the personality and activity of Paul seems an easier task. We feel as if we know him at times too well. But there are actually many different "Pauls." There is the mystical Paul and the apocalyptic Paul.[1] Closely related to these is the "Jewish Paul."[2] And as Jewish as Paul of Tarsus, Hebrew of the tribe of Benjamin and Pharisee towards the law, might have been (Phil 3:5), we also know Paul the Greco-Roman moral philosopher, who seems hardly Jewish at all.[3] Complementing these important studies we have what might be called the "New Paul."[4] Feminist scholarship has revealed both the liberating Paul and the patriarchal Paul.[5] While my approach here has been informed by a variety of scholarship, I am reading for what might be called the "social Paul."[6] The social-historical approach to Paul focuses less on the history of ideas and Paul's theology and more on how those ideas functioned to build a community, construct boundaries and norms, and form new identities within Greco-Roman society.

My focus on the "social Paul" brings two methodological issues to the foreground when reading his letters. The first is attention to rhetoric. While this signals an interest in Greco-Roman parallels, since the study of rhetoric points us to Hellenistic modes of discourse, the notion of rhetoric here encompasses Hebrew and other ancient, non-Hellenistic models.[7] My reading of Paul, moreover, highlights the apocalyptic, eschatological worldview that was central to his response to difference in these new communities or *ekklēsiai*. Second, reading for the rhetoric of the "social Paul," I focus on ideology. Drawing on the significant work of scholars who have analyzed the functions of Paul's rhetoric, we will see how Paul employs the ideology of Roman imperial power as a way to negotiate difference. I will show that Paul does not transmit a "pure" gospel from Jesus to the church but rather constructs the notion of "gospel" as a discourse of power.

The social contexts for the Pauline epistles are fairly well located, particularly when compared to the Gospel traditions analyzed in the next chapter. Here, in this chapter, I will focus more on the social and political contexts of the *ekklēsiai* themselves, reading Paul's rhetoric of difference in terms of conflicts within the communities. In Chapter 7, "The Politics of Orthodoxy," I return to Paul and the politics of Roman imperialism. While this division is only possible heuristically, here I focus on the politics of *ekklēsia* and in Chapter 7 the politics of empire, or *oikoumenē*.

In this chapter, I will analyze the ideology and rhetoric of difference in three central instances of argument in Paul's letters: the appeal to unity in 1 Corinthians; the argument with the "Judaizers" in Galatians; and the polemic against the "super apostles" in 2 Corinthians. Of course, these three letters and the exegetical problems within these instances have been extensively studied by scholars. Furthermore, the interpretation of Galatians, where the relationship of Jew and Gentile within the new *ekklēsia* of Christ and the question of adherence to Jewish *Torah* are in the foreground, has been central to the development of orthodox theology. This allows me to clarify my focus. I am not interested in doctrinal problems as such. Paul could have argued strongly for *requiring* circumcision and following Jewish *halakah* for being "in Christ," just as he could have advocated "speaking in tongues" as the highest of spiritual gifts in 1 Corinthians. Rather, my focus is how Paul discursively negotiates difference within the *ekklēsia*, rather than the substance of these important theological decisions.

1 CORINTHIANS AND THE IDEOLOGY OF UNITY

It is little wonder that 1 Corinthians has featured prominently in the social-historical study of early Christianity. The letter is an unparalleled source for the social reconstruction of the earliest Christian communities.[8] It is a unified, discrete letter from Paul's own hand.[9] The letter gives us a better glimpse at what was actually going on in this *ekklēsia* than any of his others.

As with all of Paul's letters, 1 Corinthians is situational, consisting of specific responses to particular issues.[10] And the issues in 1 Corinthians are all problems that have divided the community. These include a man living with his stepmother; traffic with prostitutes; couples, or perhaps wives, abstaining from sexual relations; betrothed men or women breaking off marriages; and mixed marriages between "brothers" and "unbelievers." And these are just the sexual issues in 1 Corinthians 5–7.[11] Before that, Paul writes an extended response in 1 Corinthians 1–4 to reports he has received from "Chloe's People" (1:11), probably slaves or freedmen traveling on business, of factions (*schismata*) within the community, with various leaders holding sway over different groups. Apollos of Alexandria, who came to Corinth after Paul left, receives particularly careful attention, as I will discuss later. Paul also writes about a host of boundary issues with "outsiders," including using the courts to resolve community disagreements (1 Cor 6); buying meat that had been offered in sacrifice at temples (1 Cor 8–10); and behavior during the weekly gatherings of the *ekklēsia* that included drunkenness at the Eucharist and privileging of ecstatic glossolalia, speaking in tongues, over other "spiritual gifts" (1 Cor 11–14). In 1 Corinthians 11 Paul also lays out an argument about the need to bind women's hair when praying or prophesying. Paul concludes the body of the letter in 1 Corinthians 15 with the contested notion of "resurrection."

Scholars have, for hundreds of years now, sought a theory that would explain the nature of the divisions in Corinth. One of the most long-standing explanations is political. Paul opens the letter by responding to reports of factions from "Chloe's people." "I say this because each one of you says: 'I'm with Paul' or 'I follow Apollos'" or 'I belong to Kephas' or 'I am Christ's'" (1 Cor 1:12).[12] Ferdinand Christian Baur, the nineteenth-century founder of the Tübingen School of the history of religions, explained the divisions in terms of "parties" and a Hegelian struggle between "Judaizing" Christian followers of Peter and Hellenistic followers of Paul.[13] This approach takes the divisions into various parties seriously as a challenge to Paul's authority. A more recent study that follows Baur's lead is John Schütz's study of apostolic authority.[14] The politics of the Corinthian situation and Paul's response are one focus here.

There is more to ideology, the relationship of ideas to structures of power, than politics. Paul makes strong theological and religious claims; perhaps the divisions stem from alternative theological perspectives? Two main theories have been advanced to explain the religious divisions in Corinth. One theory that came to prominence after the publication of the Nag Hammadi texts was the idea that the Corinthians were some type of "Gnostics."[15] The "Gnostic" proposals built on earlier studies of the Greek mystery religions.[16] But the construct of "pre-Christian Gnosticism" in mid-twentieth-century New Testament criticism has now been rejected as both anachronistic and unsupported by fuller, more careful studies of the Nag Hammadi texts.[17] A majority of conservative scholars, however, have adopted some type of theological explanation for the problems in Corinth, without ascribing the source completely to Hellenistic religion. Gordon Fee, for instance, does not recognize the parties as political at all.[18] The divisions are the result of "overrealized eschatology" or "spiritual enthusiasm" in the *ekklēsia*.[19] The Corinthians accepted Paul's Gospel and then went too far with some parts of it; Paul's concern for their over-emphasis on glossolalia in 1 Corinthians 12–14 is a prime example. This approach privileges Paul's theology as original, following the classic Christian historiography of truth preceding error. Paul's "true Gospel" precedes misinterpretations such as "over-realized eschatology"; his normative views hold the middle ground against such extremes. Contemporary notions of "mainstream" and "fringe" Christianity, moreover, become part of the reconstruction. These theological explanations developed during a period when mainstream Protestant churches could marginalize Pentecostal and Holiness Christian traditions. In fact 1

Corinthians highlights the diversity of theologies that were part of the origins of Christianity. Paul's theology is but one of many in the mix.

The pioneering study of Gerd Theissen marked social status as the primary factor for the divisions in the Corinthian *ekklēsia*.[20] In a series of essays published in Germany in the 1970s, Theissen re-examined the letter sociologically. Theissen made conjectures, based on epigraphic and literary research, about material support for traveling missionaries; the prosopography and social status of the people named in Paul's letters, such as Gaius and "the household (*oikon*) of Stephanas" in 1 Cor 1:14–16; 16:16–17 and Rom 16:23; who would pay for the food and drink referred to in 1 Cor 11:17–22; who held city offices; and who had houses for the *ekklēsia* to gather in or for the leaders to live in. Theissen turns one key verse, 1 Cor 1:26, around. Traditionally read as a reference to the relative poverty and social humility (Lat. *humiliores*) of the early Christians, Theissen noted the other side of Paul's rhetoric: "Not many of you were wise (*sophoi*) by human standards, not many were powerful (*dynatoi*), not many were of noble birth (*eugeneis*)." Some, however, were, and Theissen correlates these "wise" and "powerful" Corinthians with the positions of the "strong" in other places in the letter, such as the dispute over eating meat purchased from temple priests (*eidōlothuton*) in 1 Corinthians 8–10. Paul's argument against "human wisdom" in 1 Cor 2:1–16, as well as his argument about his own manual labor in Chapter 9, has sociological significance if he were arguing against the wealthier and more educated members of the *ekklēsia*.

Another recent approach to the divisions in Corinth focuses on gender. As mentioned earlier, many of the issues addressed by Paul concern sexual relationships and women's behavior. But the significance of gender could go much further than explicit references to women in the letter. Antoinette Clark Wire explicates these divisions.[21] First, Wire developed sophisticated method for reading Paul's rhetoric in 1 Corinthians that incorporated the insights of the "new rhetoric" of Perelman and Olbrechts-Tyteca; anthropological and sociological methodologies; and feminist scholarship.[22] Second, Wire extended the question of the role of women in the Corinthian *ekklēsia*, and the role of women prophets as part of the "problem" at Corinth, beyond the explicit statements about women in the letter (1 Cor 5–7, 11:2–6, and 14:34–35). Wire studied Paul's rhetoric to uncover what roles the women prophets could have had in the divisions over eating idol meat, the contested notions of the resurrection, and the authority of Paul versus Apollos. "In any case, [the Corinthian women prophets] ears are shaping [Paul's] mouth throughout."[23] More recently, Jorunn Økland used gender as the interpretive lens in a study of the notion of space as a gendered concept in the Greco-Roman world and in 1 Corinthians.[24]

But perhaps the search for a unifying explanation for the divisions in the community tells us more about Paul's rhetoric than the actual situation.[25] We can agree that Corinthian *ekklēsia* had notable conflict. Religious or ideological conflict is a necessary condition for the production of heresiological rhetoric. Paul's approach to difference here, however, is not heresiological. Rather, he seeks above all unity, *concordia* in Latin and *homonoia* in Greek.[26] This is the insight of the monograph on 1 Corinthians by Margaret Mitchell, who worked extensively on Greco-Roman sources for *homonoia* and Paul's rhetoric, and the starting point for Dale Martin's recent work on the ideology of "the body" in the letter.[27] With few exceptions, Paul tries to eliminate division and build up the community in this letter. Seeking only one explanation for conflict in Corinth is a response to Paul's rhetoric of *homonoia*. He connects the various conflicts because he constructs difference itself as subverting unity. His powerful rhetoric of unity functions to support the ideology of his apostolic authority.

NEGOTIATING DIFFERENCE

Unity, *homonoia* or *concordia*, was "one of the universally recognized political values" in Greco-Roman antiquity for social units ranging from the Empire and city-states to voluntary associations and the family.[28] Paul drew on an extensive *topos*, or theme, of ancient rhetoric and moral philosophy. This letter, from start to finish, is full of the vocabulary and *topoi* of *homonoia* and its opposite, strife, *stasis* or *eris* (see 1 Cor 1:11). Mitchell demonstrates that the political focus on factions, *schismata*, in 1 Corinthians 1–4 continues in the rest of the letter through numerous references to the *topoi* of unity and factionalism, even when Paul seems to be treating other substantive topics.[29]

Building from Mitchell's extensive study, I will provide one illustrative parallel of what Martin has called "benevolent patriarchalism" in the ancient world, Paul's extended simile of the *ekklēsia* as "the body of Christ" in 1 Cor 12:12–31 and Rom 12:4–8 (see Col 1:18).[30] This familiar image for contemporary Christians would have been familiar to Paul's communities as well. A well-known story of "the revolt of the belly" against other parts of the body was recorded by both Dionysius of Halicarnassus (6.86) and Plutarch (*Cor.* 6). The story was set in ancient Republican Rome during a dispute between the patricians, represented by the Senate, and the plebeians, rebelling over the tax system and money lenders. After a walkout of Rome by the people, Menenius Agrippa outlined the position of the Senate in a speech using this story. In this fable, all the other body parts rebelled against the belly because, while they were doing all the work and suffering on its behalf, the belly offered nothing in return but an appetite. The belly laughed at them, saying it took in all the food but also redistributed the nourishment to the rest of the body. Menenius then draws the analogy between the belly and the Senate, which deliberates on behalf of all the Romans and makes the decisions for them. While the conflict ended with the establishment of the tribunate, an office to represent the interests of the plebians, the message of "stay in your place" is clear (cf. 1 Cor 7:20). The central part of the body (here the belly, in 1 Corinthians the head) dominates all the others in the name of unity. This well-known ancient image functions similarly in 1 Corinthians 12 to appeal to unity or *homonoia* in the *ekklēsia*: "But God has so arranged the body, giving the greater honor to the inferior member, that there may be no dissension within the body, but the members may have the same care for one another" (1 Cor 12:24–25).

Paul's ideology of *homonoia* in response to divisions in the Corinthian *ekklēsia* acknowledges differences even while constructing one prevailing, correct view, what Elizabeth Castelli has called the "hegemony of the identical."[31] The divisions into "parties" suggest *hairesis* in its classical meaning of choice (see Chapter 1). Each of the Corinthians has "chosen" (*haireō*) a leader, according to Paul (1 Cor 1:12). A possible path here for Paul was direct confrontation, a course he follows in other conflicts ahead. But in 1 Corinthians, Paul acknowledges the validity of other points of view and figures of authority. Two examples of this approach to difference are the discussion of the roles and authority of Apollos and Paul in 1 Corinthians 1–4 and the appeal to the "strong" and "the weak" on eating idol meat in 1 Corinthians 8–10.

The section on Apollos includes several typical *homonoia* references, including the image of gardeners working together for growth (1 Cor 3:5–9) and builders working from a common foundation (3:10–15).[32] The point of these tropes is the careful, patient negotiation of his authority with Apollos'. "Think of us [i.e., Paul and Apollos] in this way, as servants [*hypēretas*] of Christ and stewards [*oikonomous*] of God's mysteries" (4:1). "Mystery" began a section earlier in the letter (1 Cor 2:1) on differences within the *ekklēsia* in a series of binary oppositions, such as "words of wisdom" and the "power of God"; the "rulers of this age" and "the Lord"; and the "unspiritual" and the "spiritually discerned." But in 4:1, Paul uses the same term as a coda to the notion that there is not any difference between him and Apollos as servants of the Lord. The elision by Paul of his and Apollos' roles is both intentional and disingenuous. The section ends with a strong assertion of his apostolic authority over the *ekklēsia* that leaves Apollos out. Here again, Paul uses a familiar *homonoia* topos, the metaphor of the family, but to quite different effects: "For though you might have ten thousand guardians [*paidagōgous*] in Christ, you do not have many fathers" (4:15). The tropes of co-equal unity between Paul and Apollos (*synergoi* or fellow-workers in 3:9) have been replaced by a metaphor of hierarchical unity under Paul's benevolent patriarchialism. He is the only father. To underscore this, Paul issues an apocalyptic warning about "the kingdom of God" and the threatening spirit with which he might return to Corinth (4:20–21).

Paul approaches other divisive issues similarly, with an ideology of unity. In 1 Corinthians 8–10, he employs the discourse of political factionalism to urge unity in the *ekklēsia* with regard to purchasing meat from the market.[33] Paul acknowledges both points of view, the concerns of the "weak" who "have become so accustomed to idols until now, they still think of the food they eat as food offered to an idol" (8:7), as well as the "strong"—that is, the more educated and wealthy members of the *ekklēsia*, who know that "no idol in the world really exists" (8:4).[34] Directing his rhetoric towards the higher-status Corinthians, and signaling his own "strong" position, he argues that they should forgo their right to eat as they please, just as he himself had given up his right as an apostle to be paid for his work. Everyone in the *ekklēsia* should put aside their own self-interests (*to sympheron*, that which is advantageous) to seek the common good (10:24).[35] But Paul cites a personal example of giving up a right as an apostle in order to assert his right as apostle with "the Spirit of God" (7:40) to make the Corinthians "imitators of me" (11:1). He anticipates in 10:17 the major *homonoia* trope of the next section, the metaphor of the body in Paul's treatment of *pneumatika*, spiritual gifts, in 1 Corinthians 12–14, "Because there is one bread, we who are many are one body, for we all partake of the one bread."[36]

Unity or *homonoia* in this section is a hierarchy of spiritual gifts (*charismata*) guided in orderly fashion by Paul's benevolent patriarchalism. Certain Corinthian leaders value ecstatic speech, tongues or glossolalia. Tongues are never dismissed as illegitimate but placed carefully at the *bottom* of the list of spiritual gifts (12:10; 14:26). Paul points out that he speaks in tongues even more than the Corinthians (14:18). The discussion of "tongues" in 1 Corinthians 12–14 negotiates the status of the different *charismata* and allows for expression of tongues within a hierarchical framework.[37] It is, to be sure, as much about ideology as theology—just as the argument upholding his right to be paid as well as his right to give up that right magnifies Paul's authority (11:1). Paul also raises a concern for "outsiders" (14:16, 23). The outsider must not witness any "discordant note," or disorder. The chapter ends with an appeal to order (*taxis*), in the face of difference. This orderly practice is the rule in "all the (other) *ekklēsiai*" (14:33; cf. 1 Cor 4:17; 7:17).

Paul does not always validate alternative positions. Chief among these is the case of "a man living with his father's wife" (1 Cor 5:1); that is, the man's stepmother.[38] While I do not think that Paul chose to oppose this case in order to highlight the degree to which he was willing to negotiate on other issues, that is one of the rhetorical effects of his pronouncement of judgment and "excommunication."[39] Even more powerful is the juxtaposition of this pronouncement in 5:3–5 with the appeal in 4:14–21 to unity over Apollo and Paul's authority, which ends with the question, "Am I to come to you with a stick, or with love in a spirit of gentleness?" Paul's judgment (*kekrika*) from afar against this man lets them know just what that stick might mean. He commands the Corinthians "to hand this man over to Satan for the destruction of the flesh."[40] This judgment, moreover, is explicitly eschatological: "so that his spirit may be saved in the day of the Lord" (1 Cor 5:5).[41] Paul is not open to negotiation on this behavior. Nor does Paul negotiate on whether women should be unveiled when praying or prophesying.⁴² The piling up of reasons in 1 Cor 11:2–16 underscores the degree to which this issue is *not* negotiable. Paul argues from tradition, common notions of beauty and "disgrace," theology, the cosmological order, scripture, the habits of angels, nature, and logic. The women are firmly subjected to Paul's patriarchal hierarchy here (see 1 Cor 14:33–35). But he does not order women prophets to be expelled, in contrast to the previous case.

Paul responds to divisions (*schismata*) and parties or factions (*haireseis*) in 11:17–22. Some Corinthians, probably the higher-status members, were gathering, eating, and drinking too much before the others arrived. Paul "does not commend" them for this practice (11:22), a reference to his "commendation" in 11:2 that introduces the stricture against women prophesying with uncovered hair. Paul's argument for order in worship has more coherence than his complicated argument for women to cover their heads. Tradition in both cases is a strong warrant as Paul "received from the Lord what I also handed on to you" (11:23).

Finally, Paul turns to problems among the Corinthians with his concept of the resurrection. Here, more than anywhere else in 1 Corinthians, we must read against the teleology of orthodoxy. Paul's position is foundational for orthodox Christian theology. But there were many different ways that Christians understood the meaning of Jesus' death, including the belief that his death was not as significant as his teaching and spiritual guidance, as suggested in the *Gospel of Thomas* and other early Christian texts. Nor should we assume unity of views about resurrection opposed to Paul within the Corinthian *ekklēsia* itself; there were likely a range of different views including the denial he confronts in 1 Cor 15:12. How does Paul negotiate these differences? As with the case of women covering their heads, Paul gives no ground and does not validate any alternative point of view. We do not find in *Paul's* rhetoric any acknowledgment of "strong" and "weak" positions on eschatology. Paul is dogmatic about restricting the meaning and significance of resurrection to his view alone. And his view—his *belief*—is critical to his authority as an apostle. For contemporary Christians and many other readers here, Paul's argument has the strength of familiarity. But it was clearly an odd view in ancient Corinth because he had to respond so carefully and forcefully to challenges from the Corinthians.

Paul foregrounds tradition and eschatology in his argument against Corinthian views on the resurrection. Tradition is primary.⁴³ The opening in 15:1–2 interrogates the Corinthians' commitment to the "gospel" and whether their faith is "in vain," immediately raising the stakes. Paul anchors his position in a succession of eyewitnesses. The chain of tradition (15:5) draws on the authority of the factions listed in 1 Cor 1:12 (Cephas; Christ himself) and destabilizes the implied counter-arguments. These people are not accessible to the Corinthians to counter Paul's positions. Furthermore, Paul's cited authorities do not include Apollos, the most notable rival leader in Corinth, who conceivably taught a different theology of resurrection.

Paul does not mention Apollos here, but his presence lingers rhetorically from Paul's argument against "the wisdom of the world" in 1 Cor 2. Paul privileges tradition and his access to apostolic witness against the alternative views of resurrection in Corinth.

He makes an eschatological argument as well. While Paul expounds his position on the resurrection more fully in 15:35–58, his critique of the Corinthians precedes this exposition (1 Cor 15:12–34). Whatever was going on in Corinth, conflicting notions of eschatology were part of it. Commentators have traditionally adopted the orthodox position in labeling these other eschatologies "collapsed" or "hyperenthusiastic" or "Gnostic." These labels mark Paul's eschatology as the original one. But Paul's struggles with the Corinthians over eschatology show that there was no reigning apocalyptic ideology for the end times in Corinth. Paul's emphatic belief expressed in 1 Cor 15:12 was clearly at odds with some Corinthians who thought that "there is no resurrection of the dead."[44] For Paul, both Christ's resurrection and the resurrection yet to come are thoroughly eschatological events. This ideology further strengthens his rhetoric, about which he leaves no room for doubt: "Then comes the end [*telos*, perhaps "the rest"], when [Christ] hands over the kingdom to God the Father, after he has destroyed every ruler and every authority and power" (1 Cor 15:24). Those who do not accept this eschatology would presumably be left out of that kingdom.

THE IDEOLOGY OF MIMESIS

Elizabeth Castelli brings a complementary perspective to this reading in her monograph on the trope of *mimesis* or imitation in 1 Corinthians as a discourse of power.[45] She examines in detail the tropes of *mimesis* in ancient Greco-Roman literary sources and in Paul, focusing on the many passages urging the recipients to "be imitators of me" such as 1 Corinthians 4:16 and 11:1.[46] Castelli argues that Paul sets himself up as a higher-status model to be emulated in order to control the communities. The discourse of *mimesis* also has important ideological ramifications for the themes I have been tracing:

> Finally, sameness is valued above difference, and this valuing under-girds the entire mimetic relationship. This elevation of sameness creates a tension in the mimetic relationship, which incorporates both a drive toward sameness and a need for hierarchy.

> Paul's invocation of mimesis indicts the very notion of difference, and thereby constructs the nature of early Christian social relationship; Christians are Christians insofar as they strive for the privileged goal of sameness. . . . Difference has only negative connotations in this mimetic economy.[47]

Castelli's insights are important. Paul's appeal to unity implies a hierarchy in the *ekklēsia* that privileges "sameness" over difference. The positive exhortation of *homonoia* suggests a negative valence for difference. And as we shall see in the next section, Paul explicitly indicts difference in Galatians in his theological constructions of "flesh" and "spirit." Postcolonial theory adds a further dimension to Castelli's work. With his appeal to unity and use of familiar *topoi* such as body and family, Paul takes the imperial position. The maintenance of order and harmony within the *ekklēsia*, the "body of Christ," corresponds to the maintenance of order and harmony within the Roman *oikoumenē*. The *topoi* of unity in 1 Corinthians also functioned to support the ideology of the ruling elite.[48] As the example from Plutarch earlier suggests, Paul's trope of *homonoia* mimics the rhetoric of the elite in Greco-Roman society. As Homi Bhabha writes, "Mimicry is thus the sign of a double articulation; a complex strategy of reform, regulation and discipline which 'appropriates' the Other as it visualizes power."[49] Paul's ideology of unity and apostolic authority is doubly implicated in power relations within the *ekklēsia* and within the *oikoumenē*, inscribing colonial power relations in the Corinthian community through a "metonymy of presence." Indeed, Bhabha has claimed that "the question of the representation of difference is therefore always also a problem of authority."[50] Paul's rhetoric of difference goes beyond inscribing binary divisions within the *ekklēsia*. The process of negotiating difference constructs a hybrid political position within Paul's imperial context.[51] I will return to the hybridity of orthodox imperial politics in the discourse of heresy in Chapter 7.

Summary: *Homonoia* in First Corinthians

When confronting division in Corinth, Paul seeks above all unity, *homonoia*, within the *ekklēsia*. On a range of issues, he acknowledges differences within the community and appeals for compromise for the sake of unity. He points to his own self-denial of rights, such as taking financial support from the *ekklēsiai*, in order to underscore the importance of unity. And yet on certain issues, Paul draws a line: the man living with his stepmother; women binding their hair during worship; and the resurrection as an eschatological event. These cracks in the ideology of unity develop larger fissures when Paul faces stronger opposition.

GALATIANS AND THE THEOLOGY OF DIFFERENCE

While 1 Corinthians is marked by the discursive negotiation of alternative positions, in Galatians Paul's ideology of "one gospel" literally splits the *ekklēsia*.[52] Paul's response to "a different gospel" (*heteron euangelion*, Gal 1:6) transforms a division over Jewish practices into a dualistic, apocalyptic

conflict paralleling the Qumran split with the sons of darkness. This bifur-
cates the community, undermining any ideology of unity in the *ekklēsia* or
"in Christ" (Gal 3:28).[53] Paul casts the sharp division between himself and
the Jerusalem faction in the rhetoric of "orthodoxy" and "heresy."[54]

Analyzing the debate in Galatia is crucial for one path that orthodox Christianity eventually took. But it could have gone the way of the
"Judaizing teachers." Eventually it did not, but we are not even sure of
the immediate consequences aside from Paul's reworking and revision of
his arguments in Romans. The battle in Galatians represents one fork on
the road towards orthodoxy, not the essential identity of Christian theology emerging.[55] Therefore we must explore this division carefully, without
resorting to a frame of reference that privileges the essence of orthodoxy.[56]
Open table-fellowship with Gentiles and no requirement for circumcision
were, for Paul, non-negotiable positions. Therefore he builds a strong theological, scriptural, and ethical defense coupled with a powerful attack on
his opponents. Because Paul's position becomes the orthodox position, his
position is almost always read as the "true" Christian position. But significantly, it is also a choice about approaches to religious *difference*. My
contrast to Paul's view on circumcision is not the so-called "Judaizers" in
Antioch and Galatia, who held a fully legitimate Jewish position, but rather
Paul's negotiation over eating idol meat in 1 Corinthians. Eating idol meat
and circumcision were just two of the issues that the followers of Jesus disagreed about. Paul stands fast on one point and negotiates on the other. We
can speculate on why Paul makes this move here but we can analyze *how*
he responds to difference and division.[57]

DIVISION IN THE EKKLĒSIA

The rhetoric of difference in Galatians exhibits four main discursive elements: a consistent, dualistic, apocalyptic ideology that theorizes the origin of difference at the social, theological, and cosmic level; the appeal to
tradition as authoritative; a polemically focused interpretation of scripture;
and the paired tropes of unity (*homonoia*) and strife (*eris* or *stasis*) as theological categories. These elements, as intertwined rhetorical gestures, are
difficult to analyze serially in this tightly composed epistle. Nonetheless I
will take them in turn, recognizing the artificiality of pulling the strands of
Paul's rhetoric apart.

In the first chapter, I identified apocalyptic dualism as one central aspect
of the early Christian notion of heresy. As Martyn has argued with respect
to Galatians, Paul's worldview is completely apocalyptic.[58] This worldview
grounds the rhetoric of difference in the letter by canalizing all opposition
as apocalyptic, and by implication satanic, opposition. Apocalyptic dualism
engenders a fixed notion of "gospel truth" that precludes fresh revelations
about his gospel (1:6–9). After admonishing the Galatians for turning to a

"different gospel," he offers a significant *correctio*, that another gospel does not even exist.[59] Even if Paul, one of his co-workers, or a heavenly angel would evangelize contrary to what had been preached already, that would be *anathema* (1:9). Betz warns "one should be careful not to create artificial problems."[60] But there is a deep contradiction between Paul's apocalyptic use of "gospel" for his own revelation and the circumscription of "gospel" as tradition (see esp. 1 Cor 15:1–3). Commentators struggle with these contradictions because of the ideology of unity preceding diversity, the basis of classic Christian heresiology.[61] I have deconstructed that ideology already. In Galatians, Paul uses "gospel" as both tradition and apocalyptic event to serve different rhetorical purposes, with sometimes polemical functions. While Paul claims strict theological and ideological monovalence for his *euangelion*, the communiqué from the Jerusalem conference (2:7), "that I had been entrusted with the gospel for the uncircumcised, just as Peter had been entrusted with [the gospel] for the circumcised," suggests that the other "pillars" might not have accepted this view. Other notions of "gospel" were circulating, and Paul's attempt to control the term suggests the nature of "gospel" itself was part of the division. He certainly denies the apocalyptic power of "gospel" revelation to anyone but himself. Multiple revelations are ideologically destabilizing; the "other" here "perverts" (*metastrepsai*, 1:7) Paul's gospel.[62] But he himself continues to receive revelations guiding his course (*apokalypsin*, 2:2).

Paul reconstructs his own history dualistically, before and after his apocalyptic call from the risen Jesus (1:15–16, *apokalypsai*).[63] This dualism is part of the background as Paul narrates what the Galatians surely could recall on their own: a deep schism among the community (2:11–16).[64] Since the Antioch incident would have been well known already to the Galatians, Paul must be seen as presenting his side of the story.[65] If Paul is trustworthy in reporting that Peter had eaten with Gentiles, it suggests that, in the power struggle between the two leaders, Peter was trying to garner followers for his own faction from within the *ekklēsia* started by Paul.[66] When Paul describes the division with Peter and Barnabas at Antioch, he is very careful to avoid blame. According to Paul, food and purity concerns create a conflict between Peter and members of the *ekklēsia* "from the circumcision."[67] Much depends, to be sure, on how to understand Gal 2:11–12; Paul suggests that the schism began with Peter's drawing back (*hypestellen*) from eating with Gentiles, apparently under the influence of "certain people [*tinas*] from James."[68] In contrast to the Jerusalem "pillars," these people are not named here.[69] Speculations about changes in Jerusalem and other political developments merely prioritize Paul's position here *vis à vis* the "Judaizers."[70] On the other hand, Paul "opposed [Peter] to his face" (2:11), suggesting, at the very least, an active role in the split.

The apocalyptic, dualistic worldview that grounds Paul's theology theorizes the origins of difference as eschatological and demonic. It also forces a schism with Peter and Barnabas. It also creates a notion of "heresy" against the "gospel" in the face of ideological difference (cf. *hairesis* in Gal 5:20). Paul constructs the schism between himself, Peter and Barnabas, and the "people" from Jerusalem at Antioch as a clash of dueling orthodoxies. Paul's real opponents here, the "people from James" must have had their own rhetoric of exclusion (note his wish for their castration, Gal 5:12).[71] They claimed they could discriminate against and even exclude the Galatians who did not follow their practices. Paul takes an orthodox position both rhetorically and ideologically, maintaining that his opponents did not act "consistently with the truth of the gospel" (2:14).[72] The Greek verb here, *orthopodeō*, perhaps "walk in line," both suggests Jewish *halakah*, from the Hebrew verb "to walk," and foreshadows Justin's claim that his Christians are *orthognōmoi*.[73] Paul presents his gospel theoretically as an orthodoxy, deviation from which is "false" (2:4) or "foolish" (3:1). To be sure, Paul resists the construct of "Law" as binding for salvation, and maintains a knife-edge dialectic between life "in the spirit" and the age to come. He nonetheless elides the "truth of the gospel" with this dogmatic position.[74]

Paul's apocalyptic dualism is cosmic as well as social.[75] The law itself is a "curse" (*katara*, 3:10). A series of dualistic antitheses structure this ideology of law and Gospel, sin and faith, flesh and spirit, all "in Christ" (3:26).[76] The spiritual elimination of social, gender, and ethnic differences for those who have "put on" Christ (3:28) is undermined by Paul's careful explication of how both social existence and cosmic existence are carved into dueling economies of law and faith (3:5). These differences remain in the *ekklēsia*. Here again we must not let Christian tradition obscure the ideological power of Paul's dualism as a rhetoric of religious difference. Perhaps Paul *is* right, theologically or philosophically, about law and faith. But the rhetoric of difference in this dualistic economy places all opposition in the realm of law and, subsequently, sin, as Paul makes a homology of law and sin in Gal 3:22. While *theologically*, all the Galatians have been baptized in the spirit by the "faith of Christ," ideologically the leaders of the opposition, and anyone in Galatia who opposes Paul, live under the economy of sin, in bondage to the "elements of the world" (4:22). They are heirs to Hagar, the bondwoman, and dwell in the earthly Jerusalem, doomed for destruction, rather than the Jerusalem above (4:25–26). Paul ties this allegory explicitly to his opponents, both the "Judaizing Teachers" and those in Galatia who follow them, in Gal 4:29: "so it is now also." Finally, in Gal 5:4, law is opposed to grace (*charis*). Again, in orthodox theology, law *is* opposed to grace, but the polemical context is primary. Difference and opposition are equated with sin and death.

A second discursive response to difference is the interpretation of scripture. Paul's interpretation of Genesis in Galatians is almost certainly a response to the opponents' readings.[77] The *midrash* on Abraham (3:6–19) is so central to Christian tradition, particularly Protestant theology read via Augustine and Luther, that it is hard to see how Paul constructs his ideology of "one Gospel" as the authoritative key to scripture.[78] For my purposes, however, since the gospel of the Teachers was as legitimate as the gospel of Paul, only different, so too their reading of Genesis was sound. Or sounder, since circumcision was the norm for Jewish men and Abraham was in fact circumcised, according to Genesis.[79] Paul needs to argue his case, despite having claimed an *apokalypsis* from Jesus and denying any possibility of "another gospel" revealed from heaven. Both sides here work within Jewish traditions of exegesis and *midrash* that were already ancient. Paul responds with an alternative exegesis of Genesis focusing on Jesus Christ. The ideology of scripture in Galatians does not depend on the interpretation per se but the idea of one correct interpretation controlled by *apokalypsis* and "spirit," dogmatically defined. Paul's reading foundationalizes the notion of one correct—that is, orthodox—interpretation of scripture and tradition in relation to Jesus Christ.[80] I will return to scripture as a theme in post-Pauline Christian heresiology in Chapter 6.

The final rhetorical element in Galatians is to make unity and difference theological categories. Paul turns again to the trope of unity or *homonoia* as he assails division, or *stasis*, in the *ekklēsia*. This dualistic rhetoric culminates Paul's argument against the opponents.[81] We see this in the stylized list of vices and virtues in Gal 5:16–26.[82] His focus is still the divisiveness of "a different Gospel"—those who would disrupt the *homonoia* of the body of Christ (3:28). In 5:15, Paul chides the *ekklēsia* for "beastly" behavior, a metaphor from the diatribe literature, in sharp contrast to the "love" commandment.[83] Humans are in concord with one another, rather than tearing at each other's throats. To engage in divisions or strife, *eris*, is to be below human. Then he turns in 5:16 to "life in the spirit."[84] This is a central, even pivotal concept for Paul's cosmology, soteriology, and ethics; he understands this as the way that Christ's resurrection delivers the baptized from sin to life. The *ekklēsia* acts out of love in the spirit and shuns the sins of the flesh. It is inherently an apocalyptic notion since, as Paul argued in 1 Corinthians 15, the resurrection of Jesus ushered in a new age of Spirit that defeats both sin and death.

While Paul understands life in the spirit as cosmically different from anything that has ever happened in human history, a result of the universe-shifting event of the resurrection of Christ, his ethics are not countercultural. In fact, the ethics of "life in the Spirit" were fairly common cultural goods of the Greco-Roman world.[85] The ethics of Gal 5:16–26 are typical, even traditional, not only in Pauline discourse but in Greco-Roman moral philosophy and Hellenistic Judaism.[86] The majority of Greeks, Romans, and Jews who were not part of the Galatian or Jerusalem *ekklēsiai* (and who had no notion of its existence) were *not* advocating "enmities, strife, jealousy, anger, quarrels, dissensions, factions" (Gal 5:20) but in fact just the opposite. The ethics of the virtues and vices listed here recapitulate the *homonoia* topos of 1 Corinthians. Paul does not advance a completely new ethic but grounds the prevailing moral discourse in the economy of the "flesh and spirit."

Difference itself is the focus in this list of vices and virtues. Galatians 5:16 expresses a "radical dualism" of flesh and spirit (*sarx, pneuma*), calling to the fore a widespread ancient concept of cosmological struggle between the forces of good and evil.[87] The traditions were widespread enough that the Galatians might have already had a large canvas of associations for this language. The apocalyptic context of this battle recalls the dualism of the Qumran sectarians.[88] As discussed in Chapter 2, the dualistic ideology of Qumran positioned the *yaḥad* politically against other Jews and the colonial powers that ruled Judea. In Paul as well, this apocalyptic dualism is not so much theological as it is political. The list of vices and virtues comes at the conclusion of an argument about leadership of the *ekklēsia* and Paul's "Judaizing" opposition. The Galatians have been given a stark choice between two leaders of the *ekklēsia* in Christ. The call to peace (*eirēnē*) in the "life in the spirit" and the derision of factions and divisiveness as part of "life in the flesh" should be read within this political context. This vice list reads like a Greco-Roman moral philosopher's definition of *stasis* (sedition or discord), the qualities opposite of *homonoia*. It would be recognized as political language, and Paul includes an inordinately high number of terms connoting political division here.[89]

This ideology of unity and difference anchors Paul's authority. Rather than negotiate difference by recognizing alternative points of view, Paul here makes strife, and therefore difference itself, a theological category "in the flesh" for political purposes.[90] Difference or divisions are the products of the "flesh" and signs of sin; *homonoia* and concord results of "spirit" and products of grace.[91] This ideology suggests the satanic origins of opposition to Paul's theology. His apocalyptic dualism places difference theologically in the realm of sin, cosmically in control of Satan, and politically in the actions of his opponents. The word *haireseis* in 5:20 is unique in Paul's vice lists. It is always negative in Paul—for instance, in 1 Cor 11:19, referring to the factions around the celebration of the Lord's Supper. *Hairesis* is the opposite of *homonoia*. To make a choice against Paul (*haireō*), to join a *hairesis*, is to be "in the flesh" rather than the "spirit."[92] But joining a faction means opposing Paul, whose now-schismatic *ekklēsia* is *not* a faction. Here, Paul foreshadows the orthodox claim that all other Christian groups are parts of factions or *haireiseis*, but that they themselves are not. The divisiveness of "a different Gospel"—those who would disrupt the *homonoia* of the body of Christ (3:28)—has been recast as a theological problem. He concludes the letter stating that "neither circumcision nor uncircumcision is anything" (6:15). Indeed, there is only unity and difference.[93]

SUMMARY

The problem of religious difference within the Galatian *ekklēsia* presents a multi-layered political crisis for Paul. First, his *apokalysis* from the resurrected Jesus Christ (Gal 1:12) sets him on a path of "life in Christ" that opposes the path taken by Peter and Barnabas, the followers of James, the Jerusalem *ekklēsia*, and indeed the entire tradition of Judaism with respect to the circumcision. Second, not only do these opponents teach a different gospel, but also their teaching challenges his ideology of "one gospel" upon which the "life in Christ" depends. Third, his authority as apostle to the Galatians is threatened and even undermined by this opposition. These differences within the community produce division that becomes schism. For Paul, this division is not just a concomitant issue that is a result of theological differences. It is the product of the flesh, the force opposed by God and the Spirit of Christ as well. Cast as theological truth within the "one gospel," this ideology has a political function against Paul's opponents.

2   CORINTHIANS AND THE RHETORIC OF SATAN

Despite the rupture within the *ekklēsia*, the theme of unity and *mimesis*, the apostolic model, is still a discursive move for Paul in Galatia (Gal 4:12). We move now to a case in which such appeals were no longer politically feasible. My final example of the rhetoric of difference in Paul's uncontested letters is from 2 Corinthians. 2 Corinthians 10–13 is most likely a different letter from 2 Corinthians 1–9, perhaps the "letter of tears" mentioned in 2 Cor 1:23–2:4 and 7:5–11. Or the "letter of tears" could have been lost while 2 Corinthians 10–13 would be a later letter.[94] We know Paul wrote complete letters to various *ekklēsiai*; he wrote more than one letter to Corinth; he mentions a "painful visit" as well as a "letter of tears"; co-workers or disciples copied his letters; and his letters were eventually collected, edited, and distributed.[95] The argument that Chapters 10–13 comprise a different letter than the rest of 2 Corinthians is solid and sufficient. Accepting that 2 Corinthians is from Paul's hand and to the same *ekklēsia*, I turn to the rhetoric of difference in this section of the canonical "epistle," 2 Corinthians. Paul's rhetoric parallels the conceptions of truth and falsehood, the anthropology of human error, and the dualism of flesh and spirit that marked the "war within" each member of the Dead Sea covenant. And Paul, too, marks his opposition as demonic, making explicit in 2 Corinthians what was implied in Galatians.

The rhetorical situation is closer to Galatians than 1 Corinthians.[96] 2 Corinthians 10–13 is an *apologia* or defense speech.[97] Recent scholarship has grouped the possibilities for Paul's opponents here along various combinations of "Judaizers," "spiritualists" or "pneumatics," "Gnostics," and the so-called "divine men" (*theoi andres*).[98] Possibly the different groups Paul negotiated with in 1 Corinthians had strengthened their positions against him. Or, comparable to documented activities of Apollos in Corinth and the "Judaizing" leaders in Galatia, new teachers whom Paul calls "super-apostles" (11:5) have gained followers in the community.[99]

The "super-apostles" of 2 Corinthians could have been from Jerusalem.[100] Paul's polemic against these opponents is not doxographic, making identification of their positions difficult. But the events had displaced Paul's authority, authority that had already been severely challenged. Paul himself had become a contentious issue.[101] In response, Paul elides the ideology of allegiance to Christ with allegiance to Paul. The various theories for Paul's opponents follow an orthodox historiography by seeing Paul in the normative, centrist position.[102] And that is precisely Paul's rhetorical strategy. 2 Corinthians 10–13 places Paul at the center and marginalizes—in fact, demonizes—the opponents. This parallels the ideology of *homonoia* in 1 Corinthians that, as we have seen, suggests to many readers a united movement in all the many conflicts and divisions within the *ekklēsia*. 1 Corinthians 1–4 calls for unity under "one father" (1 Cor 4:15). Paul's rhetoric now abandons the appeals to unity within the *ekklēsia*, the trope of *homonoia*, in favor of the ideology of apostolic authority. With "one gospel" comes one, and only one, apostle.

Rhetoric itself—Paul's appearance and humble way of speaking (*tapeinos*, 10:1)—is a synecdoche for this power struggle in Corinth. Paul does not deal with substantive theological issues but rather his standing in the community and the perception of his leadership as compared to the unnamed and undefined opponents (10:7–11). He hints at some of the issues at stake, which we can read in the context of the other Corinthian literature. This section suggests issues similar to Galatia in defining the "mission field" or "sphere of action," (*kanona*, 10:15).[103] But it is a difficult reconstruction in order to have any sense of what the content of this "other gospel" (2 Cor 11:4) could have been. Why would belonging to Christ be at all at stake? Clearly Paul belongs to Christ, as do the Corinthians (2 Cor 10:7). Paul's ironic boast of his authority (*exousia*) from the Lord for "building up and not tearing down" (*eis oikodomēn kai ouk eis kathairesin*, 2 Cor 10:8) conflicts with his use of this *exousia* in an attack on others who are also "in Christ." He claims that it is the other leaders who "belong to Christ" who are tearing the community down. He accuses them of making himself the problem (10:10). Thus the next sentence, "Let such people understand that what we say by letter when absent, we will also do when present" (10:11), echoes the implied threat of 1 Cor 4:21: "What would you prefer? Am I to come to you with a stick, or with love in a spirit of gentleness?"

Faced with attacks on his authority, Paul tries to set the terms of the debate in the introduction or *exordium*, 2 Cor 10:1–11.[104] As in Galatians, Paul's rhetoric does not suggest that he has had an active part in the division. Yet his response belies his own claims of innocence. One apparent accusation against Paul is that he conducts himself (*peripateō*) "according to the flesh," (*kata sarka*). There are a host of possible explanations for this accusation.[105] Paul's response focuses on power, divine power (*dynata tō theō*, 10:4), signaling his understanding of the charge.[106] This response recapitulates the ideology of the Galatian vice and virtue list. The "realm of flesh" discursively conjures its opposite sphere, "life in the spirit" or "life in Christ." Thus, "knowledge" has theological valence: knowledge from God (*gnōseōs tou theou*) wielded by Paul against his opponents' sinful, fleshly arguments (*logismous*, 10:4). Wield is the proper verb—with God's power Paul destroys their arguments. Within this dualistic economy of spirit and flesh, Paul does not negotiate but asserts hegemony over "every thought" (*pan noēma*, 10:5). The response is either obedience or disobedience (*parakoē, hypakoē,* 10:6). Paul expresses this "defense" in unusually strong, martial imagery, so much so he even acknowledges it (10:1, 9–10).[107]

Commentators call 2 Corinthians 11:1–12:10 "the fool's speech."[108] The significant idea in this speech is that someone else in the *ekklēsia*—that is, "in Christ" and also preaching the Gospel—is in fact a "false apostle" associated with Satan. Paul employs two dominant metaphors, satanic influence and sexual impurity, in the context of the apocalyptic dualism that grounds this rhetoric of difference. These tropes occur on either side of the speech in 11:7–11 defending his right to refuse support from the Corinthians.[109] Paul never calls the opponents satanic. Rather, he uses the rhetorical trope of *insinuatio*, typically part of the *exordium* but here in the *argumentatio*, to associate the activity of the opponents in Paul's "sphere of action" (*kanōn*, 10:15) with corruption and with Satan.[110] First (11:2), he genders the *ekklēsia* with a metaphor of the community as the bride of Christ, a metaphor that could have already been traditional.[111] Paul takes on the role of the father of the bride, a powerful position in both Jewish and Roman marriage transactions.[112] The simile follows (11:3): just as Eve was corrupted by the cunning serpent, Paul's opponents will corrupt the thoughts (*ta noēmata*) of the *ekklēsia*.[113] Paul uses the passive "corrupted" (*phtharē*), but the reference to his opponents is clear (see the "super-apostles" in 11:5), as would the reference to "thoughts" taken captive by Christ (10:4b–5) be fresh in the minds of any auditors.[114]

Paul makes this slanderous insinuation a strong accusation in the peroration, 2 Cor 11:12–15, part of the extensive argument in 2 Corinthians 10–13 over boasting.[115] The opponents are "false apostles, deceitful workers, disguising themselves as apostles of Christ." Only someone who claimed the important roles of apostle or worker could be attacked in this way, signaling the power of his opponents in the *ekklēsia*. Paul undercuts their socially recognized authority. The others "in Christ" have disguised themselves (*metaschēmatizomonoi*) in the *ekklēsia* just as Satan disguised himself as an angel of light—for the corruption of Eve and humankind. Either charge, sexual corruption or satanic association, would be strong. The combination is as fierce a condemnation as we find in the Pauline letters.[116]

Paul theorizes the origin of difference within the community. Just as a disguised Satan fooled Eve, Satan brings the false apostles into the *ekklēsia*. The charge that his opponents are disguised like Satan gives a historiographical explanation for the origin of difference. The historiography of difference and these tropes of sexual corruption and satanic power are grounded in Paul's dualistic, apocalyptic worldview. The *exordium* in 2 Cor 10:1–11 inscribes the dualistic economy of spirit and flesh. Paul then introduces the ideological formulation of "one gospel" in 2 Cor 11:4, which I marked earlier as central to Paul's ideology in Galatians (cf. Gal 1:6–9, 11–12). The content of the "other gospel" has intrigued scholars, but just as significant is Paul's rhetoric of difference in response.[117] While Paul's dualism is not always consistently expressed, we see that it is a consistent element of his rhetoric of difference.[118]

Paul attacks the notion of boasting after the peroration in 11:16–30, even while boasting of his own heritage (vv. 21b–22); his hardships (23–29); and a prison escape in Damascus (30–33).[119] Finally, he boasts of his own "visions and revelations" (*optasias kai apokalypseis*, 12:1). Most commentators understand the description of a man who was taken up to "the third heaven" or "Paradise" (12:2, 4) to be a description of Paul's own ecstatic experience. Furthermore, most scholars assume Paul is taking on the opponents on their own terms by emphasizing pneumatic experience, primarily because of the parallel argument in 1 Corinthians 12–14 but also because of the idea that these opponents were "hyper-spiritualists" (a term that, as noted earlier, privileges the orthodox position in this conflict).[120] In the ironic context of Paul's speech, this could parody the opponents' stories themselves.[121] Parody or not, this story anchors Paul's authority discursively in the ideology of mystical apocalypticism. He underscores his own "signs and wonders and mighty works" exhibited in Corinth (12:12). He concludes this letter with further echoes of 1 Cor 4:18, threatening to come to them in power (13:2–4) and exhorting them to put this *ekklēsia* in order (13:11).

The journey to Paradise results in a "thorn in the flesh," a "messenger of Satan" (12:7). Paul employs the words for Satan, as well as the only occurrence of Beliar, most often in the Corinthian correspondence of all his letters. Satan was of course active in Paul's apocalyptic worldview.[122] The activity of Paul's opponents in Corinth mimics Satan's appearance in the world. The homology between Satan's activity and the opponents' appearance echoes the rhetoric and ideology of the Qumran covenant, both in the use of Satan (or Beliar) polemically against opponents and in the apocalyptic, dualistic worldview in which God's activity in the world opposes, and is opposed by, demonic forces that will be ultimately destroyed in the *eschaton*. In the Qumran *yaḥad* and Paul's *ekklēsia*, opponents align cosmologically with Satan and the forces of evil. In a short vice list in 2 Cor 12:20, Paul expresses his fear of *stasis* within the *ekklēsia*, employing several of the same terms from Gal 5:20–21 (*eris*, *zēlos*, *thumoi*). He certainly retains the ideology of *homonoia*. But the opponents, the "super-apostles" themselves, have lost their place in the *ekklēsia*. Like the man in Corinth living with his father's second wife, they have been cast into the realm of flesh and the power of Satan.

PHILO AND JOSEPHUS

Paul had many imitators, as we shall see in Chapter 6, but no Christian textual predecessors. His writing has been most frequently compared to that
of the Greco-Roman elite. Philosophers and rhetoricians such as Plutarch
or Dio Chrysostom provide parallels for Paul's moral exhortation, literary
tropes, and epistolary style. Philosophers also negotiated ideological difference, as did medical theorists and rhetoricians.[123] But while the rhetorical
contexts of these writers might be similar to Paul's, the social contexts of
the philosophical school are quite different. Ancient Judaism offers two
closer examples for comparison: Philo of Alexandria (ca. 20 BCE–50 CE)
and Flavius Josephus (37–ca.100 CE), both of whom negotiated areas of
ideological difference within Second Temple Judaism.[124]

Philo's extensive works include descriptions of different Jewish communities as well as descriptions of difference within Jewish communities.[125]
One point of difference negotiated in Philo's treatises was the interpretation
of the Bible. Philo was an allegorical interpreter of the Torah; his biblical
interpretation influenced subsequent Christian authors in Alexandria.[126]
At several points Philo acknowledges a different approach, the "literalists"
who do not read allegorically. Philo thus deals not only with difference in
interpretation but also with difference in *how* to approach the problem of
interpretation (*hermēneia*, *Migration* 1.12; *Abraham* 2.119). He rarely confronts the literalists, let alone attack or demonize them. For instance, in *On
Abraham* 1.68, he acknowledges both literal and allegorical interpretations
for Abraham's journey from Ur. He hints at a problem with "turning plain
stories into allegory" when writing about the Passover in *Spec. Laws* 2.147.
But in *On Dreams*, Philo writes that the "stupidest person" (lit. "slow-
est," *bradytatos*) should be able to see that sometimes there is meaning
beyond the literal and that following the "allegorical rule" (*hepomenoi tois
allēgorias nomois*) reveals deeper meanings (*Dreams* 1.101–102).[127] Interpreting the Tower of Babel story in Genesis, Philo deals with both sides, the
"impious scoffers" who dismiss biblical stories as myths such as ones found
in Homer as well as "those who take the letter of the law in its outward
sense" (*Confusion* 2, 14).[128] Nonetheless, allegory, for Philo, is clearly the
philosophically superior way to read the books of Moses (*Planting* 1.36;
Posterity 1.7; *Abraham* 1.99). In *On Flight and Finding* 1.179, Philo hints
at the higher understanding for those who use allegory in comparison to
those "uninitiated" (*amyētoi*) into its meanings. But in *On the Confusion
of Tongues* 14, he indicates how the allegorically-initiated should approach
difference: "we shall take the line of allegorical interpretation not in any
contentious spirit (*aphiloneikōs*), nor seeking some means of meeting sophistry with sophistry (*ouk antisophizomenoi*)." Philo approaches hermeneutical difference with balance and conciliation.

Philo had a broad view of what might be included within Judaism. The
geography of Judaism in his writings ranges from Syria Palestine to Egypt,

in descriptions of the Essene and Therapeutae in *That Every Good Person is Free* and *On the Contemplative Life*. These essays inscribe a moral as well as physical geography; Philo sets philosophical virtues discursively in relief with these groups. Difference thus becomes exemplary. It does not matter whether these were actual desert communities, although there are enough similarities in Philo's description to align these Essenes with the Dead Sea Scrolls as well as Josephus' depiction ahead; they are clearly idealized. The importance for my argument is how Philo uses difference as an example of virtue in his descriptions of the active and contemplative life.

Philo introduces the Essenes in *That Every Good Person is Free* after a discussion of "freedom" in Stoic terms: freedom means freedom from desire, wealth, pleasure, or any other attachments. The Essenes are the main example of a Jewish group that exhibits "high moral excellence" (*kalokagathias, Good Person* 75). They are "athletes of virtue" (*athlētas aretēs*, 88), living a philosophy of freedom from attachments. They choose poverty over wealth; all are equal brothers with no slaves among them (77, 79). Money, possessions, clothing, and food are held in common (88). This practice, along with Philo's description of their Sabbath observances, parallels the *Community Rule*, but his claim that they use allegory in their philosophical study (82) does not. The Essenes are above all an example to follow of:

> piety, holiness, justice, domestic and civic conduct, knowledge of what is truly good, or evil, or indifferent (*adiaphorōn*),[129] and how to choose what they should avoid the opposite, taking for their defining standards the three, love of God, love of virtue, love of men. (*Good Person* 83)

They are an example but they are also different. They "stand alone in the whole of mankind" (*monoi gar ex hapantōn schedon anthrōpōn*, 73) in their attitude toward wealth. Their Sabbath worship differs from other Jews. They contrast most starkly with the rulers of Syria and Palestine—that is, the Herodians, who despite their cruelty have not been able to bring charges against the exemplary Essenes.

The Judaism of the Therapeutae, Philo's example of the "contemplative life," corresponds even more closely to Philo's philosophical ideals.[130] There are no clear markers of Judaism at all in the first third of the essay. Philo tends to use "Jewish" and its variations less often in his scriptural interpretations and essays and more often in the two treatises directed to Gentiles, *The Embassy to Gaius* and *Against Flaccus*. He notes, however, that they honor the seventh day (*Contempl. Life* 30–31); read and discuss the scriptures allegorically (75, 78); and keep a vigil, with hymns, for Moses, Miriam, and God's wonders at the Red Sea (84–85). Jewish identity is not central, but rather Philo's philosophical idealism and use of difference to display excellence. Their worship of the One is superior to others as they "soar above the sun of our senses" (11–12). They too give up their possessions for contemplation (13–14) and then physically separate themselves from family, friends, and their cities. Geography marks moral and philosophical excellence (18–20). The strongest difference in this essay is the descriptions of the banquets. Their gatherings are an explicit point of contrast (*antitaxas*) with the symposia of other people (40). Philo describes the debauchery and indulgence of Greek and Roman banqueting, which focus on drinking, excessive food, and entertainment (40–56). He even criticizes the *Symposium* of Socrates, which focused on love and sex (57–63). The Therapeutae, again, are a point of contrast in every way (*antitaxō*, 64). Men wear white robes and recline according to seniority; women and aged virgins share the same feast. Prayer and philosophical discussion are the focus. Youths volunteer to serve; there are no slaves. They do not eat meat and serve only water. The evening ends with the vigil and hymns to God.

JOSEPHUS

While Paul and Philo were near contemporaries, Josephus wrote some time later. Josephus knew about John the Baptist and Jesus of Nazareth, but it is very unlikely that he was influenced by early Christianity.[131] His description of the Jewish *haireseis* or schools of thought is a helpful comparison to Philo as well as Paul's responses to difference within the *ekklēsiai*. The descriptions of the Jewish *haireseis* appear in three different works: *The Jewish War*, directed to a Jewish audience; the *Jewish Antiquities*, written for the Gentile Roman audience, and his own *Life*.[132] All these texts, of course, have multiple functions, and I return to the political context of Josephus, the Romans, and the defeated Judeans in more detail in Chapter 7. While Josephus uses the model of the philosophical school to portray difference within Judaism, he is not focused on philosophical virtues and difference as exemplary, as we saw in Philo. Josephus was fully enmeshed in the politics of representation of Judaism to Romans and the Romans to Jews because of his history as Jewish general, turncoat and informer, and imperial client. Josephus employs the rhetoric of acceptance when describing the Jewish *haireseis*. The exception is the "Fourth Philosophy," which, along with the Zealots, bears the blame for the revolt and therefore helps rehabilitate the rest of the Jews.

When Josephus introduces the Pharisees, Sadducees, and Essenes in *J.W.* 2.119, he uses the verb *philosopheitai*, to philosophize, and *philosophiai* in *Ant.* 18.11. In the *Life*, he describes his experimentation with all three *haireseis* as a youth and his eventual acceptance of the Pharisees, "a sect having points of resemblance to that which the Greeks call the Stoic school" (*Life* 12).[133] This comparison to schools of philosophy marks his approach to difference within Judaism as the rhetoric of acceptance. His educated Roman audience would have understood this doxographic model for describing difference, in which Josephus elaborates on the *doxai* or beliefs of the groups.

For instance, he compares the Essenes' belief in the immortality of the soul to Greek mythology, noting how they share "the beliefs of the sons of Greece" on punishments in the afterlife (*J.W.* 2.155–57). He then describes and compares the beliefs of the Pharisees and Sadducees about fate and the soul (*J.W.* 2.162–65). The other descriptions of the Jewish schools employ similar doxographic methods. In *Ant.* 13.171–73, he describes the "different opinions [*diaphorōs hypelambanon*] concerning human affairs" among these three *haireseis* and their views on fate and in *Ant.* 18.11–22 the doctrines (*logoi*) of these three philosophies.

Josephus treats the Essenes in much more detail than the other two schools in *J.W.* 2.120–60 and slightly longer detail in *Ant.* 18.18–22 (one chapter more than the Pharisees, 18.12–15). As we have already seen, they were the most exclusive and sectarian, as well as dualistic and hierarchical, of Second Temple Jewish groups. For the most part Josephus avoids the idealization of Philo, who presents them as moral exemplars. He notes their reverence (*semnotēs*), avoidance of pleasure, and rejection of wealth in community (*J.W.* 2.119–22). Josephus is even-handed and descriptive. He then devotes only a few short paragraphs to the Pharisees and the Sadducees, noting that the Pharisees are affectionate and harmonious, employing the *topos* of *homonoia*, while the Sadducees are "rather boorish" (*agiōteron*). Regardless of whether his observations were socially accurate, Josephus inscribes the politics of representation in post-war Judaism. The Essene community at Qumran was destroyed in the war; in the *Jewish War* they are constructed as a social and philosophical curiosity, removed from society. The aristocratic Sadducees were most closely attached to the now-destroyed Temple hierarchy. The Pharisees, to whom Josephus himself claimed allegiance, were the most successful survivors in the post-war climate.

Josephus also describes the infamous "Fourth Philosophy" started by Judas the Galilean (*Ant.* 18.23–25). The politics of representation come to the fore here as well. Josephus attempted to blame the war against Rome on undesirable elements within Judea rather than Judaism itself. He represented traditional aristocratic interests in Judea as well as imperial politics in Rome. The Fourth Philosophy, often elided in scholarship with Jewish "Zealots," shares the blame in Josephus' historiography for the revolt (see Chapter 7). Josephus treats them doxographically, if negatively, describing their attachment to liberty and their belief that God alone is ruler. This revolutionary political position would have been perceived as very negative in Rome after the Judean War. Josephus continues his description, noting that they do not fear death and exhibit tolerance for pain. But he characterizes this philosophy as foolishness (*anoia*) that sickened the nation and cuts off further discussion.

All of these responses to difference within Judaism are political. Philo's use of allegory was a response to the social-political context of Alexandria, as Dawson has shown. And Paul turned to allegory in Galatians as part of his response to the Judaizing teachers. So too Josephus' doxographic description of the *haireseis* expressed the politics of representation of Judaism in post-war Rome. With the exception of the radical "Fourth Philosophy," difference was accepted. Josephus' doxography of the Jewish philosophies places them discursively on par with the Platonists, Peripatetics, Stoics, and Cynics of the Greco-Roman world. These approaches are non-heresiological responses to ideological difference in Judaism by Philo and Josephus.

CONCLUSION: FROM SIN TO SCHISM TO HERESY

The comparison with Philo and Josephus highlights Paul's rhetoric of difference. The three discursive moments of division earlier have shown how Paul employed the rhetoric of difference to bolster the ideology of apostolic authority. In 1 Corinthians, Paul employed *homonoia* as a discursive trope to negotiate divisions in the *ekklēsia*. While Paul recognized alternative points of view on several positions, such as the role of Apollos and the eating of meat from temple markets, he takes firm stands on others, such as the incestuous man, women's roles and authority in the *ekklēsia*, drunkenness during the Eucharist, and the belief in the Resurrection. But in each case he appeals for unity under his leadership. In making this argument, Paul foregrounds tradition, eschatology, and apostolic witness as unifying ideologies subsuming different theological positions. These three ideologies are central to orthodox Christian heresiology. Furthermore, his appeal to the Roman imperial ideology of unity elides the power of the apostle with the power of the elite in the Greco-Roman world.

A stronger political challenge in Galatia pushed Paul beyond the *homonoia* trope. There, the discourse of apocalyptic eschatology, the ideology of "one gospel," and the dualistic economies of "flesh" and "spirit" were rhetorical tools against his opponents. Within these dualistic economies, difference and opposition have theological valence as part of the apocalyptic, demonic realm of the flesh. Finally, in 2 Corinthians, Paul demonized his apostolic opponents by associating their activity and "other gospel" with the mythology of Satan's corruption of Eve. Here he added the two dominant tropes of subsequent Christian heresiology, satanic influence and sexual impurity, to the ideology of tradition, apostolic witness, and apocalyptic dualism that grounds Paul's rhetoric of difference. In both of these letters, Paul's apocalyptic, eschatological worldview is essential to the confrontation with his opponents.

The key points in Paul's heresiology include:

1. *Homonoia*, the political ideology of unity that privileges sameness over difference
2. Apocalyptic dualism in the cosmic realm mapped onto the social world and his opponents

3. Authority grounded in apostolic tradition and the "correct" interpretation of scripture
4. The tropes of satanic origins and sexual slander against his opponents

While Paul's dualistic apocalypticism in Galatians and 2 Corinthians recalls
the Dead Sea Scrolls, his rhetoric of difference is a reversal of the Qumran
rhetoric of separation. Where the Qumran covenanters used apocalyptic
rhetoric against the Jerusalem authorities and forged an identity in the desert apart from other Jewish groups, Paul takes the same Essene rhetoric of
light and darkness to expunge unwanted doctrine and leaders from within
his *ekklēsia*, a discursive move that attempts to eliminate opposition and
to extend his authority over the community at the same time. This rhetoric of difference and exclusion runs counter to the ideology of *homonoia*
prevalent in both Roman political discourse and Paul's own letters. Elsewhere, Paul implicitly adopts (in 1 Corinthians) and explicitly employs (in
Romans 13) a political theology of *homonoia* by means of God-ordained
Roman rule. The maintenance of order and harmony within the *ekklēsia*,
the "body of Christ," corresponds to the maintenance of order and harmony within the *oikoumenē* of the Empire. I will trace the development of
this imperial discourse of hegemony in Chapter 7. First, I turn to further
developments in the Gospel traditions.

5 The Christian Gospels as Narratives of Exclusion

When they saw him, they worshipped him; but some doubted.

Matt 28:17

INTRODUCTION

We saw in the previous chapter Paul's defense of his gospel against any other. I will focus here on a different and likely later moment in the history of Christian discourse when "gospel" becomes a literary genre as well as the content of preaching. The Gospel narratives present a new set of complex literary problems, but can be read as discourses of exclusion.[1] I will trace this theoretical move in the earliest collections of sayings and Christian narratives about Jesus for the rhetoric of exclusion against other Christians in the first century.

These texts are critical in the genealogy of heresy. But the opponents in the Gospels are harder to identify than even in Paul's letters. Despite the best scholarly efforts, they remain relatively dislocated, historically and socially. In a history of dogmatic conflicts and "heretics," this would be problematic. But in a history of *discourse*, this is methodologically possible. Working with literary theory as much as social history in this chapter, I focus on the internal conflicts and politics in these documents—Q, Matthew, and the *Gospel of Thomas*—and how they construct a heresiological rhetoric of difference in response.

Mark was almost certainly the earliest narrative Gospel, although not necessarily the first written one.[2] Important studies have read Mark as written against other, "heretical" Christians.[3] But it lacks a community focus. Without precluding readings of Mark as a heresiological narrative, I will turn to other gospels that contain clearer instances of argument. I will begin with two Sayings Gospels, one hypothetical, both controversial: the Sayings Source Q and the *Gospel of Thomas*.[4] Both have figured significantly in recent scholarship on the historical Jesus as well as early Christian origins. It is the latter issue that I focus on here as part of genealogy of the notion of heresy. I compare these to the responses to ideological difference in the Gospel of Matthew and the early church order *Didache* (*Teaching of the Apostles*). While these Gospels differ with regard to the salvific importance of the death and resurrection of Jesus, at certain stages in their composition they adopt similar rhetorical strategies for dealing with difference within their communities. The rhetorical patterns of argument form around an apocalyptic worldview, which drives confrontation and expulsion of opponents, while the *Gospel of Thomas* inscribes strategies of avoidance.

Gospel texts can be read as narratives about the communities themselves rather than reports of what Jesus actually said or did. This insight is significant for the genealogy of heresy. These are texts in which the strategies of exclusion are narrated in the words of Jesus himself. Heresiology becomes, in the Gospel of Matthew, a discursive move by the eponymous founder of the religion, Jesus Christ. Where we saw in Chapter 3 that Jesus, as a Jewish apocalyptic prophet, engendered conflict with other Jewish communities, this Gospel reconstructs Jesus as the arch-heresiologist of Christianity.

THE PROBLEM OF Q

The hypothetical Q (from the German *Quelle*, "source") was postulated in the nineteenth century by source critics of the New Testament delineating the relationship of the Synoptic Gospels Matthew, Mark, and Luke. The classic two-source theories held that Mark and Q were sources for Matthew and Luke.[5] Q was thus defined as the material contained in both Matthew and Luke but not in Mark.[6] The discovery of the *Gospel of Thomas* at Nag Hammadi strengthened the case for Q by proving the existence of an early Christian Sayings Gospel without narrative, miracles, or a passion account. The scholarly project of the recovery and analysis of Q includes the reconstruction of the original text; recovery of the stages in the redaction of Q before it was used by Luke and Matthew; and the social context of the Q community.[7] Scholars have postulated that Q was a written Greek document, preserved more faithfully in Luke than in Matthew, and that it went through two major redactions.[8] Study of Q and the history of its community has gone far beyond recognizing the double-tradition in Matthew and Luke.[9]

Kloppenborg's analysis of the genre and redaction of Q divides it into three different types of material that correspond to different redactions of the documents: sapiential (wisdom) sayings, conflict sayings, and apocalyptic sayings. Kloppenborg argued that the sapiential sayings and admonitions were the "formative element" in Q. The *written* form of these wisdom sayings preceded the addition of apocalyptic and conflict sayings.[10] He emphasizes that literary history does not map directly onto tradition history: the secondary material could be as old as the primary elements, while the primary elements could contain newer sayings than the secondary elements.[11] His research places the original Q (Q[1]) document in the Hellenistic wisdom tradition rather than the apocalyptic Jewish context in which I, with many other scholars, place the historical Jesus. Wisdom traditions were part of Second Temple discourse, including apocalyptic texts.[12] Nonetheless it is significant that Kloppenborg's Q[1] suggests a community focused entirely on the teachings of Jesus rather than the ministry or death of Jesus. Many scholars have challenged this reconstruction of the stages of Q as well as the implications of Kloppenborg's literary analysis, finding instead a more traditionally Christian Q community as read through the Synoptic Gospels, Paul, and Acts.[13] A particular criticism is whether Q, despite lacking a passion narrative, presupposes the crucifixion of Jesus as part of its ideology (cf. Luke [=Q] 14:27). But others have pushed the notion of the "Q Community" even further from traditional reconstructions of Christian origins that follow the Synoptic Gospels and Acts, proposing more radical revisions of the beginnings of early Christianity.[14]

There is a danger of circularity on both sides of this debate. Genre analysis that hypothesizes the sapiential Q[1] document as formative relegates the apocalyptic elements to secondary status, which in turn sets the presuppositions for the historical reconstruction of the Q community.[15] Kloppenborg also puts the most eschatological passages in the same strata as the passages grappling with the *delay* of the parousia.[16] More traditional scholars, on the other hand, presuppose an early, normative Christianity that preached a crucified, salvific Christ and shape their interpretation of Q according to its Synoptic strata and Pauline theology.[17] Their assumptions of an originally unified Christian *kerygma* preclude an early, wisdom-oriented Christian community.

Placing the wisdom material in Q before the apocalyptic material does not mean we must place the Christology of Q[1] before every other early Christian tradition. Such a move would follow the Hegesippian ideology of pure Christian truth preceding error, where in this case the "original Q" is the pure doctrine of Christ. It is important to remember that the *Jesus movement itself* was highly diverse, lacking the unity implied by the reconstructed Q[1]. Q represents one early Christian movement among many, communities that were both apocalyptic and sapiential. But other scholars have taken these literary stages in the Q document as historical phases in a Q community that preserved the original sayings of the historical Jesus.[18] As discussed in Chapter 1, Mack has mapped an elaborate history of the Cynic Jesus and the Q Community that develops through the various stages corresponding to the redaction of Q outlined by Kloppenborg.[19]

Furthermore, in Chapter 3, I argued that Jesus was an apocalyptic Jewish prophet leading a renewal movement that focused on the Temple and ultimately ended in his crucifixion. My view does not separate the historical Jesus, as prophet and teacher, from the wisdom traditions of the earliest Q document, since these traditions have deep Jewish apocalyptic roots.[20] But I reject the *non-apocalyptic* Jesus. The apocalyptic elements of Jesus' ministry would more likely be *excluded* by wisdom-oriented followers who held a non-apocalyptic, sapiential interpretation of Jesus than be *added* as part of the manufacturing of a "Christian myth of origins." This portrait of Jesus in Q[1] (as reconstructed by Kloppenborg and others) would appeal more to philosophically-oriented Jews and Gentiles as a noble Sage of Wisdom or a Cynic philosopher than an executed political prisoner. The existence of a "Q community" points to the diversity of Jesus' followers and post-crucifixion movements, but we do not need to map this onto the historical Jesus himself. Rather, the hypothesis of the Q community supports the theoretical approach I outlined in Chapter 1 that rejects any original purity to the Jesus movements. The Q document and communities show the inherent diversity of responses to and interpretations of Jesus' teaching and death.

CONFLICT IN Q

The rhetoric of difference in Q also reveals conflict among the early followers of Jesus. The redaction of the Q^1 sapiential sayings with a layer of polemical sayings and stories against "Israel"—that is, with the apocalyptic sayings in Q^2—reflects deep ideological differences within early Christian communities. The wisdom message of the Q^1 community met opposition in Palestine and Syria, just as Paul did in Antioch and Corinth. As reconstructed by Kloppenborg, the sapiential Q^1 material transmitted the words of Jesus in six major wisdom speeches that followed the "instruction genre" of ancient Near Eastern wisdom collections.[21] But Q^1 departs from the genre with radical and sometimes confrontational statements about the kingdom and discipleship. It includes statements such as Q (=Luke) 9:60, "Follow me, and leave the dead to bury their own dead" and the countercultural admonition against earthly wealth in Q 12:33, "Do not treasure for yourselves treasure on earth."[22] This stream of radical sayings in the Q^1 material could have led to the conflict and rejection of the message.

The polemical passages in the apocalyptic Q^2 inscribe a dualistic, sectarian rhetoric of difference. Q begins with John the Baptist traditions that have been assigned to the second redaction (Q 3:3, 7–9, 16–17).[23] Images of eschatological judgment include warning of "impending rage" (*mellousēs orgēs*); the ax ready to cut the trees; and the burning of the unhealthy trees. John attacks the crowds of common people (*'am ha-'aretz*), Pharisees, and other Jews coming to see him; they are "snakes' litter" (*gennēmata enchidnōn*) who falsely claim identity as Israelites by birth alone. This grounds Q in the twin ideologies of apocalyptic judgment and a contested identity of Israel, ideologies found in the Qumran sectarian writings and central to early Christian heresiology.[24] John's condemnation of Pharisees and Sadducees parallels the rhetoric against other Jews at Qumran. The rhetoric of this intra-Jewish polemic feeds Christian heresiological discourse. But the focus on the identity of Israel in Q^2 contextualizes the polemic politically. By challenging others' claim to the birthright of Abraham, the community of Q lays claim to this identity of Israel for themselves.

Other passages in Q portray conflict between the early followers of Jesus. The beatitudes reflect rejection of those who follow Jesus; "Blessed are you when they insult and persecute you, and say every kind of evil against you because of the son of humanity" (Q 6:22; cf. Q 7:23). I read this as a community saying attributed to Jesus. Their sapiential ideology set the Q community against other followers of Jesus. Jesus condemns "this generation," for missing the meaning of his and John's missions (Q 7:31–34), proclaiming that "Wisdom was vindicated by her children" (Q 7:35). This apothegm connects the Q community to the Jewish wisdom traditions of Prov 1:20–33 and 8:1–21 and the deuteronomistic tradition of the prophetic judgment of Israel.[25] Israel is a synecdoche for the opponents of the Q community. The children of Wisdom are the Q community that have accepted Jesus' message while "Israel" has rejected Jesus—and them. In Q 11:49–51 and 13:34–35, Wisdom sends messengers to Israel who are rejected and killed. The healing of the centurion's boy (*pais*, Q 7:1–10) signals the inclusion of Gentiles in the Q community as well as the lack of faith in Israel (7:9).

Conflict in Q[1] inscribes resistance to Jesus' historical activity as well as the community itself. We see resistance to Jesus in the Beelzebub accusation and response (Q 11:15–20) and the response to a request for a sign and the sayings on light (Q 11:29–35).[26] But the programmatic Q 11:23 goes much further: "the one not with me is against me," both Israel (so 3:16) and Gentiles (7:10; see also Q 12:54–56).[27] While the Beelzebub accusation and the response to a request for a sign are likely original to Jesus himself, Q 11:23 rhetorically shifts from a controversy caused by Jesus' healing to a dualistic ideology in which all opposition is demonic. As Kloppenborg notes, this accusation is broader in Q than in Mark, where the accusation is made by "scribes from Jerusalem."[28] The apocalyptic passages are not all polemical, however, further challenging the idea that only Q[2] inscribes opposition to the community. For instance, Q 16:16 is apocalyptic—John inaugurates the new age—but it is not polemical. The Q or "Logia Apocalypse" preserved in Matthew 24 and Luke 17 (Q 17:23, 24, 26–30, 34–35, 37),[29] while strongly eschatological, lacks the polemical and heresiological features of the Synoptic Apocalypse. For instance, the separation statements in Q 17:34–35, "one is taken and one is left," do not explicitly signal judgment within the Q community or against its opponents but rather universal, eschatological judgment. The Q Apocalypse lacks the paraenetic and polemical themes of the Matthew's Synoptic Apocalypse, explored ahead.[30]

The polemical woe oracles in Q, against named Jewish groups, include the doxographic exposition of their positions (again, see ahead on Matthew). While not systematic, the bundle of different accusations, actions, and positions opposed here foregrounds the theme of conflict with other Jewish groups.[31] Q 11:39–42 condemns the Pharisees for focusing on minute aspects of the law, metonymically construed as the tithing of herbs and washing of cups, rather than justice, mercy, and faithfulness, and their own internal pollution;[32] Q 11:44 also focuses on their exterior appearance opposed to their interior qualities. Q 11:43 condemns the Pharisees' love of high positions and accolades. Q 11:46–48, 62 brings even harsher condemnation against the "exegetes of the law" (*tois nomikois*) for their burdensome interpretations. Jesus accuses them of shutting people out of the kingdom of God and building tombs for the prophets, the very prophets killed by their forefathers. The Q woe oracles conclude with a wisdom saying, "I will send them prophets and sages, and some of them they will kill and persecute, so that a settling of accounts for the blood of all the prophets poured out from the founding of the world may be required of this generation" (Q 11:49–50).[33] Jesus' demand here for an accounting (*hina ekzētnthē*) from this generation connects the charges against the labeled Jewish opponents in the woe oracles (scribes, Pharisees, lawyers) to the universalized dualistic opposition expressed by Q 11:23, "those who are not with me are against me" (cf. Q 11:29–30). While these oracles reflect different settings and sources, the rhetoric of difference marks excluded opponents, delineates their positions and evil actions, and then broadens the polemics to the "generation" of Israel.[34]

The problem of the delay of the parousia appears in the parable of the faithful and unfaithful slaves waiting for their master's return (Q 12:42–46). This problem faced only communities that had adopted the notion of the return of Jesus. The use of slave here (*doulos*) signals this as a warning to the leaders of the community.[35] The neglectful, drunkard slave expects his master's return, but not at this point. Only believing members of the community could be excluded for dereliction rather than for not accepting the apocalyptic message (cf. Q 11:29–32).[36] The notion of heresy requires an "intimate enemy," someone who shares the ideology of the group enough to be a political threat to the community. The parable of the unfaithful slave, therefore, conveys judgment against members or former members of the community, as opposed to "this generation" that does not accept the Q message. The remainder of 12:39–59 consists of apocalyptic judgments and pronouncements. While Kloppenborg places these in a secondary redactional layer, most of this material springs from the apocalyptic roots of Jesus' prophetic activity.

Working from a hypothetical document, however carefully reconstructed, does not allow us to be more specific about the social contexts for the disputes between the Q community and the other followers of Jesus. But clearly the document inscribes such a context of conflict. While some scholars have tried to keep the origins of the wisdom-oriented Q community pristine within the hurly-burly of early Christianity, the polemical sayings and stories in the apocalyptic layer Q[2], which are intricately connected to Q[1], contain many of the rhetorical features of Christian heresiology: the ideology of apocalyptic judgment; a dualistic, sectarian worldview; polemics against identified opponents with doxographic exposition of their opposed beliefs and practices; and the contested politics of the identity of Israel.

These rhetorical components fully involve Q with the conflicts that marked the origin of Christianity. We do not see here a genealogical relationship between the various opponents; rather the sectarian rhetoric employs the dualistic trope of opposition to Israel. Nor do we find satanic or demonic explanations for the origin of error. Q includes aspects of the rhetoric of heresiology but not the fully formed notion of heresy that includes a myth of origin for error.

THE GOSPEL OF THOMAS

Discovered in 1948, the *Gospel of Thomas* is one of the central texts in re-imagining the origins of Christianity.[37] While its final form is a second-century text, it has first-century origins, including some authentic Jesus traditions. In its development over two centuries, the *Gospel of Thomas* represents a trajectory that Q might have taken. There are numerous parallels in Q, the Gospels of Matthew and John, and *Thomas*, showing the degree to which Gospel traditions overlapped in the late first century. As I noted in Chapter 1, this shows the degree to which early Christian communities interacted as well. The enigmatic nature of the *logia* (sayings) and lack of narrative context have led scholars to interpret various logia in completely different ways. Thus the historical reconstruction of the text and community (or communities) determines readings of the text itself.[38] Attention on *Thomas* has focused primarily on the text as a source for earliest Christianity—that is, what the text reveals about the actual teachings of Jesus and the beliefs of his earliest followers—and on the final form of the Gospel as a source for second-century Gnosticism.[39] I will look here between those two main issues at the discourse of difference in the *Gospel of Thomas* as evidence of interaction and conflict between various Christian groups in the first century. *Gospel of Thomas* inscribes both apocalyptic responses to difference and other strategies of avoidance that become features of second-century Gnostic Christianities.

April DeConick has proposed a hypothesis for the tradition history of a "Kernel" of sayings in the *Gospel of Thomas* and subsequent accretions to the text that resulted in the final version.[40] DeConick employs what she labels a "new *Traditionsgeschictliche* approach" that revises older history-of-traditions analysis with more recent work on social memory, the sociology of communal conflict, and research on oral performance and composition.[41] She argues that *Thomas* was an orally derived text, a "rolling corpus" of versions that retained the character of oral performance and composition even after being scribed, as opposed to a "statically-authored" text, in which an author composed the Gospel from various written sources.[42] In the context of the oral consciousness of the Thomas community, a series of community crises or conflicts produced new sayings and reinterpretations of sayings that can be analyzed as redactional layers in the final text.[43] DeConick identifies three important crises: the death of eyewitnesses; the delay of the eschaton; and the accommodation of Gentile converts.

In addition to developing this methodology for reading *Thomas*, DeConick identifies the "Kernel" of *Thomas* as apocalyptic and the Jesus of the Kernel as an eschatological Jewish prophet, as opposed to non-apocalyptic, sapiential reconstructions of Jesus in *Thomas* similar to the ones discussed in Q[1] above. This places the earliest *Thomas* traditions within the eschatological milieu of other early Christian traditions. She further connects *Thomas* to the Jerusalem community of Jesus' followers led by James the Righteous, which she labels a "conservative Christian Jewish community."[44] Of particular importance here is how DeConick identifies the polemical passages in *Thomas* as accretions produced in a community in crisis or conflict. In a path similar to the discursive history of the Q document analyzed earlier, the Thomas community developed ideologies that conflicted with other Christian communities.

There are about fifty logia in the *Gospel of Thomas* that could be read as expressing difference or conflict (3.1; 6.1; 14.1–3, 5; 16.1–4; 31; 39; 43; 53; 57; 60; 61.1 [2–4?] 5; 64.12 [1–11?]; 65.1–7; 68.1–2; 69.1; 71; 89; 93; 102; 112?; 113). Of these polemical logia, DeConick has marked 16.1–3, 31, 39, 57, 61.1, 64, 65.1–7, 68.1, 71, 89, 93, and 102 as part of the original Kernel of *Thomas*. Each of these Kernel passages has Synoptic parallels, showing the conflict experienced at the earliest levels of the Jesus tradition, perhaps in the ministry of Jesus himself.[45] I argued in Chapter 3 that Jesus experienced resistance from other Jewish religious leaders as well as the Roman authorities. The polemical logia in the Kernel of *Thomas* support my reconstruction of Jesus and DeConick's argument that the original *Thomas* was an apocalyptic document.

The expansion of the polemical passages in the accretions to the *Gospel of Thomas* from 60–100 CE shows that the Thomas community met increasing resistance from other Christian groups in the second half of the first century. Of the polemical passages earlier, DeConick places 68.1–2 before 60 CE, in the period of relocation and leadership crises. The beatitude in 68.1, "Blessed are you when you are hated and persecuted" (cf. Matt 5:11; Luke 6:22) is part of the Kernel, while 68.2, "and no place will be found where you have not been persecuted" is an accretion that interprets the original logion.[46] DeConick assigns the polemical passages 3.1; 6.1; 14.1–3, 5; 43; 53; 60; 64.12; 69.1; and 113 to the period of 60–100 CE, during which the crises included delay of the eschaton and accommodation to Gentiles. She places significantly fewer of the polemic logia in the final stage during 80–120 CE (16.4; 61.[2–4?] 5; 112?). During this period, the Thomas community was facing the death of the eyewitnesses and a continuing eschatological crisis. This was also the period of the development of the hermetic and encratic traditions that give the final text of *Thomas* a "Gnostic" character (e.g., *Gos. Thom.* 1, 13, 112, 114). In this final stage, the Thomas community had distanced itself ideologically and perhaps spatially from other Christian communities and was experiencing less resistance and conflict.

Most of the polemical passages in the *Gospel of Thomas* are from the earlier layers and almost all of these also have Synoptic parallels. These logia exhibit a dualistic, eschatological worldview. "There is light within a man of light, and he [or, it] illumines the whole world (*kosmos*); when he [or, it] does not shine, there is darkness (*Gos. Thom.* 24.3; cf. 45). This Kernel logion expresses a dualistic anthropology similar to the "Two Ways" motif found in the Dead Sea Scrolls (1 QS iii, 12–iv, 55) and *Did.* 1–6 (see ahead). Other eschatological motifs include the fiery judgment of the world (*Gos. Thom.* 10 and 82; cf. Luke 12:49; Dan 7:9; *1 Enoch* 14:13) and prostrating oneself before the throne of God at the eschaton (*Gos. Thom.* 15; Dan 8:18; Ezek 1:28; *1 Enoch* 14.24).[47] Logion 57 is a parable of weeds sowed by an enemy in a man's field. As in the parallel in Matt 13:24–30, the parable ends with the pronouncement of judgment, "For on the day of the harvest the weeds (*zizania*) will appear; they will be pulled up and burned down." *Gos. Thom.* 61.1, "Two will be resting on a bed; one will die, (and) the other will live," parallels the Q saying in Luke 17:34 and Matt 24:40–41, "one will be taken and one will be left." The polemics of the Kernel of *Thomas* inscribe an eschatological worldview typical of Second Temple Jewish and early Christian literature.

Two of the polemical logia in *Thomas* delineate practices that the community opposes and condemn named opponents. *Gos. Thom.*14.5, "For what will go into your mouth will not defile you, but what comes out of your mouth, that is what will defile you," closely parallels Mark 7:15 and Matt 15:11. In the two Synoptic Gospels, the saying occurs in the context of a dispute with the Pharisees and scribes from Jerusalem over the washing of hands, a charge broadened against Jesus' disciples for breaking the "tradition of the elders" (*tēn paradosin tōn presbyterōn*, Mark 7:5; Matt 15:2), referring to the oral traditions of the Pharisees. In the *Gospel of Thomas* the logion is part of a broader polemical context discussing fasting, prayer, and alms (*Gos. Thom.* 14.1–3). As in Mark and Matthew, the logia delineate practices that separate different Christian groups. Fasting, prayer, the giving of alms, and dietary laws were points of conflict and negotiation in later first-century Christian communities that retained aspects of Jewish practices.

The *Gospel of Thomas* also polemicizes more directly against these shared opponents: "Jesus said: The Pharisees and the scribes have received the keys of knowledge and have hidden them. They did not enter, and those who wished to enter, they did not allow. But you be wise as serpents and innocent as doves" (*Gos. Thom.* 39; cf. Matt 10:16; Luke 11:52, Matt 23:23). This polemic against the Pharisees in both *Thomas* and Q was part of defining new Christian identities within the range of Jewish practice in the late first century, when there was no authority, rabbinic or otherwise, with religious hegemony.[48] To be sure, the communities of Q, *Thomas*, and Matthew might be called Jewish insofar as all early Christian communities drew from Jewish traditions. The attention to Jesus as guide or savior, however, marks these as early Christian texts. While the interpretation of Jesus differs in these Gospels, the rhetorical function of the polemical logia in *Thomas* parallels the Synoptic traditions against the Pharisees and scribes. I return to this problem with Matthew ahead.

The polemical logia from 60–100 CE that do not have Synoptic parallels inscribe the rhetoric of difference in the most characteristic way for *Thomas*. In *Gos. Thom.* 43, the disciples pose the question to Jesus, "who are you that you say these things to us?" The response suggests intra-community division over Christology: "In what I say to you, you do not know who I am." The lack of narrative context in *Thomas* makes it difficult to identify the disciples here as members of the actual community or intimate enemies from other Christian communities. The important *Gos. Thom.* 13, from the final layer, explicitly compares Thomas to Peter and Matthew, most likely representing different Christian communities and Christologies.[49] In *Gos. Thom.* 43, Jesus further negatively characterizes the Christians who do not have "insight" or express a different Christological view as "like the Jews, for they love the tree but hate its fruit, and they love the fruit but hate the tree." The logia maps the disagreement within the community with "those who do not know who I am" onto the opposition between the Thomas Christians and the "Jews," a synecdoche for any range of Jewish groups in the late first century, including Christians, as in the Gospel of John. The accretion comes from a period in the late first century when the Thomas community was further distanced from Jewish communities.[50] By condemning some Christians as "Jews," the logion suggests an ideological split in which powerful discursive formations (the "Jews") were leveraged against internal enemies.[51]

Two of the other three polemical logia without Synoptic parallels oppose Jewish practices. *Gos. Thom.* 53 is a polemic against circumcision: "if [it] were profitable, their father would beget them circumcised from the mother." *Gos. Thom.* 60, a conversation about a Samaritan going to Judea with a lamb for sacrifice at the Temple, represents a shift away from the Temple for the Thomas community, probably post-70 CE.[52] The rejection of the Temple cult could also be part of the separation from other Jewish communities. Finally, *Gos. Thom.* 64.12, against merchants and buyers, is unique within the polemical logia.

These polemical logia parallel the eschatological rhetoric of difference found in other early Christian literature. The *Gospel of Thomas*, however, took a different turn from orthodox Christianity in its final phase. As Elaine Pagels has shown, the theology of the final version directs the spiritual seeker inward, for his or her own mystical, salvific experience.[53] Pagels emphasizes in particular the realized, as opposed to apocalyptic, eschatology of the *Gospel of Thomas*, the notion of light within each person who follows Jesus as opposed to the orthodox Christology that Jesus is the "only-begotten" son of God; the *incipit* of *Thomas* that directs the reader to find the way for herself; and the "twinning" motif, that a believer might, with Thomas, recognize himself as Jesus' spiritual twin. DeConick's thesis that the mystical and encratic elements in the Gospel were a later interiorization of the original eschatological ideology fits with this reading. The final Gospel recontextualizes the polemical passages in a non-heresiological discourse of difference. A heresiological response to ideological difference includes the theory of demonic origin and the rhetoric of eschatological judgment. An apocalyptic worldview is central to this conflict. But when a person can find the path to the light within to become a twin of Jesus, the polemic of heresiology transmogrifies into the exclusionary ideology of the spiritual elite. Rather than condemn heretics, Thomas Christians can ignore them, secure in their esoteric knowledge and enlightenment. The interiorization of the eschaton and the adoption of mystical practices produced a discourse of difference that sharply contrasts with orthodox heresiology.

MATTHEW: A HANDBOOK FOR DISCERNING DIFFERENCE

Jewish and Christian Identity in the Gospel of Matthew

I return to the problem of these vexing terms as labels designating identity in the first century. As with the letters of Paul, the Gospel of Matthew forces us to grapple empirically with the questions raised theoretically in Chapter 1. The fuller narrative of Matthew gives us better footing than Q or *Thomas* when treading this slippery terrain. The Gospel of Matthew was written in the last quarter of the first century, perhaps in the 80s. Numerous parallels between Matthew, the *Gospel of Thomas*, and the *Didache* suggest a shared Syrian provenance, perhaps in or around Antioch.[54] The majority of scholars have placed Matthew within a Jewish context and a few in a Gentile Christian community.[55] The prevailing view is that the Matthean community expressed a type of "Christian Judaism"; that is, a minority sect within formative Judaism of the late first century that interpreted Jewish belief and practice through Jesus traditions.[56] Many scholars fall on either side of this centrist position. Some have argued that Matthew's community was completely Jewish in belief and practice.[57] Others have argued that the thesis of Overman and Saldarini places Matthew too close to Judaism, diminishing the dramatic reinterpretation of Judaism in Matthew's Christology.[58] For Donald Hagner, then, Matthew is not "Christian Judaism" but "Jewish Christianity," a group that had by this time split from the synagogue.[59] And yet, given that all varieties of Christianity are a form of Judaism, this term hardly defines Matthew's social context with any precision.

Hagner's thesis of the relation of the Matthean community to the Jewish synagogue raises the debated issue of the *Birkhat ha-Minim*, the Jewish benediction against the *minim* or heretic. The theory around this developed by J. L. Martyn for the Gospel of John has been very influential in New Testament scholarship. [60] According to Martyn, the references in the Gospel of John to being cast out of the synagogue for claiming Jesus was the Messiah (John

9:22; 12:42; 16:2) refer to a stage in the life of the Johannine community in the 80s when the publication of the *Birkhat ha-Minim* by the Rabbinic Council of Yavneh forced the separation of the Johannine and rabbinic communities.[61] Each aspect of this theory has been critiqued. First, the Genizah text, with its reference to "Nazareans," is unlikely to be original.[62] Many scholars have dismissed Martyn's idea that the *Birkhat ha-Minim* was the cause of this crisis in the Johannine community.[63] The word *minim* most likely did not mean Christians at all but implied condemnation of other Jews in the later first century.[64] Stephen Motyer has recently written of a "near consensus" that the Yavnean sages issued the curse near the end of the first century, but that we cannot be sure who the *minim* were, what the curse actually said, or what its purpose might have been.[65] Daniel Boyarin has gone further to question the first-century origins of the myth of the Yavneh council as well as the curse, seeing the council as a third-century Palestinian myth of origin for later rabbinic Judaism.[66]

I do not, then, read Matthew as a discursive response to early rabbinic proclamations excluding the followers of Jesus from the synagogue. But questioning the validity of the Council of Yavneh or the *Birkhat ha-Minim* does not eliminate the considerable tension inscribed in the Gospel, tension expressed in both direct polemic against Pharisees and Jews as well as submerged narratives and allegories of exclusion. The rhetoric of difference is real enough, whenever and whatever the historical process was in rabbinic circles for excluding Christians. I consider, therefore, the reformulations of the notion of identity in both Christianity and Judaism in the first two centuries of the Common Era, a process that continued throughout late antiquity.[67] I will show how the heresiological narrative of exclusion in the Gospel of Matthew inscribes the deep tensions in communities forming boundaries between insiders and outsiders who used to be insiders, the intimate enemies of the communities. Should we read these deep tensions and inscribed polemics as Jews versus other Jews, Christians versus other Christians, or some combination of these categories? To figure out how "Jewish" the Matthean community was implies a notion of what Judaism was and was not in the late first century. The categories remain in flux for centuries.[68] Confusion between Jews and Christians by outside observers such as Galen and Lucian was evident in the second century and within both Jewish and Christian communities until the fourth, periods beyond my scope.[69]

For Matthew, I am focused on first-century Jewish identity after the Roman war and the destruction of the Temple (66–70 CE). Overman compares Matthew's Judaism to the normative or formative Judaism theories of Sanders and Neusner as a measure of how Jewish the Matthean community was.[70] But if neither formative nor normative Judaism works as a historical measuring stick in the later first century, I will hold here to a heuristic notion of Judaism that includes both the earliest rabbis and Matthew. The term *Ioudaios* was a recognizable marker in the first century, even if the boundaries for who was and was not a Jew were broad and flexible, shown by Philo in Chapter 4.[71] *Ioudaios* included a range of Judaisms—apocalyptic and aristocratic inheritors of

Essene and Sadducean traditions, rabbinic or Pharaisaic teachers, scribes, the majority '*am ha-aretz* reeling from the war with Rome, and Diaspora Jews of multiple ethnicities.[72] I retain "Jewish" to analyze the polemical construction of self-identity in Matthew, recognizing that the polemic against "Jews" in the New Testament texts implies a more fixed social formation than the social historical setting allows for. The Jews of the New Testament texts are discursive formations as construed by Foucault, "objects that emerge only in discourse."[73] The Gospel of Matthew inscribes a "body of rules that enable them [i.e., the Jews] to form as objects of discourse and thus constitute the conditions of their historical appearance."[74] As discursive formations, not social formations anterior to the discourse, the Jews are "real" enemies in Matthew's community. I look then for the system of relations that make the discursive formations possible by reading for polemical constructions and the rhetoric of difference in the Gospel.

The problematic terms "Christian Jewish" and "Jewish Christian" both imply a fixed pole of Judaism against which the Gospel's community should be measured.[75] The Matthean community was engaged in an identity struggle with other Jewish communities, some of which recognized Jesus and others of which did not. Insofar as all of these could be described as some form of Judaism, Matthew is a Jewish text. With Meeks, I see the focus in Matthew as "Jesus with Judaism."[76] The Gospel of Matthew was written in a context of multiple conflicts, within and between followers of Jesus as well as Jews who rejected or neglected Jesus. Perhaps the Matthean community considered itself "truly Jewish" and was defining itself against another Jewish group with whom it had a close relationship. Or perhaps opponents advanced alternative Christologies. In either case, whether the opponents rejected Jesus or adopted a conflicting interpretation of Jesus, the discursive conflict can be placed within Judaism. Regardless of whether we can precisely define it, it was in fact some type of *Judaism* against which and through which the Matthean community defined itself.[77]

I contextualize this negotiation of identity and rhetoric of difference in the Gospel of Matthew as Jewish discourse. But Matthew's Judaism has an important rhetorical actor: Jesus Christ occupies the central role.[78] What is central theologically has considerable significance rhetorically. Matthew's Jesus articulates the identity of the community.[79] In the special Matthean ("M") material as well as the redaction of Mark and Q, Matthew constructs a Jesus who articulates the notion of heresy, the rhetoric of difference *against* other Jews. Matthew intensifies the process we have seen in Q and *Thomas*, in which Jesus' sayings have been polemically reconstructed to heighten the ideological divide with other communities.

Community Tensions in Matthew

The idea that the Gospel of Matthew reflects a divided Jewish community contesting both Christology and adherence to the Torah is supported by its polemics against other Christians. There are polemical passages in

Matthew against outsiders as well, particularly against the scribes and Pharisees (examined ahead), but the intra-community divisions in Matthew are unique among the Gospels. "When they saw him, they worshipped him; but some doubted" (Matt 28:17). While the forceful conclusion of the Gospel attempts to quiet these doubts, intra-community tensions abound. Matthew includes, of course, most of the Gospel of Mark as well the polemical passages from Q discussed earlier: John the Baptist's apocalyptic message (Matt 3:7–10); the blessings for those who are persecuted on account of Jesus and for those who are scandalized by him (5:11; 11:6); the dualistic charge, "the one not with me is against me" (12:30); and the woes against the scribes and Pharisees (23:1–36).[80] Matthew's redaction of these sources reveals the tensions with the enemies within.

The famous Sermon on the Mount (Matt 5:3–7:27) shows this pattern. The Sermon is a didactic discourse of Torah teaching and practice that inscribes the divisions within Matthew's community as well as divisions between the community and other Jews.[81] The full range of teachings that make the Sermon on the Mount a "cult-*didache*" also describes the theological and practical points of difference.[82] The beatitude Q 6:22, discussed earlier, anticipates rejection of the followers of Jesus. Matthew's version include a general blessing for those "persecuted for righteousness' sake" (5:10), which is absent from Luke, as well as an elaboration of Luke 6:22. This eighth blessing in Matt 5:10 forms an *inclusio* with 5:3, repeating "for theirs is the kingdom of heaven," and draws on a larger Jewish wisdom and Greco-Roman motif of persecution.[83] The next beatitude then focuses on persecution as followers of Jesus in particular. Significant changes in Matthew include substituting "persecute" (*diōxōsin*, Matt 5:11) for Luke's "exclude" (*aphorisōsin*) and "uttering all kinds of evil falsely" (*pseudomenoi*) where Luke has "cast your name as evil."[84] The *pseudo-* words, "false," are Matthean favorites that indicate internal divisions.[85] The persecution is "on my account" rather than "on account of the Son of Man" (Luke 6:22); that is, divisions within the Christian community. While Luke's Sermon moves to the "woe section" next (Luke 6:24–26), Matt 5:11–12 concludes Matthew's beatitudes with the theme of persecution of the *ekklēsia* (cf. 5:44).

The pronouncement of the principles of Torah interpretation in Matt 5:17–20 is a central theological statement for Matthew's Judaism.[86] Jesus fulfills the law and charges the community to keep every stroke of every letter of the law (*iōta hen ē mia keraia*, 5:18). The pronouncement opposes those who break the commandments and, significantly, "teaches others to do the same,"[87] although the judgment against them, that they will be "least in the kingdom of heaven," is not as harsh as the apocalyptic condemnation in Matthew's parables of judgment studied ahead. The Christian reinterpretation of the Torah in Matt 5:21–48 delineates the Matthean position against their Jewish opponents. Matthew's community was divided from, and perhaps slandered or persecuted by, other Jews both in their Christology and their interpretation of the Torah. For Matthew, their righteousness must exceed "the scribes and Pharisees" (5:20); they must be perfect, as God is perfect (5:48). Matthew moves from interpretation of the Torah to matters of *halakah*: alms, fasting, and prayer (Matt 6:1–18; cf. *Did.* 8.1). The Sermon of the Mount is a doxographic exposition of Matthew's positions against this opposition and the basis for a fully developed heresiological discourse.

The Sermon expresses judgment against other believers in Christ as well as against the "scribe and Pharisees"—that is, other Jews who do not accept Jesus' principles of Torah interpretation.[88] Matt 7:13–27 consists of polemics against those who accept Jesus Christ, but who do not accept Matthew's theology.[89] The rhetoric of difference inscribes the problems of community boundaries.[90] The Q saying reworked in Matt 7:13–14, on the "narrow gate," suggests the winnowing of the community in the parables of judgment. But more immediate judgment is at hand in the eschatological warnings that conclude the Sermon on the Mount. In Matt 7:15, Jesus warns of "false prophets" (*pseudoprophētōn*) who appear in "sheep's clothing." "False prophet" is a heresiological term that refers to *internal* enemies with access to the community. A false teaching is one that is close enough to believe. For Matthew's community, the question of which prophet is legitimate is a critical social issue. The phrase "narrow gates" suggests blurred lines in the community over those who will "pass through" despite their prophecy, casting out demons, or miracles. The disguised enemies will be judged at the end. Matt 7:21 describes the same situation as Justin in the *Dialogue with Trypho*. There are many who call Jesus "Lord" but who are not true Christians. For Matthew, they are heretics. A concluding Q parable, 7:24–27, recapitulates the "Two Ways" theme in the image of the houses of the wise and foolish built on rock and sand, the latter destroyed in an apocalyptic storm. The Sermon on the Mount, a formative heresiological text, describes the diversity of praxis and belief within the community that acknowledges Jesus as Lord;[91] delineates proper ("orthodox") theology, focusing on Torah interpretation and the Christian cult; and condemns opponents to eternal damnation.

The Community Discourses

Within all the early Christian Gospels, community problems come to the fore most clearly in the Gospel of Matthew. This contrasts with the more enigmatic Sayings Gospels such as Q and *Thomas*, from which community issues must often be deduced, and Gospels such as John, the *Gospel of Mary*, and the *Gospel of Judas*, in which community concerns have been narrated symbolically and must be read allegorically. Two examples of this are the "Missionary Discourse" in Matthew 10 and the "Community Handbook" in Matthew 18.[92] In these sections, the author has placed a variety of passages from Mark and Q with special Matthean ("M") material in clearly delineated discourses with a community focus.[93] Both end with the formulaic conclusion that frames the Matthean discourses (11:1; 19:1). These two discourses highlight both the divisions within the Matthean community and the focus on dealing with difference by reproof, condemnation, and expulsion.

Matthew's redaction of this material focuses on division and disagreements, even in the missionary discourse that describes actions outside of the community. This discourse has a church focus. The Christological summary from Mark 6:34, which describes Jesus' compassion for the crowds, introduces the problem of mission in Matt 9:35–36. The church does Christ's work here (cf. 10:24–25).[94] Q 10:2, "the harvest is plentiful but the laborers are few," follows in Matt 9:37–38 as a bridge to the sending out of the twelve with "authority over unclean spirits, to cast them out, and to cure every disease and every sickness" (Matt 10:1). This commission, emphasizing apostolic, or church, authority, has been moved forward in Matthew's narrative from Mark's (Mark 6:7), followed by the naming of the twelve (Matt 10:2–4), which Mark places earlier in Jesus' ministry. An important M passage then spells out divisions in the mission field that implies divisions within the community itself: "Go nowhere among the Gentiles, and enter no town of the Samaritans, but go rather to the lost sheep of the House of Israel" (Matt 10:5–6). But this discourse includes a warning; they go "like sheep into the midst of wolves" (Matt 10:16/Q 10:3). Matt 10:17–25 (M) further describes the perils of the mission: "they will hand you over to councils and flog you in their synagogues; and you will be dragged before governors and kings because of me" (10:17–18; cf. Matt 24:9, 13). Internal division follows external persecutions. Families divide over Jesus and "you will be hated by all because of my name" (10:22). A series of Q passages follow, on fear of persecution and comfort in distress; more divisions within the family; and the radical loyalty demanded of the audience (10:26–39). The discourse concludes with four correlative apothegms equating the work of the missionaries with the work of Jesus. These exhortations for the community to welcome prophets and righteous ones and to support "these little ones," within the Matthean dualistic worldview, suggest that anyone who is not for the mission of the church is in fact against it.

When read as a document of a Jewish community that worships Jesus seeking new members "from among the house of Israel," this discourse reveals significant conflict with other Jews. The "mission field" is compared to a pack of wolves, lying in wait, allied with "governors and kings" who will physically punish them. Difference within families becomes open war as father betrays child and brother sends brother to death. The community should be prepared for strong resistance. The houses and towns that do not accept the message will be cursed like Sodom and Gomorrah, while the apostles can grant "peace" to those who support them. Since the apostles of the church (and perhaps "the little ones") have spiritual powers, such curses have authority. This dispute is spiritualized, since the

Spirit speaks on behalf of the ones captured. Difference is thus thematized apocalyptically as those with the Spirit (of truth) and those condemned, like Sodom, to eternal fire.

Matthew places the community discourse in Matthew 18 after the Markan story of the disciples arguing over "who was the greatest" (Mark 9:34).[95] Matthew changes the question of Jesus to the disciples, "What were you arguing about on the way?" (Mark 9:33), to a question from the disciples to Jesus: "Who is the greatest in the kingdom of heaven?'" (Matt 18:1). This redactional change softens Mark's harsh portrayal of the disciples and has them, standing for the community, initiate the discourse. Jesus explains how the church should conduct its internal business, beginning with the exhortation to change to be like the children (*paidion*) and to welcome them in Jesus' name (18:2–5; cf. Mark 9:37; Matt 10:4). Matthew omits the exorcism story that follows in Mark 9:38–41 (cf. Luke 9:49–50), keeping the focus on community. The shift from *paidion* to "these little ones" (*tōn mikron toutōn*, Matt 18:6, 10, 14; cf. 10:42), then, clearly indicates divisions within the community over the treatment and status of this group.[96] The phrase "little ones" in Matthew describes itinerant disciples who need community support; the *Didache* (discussed ahead) attests to the continuance of wandering prophets into the second century.[97] Here the concern is how to deal with difference within the community. They are warned not to bring any cause for stumbling (*skandalizō, skandalon*), a warning heightened with extreme sayings about maiming oneself in order not to stumble (18:6, 8). They should "not despise" them (*orate mē kataphronēsēte*, 18:10); the "little ones" are a divisive group. The Q parable of the lost sheep (Luke 15:3–7) follows as a strong exhortation to support them (18:10–14). The parable in Matthew, which in Luke is aimed at redeeming or welcoming *sinners* into the Christian community, here describes the importance of the *mikra*, the little ones.[98] The M introduction and conclusion with "little ones" reframe this parable about God seeking out a sinner as seeking and supporting these controversial points of internal division.

Two special M passages conclude the discourse on negotiating difference within the community. Matt 18:15–20 presupposes serious disagreements; the situation here parallels the situation in 1 Corinthians 6, in which members of the *ekklēsia* are taking each other to court. Matthew gives specific instructions for confronting and reproving a member who sins against another based on biblical rules for the evidence of witnesses (18:15–17; cf. 5:23–27).[99] The penalty for the convicted offender reveals the depth of the divisions here: they should be treated "as a Gentile and a tax collector," groups explicitly *outside* the community. Matthew had already contrasted the ethical standards of the community to Gentiles and tax collectors in 5:43–47, extolling the community to "be perfect, therefore, as your heavenly Father is perfect." The decision makers in 18:15–20, the "two or three gathered in my name," are the leaders of the community, whose authority to "bind and loose" on earth and heaven was augured in the proclamation to Peter at Caesarea Philippi in 16:18–19 (*deō* and *lyō* in both 16:19 and 18:18).[100] This is a church order for a leadership that has divine authority to make decisions about what is permitted and who remains in the community. Matt 18:18–19 explicitly makes the decisions of community leaders in divisive situations homologous to decisions made by God.

Peter, representing the church leadership, then asks another question of Jesus about forgiveness. The response to forgive "not seven times, but I tell you, seventy-seven times" (18:22) tempers somewhat the rules for reproof.[101] The parable of the unforgiving servant follows (Matt 18:23–35).[102] In response to a question about *forgiveness*, Matthew places an allegorical parable of *judgment*.[103] Recent research has identified the context of the parable as a Gentile king collecting payment from tax farmers; the word translated "debt" in 18:27, *to daneion*, might better be translated "loan."[104] The slave owes the king the fantastically large sum of 10,000 talents but receives forgiveness.[105] This slave does not extend the same mercy for a debt owed by a fellow slave and is reported to the king, who revokes the offer of forgiveness and sends him to the "torturer" (*basanistēs*) for punishment. In the conclusion to the parable, Matthew makes the allegorical interpretation explicit: "So my heavenly Father will also do to every one of you, if you do not forgive your brother or sister from your heart." The king (*anthrōpō basilei*, 18:23; *kyrios*, 18:25–34) is "your heavenly Father" and the slaves (*douloi, syndoulos*) are the community. The charge from Jesus in 18:22 to forgive limitlessly resonates in the punishment for the slave who does not forgive once. The king, however, the "heavenly father," does not follow Jesus' exhortation, forgiving then revoking his own forgiveness and handing the slave over to be tortured (18:34).[106] The other slaves report the behavior of the unforgiving servant to the *kyrios* (18:17), rather than reproving him first, as extolled in 18:15. The exhortation to forgive becomes a story of judgment. Thus we see in both the mission and community discourses a community facing divisions over mission, Gentiles, the "little ones," families, and internal disagreements, and prepared to reprove and expel the enemies within.

The Synoptic Apocalypse

Matthew's version of the "Synoptic Apocalypse" (Matthew 24:1–35 =Mark 13:1–13) marks divisions within the community as signs of the eschaton. This eschatological theory of the origin of difference, stemming from dualistic, apocalyptic Jewish worldviews such as we saw at Qumran, is central to orthodox heresiology. The theory of an eschatological genesis of internal division drives the discursive confrontations with ideological opponents.

The discourse begins with a question from the disciples about the destruction of the Temple and the "signs of your coming (*parousias*) and the end of the age (*synteleias tou aiōnos*)" (Matt 24:3). Matthew follows Mark 13 closely, with the exception of moving Mark 13:9–13 to the mission discourse (Matt 10:17–21), which I noted earlier as part of the theme of conflict in that community address. Matt 24:5 (= Mark 13:5) raises the specter of internal Christian divisions at the parousia, when many different people claim to be the returned Christ. The first significant Matthean addition, 24:10–12, recapitulates the themes of internal conflict, division, and false prophecy expressed in Matt 7:13–72, 10:17–25, and 18:15–20. The end times are marked by apostasy, deception, and backsliding.

This apocalyptic scenario combining the eschaton, false messiahs, and false prophets precedes Matthew to be sure. Mark 13:21–23 (= Matt 24:23–25) expresses the same idea, including the key phrase "false Christs and false prophets" (*pseudochristoi kai pseudoprophētai*).[107] I showed earlier that both Q and *Gospel of Thomas* include apocalyptic scenarios of strife and division. But this theme is magnified in Matthew. Matt 24:23–25 marks the core heresiological identification of the *eschaton* with the arrival of false messiahs and false prophets. These figures will "lead astray, if possible, even the elect" (*eklektous*, the "chosen"). This eschatological rhetoric of difference in Matthew has a political function in the context of division and difference *within* the community. As we have seen, Matthew's community was already divided internally and in conflict with Jews and other believers in Christ. The discourse of apocalyptic error, "false prophets and false Christs" leading people astray, inscribes the current situation of conflict rather than predicts a future event. Matthew's discursive move makes opposition an apocalyptic act. The parable of the weeds and wheat (Matt 13:24–30) connects opposition in Matthew's community to Satan himself.[108] Matthew's Gospel is thus foundational for the orthodox notion of heresy. An apocalyptic worldview and an eschatological theory for the origins of difference drive confrontation in Christian heresiology. Rather than avoid or ignore opponents, or elide opposing ideologies, the orthodox approach is eschatological confrontation with the satanic enemies within.

Allegories of Exclusion in Matthew

As we have seen, the Sermon on the Mount defines the boundaries of theology and praxis against Matthew's Jewish and Christian opponents. The mission discourse in Matthew 10, while focused on reaching outside of the community, inscribes divisions within the community while Matthew 18 explicitly describes the problems and procedures for a divided community.[109] My reading of these discourses signals a way of reading the parables in Matthew as allegories of exclusion, in which eschatological judgment is the discursive response to the social problem of difference within the community. My allegorical reading of the parable of the unforgiving servant earlier provides a model. Matthew features such parables in the Judean section (see Matt 19:1) after the discourse on community behavior in Matthew 18 and in the fifth "eschatological discourse" (Matthew 25–26) that follows Matthew's Apocalypse.[110] Two parables that can also be read as allegories of the community, the laborers in the vineyard (Matt 20:1–16) and the parable of the wedding feast (22:1–14), inscribe the social tensions over the negotiation of ideological difference within Matthew's community. Jesus Christ himself narrates the heresiological ideology of apocalyptic judgment as a solution to difference in the *corpus mixtum* of the Matthean community.[111]

The parable of the laborers in the vineyard exists only in Matthew but could well have originated with Jesus.[112] It warns against any presumptions by those who are "first" over those who are "last" and exhibits several typical themes of Jesus: agricultural imagery; "odd behaviour to represent divine activity"; and excessive grace.[113] Reading as an allegory of Matthew's community rather than as a parable of Jesus, I highlight the mixed community in which some arrive early and some later. Matthew turns Jesus' message of surprising, over-abundant grace into a message of judgment against those who presume superiority over others, similar to how Jesus answers Peter's question about forgiveness with a parable of judgment in Matt 18:23–35. The "early laborers" (20:3) could be those born as Jews and the "late laborers" (20:9) the Gentiles who join the church later.[114] But that would assume clear boundaries for Jewish and Christian identities that did not exist at this time. It would also reduce Matthew's four groups of laborers into two. We should not ignore the groups who appeared at noon and 3:00 (20:5). The internal mixture of this *ekklēsia* is what is important. While the original version might not have included four different groups, their presence in the parable foregrounds the Matthean *corpus mixtum*.[115] The parable is not an allegory of Jews and Gentiles but an allegory of difference within the church.

The complaint against the landowner (20:12) displays the tensions and struggles within Matthew's community. The parable expresses an ideology of equality in which social difference, represented by the four groups of laborers, has been overcome by the unexpected behavior of the landowner. The landowner pays all of them the same promised wage. He is extravagant (*agathos*, 20:15) in paying the latter groups a full day's wage but radically egalitarian in paying the full-day workers the same as the other groups (they grumble that the last ones would be *isous hēmin*, "equal to us," 20:12). Just as the wicked servant in Matt 18:23–25 allegorizes disputes within the *ekklēsia*, this parable allegorizes difference that leads to division and must be ideologically theorized as well as discursively negotiated.[116] But there is no negotiation here. The landowner enforces an ideology of equality but not one of unity (*homonoia*). As with the rules for expulsion in Matthew 18, this is a discourse about difference that does not include a script for unity. Equality is forced and the grumbling stands unresolved.

Matthew adds an editorial comment at the end of the parable, "So the last will be first, and the first will be last" (20:16), which, while possibly dominical, connects the problem of difference in the community with the ideology of eschatological reversal.[117] The theme of forced equality in the parable of the laborers is undermined by the many parables in the Gospel of Matthew that describe judgment *within the community itself.* Emblematic of these is Matthew's version of the parable of the wedding feast. The parable is almost certainly an authentic Jesus tradition for which we have multiple, and likely independent, attestations in the Gospels of Matthew, Luke, and *Thomas.*[118] The host's radically inclusive action of inviting "those from the streets" (*Gos. Thom.* 64) and "the poor, the crippled, the blind and the lame" (Luke 14:21) to attend his banquet, one that others originally considered more worthy had refused, fits the pattern of Jesus' eschatological preaching about the kingdom of God. Here again, Matthew turns Jesus' parable into a community allegory.[119] The host has become a king, representing God, the son is Jesus, and the wedding banquet is the eschatological feast. The king sends out slaves twice, who stand for the prophets as well as Jesus in a second role. After the second invitation, the people "made light of it . . . while the rest seized his slaves, mistreated them, and killed them" (22:5).

Redactional changes highlight Matthew's ideology of eschatological judgment. *Gos. Thom.* 64 reads that, upon receiving the rejections of his original guest, the man instructs his servant to "Go out to the streets, bring those whom you will find, so that they may dine (*deipnein*)." In Luke, the householder (*oikodespotēs*) becomes angry and instructs the slave to bring in (*eisagage*) the "poor, the crippled, the blind and the lame" (Luke 14:21). When the slave tells him there is more room, the master extends the invitation to "the roads and lanes" (14:23). In Matthew, the king's response is decisively martial and excessively judgmental—he sends troops to kill the guests and burn the city (20:7). It is also inclusive to the point of universality: "Go therefore into the main streets, and invite everyone you find to the wedding banquet" (Matt 22:9). This broader "whomever you might find" (*hosous ean heurēte*) is strengthened by a universalistic addition: "Those slaves went out into the streets and gathered all whom they found, both good and bad (*ponērous te kai agathous*); so the wedding hall was filled with guests" (Matt 22:10). These two verses shift the focus of this parable from the radically inclusive nature of the kingdom of God, which was likely an original point, to an allegory of universal judgment. By gathering "the good and the bad," Matthew explicitly refers to all humanity.[120] As with the parable of the last judgment, in which the Son of Man gathers "all the nations" (*panta ta ethnē,* Matt 25:32), this parable directs the message of eschatological judgment beyond Matthew's community.

The universal eschatology of the parable, however, includes a message of judgment within the mixed community of Matthew. This internal judgment is figured by the man at the feast who does not have a wedding robe. He is within the gathered community of the feast but completely unprepared. The concluding aphorism in Matt 22:14, "For many are called, but few are chosen," directs the message against those called into Matthew's *ekklēsia.* Do not presume that you are safe, this warns the auditors. Will your "garment" be acceptable on the last day? Within this mixed community, the negotiation of difference will lead to hell itself. Matt 22:13 is unequivocal about the punishment for the speechless man who lacks the proper garment.

This theme of judgment within the community is expressed in the parables in Matthew 25–26, in which Matthew maps the theme of universal eschatological judgment back onto the community. The Matthean parables of the ten bridesmaids and the last judgment, as well as Matthew's reworking of the parable of the talents, have been read consistently as eschatological allegories. Each of these stories includes the motif of separation of a group living or working together—in the fields, as slaves in the same household, as bridesmaids meeting the same bridegroom. The parables emphasize community associations that end in a divisive judgment in which some pass and others do not. It is significant that in the parable of the last judgment, the rejected goats know Christ. "Lord, when was it that we saw you hungry or thirsty or a stranger or naked or sick or in prison, and did not take care of you?" (Matt 25:44). The accursed recognize the Lord, but do not share the insights that the righteous have. Again, for Matthew, the problem is difference within the church. These accursed "goats" find themselves in the position of the man without a wedding garment. The community will be winnowed. And as programmatically expressed in the Sermon on the Mount, we see here the emphasis on halakah, *practice*, whether it's the "wedding garment" or things done "for the least of these."[121] The eschatological parables in Matthew are allegories of exclusion, heresiological narratives that construct a theory of difference and judgment within the community.

As we saw in Chapter 2, dualistic apocalyptic ideology was central to the Dead Sea Scroll community. But the rhetoric of difference in the Qumran sectarian texts contrasts with the internalized notion of difference in Matthew. In *The Community Rule*, while it is true that God plants equal shares of the warring spirits in each person, those in the community are the "sons of light" while the "sons of Belial," Judeans and Romans alike, are outside of the Covenant. Difference is external to the Covenant community while apostasy is a threat within. The Rule inscribes a technology of control to maintain sectarian identity as the Sons of Light. Matthew, in contrast, notes that "many are called, but few are chosen." The Matthean community expects winnowing of the *ekklēsia* as well as of the world.

The Other as Heretic

The Gospel of Matthew includes extensive polemics against outsiders, named Second Temple Jewish groups, a polemic that is part of the Synoptic tradition but magnified in Matthew. Pharisees were part of first-century Jewish social life and the social context of Matthew's community as well.[122] While Matthew opposes other Jewish groups and leaders, the Pharisees, with the scribes, are the chief target of polemics.[123] Here my interest is the Pharisees as discursive formations in the Gospel. I read the Pharisees in particular, along with the scribes and Sadducees, as metonymic markers for opposition to the community. The term "Pharisee" in Matthew is somewhat anachronistic and simplistic as a social-historical referent. With the scribes, they represent some group within formative Judaism in the late first century, probably precursors to rabbinic Judaism.[124] Labeling Matthew a sectarian text from a sectarian community suggests that the opposing "scribes and Pharisees" have more power than the leaders of the Matthean community, but that does not mean hegemony. Polemical and heresiological rhetoric can be directed against powerless minority groups as much as powerful leaders. Clearly there was an ideological struggle. The Pharisees and scribes, as discursive formations in the Gospel of Matthew, are the model for the religious opponent, the co-religionists with enough shared ideology to mark them as dangerous. In short, Pharisees are heretics.

The scribes and Pharisees are portrayed in negative terms throughout the Gospel.[125] Both the scribes and Pharisees are labeled "evil" (*ponēros*, 9:4; 12:34; *ponēria*, 22:18), a dualistic term that in Matthew is also associated with Satan ("the evil one," *ho ponēros*, 5:37; 6:13; 13:19, 38) and "this evil generation" (*genea ponēra*, 12:38–42; 16:1–4).[126] The harshest attack comes in the woes against the "scribes and Pharisees, hypocrites" in Matthew 23:1–36. The accusations against the scribes and Pharisees is significantly magnified in Matthew from the Markan and Q versions (Mark 12:37–40; Luke 11:39–52; 20:45–47). The Pharisees are Jesus' chief opponents in the Gospel of Matthew, completely opposed to Jesus on matters of law such as Sabbath practice, purity, divorce, and interpretation of the Torah.[127]

The harshness of the polemic has motivated several scholars, in the post-Holocaust environment, to try to contextualize and separate Matthew's charges from Christianity itself.[128] Careful research into the parallels and context in ancient rhetorical polemics, both Jewish and Greco-Roman, is important, and these scholars have made a significant contribution, as have the scholars who have placed Matthew's community *within* Judaism rather than *against* Judaism.[129] But it is important not to let apologetics override analysis of the ideological force of this rhetoric, distasteful and violent as it might be. Matthew's community formed its identity in part by demonizing other Jews. That said, it is not necessary to draw a straight line from Matthew 23 to the Holocaust. David Nirenberg, in his history of the persecution of Jews and other minorities in Spain in the Middle Ages, argues against reading such events teleologically as evidence of increasing intolerance and irrationality leading inexorably to the Holocaust.[130] Thus, while acknowledging and abhorring the ways that these polemics have been used as texts of terror, I read this rhetoric in the context of the discourse of difference and heresiology in the Gospel of Matthew. The fierce polemics against the scribes and Pharisees functioned to construct and legitimate community identity and boundaries.[131] The identity of Matthew's community, and eventually of orthodox Christianity itself, formed around this rhetoric of demonization. This is the discourse of heresy. The Pharisees are heretics in the narrative world, and probably the social world, of Matthew. As discursive formations in the Gospel, they receive full heresiological treatment. The Pharisees are dualistically demonized as "evil"; associated with Satan, the "evil one"; and discursively elided with other Jewish groups in a universalized web of opposition.

The woes are a doxographic delineation of the Matthew's opposition's principles of Torah interpretation and *halakah*. As I argued earlier, the Sermon on the Mount functions as an exposition of the Torah principles and practices of the Matthean community. The Gospel opposes the "traditions of the elders" (Matt 15:2), which refers to the Pharisaic and rabbinic oral Torah. Matthew 23 is in essence the *reverse* of the Sermon on the Mount, a polemical heresiology of opposition beliefs and practices.[132] The opening injunction to "do whatever they teach you and follow it; but do not do as they do" (*poiēsate, mē poieite, ou poiousin*, 23:3) recalls the closing admonition in the Sermon to "hear these words and act on them" (*poiei, mē poiōn*, 7:24, 26). The Pharisees tie heavy burdens (23:4) while Jesus' yoke is light (11:28–30). They make a public show of their cultic practices, such as phylacteries and fringes, and claim the places of honor in public and in honorific titles (23:5–7). Matt 6:1–6, 16–18 instructs the community to hide their almsgiving, prayer, and fasting from others. The exhortation to "turn the other cheek" (5:38–41), which calls for submitting to others, parallels Matt 23:8–12, which instructs the community to avoid the title "rabbi" and to humble themselves.

The polemic against the "hyprocrites" for seeking converts contrasts with the mission discourse in Matt 10:1–42, which contains the directions for how to seek converts in a context of opposition, as noted earlier (cf. also 5:19, "and teaches others to do the same"). It derides them for valuing their oaths on gifts in the Temple more than altar, sanctuary, or heaven itself (23:16–22). The Sermon on the Mount both forbids making oaths on heaven, earth, and Jerusalem (5:33–37) and exhorts the community to eschew earthly gold for "treasure in heaven" (6:19–21). It includes rules for almsgiving (*poiēs eleēmosynēn*, 6:2) but not tithing (*apokedatoute*, 23:23), one of the accusations from the Q tradition (Luke 11:42). Matthew accuses the Pharisees and scribes of abandoning "the weightier matters of the law," justice, mercy, and faith, a phrase that evokes summaries in Matt 7:12 and 22:34–40.[133] The rhetoric implicitly commends the Matthean insiders for keeping to this higher standard. Matt 23:25–26 accuses the hypocrites of ritually cleaning dishes while remaining immoral in their soul, recalling the controversy between Jesus and his disciples and the Pharisees and scribes over the "traditions of the elders" about ritual purity and what truly defiles a person (Matt 15:1–20; Mark 7:1–23).

The charges to this point in the "woe discourse" have a clear *halakhic* basis, even if the charges are hyperbolic or false.[134] The final two woes (23:27–33) have no such grounding. In fact, they are nothing short of vicious, slanderous insults. The sixth woe compares the Pharisees and scribes to whitewashed tombs, which are clean on the outside but "inside are full of bones of the dead and of all kinds of filth" (23:28). The revulsion we might feel from this image today would only be magnified in an ancient Jewish context in which corpse impurity rendered a person unclean for participation in the cult. Matthew's Jesus goes on to charge the scribes and Pharisees with the deaths of the prophets and the sins of their Jewish ancestors (23:30–31). The dualistic condemnation of the "evil" Pharisees noted earlier reaches a heresiological climax when Matthew's Jesus condemns these Jewish opponents to gehenna, or hell (23:33).

The concluding pronouncements of apocalyptic judgment in 23:34–36 (*Dia touto idou*, 23:34) broaden the polemic and connect the woes against the scribes and Pharisees to larger themes in the Gospel. The motif of the persecution and assassination of "prophets, sages, and scribes . . . . from the blood of righteous Abel to the blood of Zechariah son of Barachiah, whom you murdered between the sanctuary and the altar" (23:34–36) recalls, of course, the execution of Jesus, which Matthew blames more explicitly on the Jews than any of the canonical Gospels (Matt 27:25; cf. *Gos. Peter* 1, 23). Matt 23:36, "all this will come upon this generation," evokes the eschatological parables of judgment throughout the Jerusalem section. And the lament over Jerusalem that follows in 23:37–39 transitions to the destruction of the Temple, the apocalyptic discourse, and trial of Jesus himself.

Matthew places this polemical "woe discourse," moreover, after the parable of the wedding banquet and close to the Matthean Apocalypse, both of which I analyzed earlier. The juxtaposition of these woes with the parable of judgment and the apocalyptic discourse shapes this rhetoric of condemnation. The Pharisees and scribes are the eschatological agents of difference constructed in the Matthean Apocalypse. As heretics, they represent the proximate enemies of the community, with a shared Jewish ideological worldview. The mixed community that hears stories of sudden judgment on bridesmaids, wedding guests, or crops in the field imagined as one group has every reason to fear this eschatological judgment.

Summary

The significance of questions of identity, with which I began this treatment of Matthew, should be clear now for reading the rhetoric of difference and notion of heresy in this Gospel. This is not a "Christian" community opposed by "Jews," nor "Jewish Christians" arguing against "Gentile Christians." Rather, Matthew's Gospel inscribes deep divisions with other Christians and Jews that share aspects of belief, in both Jesus and the Torah, along a spectrum. As such, these others are heretics: intimate enemies of the community. Sometimes they are metonymically figured in the text, as in the case of the Pharisees. But as the allegories of exclusion in the eschatological parables show, Matthew's community expected eschatological judgment to fall within the community as well. Elements of heresiological rhetoric include the demonization of opponents; polemical doxography of their *halakah*; and an eschatological theory of origin for difference that drives discursive confrontation with opponents. The group identity of Matthew's community is formed via this heresiological rhetoric. And, as such, Matthew becomes the "Church's Gospel" in orthodox Christianity.

THE DIDACHE

Comparison casts the heresiological rhetoric of the Gospel of Matthew in high relief. A later text, the Teaching of the Apostles or *Didache*, provides a further comparison from what was likely an orthodox perspective. *Didache* has been placed in the first and second century and in Egypt as well as Antioch.[135] I place it here because the text contains references to the Gospel of Matthew, in particular the Sermon on the Mount, although if it is from Antioch, we could also compare it to the epistles of Ignatius of Antioch in the next chapter.

While *Didache* describes differences within the community, including techniques of identification of differences and tactics for dealing with it, it is not heresiological. The text begins with a treatise on the "Two Ways," a familiar theme in early Christianity (cf. *Ep. Barn.* 18–20) as well as Second Temple Judaism (1QS III, 12–IV, 25; see Chapter 2). *Didache* describes the "Two Ways" but does not connect them to either a dualistic anthropology or the rhetoric of difference. "There are two paths, one of life and one of death, and the difference between the two paths is great" (1.1). The exhortations in *Did.* 1.2–2.6 are not polemical. *Did.* 2.7 could be taken as explicitly non-heresiological: "Do not hate anyone—but reprove some, pray for others, and love still others more than yourself." Significantly, the treatise exhorts the audience to "not create a schism (*schisma*) but bring peace to those who are at odds (*machomenous*)," another non-heresiological admonition (4.3). Nor is choice predestined. The evil "path of death" includes "persecutors of the good, haters of the truth, lovers of the lie, who do not know the reward of righteousness, nor cling to a fair judgment" (5.2) but is not associated with religious dogma or matters of practice that follow.

The second section of *Didache* describes specific practices for baptism, the Eucharist, and the treatment of prophets (*Did.* 7–15). The rhetorical tone, however, is more instructive than combative. Since whatever Christian communities used *Didache* did so in a diverse context, I should not overstate this. But the text lacks the eschatological judgment and heresiological rhetoric of Matthew. The issue of fasting in *Did.* 8.1–2 follows Matthew's use of "hypocrites" in Matt 6:5. Matthew elaborates on the misguided practices of the opponents whereas *Didache* merely draws the distinction from the hypocrites' fasting on the wrong days. *Didache* 11–12 indicates more clearly a context of division by indicating which teachers, itinerant prophets, and apostles should be received or not, according to standards set out in the text.[136] Asking for money or excessive hospitality is a particular problem here (11.5, 9; 12.5). But these false prophets and rejected "Christmongers" (*christemporoi*) are not demonized or judged eschatologically.[137] The apocalyptic conclusion includes the line from the Synoptic tradition theorizing difference: "For in the final days the false prophets and corruptors of the faith will be multiplied" (*Did.* 16.3). The text does not emphasize any heresiological connection of the eschatological conclusion to the differences in practice in *Did.* 7–15. This contrast will become clearer in Chapter 6, in which I treat similar passages in 1–2 John that are heresiological.

There are any number of reasons that *Didache* could have adapted Matthean and other early Christian sources in non-heresiological way. Source issues suggest a laconic editor without a clear ideological agenda. It could be a document for instruction for which such issues seemed tangential. Without specifying a reason, the *Didache* uses various Christian traditions to describe difference in practice without heresiological rhetoric.

CONCLUSION

I have traced the rhetoric of conflict in Q, *Thomas*, Matthew, and *Didache*. The apocalyptic Q[2] contains many of the rhetorical features of Christian heresiology: the ideology of apocalyptic judgment; a dualistic, sectarian worldview; polemics against identified opponents with doxographic exposition of their beliefs; and the contested politics of the identity of Israel. These rhetorical features fully involve the Q community in the conflicts that marked the origin of Christianity. The *Gospel of Thomas* in contrast recontextualizes polemical passages from the Synoptic tradition in a non-heresiological discourse of difference. Rather than condemn heretics, Thomas Christians found strategies for avoidance in the interiorization of the eschaton and esoteric knowledge. This sharply contrasts with the heresiological rhetoric and allegories of exclusion in the Gospel of Matthew.

The Gospel of Matthew enshrines Christ as Emmanuel, "God with Us," for the Christian community (Matt 1:23; 28:20). Even as Jesus asserts this identity as Son and representative of God, Matthew records that "some doubted" (Matt 28:17), which is indicative of the tensions within this community evident in the Gospel. Q and *Thomas*, in contrast, hardly focus on the death or resurrection of Jesus at all, focusing instead on enlightenment of the individual enabled by the teaching of Jesus. Q would have been unacceptable for the orthodox canon without the resurrection narratives of Matthew and Luke, while *Thomas* was rejected. And yet both Q and *Thomas*, in their earlier forms, include the dualistic apocalyptic rhetoric that marks Christian heresiology. The sapiential Q traditions and Gnostic-oriented *Thomas* traditions might be connected ideologically to second- and third-century Gnosticism. But texts labeled Gnostic, such as the *Gospel of Mary* treated in Chapter 6, employ different, non-heresiological strategies for dealing with difference. My analysis of Q and *Thomas* points to a much more diverse portrait of early Christianity than "proto-orthodox" and Gnostic. They are further evidence of a wide ideological spectrum of early Christian ideologies that resists the categorizations of both orthodox heresiologists and contemporary historians.

The Gospel of Matthew expresses a fully formed discourse of heresiology against opponents. This explains how such a "Jewish" text, with theologies strongly at odds with Paul and John and radically different from the ecclesiology of Luke-Acts, could be central to the orthodox project of hegemony and eventually included in its canon. Christian orthodoxy needed a Jesus who articulates difference as an ideological notion; that is, a Jesus who employs heresiological rhetoric. Matthew's Jesus does just that.

Part II
The Politics of Heresy

6 Policing the Boundaries
The Politics of Heresiology

They went out from us, but they did not belong to us; for if they had belonged to us, they would have remained with us. But by going out they made it plain that none of them belongs to us.

1 John 2:19

The words "police" and "politics" have the same root, the Greek word *polis*, "city."[1] And it was in the *poleis* or cities of the eastern Roman Empire that the Christian discursive response to difference took shape as heresiology. Of course, all groups have to maintain their identity in part by identifying boundaries and by defining insiders and outsiders.[2] The early orthodox Christians were no exception to this social dynamic. The discourse of heresy, however, was not the only way to do that. Perhaps it has become so naturalized in our culture that it is hard to see now how these particular moves were formed and employed. The genealogy of heresy reveals the response to difference that has become part of "common sense" in the Christian and post-Christian social world.[3]

I have traced the negotiations with ideological difference and the development of heresiological responses in Part I, from Qumran to the early Gospel traditions. In this chapter, I will focus on how the notion of heresy functioned to police the boundaries within each community; that is, its internal political functions. In the next chapter, I will turn to the external politics of heresy in the appeal to Empire by early orthodox Christians. The politics of heresy overlap, of course, but this division allows me to delineate these multiple functions. The texts in this chapter inscribe a clearly defined ideology of heresy as a strategy for negotiation with difference within Christian communities: Colossians and the Pastoral Epistles; the Apocalypse of John; the Johannine epistles; and the letters of Ignatius of Antioch and Polycarp of Smyrna. The peril of deception and importance of discerning the "false" teachers permeate these late first- and early second-century Christian texts. Difference is not innovation but error. And an apocalyptic, eschatological worldview drives the ideological confrontation with opponents. Several of these texts employ the word *hairesis* in a technical sense for the first time; all exhibit the ideology of heresy and the rhetorical markers of heresiology as outlined in Chapter 1. I will compare these to alternative discursive strategies for difference in the *Gospel of Mary* and the *Gospel of Judas*. Here, rather than heresiology, we see the rhetorics of elision and derision, and strategies of accommodation and avoidance.

Some of these texts are as well grounded in a social-historical context as any other early Christian texts, particularly in comparison to the Gospel traditions studied in the previous chapter: the Apocalypse, Ignatius, and Polycarp in particular, with specific urban settings in Asia Minor and extensive literary connections with the Pauline texts. Others are contextualized only within literary-rhetorical traditions: Colossians and the Pastorals, written pseudonymously as Pauline epistles; and the three letters of John, with strong thematic connections to the Fourth Gospel and specific social situations outlined in 2–3 John. Social location is hypothetical beyond scholarly estimates of decade and provenance. Finally, the Gospels of *Mary* and *Judas* are as socially dislocated as any early Christian Gospel traditions. But all of these texts explore, and *contest*, the significance of Jesus Christ with other Christian leaders and communities (rhetorically and metonymically). The discursive responses to difference in these texts provide the guy-wires to construct a comparison of early orthodox heresiology with the rhetoric of difference in other Christian texts.

I begin this chapter with the ideology of tradition and notion of heresy in Colossians, Revelation, and the Pastoral Epistles, which I compare to the *Gospel of Mary*. I then turn to Ignatius of Antioch and Polycarp of Smyrna, two second-century bishops who consciously place themselves as the discursive inheritors of Paul's legacy. Finally, I compare these early orthodox responses to difference to the rhetoric of derision in the *Gospel of Judas*.

AFTER PAUL

In Chapter 4, I examined Paul's rhetoric of difference and the ways he labeled, marginalized, and demonized opponents within the *ekklēsiai*. Despite often pointed rhetoric in 1 Corinthians, however, the ideology of unity often leads to negotiation of difference or displacement of resolution to the next age. By emphasizing *homonoia*, Paul elides divisions that might have otherwise produced social fissures. And by retaining a sharp eschatological edge, Paul displaces the task of dealing with opponents to God and Christ (or, in the case of the man sleeping with his mother-in-law, Satan). Eschatology works the other way, however, when Paul forces a schism in Galatia and exhorts the Corinthians to identify and avoid "agents of Satan" such as the "super apostles" of 2 Cor 11–12. These two conflicts mark heresiological responses to difference.

Battles between Paul, the Jerusalem leaders, and other apostles shift to battles over the legacy of Paul himself in the Deutero-Pauline epistles. The authors of these letters consistently appeal to tradition against Christian opponents within the communities. The ideology of tradition is expressed as a Christian *mos maiorum*, the Roman value of the tradition of the elders, and the *ekklēsia* is represented as a well-ordered Roman family. The ideology of tradition moreover supports the heresiological historiography of truth before error, through which the authors accuse their opponents as deviating or swerving from an "original," and now traditional, truth. Further heresiological rhetoric in these texts includes slandering opponents; uniting enemies in one monolithic opposition; and theorizing the origins of difference as satanic and eschatological. This eschatological worldview drives these discursive confrontations.

The Ideology of Tradition in Colossians

Prophetic authority was central to the formation of early Christian communities in the first century. But by the second century, prophetic challenges to received tradition could be viewed with skepticism and alarm by orthodox Christians, as the case of Montanus' "New Prophecy" demonstrates.[4] Paul himself appeals to the tradition of the Last Supper as a warrant in quelling the divisions (*haireseis*, 11:19) in the Corinthian *ekklēsia*. "For I received from the Lord that which I handed on to you, that on the night in which he was handed over, the Lord Jesus took bread" (1 Cor 11:23). He also appeals to tradition with the same formula in 1 Cor 15:3 to introduce the extended refutation of alternative ideas about the resurrection among the Corinthians. In the post-Pauline *ekklēsiai*, the authority of received tradition began to replace prophetic authority as early as the second generation (cf. 1 Cor 14:5 vs. Col 2:6–7). Turning Jesus traditions into written texts in the mid-first century could signal an effort to construct tradition as authoritative. The variety of Gospel traditions, from narrative to sayings Gospels to Matthew and Luke's inclusion (or absorption) of Q, shows that different and opposing communities anchored their authority within written Gospel traditions.[5] Other Christian communities, however, continued to honor prophets with new revelations and visions, such as the apocalyptic prophet John of Patmos and the various communities often labeled as "Gnostic Christians," even if these revelations challenged received traditions.

One of the earliest Deutero-Pauline epistles, Colossians, emphasizes the ideology of tradition polemically against other Christian opponents. Commentators tend to call the Colossian opponents "errorists" or even heretics, privileging the Deutero-Pauline epistle as preserving the "truth" of Christian theology. The opponents are then construed as some combination of Jews, Gnostics, or Hellenistic philosophers. But the most likely conversation partners within the Christian community, and hence the targets of polemic, would be other Christians. Col 2:16–23 describes an intimate relationship between the opponents and the Colossian community. The opponents are able to condemn (*krinetō*) and disqualify (*katabrabeuetō*) other Christians in Colossae, Hierapolis, and Laodicea on the basis of whether they eat or drink certain items, celebrate festivals or Sabbaths, or have mystical visions of angels in heaven. It is unlikely that someone *outside* the Christian community would be able to judge or condemn in this manner. The opponents must therefore have authority *within* the Christian community. The epistle inscribes deep ideological disagreement between "Paul" (a name chosen to enhance the authority of his position) and opposing Christian prophets who challenged the emerging Pauline church hierarchy, whose authority derived from received tradition rather than charismatic revelation.[6]

The inclusion of the Christ Hymn, which was already a received Christological formulation, just after the thanksgiving and benediction (Col 1:15–20) shows the importance of tradition for this author and community.[7] The myth of the foundation by the *syndoulos* Epaphras (fellow-slave, 1:7) strengthens the author's emphasis on received tradition by connecting the Colossians to the imagined Paul. And even more significantly, the letter refers to the authority of tradition itself. First, when applying the Christ Hymn to the Colossian situation, the author warns his audience to stay within the boundaries of established faith (*tē pistei tethemeliōmenoi*) and not to shift from the message of the gospel that they had heard (1:23). Second, in an even more direct appeal, the author cites established tradition as a warrant and guide for the Christian life (Col 2:6, note *peripateite*).[8] The Colossians are to live their lives in Christ, "rooted and established," "as you have received" (*hōs oun parelabete*), and "just as you were taught" (*kathōs edidachthēte*, 2:7).[9] In this meta-traditional appeal, tradition is more than received formulations; it is a warrant for its own sake.

Furthermore, the opponents base their authority on visionary revelation rather than received tradition. The two main characteristics of the opponents described in Col 2:16–23 are the observance of some type of Jewish *halakah* relating to food, Sabbath, new moons, and festivals; and visionary ascent as a source of authority.[10] The claim by the author of Colossians that the opponents' teaching is *human* tradition (Col 2:8) directly challenges their "heavenly" revelations, which Colossians characterizes as "earthly" teaching. The author of Colossians, responding to the threat against his authority from apocalyptically-oriented Christian leaders, tries to turn his audience's attention away from vision of angels in the heavenly throne room. He foregrounds established tradition handed down in the churches over prophetic visions that challenge his authority. For the author, teaching *kata Christon* means teaching what has been received (*paralambanō*) rather than what comes from new prophetic revelations.

The Apocalypse of John

John of Patmos and his disciples were an apocalyptic Christian community in Asia Minor that drew authority from heavenly revelation, such as the one opposed by the author of Colossians. There is no mention of bishops or deacons in Revelation, whereas the evidence of Deutero-Pauline letters and Ignatius clearly shows that some Christian communities in Asia had a structure that included these offices.[11] The address of each message to the "angel of the church," moreover (Rev 2:1, 8, 12, 18; 3:1, 7, 14), could signal an attempt by John, the apocalyptic prophet, to circumvent the authority of leaders holding the offices of elder, deacon, or *episkopos* (Phil 1:1; 1 Pet 5:1–5; 1 Tim 3:1; Tit 1:7).[12] Such an attempt would mark a classic Weberian conflict between received and charismatic authority. Revelation thus represents an attempt to use prophetic authority against Christian opponents with different social legitimations.

John's own discursive response to opponents is heresiological. The messages in Revelation 2–3 focus on how each *ekklēsia* has responded to other Christian groups or leaders: "apostles" (2:2); the "Nicolaitans" (2:6, 15); "Balaam" (2:14); and "Jezebel" (2:20–25). The condemnation of these other Christian teachers and prophets in the Asian churches suggests that John saw their authority as a threat to his own. The Ephesians are praised for testing "those who claim to be apostles" and for finding them to be false (cf. *Did.* 11.3–6). We do not have any more information here nor any reason to connect them to other teachers whom John opposes. In Revelation, apostles are part of the past, in heaven (18:20) and the New Jerusalem (21:14). The messages to Ephesus and Pergamum mention the "works" (*erga*, Rev 2:6) and "teaching" (*didachē*, Rev 2:15) of the Nicolaitans. Again there is no description of what the Nicolaitans taught. Commentators usually assume that the Nicolaitans hold to "the teaching of Balaam" (Rev 2:14), permitting Christians to eat meat purchased from pagan temples (see 1 Cor 8–10). The message to Pergamum refers to two different groups, some who hold to the teaching of Balaam and some who also hold to the teaching of the Nicolaitans. This lack of specificity allowed later Christian heresiologists, from Irenaeus onward, to elaborate in greater and greater detail the outrages of the Nicolaitans.[13] The messages to Smyrna and Philadelphia also mention "those who call themselves Jews but are the synagogue of Satan" (2:8; 3:8), suggesting a struggle over the identity of "Jew" in the Asian *ekklēsiai*.[14]

Finally, John attacks "Jezebel," a prophet and teacher supported by the *ekklēsia* of Thyatira.[15] Her leadership was clearly a threat: "I gave her time to repent, but she refuses to repent of her fornication" (Rev 2:21). The use of "fornication" (*porneia*) here, as with the name "Jezebel," is almost certainly slanderous rather than descriptive.[16] We learn a bit more about this opponent. Her disciples are her "children" (Rev 2:23), the customary term for students in Greco-Roman culture. Her teaching of "the deep things of Satan" (Rev 2:24) suggests speculation on cosmic origins such as we see in *The Apocryphon of John.*[17] The description of part of her moral teaching is the same as the description of the teaching of Balaam in Rev 2:14, allowing the purchase of meat sacrificed in Greek temples. "Jezebel" challenged John's authority on issues such as eating meat purchased from pagan temples by means of prophecy and teaching and therefore posed a threat, which John prophetically faced in Thyatira. Nonetheless she retained a following and support there.

When faced with difference, John slanders or demonizes other leaders and ridicules their teachings and beliefs. Revelation rhetorically constructs one unified, satanic opposition to John and his circle of prophets from this array of different Christian or Jewish groups.[18] While the scholarly tendency has been to elide these groups and teachers, with the exception of the "so-called Jews," as "heretics," Gnostics, or some other group, that position yields to John's rhetoric. In fact, Revelation 2–3 describes the broad diversity of late first-century Christianity. Here we see clear instances of heresiology discursively policing the boundaries of the *ekklēsiai* in Asia, paralleling the heresiological response in Colossians, which opposed an apocalyptic community such as John's. This response was not always successful, as "Jezebel's" continuing activity in Thyatira shows. I will return to the imperial politics of Revelation in the next chapter.

THE PASTORAL EPISTLES

I turn now to 1 and 2 Timothy, the New Testament texts in which the notion of heresy is most fully expressed. These letters could in fact have been written after the letters of Ignatius and Polycarp, analyzed ahead. In this section, I look at the multiple heresiological functions of the ideology of tradition in these letters. These include attacks on opponents who have "deviated" from the traditions handed down as well as appeals to Roman values, including gender issues that link these epistles to the *Gospel of Mary*. Furthermore, scripture functions metonymically for tradition in the Pastoral Epistles, where it is not only cited but also valorized as authoritative. The famous description of "good Christian citizenship" in these epistles reveals a heresiological agenda.

Tradition and the *Mos Maiorum*

The Paulinist author of 1 Timothy foregrounds the "established faith" of the author against "different doctrine" in the first sentence after the greeting (1:3). Opposing Christian teachers, who "occupy themselves with myths and endless genealogies that promote speculation rather than divine training" (*oikonomian theou*, 1:4), are the main problem for this Christian leader. In this opening salvo, the author thematizes the origin of difference with a genealogy casting "truth" before "error." The opponents, "some people," have deviated (*ektrepō*) from God's economy and gone the erroneous way of these myths. The teaching that "Timothy" preserves is cast as the original, pure teaching against the mythic deviations of the opponents. Timothy himself is a personification of the Christian tradition (elaborated in 1:12–17); as prophesied he embodies the good fight of the "sincere" (*anypokritos*) Christian. The example of Timothy, whose faith was prophesied in his youth, contrasts with Hymeneus and Alexander, who have been turned over to Satan for having rejected "conscience" and suffered a "shipwreck in the faith" (cf. 1 Cor 5:5). As with others who have "turned away" (1:6), these heretics have deviated from the tradition held fast by Timothy and are now outside of the *ekklēsia*. Since truth precedes error in this formulation of doctrine, their transgression is deviation from what is "sure and true."

The appeal to pray for kings follows immediately on the identification of the two heretics. The ideology of empire is twinned with the appeal to tradition set forth in the rejection of alternative points of view as "heresy." While there is clearly an apologetic function to this appeal, "so that we may lead a quiet and peaceable life," this phrase ends with *en pasē eusebeia kai semnotēti*. As Mary R. D'Angelo has shown, the word *eusebeia* here conveys "the imperial virtue of *pietas*, a combination of devotion to the deity with the proper respect for one's superiors and responsibility toward one's dependents, especially as familial duty."[19] Martin Dibelius and Hans Conzelmann had already recognized the "ideal of good Christian citizenship" expressed here and throughout the Pastoral Epistles, marking the words *eusebia*, *semnotēs*, and especially *sōphrōn*, "prudent," as indicative of this Christian life in the world, a world in which the *parousia* is further and further in the distance.[20] I stress that the appeal to empire in 2:1–2 fits with the polemic against other Christians in 1:19–20. Those who deviate from the established faith are by implication socially deviant and do not share in the notion of "good Christian citizenship."

God approves of this idealized Roman life; prayers for the emperor are "right and acceptable" (*kalon kai apodekton*) to God, just as God finds it pleasing when families support widows (5:4). First Timothy pays significant attention to marital relations and family order (see "Gender" ahead). The connection of 1 Tim 2:9–15, enjoining women to remain modest, submissive, and quiet, to the injunction for the men to pray (2:8) is not immediately obvious. But this apparent disjunction becomes clear when we recall who the men are praying *for*: "for kings and all who are in high positions" (2:1–2, *proseuchē*; cf. *proseuchomai*, 2:8). Good Christian citizenship is again the goal, here tied to well-ordered families and submissive, modest women. The analogy of state and household was a familiar one in the Greco-Roman world (Aristotle, *Nichomachean Ethics*, 1161a6). The author of 1 Timothy appeals to imperial hierarchy in the injunction to pray for kings and rulers, connecting this to the submission of women in 1 Timothy 2.

When writing about the ambivalence of colonial discourse, Homi Bhabha describes mimicry in a way that illuminates the author's discursive moves here.

Mimicry is thus the sign of a double articulation; a complex strategy of reform, regulation and discipline, which "appropriates" the Other as it visualizes power. Mimicry is also the sign of the inappropriate, however, a difference or recalcitrance which coheres the dominant strategic function of colonial power, intensifies surveillance, and poses an immanent threat to both "normalized" knowledges and disciplinary powers.[21]

The homology of *oikoumenē* and *oikos* is reversed in 1 Timothy, as the well-ordered and hierarchical *oikos* is now mapped back to the *ekklēsia*, re-inscribing imperial values within Christian discourse. By implication the *ekklēsia* of 1 Timothy models the empire itself and posits the notion of a Christian *empire*. I shall return to this theme more fully in the next chapter, focusing here on how this functions heresiologically to police the boundaries of the community.

The author returns to opposing teachers and teachings in 1 Tim 4:1, after the discussion of church offices and order. Here, the writer theorizes more fully the presence of different Christians within the social and discursive world of the community as a sign of the end times (*en hysterois kairois*, 4:1). This eschatological worldview is central to heresy. And given the delayed eschatological horizon in the Pastoral Epistles, the references to the last days in this letter are more heresiological theory than eschatological ideology. In a double attack, the author places these other Christian teachers within this heresiological framework and then attacks their ideas as demonic. To elaborate on the first attack, people have "renounced the faith" (*apostēsontai tines tēs pisteōs*) by turning to other teachers. The author again maintains that truth precedes error, the classic heresiological formulation. But second, he pays even more attention to the demonic origin of these other teachings. The role of Satan, the enforcer for Hymeneus and Alexander (1:20), is more active here; people heed "deceitful spirits" (*pneumasin planois*) while demons actually teach doctrine (*didaskalias daimoniōn*), albeit false doctrine (*pseudologōn*, 4:2). The doxographic description of opposed Christian teachings in 4:3 echoes 1 Tim 1:4–7, notably adding sexual abstinence and restrictions on food. Taken together, the heresiological doxography in 1 Timothy suggests some aspects of a Gnostic worldview. The response is traditional doctrine (1 Tim 4:4–5) followed by an affirmation that marks the doctrine as just that, tradition, for "these instructions" (*tauta hypotithemenos*, 4:6; cf. 4:11) are "the words of the faith and sound teaching that you have followed." What has been followed (*parēkolouthēkas*), sound doctrine received and carried forth, is contrasted with the "profane myths and old wives' tales" promulgated by the opponents.

The remainder of this section attacking other Christians (to 4:16) includes numerous appeals to tradition. The refrain in 4:9, *pistos ho logos*, "the saying is sure," marks such appeals throughout the Pastoral Epistles (1 Tim 1:15; 3:1; 2 Tim 2:11; Tit 3:8). And despite his youth, the recipient has the blessing of elders (4:14). The concluding exhortation to persist (*epimene*, 4:16) in what has been received and taught signals the importance of tradition as a warrant against other Christian leaders and teachers. Given the importance of antiquity and the *mos maiorum* in religion and morality in the Greco-Roman world, this would be a powerful appeal. But the appeal to Roman imperial ideology is not only to position "Timothy" and this community firmly within the Roman Empire, but also to place Christian opponents outside of it. In a colonial appropriation of the "master's tools," the author of 1 Timothy claims the power of Empire as a hegemonic move against other different Christian teachers. Invoking the authority of Christian tradition in 1 Timothy by claiming the opponents have deviated from the economy of God mimics the widespread respect for tradition in the Greco-Roman world.

2 Timothy employs the same heresiological theory of truth preceding error. Difference is deviation from an original, traditional truth. The Paulinist author grounds his own faith and that of Timothy in a succession of generations, the Christian *mos maiorum*, citing continuity of worship (*latreuō*) with his ancestors (*progonoi*, 1:3) as well as Timothy's third generation in the faith (1:5). He emphasizes continuity of "sound teaching" (*hygiainontōn logōn*, 1:13) passed from "Paul" to "Timothy." This faith from "before the ages" (1:9) should be guarded as a treasure (1:15). Phygelus and Hermogenes have "turned away" (*apostrephō*) from "Paul"; difference is therefore deviation. The author warns against even debating or disputing these ideas (*logamachein*, 2:14). They are not even teachings but "empty sounds," (*kenophōnias*, translated as "chatter" in the NRSV), which spread like gangrene and lead orthodox Christians into impiety. This same "chatter" was linked with "false knowledge" in 1 Timothy (*tēs pseudonymous gnōseōs*, 6:20). Hymenaeus and Philetus are another example of deviation for swerving (*ēstochēsan*) from the truth by challenging the bodily resurrection (2:18). The "true faith" in contrast is a firm foundation (*themelios*). In 4:3–4, while maintaining the continuity of tradition in what he has handed down, the author again portrays these heretical opponents (with "itching ears, *knēthomenoi tēn akoēn*) as deviating (*apostrephō*) from the truth, thus claiming to maintain the one pure teaching of Jesus. The author dismisses the intellectual or theological validity of alternative Christian teachings; indeed, he dismisses intellectual dialectic itself.

Scripture and Tradition

"All scripture is inspired by God and is useful for teaching, for reproof, for correction, and for training in righteousness, so that everyone who belongs to God may be proficient, equipped for every good work" (2 Tim 3:16). The scriptures of ancient Israel, via typological readings of the Septuagint, become central to orthodox Christian dogma. Justin's *Dialogue with Trypho* develops this argument at length and Irenaeus argues for and from these scriptures at the end of the second century. We saw in Chapter 4 how Paul argued midrashically from Genesis against the necessity of circumcision and allegorically against his opponents in the story of Sarah and Hagar. The appeal to scripture in the Pastoral Epistles functions metonymically for the ideology of tradition, a warrant for ecclesial authority for the post-Pauline leadership in Asia Minor. Thus, this ideology was a *heresiological* move against other Christian communities that privileged direct and ongoing prophetic or spiritual revelation over received tradition. A number of their texts that have survived were labeled "heretical" by second-century orthodox leaders. The *Gospel of Mary*, which I will compare to the Pastorals, is one such text.

Gender

I first turn to the issue of gender as a way to connect these texts. 1 Timothy expresses fully the standard Roman ideology of women's roles within the household. In Chapter 2, the author produces an unqualified circumscription of women's roles as prudent wives and mothers, opposing any notions of gender equality that might be read from Paul's authentic letters. Men pray for the emperor (2:8) while the women remain modest, submissive, and quiet. As noted earlier, the letter marks a homology between *oikoumenē, ekklēsia,* and *oikos.* Opposing teachers and teachings are specifically gendered in the letter, inscribing imperial hierarchy not only within the household but also against other Christians. Further, the bishop must manage his own household well (3:5), including both his wife and his children, in order to demonstrate his ability to care for the church. Family, household, and church are as well ordered as the Roman Empire. The *Haustafel* or Household Code in 1 Tim 2:8–16 and 6:11–17, which was already traditional by this point (Col 3:18–4:1; 1 Pet 2–3; see Chapter 7), supports this imperial ideology.

The gendered language in 4:7 to describe the opponents' teaching as "profane myths and old wives' tales" underscores the strict limitation of women's roles as spiritual leaders within this community (1 Tim 2:9–15). Not only does this suggest at least one opposing community in the author's social world that privileged the authority of women (for instance "Jezebel" of Thyatira in Rev 2:19–25 or a community reading the *Gospel of Mary*), but it also inscribes Roman imperial ideologies of gender against alternative Christian teachings. Just as married women must be controlled within the family, widows, as unattached women, pose a threat to the community order. Thus the letter pays particular attention to the enrollment of "real" widows supported by the *ekklēsia.* Those who receive support must have given support in their own time: "she must be well attested for her good works, as one who has brought up children, shown hospitality, washed the saints' feet, helped the afflicted, and devoted herself to doing good in every way" (1 Tim 5:10). Younger widows pose a greater threat because they might remarry out of carnal desires, thus violating their vows. And they undermine church doctrine: "they learn to be idle, gadding about from house to house; and they are not merely idle, but also gossips and busybodies, saying what they should not say" (5:13). But gossip and idle tales are not the real threat; rather, it is alternative teachings that might validate the power of women in the *ekklēsia.* The charge here of "forbidden" talk clearly suggests the "profane myths and old wives' tales" of the author's opponents. Indeed, "some have already turned away to follow Satan," which might give outsiders a chance to revile the Christians.

The attack on other Christian opponents in 2 Timothy is both gendered and explicitly heresiological. The author theorizes dissent, difference, and opposition eschatologically as signs of the last days; slanders these opponents morally; and takes special aim at a different form of Christianity that espoused gender equality (3:1–9). The distressing times of the last days are marked by vice-ridden, godless, unholy people who target the unfaithful. Women, "little women" in particular (*gynaikaria*), are their targets within the *ekklēsia*. They are unable to come to the truth itself. He then links his current opponents, other Christian teachers, to the *scriptural* opponents of Moses, Jannes and Jambres, thereby constructing a unified opposition in which all opposing Christian teachers (i.e., heretics) are united against the people of God. This theory of origin and construction of a unified, demonized opposition marks 2 Timothy as heresiological.

The Gospel of Mary and the Rhetoric of Ellipsis

Controversy over women's leadership and the value of women's teaching in the Christian community discursively connects the *Gospel of Mary* to the Pastoral Epistles. The *Gospel of Mary* in essence re-narrates the strictures and prohibitions against women in the controversy among the apostles over Mary's teaching, challenging the ideology of the Pastorals on several key points.

The first four chapters of the surviving *Gospel of Mary* focus on Jesus' teaching. When he departs (4:1), the disciples are distressed and confused. Mary emerges as the leading disciple. She immediately takes charge, comforts the others, and leads them to debate the meaning of Jesus' words. Her authority to lead is clear. Peter then asks Mary to *teach*, focusing on her gender: "Peter said to Mary: 'Sister, we know that the Savior loved you more than all other women'" (6:1). And he acknowledges she has received special instruction hidden from the others.

This view of gender is quickly recast in ways that further challenge the ideology of the Pastoral Epistles. After Mary finishes her account about the ascent of the soul, she stops and is silent after what must have been an even more complex recounting of this ascent "since it was up to this point that the Savior had spoken to her" (9:30).[22] This alone reflects positively on her authority as an authentic witness who transmits the revelations of Jesus accurately to his followers. The positive image of Mary, developed in the first nine chapters of the *Gospel*, is challenged by Andrew and then Peter. The brothers present two pillars of the formative doctrine of the orthodox party. First, Andrew focuses on the problem of difference. Mary's teachings are, to the orthodox, "strange ideas" (10:1). Andrew's response points to the dogmatic difference between orthodox and other Christian teachings. But the nature of the teachings as different (and hence targets for the heresiological attack in the Pastorals) is not further explored because the community of the *Gospel of Mary* found these to be true revelations from Jesus. Andrew, however, stands in for the orthodox Christians who are attacking the Magdalene community. And whereas the orthodox Pastoral Epistles theorize difference heresiologically as satanic and eschatological, the *Gospel of Mary* ignores it by leaving Andrew's challenge hanging. This discursive ellipsis of difference contrasts sharply with orthodox heresiology. Difference is not only unchallenged, it is implicitly valued.

Peter then attacks the messenger herself: "Are we to turn around and listen to her? Did he choose her over us?" (10:3). Two issues emerge in his response to her teaching, both of which challenge the doctrine of the Pastorals. First, he questions that Jesus would have given her "private" information without the male apostles knowing about it. The point of contention could also be the private revelation itself, but he is emphatic that it is "with a woman" that is the problem. The tradition, moreover, of private revelations to the apostles in different Gospels (*Thomas*, Matthew, John) would have been known across different Christian communities in the second century. The second ideological issue in Peter's response is women's authority in the community. He focuses on a woman as leader in the church. In the Gospels of both Matthew and John, Peter receives special authority from Jesus over the other apostles.[23] This question from Peter foregrounds the ideology of Petrine as well as male authority in Christian churches. Peter's question in essence encapsulates the prohibitions of women's authority inscribed in 1 and 2 Timothy. Just as Jesus' revelation to women is questioned by Peter, so too is their authority to lead in the church. The *Gospel of Mary*, however, affirms this authority.

Scripture as Tradition

1 Tim 4:13 urges the recipient to "read aloud," a probable reference to scripture. The appeal to scripture to support the ideology of tradition is even stronger in 2 Timothy. As noted earlier, the epistle opens with a Christian *mos maiorum* in reference to the worship of "Paul's" ancestors and the multiple generations of faith present in Timothy. Indeed this is not a new religion but one from "before the ages" (1:9). The author marks Jesus as a descendant of David (2:8). This traditional Christian formulation is scarce in Pauline literature, appearing only in Romans and 2 Timothy (see Ign. *Trall.* 9; *Smyrn.* 1.1).[24] And, we should ask why *this* tradition at this point, rather than assume the inevitability of orthodox formulations. Here it more firmly connects the "sound faith" with the scriptures. Then, in 2 Timothy 3:1–9, discussed earlier for its gendered polemics, the author links his Christian opponents to Jannes and Jambres, the apocryphal names for Moses' scriptural opponents in Exodus 7:8.

"Paul" then cites his own example of patience, steadfastness, persecution, and suffering (2 Tim 3:10). The focus is really on other Christians, not persecution: "Indeed, all who want to live a godly life in Christ Jesus will be persecuted. But wicked people and impostors will go from bad to worse, deceiving others and being deceived." Deceiving (*planōntes*) is not persecution (*diōchthēsontai*). It is in this heresiological context that the author cites the authority of scripture, linked by the themes of continuity and tradition. To "continue in what you have learned and firmly believed" (3:14) means to continue holding to the authority of scripture. "Timothy" himself has known the scriptures since he was a baby (*brephos*, 3:15), demonstrating continuity of tradition in *oikos* and *ekklēsia*. This takes us to the quote cited earlier on the inspiration of scripture, 2 Tim 3:16. It is not just a doctrine of scripture that is important here, but also the ideology of tradition, of preserving truth against new "deviations" by heretics. Scripture is part of tradition, and both have heresiological functions.

Revelations from the Risen Christ

Just as it challenges the Pastoral Epistle's ideology of gender and prohibition of women's leadership, the *Gospel of Mary* challenges this ideology of tradition and the authority of scripture. Once again, this is a submerged narrative in the Gospel. These can be read in the content of Mary's revelation and the presentation of that revelation to the other apostles.

First, the *Gospel of Mary* challenges the content of orthodox theology. In Pauline texts, sin is a powerful force but in the *Gospel of Mary* sin does not have an ontological status separate from the individual. Peter asks Jesus, "What is the sin of the world" and Jesus answers that there is no such thing as sin! Rather each person produces sin when he or she swerves (troped as adultery, 3:4) from the good that is within. Good rather than sin exists within each person (4:3). Jesus is not the salvific Christ whose atoning sacrifice defeats sin but the guide who instructs the apostles how to find the "child of true Humanity" within. Most significant is Jesus' declaration: "Do not lay down any rule beyond what I determined for you, nor promulgate law like the lawgiver, or else you might be dominated by it" (4:9–10). I noted earlier the many creedal formulations in the Pastoral Epistles that had developed as traditional beliefs within that Pauline community. 1 and 2 Timothy are texts dominated by laws, laws including scripture. The *Gospel of Mary* opposes both this ideology of scripture and such laws that go beyond the revelations from the spirit of Jesus.

Mary's vision (*Gos. Mary* 7–9), while unfortunately fragmentary, elaborates allegorically and ethically this theology of inner illumination. She describes the ascent of the soul past a series of four powers, including Desire, Ignorance, and a seven-formed Power of Wrath that comprises darkness, desire, ignorance, zeal for death, the realm of the flesh, foolish wisdom of the flesh, and the wisdom of the wrathful person. The soul avoids and defeats these powers: "I saw *you* . . . and you didn't recognize me" (9:4–6). Jesus does not defeat these powers (as in the Pauline epistles;

e.g., Rom 6:6–12; Col 2:15) but rather offers the guidance for the "mind" to see this vision and for the soul to pass the Powers on the way to the spiritual realm.[25] Mary's vision offers direction for how to find the child of humanity within each person. These theological differences between the *Gospel of Mary* and the Pastoral Epistles are stark indeed.

The manner of Mary's instruction to the other apostles, as well as its content, opposes received tradition. She sees Jesus "in a vision" and discusses this vision with him. Her vision communicates her own purity of mind (7:7) and ability to converse with Jesus and God, in the heavenly realm.[26] The conversation and vision distinguish Mary from the rest of the apostles, as does her stability in "not wavering" at the sight of Jesus.[27] The vision is almost certainly a post-departure (in orthodox terms, post-resurrection) vision; that is, the text maintains that Mary receives visions and instructions from Jesus after he has departed from the apostles. The visionary authority Mary wields in the community contrasts with the emphasis on received tradition in the Pastoral Epistles. Interestingly, Mary stops her description of the ascent of the soul a bit abruptly, "since it was up to this point that the savior had spoken to her" (9:31). While this sounds at first glance as if it supports an ideology of tradition, that Mary hands down what she has received, it is important that this is a post-resurrection vision. In other words, this is new to the apostles and the Marian community. But the hesitancy underscores her authority as a visionary prophet. She says no more than what she saw in her vision. Levi's closing proclamation underscores both the content of Mary's teaching and the authority of her vision: "We should clothe ourselves with the perfect Human, acquire it for ourselves as he commanded us, and announce the good news, not laying down any other rule or law that differs from what the Savior said" (10:11–13). Levi summarizes the double challenge to the orthodox party, in the *Gospel of Mary*, to both the ideology of tradition and the authority of scripture.

Summary

This comparison of the Pastoral Epistles and the *Gospel of Mary* has highlighted key aspects of the heresiological responses to difference within the early orthodox *ekklēsiai*. 1 and 2 Timothy both respond to Christian opponents, named or unnamed, who are ideologically heretics, although the word itself does not appear. But as I argued in Chapter 1, there is clearly a notion of heresy before the word "heresy" is used. The heresiological response by the author (or authors) includes the ideology of tradition, a Christian *mos maiorum* that mimics Roman imperial values while condemning other Christians; scripture as a source of authority and metonym for tradition; and difference as construed as deviation from the truth, as error rather than innovation or inspiration. While the text or community of the *Gospel of Mary* might or might not have been in the sights of this author, my comparison not only sketches out one alternative Christian theology, but also shows an alternative response to difference itself, the rhetoric of elision, instead of heresiological confrontation.

THE JOHANNINE COMMUNITY AND THE EPISTLES OF JOHN

The Johannine epistles are an early orthodox parallel to the Pastoral Epistles. They too are written within a theological and discursive tradition, in this case the Gospel of John. But whereas the pseudonymous Pastorals adopt the name of Paul, the author of 1 John and the "elder" of 2–3 John (possibly the same person), do not make any claims to be the Beloved Disciple of the Fourth Gospel.[28] These epistles are closely connected to the Gospel, particularly 1 John in vocabulary and theology. They mark an intermediate discursive stage between the pseudonymous Pastorals and the letters of Polycarp and Ignatius, who claim ideological continuity with the apostle Paul but do not write in his name. 1 John is an unsigned theological essay while 2–3 John are actual letters from an elder (*presbyteros*, 2 John 1, 3 John 1) to two different individuals who supported *ekklēsiai*, an "elect lady" (*eklektē kyria*) and a man named Gaius. 1 John is quoted by Polycarp in his *Epistle to the Philippians*, and Ignatius might have known the text or a shared tradition.[29] The Johannine epistles share a heresiological ideology with these bishops.

The Fourth Gospel tells the story of Jesus, from John the Baptist to crucifixion in Jerusalem and resurrection appearances in Judea and Galilee. For almost forty years now, scholars have read the story of Jesus as the story of the Johannine community as well, a "two-level" narrative in which the development, controversies, and schisms of the community and between the community and the "Jews" have been re-inscribed in the narrative of Jesus' actions.[30] As noted in Chapter 5, the idea that we can read the Gospel as the story of a *community* as much as a theological story about Jesus remains fundamental to the social history of the Johannine community. The central story of the man blind from birth, whose parents fear the Jews, "for the Jews had already agreed that anyone who confessed Jesus to be the Messiah would be put out of the synagogue" (John 9:22), signals a break with a Jewish community as a critical moment in the community. As with Matthew's Pharisees, the Jews in John are metonymic markers of the opponents.

While the identities of opponents in the Fourth Gospel are complicated both by the symbolic narrative and the difficulty of labeling "Jews" and "Christians" in the first century, the lines become clearer in the Johannine epistles. 1 John includes key aspects of heresiology: demonization and moral condemnation of opponents and a theory for the origin of difference. 1 John 2:19 states that the "antichrists" opposed by the author "went out from us, but they did not belong to us." The author theorizes identity by affiliation; the schism defines two Christian communities where there was formerly one. These "antichrists" were therefore part of the same community as the author's and recipients', the type of proximate enemy inscribed and demonized in the messages of Revelation as well. This other Christian community, when faced with theological difference, chose to separate, a strategy of avoidance. The author of 1 John, with an eschatological worldview, chooses in contrast a heresiological response. Those who were once "of Christ" are now against Christ and associated with the antichrist of the end times. Furthermore, the term theorizes the origin of difference within the Christian community, a critical aspect of the notion of heresy. Those who have accepted Christ have turned against Christ, as heretics, because "it is the last hour" (*eschatē hōra estin*, 2:18). 1 John applies the eschatological theory of the origin of heresy, here a self-fulfilling prophecy that explains internal Christian difference as both sign and cause of the end times. These other Christians, moreover, receive harsh moral condemnation (1:6–10; 2:4, 9–11; 4:20). The rhetoric of heresiology includes the moral depravity of Christians who have different beliefs.

1 John also includes some doxographic elements in its characterization of opponents. The precise beliefs of the two Christian groups are hard to define but their differences center on Christology. The attack in 1 John 2 continues that the "antichrist" is the "liar" (*pseustēs*) who denies that Jesus is the Christ and denies the Father and the Son. The Johannine language in 2:24–25 ("abide," *menō*, "eternal life," *tēn zōēn tēn aiōnion*), references to Christological passages in the Fourth Gospel, suggests that there could have been a division over the divinity of Jesus and his equivalence with God the Father.[31] But in 4:1–3, the author warns of "false prophets" and "antichrists" who hold a docetic Christology; that is, the idea that Jesus was not fully human but only appeared (*dokeō*) to be. This "heretical" outlook would have been eminently sensible in Greco-Roman culture, with its many myths of gods appearing on earth in human guise. Several different Christian teachers and communities embraced docetism (a descriptive term, not a particular Christian school of thought) in different varieties, but it was consistently attacked by orthodox Christians. The author of 1 John expressly states that Jesus came in the flesh and emphasizes the actual physical, atoning sacrifice of Jesus (1:1–2; 1:7; 2:2; 4:10; cf. John 20:24–29). The more specific warning in 2 John 7–11 not to give hospitality to "those who do not confess that Jesus Christ has come in the flesh" lends weight to the idea that docetism is the heresiological issue. And while the author labels them again as "antichrists" (2 John 7), the practical issue of hospitality in other *ekklēsiai* for travelling Christians highlights that these proximate enemies, or heretics, were in fact Christians as well, who could be welcomed in Christian households.

The heresiological nature of these responses to difference within the Christian community in 1–2 John becomes clearer when compared to the problems addressed by the elder in 3 John. In this short letter, problems are not met with heresiological responses. Gaius, the recipient, is commended for the hospitality he has shown to travelling Christians in his *ekklēsia*, even providing support for their journey (*propempsas*, 6). But Diotrephes, "who likes to put himself first" (*philoprōteuōn*, 9), does not recognize the elder's authority and has not received Christian travelers with hospitality. Rather, Diotrephes has attempted to exercise his own authority over the *ekklēsia* and expelled those who continued to welcome Christians; that is, those who have continued to recognize the elder's authority. There is clearly a power struggle in the *ekklēsia*, but this is not a heresiological response. Presumably Diotrephes holds to the correct Christological dogma. The elder wants to rein him in, prevent his actions against other Christians, and limit his authority over the church. But the elder does not use any heresiological rhetoric when dealing with an *orthodox* opponent.

Summary

As with the Pastoral Epistles, the Johannine epistles use heresiological constructions against Christian opponents, "antichrists" who had once been part of the same Christian community. They are demonized, morally slandered, and their existence is theorized eschatologically. Other problems within the *ekklēsiai*, however, are not met with heresiological responses, as shown by the case of Diotrephes.

IGNATIUS AND POLYCARP

Ignatius and Polycarp, two early second-century bishops (*episkopoi*) in Asia Minor, mark the final stage in this book for the development of the notion of heresy. While it is possible that their activity actually preceded the authorship of the Pastoral Epistles, they position themselves differently. The author, or authors, of the letters to Timothy and Titus write as Paul himself, but Ignatius and Polycarp claim the mantle of Paul's heirs.[32] In other words, whereas the author of 1 Timothy forged a letter as Paul, Ignatius and Polycarp acknowledge Paul as predecessor and authority. These leaders do not see themselves as exploring new revelations from Jesus or the spirit of God. Rather, they place themselves as explicitly post-apostolic and in continuity with Pauline, Johannine, and Gospel traditions. Their letters include the conscious appropriation of Christian writings such as Paul and 1 John; a heresiological response to difference in the churches; and the ideology of traditional apostolic authority now relocated to the bishop.

Ignatius places himself as discursively close to Paul as he can. He frequently calls attention to his own act of writing.[33] In *Eph.* 12.2, Ignatius yokes his hopes for his own eternal fate to that of Paul, "the holy one who received a testimony and proved worthy of all fortune."[34] He opens *Trallians* with greetings "in apostolic manner," a reference to Pauline greetings.[35] In *Rom.* 4.3, he invokes the legacy of both Peter and Paul, even using a Pauline turn of phrase when contrasting their freedom (*eleutheroi*) to his slavery (doulos); "But if I suffer [death by wild beasts in the arena], I will become a freed person (apelutheros) who belongs to Jesus Christ, and I will rise up, free in him" (cf. Rom 6:4; 1 Cor 7:22).[36] While Ignatius carefully distinguishes himself from Paul, he takes on Paul's epistolary posture and authority quite intentionally: "I am writing to all the churches and giving instruction to all" (Ign. Rom. 4.1; cf. 1 Cor 4:17; 7:17; 14:33).

In his letter to the Philippians, Polycarp consciously evokes the memory of Paul and the Pauline traditions that he upholds. His own act of writing (graphō) to the Philippians recalls Paul's example; he is at pains to note that he writes at their request rather than his initiative (Pol. Phil. 3.1–2). And, in what is possibly the original concluding section of his second letter, "Paul and the rest of the apostles" function as metonyms for tradition itself (9.1): "Therefore I urge you (parakalō) to obey the word of righteousness and practice all endurance."[37] Paul and the apostles, along with the now-martyred Ignatius, serve as examples of this endurance. The traditional language here is part of the concluding peroration (Chaps. 8–10) that follows the attack on false teaching in Chapter 7. All three chapters begin with emphatic "therefores" (oun, ergo) and appeals to tradition. The "faith" in which he exhorts the Philippians to stand firm (10.1) and the "truth" in which they should be united parallel the dogmatic traditions we saw in the Pastoral Epistles: the salvific, atoning death of the sinless Jesus (8.1); the examples of Paul and the apostles (9.2); charitable works (10.2, cf. the warning against philargyria, Pol. Phil. 4.1; cf. 1 Tim 6:10); and attention to the values and sensibilities of "outsiders" (gentibus, 10.2).

Both authors use heresiological constructions to deal with difference in the churches. Polycarp mentions an "error that deceives many" in 2.1–2, drawing on a basket of phrases from texts that would later be included in the New Testament.[38] This "error" is again some type of docetic Christology. For Polycarp, a docetist is not a Christian but an antichrist (7.1, citing 1 John 4:2–3); the one who denies the cross is "of the devil." This was likely the version of docetic Christology that held that the Logos inhabited the body of the man Jesus but departed before his death on the cross. Polycarp attacks the ways these opposing teachers corrupt the traditions of the Christian orthodox: "whoever distorts [methodeuē] the words of the Lord for his own passions, saying there is neither resurrection nor judgment [krisin]—this one is the firstborn of Satan" (7.1). Since the gospel traditions and sayings sources were forming throughout the second century, Polycarp likely refers to oral rather than written traditions here.[39] Just as the orthodox Christians grounded their beliefs in resurrection accounts in the Gospels of Luke and John, other Christians quoted words of the Lord to support their theologies. But Polycarp attacks these different Christians traditions as satanic "distortions," while describing their theology of no resurrection or judgment.

In contrast, Polycarp claims he preserves the original truth that preceded error. Evoking the language of conversion and redemption, he urges the recipients to "turn back" (*epistrepsōmen*) from these "satanic anti-christs" with their "false teachings" (*pseudodidaskalias*) to "the word that was delivered to us from the beginning" (*ex archēma hēmin para-dothenta logon*, 7.2).[40] Contrasting the word (*logos*) of his own orthodox Christians with the deceitful sayings (*logia*) that the opponents claim come from Christ, Polycarp claims that his side preserves the *original* truth and that the teachings of docetic Christians are perversions of that truth. The ideologies of truth preceding error, the valorization of apostolic tradition, and the polemical attack on the other Christians as satanic antichrists who distort the words of Jesus mark Polycarp's heresiological attack on other Christians.

He does not always respond to difference in this way. Polycarp has another problem to address in the letter, the presbyter Valens, who apparently robbed or misappropriated church funds (11:1). Polycarp explicitly condemns this evil (*malus*) and inability to exercise self-control (*gubernare*).[41] The perils of the "love of money" are a theme across the letter in his exhortation for life in the church, deacons, and elders (*avaritia*, 11.1; cf. *philargyria*, 2.2; 4.1, 3; 6.1). But Valens' sin does not make him a heretic. Rather, he is "defiled by idolatry and will be judged as if among the outsiders [*gentes*] who know nothing about the judgment of the Lord" (11.2). This evil act makes Valens, in the words of Matthew, "like a Gentile and a tax-collector" rather than a heretic. The condemnation of Valens, as with the rebuke of Diotrephes in 3 John noted earlier, highlights the specific nature of orthodox heresiology in these texts. Neither Valens nor Diotrephes is a heretic. In fact, Polycarp prays that the Lord will give him and his wife "true repentance" (*paeniten-tiam veram*).

Ignatius also exhibits a sharp sense of policing the internal boundaries of the *ekklēsiai*, with a wider array of opposing teachers and Christian communities in a fuller set of letters. Indeed, Ignatius' heresiology is more pronounced than any other early Christian writer before Justin. Ignatius is the first of the "apostolic fathers" to use the words heresy and heterodox (*hairesis*, Ign. *Eph.* 6.2; *Trall.* 6.1; *heterodoxia*, *Magn.* 8.1; *heterodoxeō*, *Smyrn.* 6.2). Schoedel calls his use of these terms "quasi-technical," pre-sumably in comparison to non-pejorative uses in Josephus and Acts and the heresiologists following Justin.[42] The word *hairesis* is never positive in Paul and even more negative in Ignatius: "Therefore I am urging you—not I, but the love of Jesus Christ—make use only of Christian (*christianē*) food and abstain from a foreign plant, which is heresy" (*Trall.* 6.1). My claim is that this is a technical term and that the ideology of heresy is fully developed in his letters. Ignatius therefore provides an orthodox finale to my study of the genealogy of heresy and the discursive hinge to the heresiologists of the second century.

Every letter save *Romans* expresses Ignatius' concerns with error in the churches. He seems to have at least two sets of opponents in mind, those Christians who hold a docetic Christology and "Judaizers." His different responses to these two perceived errors show different internal politics between the ideology of heresy on the one hand and the negotiation with difference on the other. The docetic, and therefore heretical, Christians receive the longest treatment in *Smyrn.* 1–7. Ignatius' heresiological rhetoric against these "wild beasts" includes dogmatic assertions of early orthodox creedal formulas and slanderous attacks on the opposing Christians' beliefs, actions, and moral character. He opens the letter with a creedal statement about Jesus (*Smyrn.* 1–3): "both flesh and spirit"; of the family of David "according to the flesh" but also Son of God "according to the will and power of God"; born from a virgin; baptized by John; "nailed in the flesh" under Pontius Pilate and Herod (1.1–2).[43] Jesus suffered this death and "truly raised himself" (2.1).[44] Finally, he completes his creed of "these things" (*tauta*, 2.1, 4.1) with assertions of Jesus' physical resurrection.[45] Scripture supports him as well (5.1). Ignatius' theology reveals the outline of early orthodox dogma. Just as important is the *rhetoric* of the creed itself. A statement of common dogma is foundational for the ideology of heresy (4.1; cf. "gospel" in 5.1).[46] Even angels would be judged for not believing this (6.1), a probable reference to the Christian leaders of the group who do not agree with Ignatius' creed.[47]

The heresiological attack follows this creed. Ignatius slanders these other Christians whom he opposes, "wild beasts in human form" (4.1), extensively in this letter. The phrase is ironic given his fate of death from wild beasts and labeling of his Roman guards as "ten leopards" (*Rom.* 5.1). But he draws that comparison because these Christians, like the beasts in the arena, are not human: "if possible you should not even meet with them" (*Smyrn.* 4.1; 7.2). He does not even write their names (5.3). Dogmatic difference leads to moral accusations: these other Christians do not express love or charity for widows, orphans, and prisoners (6.2).[48] This slander is typical of his approach to "heretical" Christians.[49] In *Eph.* 7.1 he attacks those who "bear the name [Christians] in wicked deceit" (*dolō ponērō*; cf. 8.1 *exapataō*) as "wild animals" and "raving dogs"; in 16.1–2 he accuses them of deceit, corruption, and filth (*hryparos*). They are destined for the "unquenchable fire." Heretical teachers are beyond the pale and should be completely avoided (*Smyrn.* 4.1; 7.2).[50] In contrast to the heretical teachers (*Eph.* 9.1–2), Ignatius urges the Ephesians to pray for outsiders.[51] Whereas "gentiles" are redeemable, heretics are not.

But heretical teachers might appear trustworthy (Ign. *Phil.* 2.2; *Trall.* 6.2; *Poly.* 3.2). Ignatius therefore counters this threat to the orthodox creed with doxography. He turns their docetic theology around. Just as they believe that Christ only appeared as human, they themselves are "only an appearance"—indeed, demons without bodies (*Smyrn.* 2.1). He emphasizes suffering, physical death, and flesh in opposition to their docetic Christology (*Smryn.* 5). The docetic Christians are "public advocates of death, not truth" (5.1) and "corpse bearers" for denying that Christ "bore flesh" (*nekrophoros, sarkophoron,* 5.2).

Ignatius claims that they abstain from the Eucharist and prayer (7.1). There is no more reason to accept this accusation than his slander in *Smyrn.* 6.2 that they did not practice love or charity. But these Christians might have adopted the same strategy for difference as the Johannine "antichrists" discussed earlier: separation, a strategy of avoidance (cf. *Smyrn.* 8.2). That would not necessarily be a heresiological strategy. In the absence of textual evidence we cannot know whether they demonized and slandered Ignatius and his creed. But if the Christians opposed by Ignatius produced or valued a text such as the *Gospel of Mary*, separation would clearly be a non-heresiological strategy of avoidance. These Christians might have split from the others with whom they disagreed. Christians did not always separate when they disagreed with the orthodox hierarchy. John of Patmos strongly condemns "Jezebel" and the *ekklēsia* of Pergamon for supporting her. This is an example of a mixed community that also recognized John's authority as a prophet (short of heeding his pronouncement against her). And, later in the second century, Irenaeus wrote against "gnosis falsely named" in part because the esoteric exclusivism of some Christians allowed them to remain part of orthodox communities.

While Ignatius argues from scripture and the Hebrew prophets for Christian tradition, he argues against Judaism and "judaizing" (*ioudaizen, Magn.* 10.3) in *Magnesians* and *Philadelphians*. Ignatius seems to have a clearer sense of what Judaism is at this point than recent scholarship of Jewish and Christian identities in the first and second century (as discussed in Chapters 1 and 5). He discredits Judaism as "false opinions and old fables" and urges the Christians to celebrate the Lord's Day rather than the Sabbath (*Magn.* 8.1, 9.1). Ignatius goes as far as to claim Christianity has *replaced* Judaism—similar to the argument of supercession in the Letter to the Hebrews, but demonstrating much less understanding of the scriptures. His convoluted assertion is that "Christianity did not believe in Judaism, but Judaism in Christianity" (*Magn.* 10.3). Even the Hebrew prophets lived "according to Jesus Christ," as disciples "in the spirit" (*Magn.* 8.2, 9.2).[52] He seems to mean that the Hebrew scriptures anticipated Christ and Christianity. This becomes the standard orthodox interpretation of what comes to be the Old Testament, but Ignatius does not include typological interpretations of the law and prophets, only dogmatic assertions that they anticipated or believed in Jesus Christ.

The universality claimed for orthodox Christianity here (*pasa glōssa, Magn.* 10.3) is typical of the theme of unity in Ignatius' epistles. He uses the word *homonoia*, concord, eight times in his epistles, drawing on the political *topos* discussed in Chapter 4.[53] This theme features prominently at the beginning of *Philadelphians*, also focusing on Judaism; Ignatius warns against division and schism (*Phld.* 2.1; 3.1–3). He constructs homologies between the "unity of the church" (*tēn henotēta tēs ekklēsias,* 3.2), the oneness of the Eucharist, and the monarchical episcopate (*Phld.* 4). He stresses unity in *Philadelphians* also because of the divisive prophetic encounter referred to in *Phld.* 7–8, in which Ignatius apparently spoke prophetically to support the authority of the bishops, priests, and deacons (*Phld.* 7.1).[54] Unity is an important theme throughout, but when dealing with Judaism even more so, because Ignatius affirms Jesus' and Christianity's origins in Judaism as well as the succession from Judaism to Christianity. This is a careful balancing act. The universal Christianity proclaimed by Ignatius must contain the right amount of Judaism, in the right proportion and relationship to Christianity: no more and no less.[55] Ignatius shifts the meaning of Judaism to define its value only insofar as it has witnessed and yielded to Christianity.

The rhetoric of difference for "Judaizers," then, is not heresiological. Rather, acknowledging Christianity's Jewish origins, Ignatius negotiates with these "Jewish" Christians under the *topos* of unity.[56] The "Judaizing" Christians remain part of the church, unlike the docetists who have withdrawn and whom Ignatius refuses to recognize, only demonize. Ignatius realizes that there will be conversations between different Christians over the relationship of Christianity to the Hebrew scriptures (*Phld.* 8.2). He attempts to stifle this by warning the Philadelphians not to listen to these discussions (*mē akouete, Phld.* 6.1; *pheugete oun,* 6.2), even associating such "evil designs and snares" with the demonic "ruler of this age" (6.2). This strategy of avoidance does not lead to heresiology but an appeal to unity: "all of you should stand in agreement (*epi to auto*) with an undivided (*ameristō*) heart" (6.2).

Ignatius thus firmly places himself in the rhetorical center among these other Christians: docetic, Jewish, charismatic, and no doubt other varieties unknown to us. Channeling opposition into one united group is a heresiological move. It has been argued recently that some of his opponents valued prophetic charisma over episcopal authority.[57] Christians writing in Paul's name in the late first and early second century, from Colossians to 1 Timothy, argued against revelatory visions in favor of traditional authority. While Ignatius spoke prophetically at Philadelphia, his prophecy supported the ecclesiastical hierarchy over new prophetic revelations: "I cried out while among you, speaking in a great voice, the voice of God, 'Pay attention to the bishop and the presbytery and the deacons'" (*Phld.* 7.1).[58] Ignatius was the earliest advocate, and one of the strongest, of the monarchical episcopate. Schoedel's significant contribution was reading this as a rhetorical posture rather than reflection of actual ecclesiology in Antioch or Asia. In other words, Ignatius believed that the bishop should rule the churches absolutely and wrote as if this were the case, when in fact all Christians did not accept this authority. The power of the bishop comes from the office itself rather than prophetic charisma. In Weberian terms, Ignatius thus links traditional and institutional authority. Ignatius demurs that his authority approaches the apostle (*Trall.* 3.3), but is clear that the bishop has replaced the apostle. The bishop is the "image of the Father" while presbyters are the council of apostles and the deacons associated with the service of Jesus Christ (*Trall.* 3.1; cf. *Magn.* 6.1). While this analogy places the bishop in God's position rather than the apostles', in practical terms the bishop takes the place of Peter or Paul.

The monarchical bishop guides and represents the unity of the church and hence the universality of its dogma. Ignatius warns the Smyrnans to "flee divisions" (*Smyrn.* 7.2) even though he has also exhorted them to "avoid such people" in the previous sentence, creating the very division he warns against. As with Paul in Galatians, Ignatius creates schisms and then claims his opponents are part of a faction (*hairesis*) while he and his followers are not.[59] And he moves immediately from this ironic appeal to unity to exhortations about the bishop (*Smyrn.* 8.1). The episcopate unifies the church, in Ignatius' mind. It also unifies *opposition* to the church against the authority of the bishop, whether by docetic separatists, Judaizing traditionalists, prophets, or some other Christian group opposed by Ignatius. The ideology of heresy constructs a unified web of opposition to the one true church, a church that Ignatius equates with the bishop.[60]

In contrast, the *Epistle to the Romans* is a non-heresiological response to difference in the Christian *ekklēsiai*. As noted earlier, Ignatius writes in the company of "ten leopards" (*Rom.* 5.1), Roman soldiers taking him to die in the arena in Rome. He embraces this fate "that I not only be called a Christian but also be found one." Ignatius argues, in graphic phrases, that he must die for Christ to be a true disciple of Christ (*Rom.* 2.1–2; 4.1–2). But there were clearly different views on the necessity of martyrdom in the church.[61] Ignatius signals his concern early in the letter that he is "afraid of your love, that it may do me harm" (1.2). He is arguing against other Christians with the will or means to prevent his death in Rome; this is the main point of the letter. The necessity of martyrdom was clearly a matter of difference. But this was not a dogmatic issue. Therefore, Ignatius does not view this difference as an example of heresy nor does he employ heresiological rhetoric. Rather, he cajoles, begs, and attempts to persuade them not to assist "the ruler of this age" (7.1). Like Odysseus before the Sirens, he anticipates changing his mind but urges them "instead be persuaded by what I am writing to you now" (7.2). He cannot order them to do this "as Peter and Paul did" (4.3), since he is not their bishop. This rhetoric of martyrdom in *Romans* marks a clear difference from his heresiological response to docetic Christians in the other epistles.

Ignatius uses the words Christian and Christianity more than any writer to this point and among the most frequently of the "Apostolic Fathers." As with Judaism earlier, he has a clear idea of what it means. Indeed, Ignatius takes for granted terms that Justin Martyr contests in his *First Apology*, as discussed in Chapter 1. "Christianity" in the epistles of Ignatius expresses the politics of one orthodox, universal church. This is the rhetorical posture of political hegemony, even if the posture did not fit the social context of the diverse Christian churches. He uses variations of Christianity in contrast to Judaism in *Magnesians* and *Philadelphians* (*Christianismos*,

Magn. 10.1, 3; *Phld.* 6.1). He uses "Christian" (*Christianos*) in *Trall.* 6.1 against docetists, linking them with "heresy." He uses Christianity in *Rom.* 3.2–3 in connection with his anticipated martyrdom (cf. 7.3). And he associates Christianity with subservience to the bishop (*Magn.* 4.1). Thus when he writes to the Ephesians that he hopes to "share the lot of the Ephesian Christians, who have always agreed with the apostles by the power of Jesus Christ" (11.2), Ignatius expresses the ideology of orthodox Christianity, a universal church with unified dogma and hegemony under the authority of one bishop.

THE GOSPEL OF JUDAS

The final text in this chapter is the *Gospel of Judas*. The title has been known for centuries from Irenaeus' mention of "Cainites" who base their beliefs on a "fictitious *Gospel of Judas*" (*Haer.* 1.31.1). Part of this text was re-discovered in the Codex Tchachos and recently published.[62] As with the *Gospel of Mary* earlier and the Gospels studied in Chapter 5, I read the theology of the community and its relations with other Christians, Jews, or outsiders symbolically through the story of Jesus and the twelve disciples. The opposition in this second-century text could reflect interactions with communities that wrote or read the Pastoral Epistles or letters of Ignatius as well as other Gnostic Christian communities.

The theology of the Gospel of Judas exhibits a Sethian Gnostic perspective. The latter word, "Gnostic," I employ as a descriptive term for a religious worldview rather than a label for a specific community, the "Gnostic Christians." Sethian Gnosticism refers to a group of texts, called "Classic" Gnosticism by Bentley Layton, which receives its fullest exposition in the *Apocryphon* or *Secret Book of John*.[63] The details of this complex cosmology are not central to my argument, except the degree to which they marked ideological differences between the community of Judas and other Christians. Key features and characters of the cosmology in the *Gospel of Judas* include the origin of the spiritual universe in the One; Autogenes the Self-Generated and Barbelo, who make up the divine triad; the four heavenly luminaries; the "corruptible Sophia" and her offspring, the creator of the material world, called Nebro and Yaldabaoth, and his collaborator Saklas. Central to this worldview is that Yaldabaoth and Saklas rule this world and have imprisoned the spiritual ones in bodies. Christ/Seth was sent to free the spiritual ones and bring them back to the heavenly realm. The Gnostic worldview, more so than its mythology, is important to the rhetoric of difference because it is an esoteric worldview. People with gnosis (variously defined in different texts) have special insights into the nature of God and the universe that most people do not. This creates a divide between the "insiders," often self-labeled as *pneumatikoi* or "spiritual ones," and the majority without gnosis, the *psychikoi* and the *sarkikoi*, the "fleshy people."

Given the range of Christianities in the second century, it is certain that the community that produced the *Gospel of Judas* would have contentious relations with orthodox and other Christians. The choice of the anti-hero Judas alone marks this as an exceptional text. To be sure, there is a certain logic in honoring Judas, who managed to make the arrest and execution of Jesus possible in the canonical Gospels, in Christianities that believe the death of Jesus was a salvific and atoning act for humanity.[64] Jesus' death is theologically good and Judas engineered it. But this position does not seem to have held in orthodox Christianity at all. Paul never mentions Judas but he is demonized in the canonical Gospels and later traditions as the arch-traitor. The choice of Judas as hero, therefore, signals contentiousness with other Christian communities that the choice of Thomas, Phillip, or Mary in other Gospels does not.[65] Cain might have been honored as well because Cain opposed the God of this world.[66]

There are concentric rings of contentiousness in the *Gospel of Judas*: Judas against the other disciples; spiritual ones against the material world of Yaldabaoth; Yaldabaoth against Sophia; and Sophia against the other spiritual luminaries. Only in the One does contentiousness and division end. The Sethian Gnostic vision, therefore, is a vision of the end of division and restoration of unity. And the religious worldview reveals opposition to and from everyone else in the world until that unity has been achieved. The text itself includes contentious interchanges between Jesus and Judas on the one hand and the rest of the disciples on the other. In the opening dialogue (34), Jesus laughs, an unusual reaction in most Christian literature but relatively frequent in *Gospel of Judas*, when he sees the disciples giving thanksgiving over the food (or perhaps offering the Eucharist). While he is not laughing at them, he clearly sees them as misguided, even remarking that they and none of their "generation" know who he truly is.[67] The disciples represent other Christians, such as orthodox Christians, who do not have the gnosis of Sethian spiritual ones. The opposition between the communities of Judas on the one hand (the so-called "Cainites") and other Christians has been mapped onto the opposition between Judas and the disciples. They become angry while Judas confesses Jesus' true identity, "from the immortal realm of Barbelo" (35; cf. *Gos. Thom.* 13). He then receives special instruction from Jesus (36).

The next morning, Jesus appears to the disciples again, laughs at their lack of understanding, and then offers an alternative interpretation of the Temple in Jerusalem. He indicts the disciples for "the many people you lead astray before the altar" (38–41). Reading the social conflicts of the Judas community symbolically in the narrative of Jesus and the apostles, the Temple represents the ecclesial hierarchy of second-century orthodox Christianity, such as we saw inscribed in 1 Timothy and Ignatius. The Jerusalem Temple and authorities are fully indicted in the *Gospel of Judas* as enemies of Jesus and therefore stand for the enemies of the Judas community. The Gospel also marks the high priests and scribes as the enemies of Jesus in the concluding betrayal in the text (58). In a second dialogue between Jesus and Judas, Judas reports a vision in which "I saw myself as the twelve disciples were stoning me and persecuting me" (44–45). When Judas asks about his fate, Jesus responds "You will become the thirteenth [disciple] and you will be cursed by the other generations—and you will come to rule over them" (46–47).

Jesus then offers a more extended teaching about "[secrets] no person [has] ever seen," (47–53); that is, the Sethian cosmology sketched earlier. The divisiveness in the cosmology mirrors the Gnostic anthropology of spiritual against fleshly persons. Jesus describes the powers that Jews and other Christians worship as creator, El or God, speaking:

> "Let twelve angels come into being [to] rule over chaos and the [under-world]." And look, from the cloud appeared an [angel] whose face flashed with fire and whose appearance was defiled with blood. His name was Nebro, which means "rebel"; others call him Yaldabaoth. Another angel, Saklas, also came from the cloud. So Nebro created six angels—as well as Saklas—to be assistants, and these produced twelve angels in the heavens, with each one receiving a portion in the heavens. [51]

These are the divine rulers of the world who create Adam and Eve (or Zoe, 52–53). The dualistic Gnostic anthropology expressed here divides most people, who only receive spirit on loan from Michael, from the "spirits of the great generation," who receive spirits from Gabriel that resists the rulers of this world (53; cf. 36–37). God (the Great One) gives "knowledge" (gnosis) to Adam and descendants of the great generation to gain power against the "kings of chaos and the underworld" (54). Jesus identifies Judas as the one who will "sacrifice the man that clothes me" (56) by turning him over for death at the hands of the priests and the scribes (the betrayal, 58, which parallels the canonical accounts). This sets Judas apart from the other disciples, those "who have been baptized in your name . . . who offer sacrifices to Saklas" and have some association with "everything evil" (56): "But you will exceed all of them."

Jesus laughs again here at the end of the Gospel as he finishes his account of Gnostic cosmology and the plan for Judas to free his spirit. Judas alone understands Jesus' true identity and mission, similar to Thomas in the *Gospel of Thomas*, and receives instruction in a mythology with parallels to the *Apocryphon of John*. Judas betrays Jesus to his death, freeing him from his body and the rulers of the world and pointing the path to the Great One.[68] Death is essential. But in the *Gospel of Judas*, the essential death of Jesus is a double-reversal of the Pauline theology adopted by orthodox Christians. Paul struggled with the irony of the foolishness (*mōria*) of the cross, the humiliation that brings honor (1 Cor 1:18; 2:14; 3:19). In the *Gospel of Judas*, death is not humiliation but liberation for those with gnosis. Jesus shows Judas his star and he is transfigured at the end of the Gospel (57–58).

Others do not understand this: not only the high priests, who believed that they defeated Jesus, but also the orthodox, who still regard the crucifixion as shameful according to the standards of this world. They do not understand who or what they worship, or even why.

The rhetoric of difference in the *Gospel of Judas* complements the irony of this theological reversal. Jesus laughs because his "followers" are benighted; the joke is on them. Irony is key to this rhetoric of difference. Where the *Gospel of Mary* treats difference by means of elision, the *Gospel of Judas* employs the rhetoric of derision. Jesus, the Sethian Christ and second Adam who delivers the Gnostic message of salvation, ironically mocks the befuddled disciples for their ignorance. The dualistic divisions in the cosmos and soteriology of the *Gospel of Judas* mirror the differences between the Christians who followed these teachings and orthodox Christians. In the esoteric soteriology of Sethian Gnosticism, there is no eschatological imperative to confront the *sarkikoi* who lack gnosis. Laughing at them is the best course of action. This discursive response likely reflects a social reality in which various Gnostic Christian groups either withdrew from orthodox communities or remained within as an esoteric cell. Gnostic soteriology does not demand confrontation of the satanic other but rather allows for avoidance, pity, or, here, ridicule. The rhetoric of derision in the *Gospel of Judas* presents an alternative rhetoric of difference to both the *Gospel of Mary* and orthodox heresiology.

CONCLUSIONS

The full expression of early orthodox heresiology for policing the boundaries of the community emerges in late first- and early second-century Christian texts. The valorization of received tradition is central to the ideology of heresy. Notions of apostolicity, scripture, and patriarchal authority function as metonyms for tradition. Other important elements include the authority of ecclesial officers over prophets; the centrality of dogma; and the demonization and doxography of difference. The two texts with clear instances of multiple opponents or errorists, Revelation and Ignatius, unify these other Christian teachers in a web of opposition to the true faith. Ignatius labels this as heresy. In the other texts it is not clear whether there are multiple opponents: for instance, the Colossians' "someone" and Johannine "antichrists." In the Pastoral Epistles, any deviation from the received tradition, whether by heretics or young widows, is condemned. Above all, the eschatological worldview of orthodox Christians supports the imperative to confront demonic opponents.

I compared these early orthodox responses to religious difference as heresy with the *Gospel of Mary* and the *Gospel of Judas*. In contrast to the orthodox texts that assert the salvific, atoning death of Jesus Christ, the *Gospel of Mary* emphasizes Jesus and Mary as guides for the ascent of the soul. In contrast to the Pastoral Epistles and Ignatius, Mary receives new revelations from Jesus and authorizes continuing illumination of the church. The *Gospel of Judas* is a counter-orthodox, Sethian Gnostic text opposing both the God of the Bible (Yaldaboath) and the apostles of the church. Judas realizes Jesus' true identity and Jesus gives him insight on escape from this world. In addition to these different Christologies and theologies, we saw different approaches to difference in these Gospels from the orthodox texts: the rhetoric of elision and the rhetoric of derision. Mary avoids contesting points of dogma with the other apostles. She sets out the extent of her vision and no more. By eliding the differences among the apostles, she achieves unity within the bickering group. Jesus, in contrast, in the *Gospel of Judas*, mocks the apostles who do not understand his true identity. While the other apostles will condemn Judas, he and Jesus know that their ignorance leads to perdition rather than life in the spiritual realm.

All religious communities have to police boundaries and mark insiders and outsiders. Each of these texts testifies to ideological differences within early Christian communities. These different *approaches* to difference, however, identify orthodox heresiology as a unique strategy, an ideological theme for Foucault. Ignatius, Polycarp, and the authors of 1 John and 1 Timothy did not seek reconciliation, unification, or common ground with their opponents. Nor did they take a strategy of mockery and avoidance, fully aware that these other Christians were doomed. That is the path of esoteric Christians with special knowledge; they have no need to confront others because they have the true insight into salvation. The apocalyptic, eschatological theory of the origin of difference and division leads to these political practices within the *ekklēsiai*. The orthodox leaders confront the demonic forces in their midst. These early orthodox leaders, armed with the ideology of heresy, attacked their opponents with a full range of polemical rhetoric. Both the orthodox and Gnostic texts are dualistic. Dualism is, however, necessary but not sufficient for heresy. The cosmology of *Judas* provides the origin of error in the rebellion of El, Yaldaboath, and Sakal. And the origin of error in Gnostic cosmology results in an esoteric dualism that leads to avoidance, elision, or derision of others rather than heresiological confrontation.

In addition to policing the internal boundaries of the *ekklēsiai* for demonic forces, the orthodox Christians sought hegemony within all the Christian communities. The ideology of heresy is an inherently imperialistic discourse; orthodox Christianity seeks hegemony in the *ekklēsia* and the *oikoumenē*. We touched on some imperial themes earlier in the Pastoral Epistles; I now turn to the imperial rhetoric of heresy.

7 The Politics of Orthodoxy

The tribune came and asked Paul, "Tell me, are you a Roman citizen?" And he said, "Yes."

The tribune answered, "It cost me a large sum of money to get my citizenship." Paul said, "But I was born a citizen."

Acts 22:27–28

How could an association of Christians that valorized martyrs and martyrdom at the hands of the Roman authorities become the official religion of imperial Rome? Justin embodies a contradictory stance by arguing that his party of Christians was composed of worthy citizens of an empire destined to be destroyed by the hand of God at any moment. In the previous chapter we examined the internal political functions of heresiological rhetoric in late first- and second-century Christian social formations. But these early *ekklēsiai* were also colonial locations. The discourse of empire was integral to the rhetoric of heresy. In this chapter I will examine the foundations in the first- and second-century texts for what becomes imperial orthodox politics in the fourth century CE.

In Chapters 2 and 4, I examined respectively the imperialistic Hellenistic propaganda of the Hasmoneans and Paul's appeal to empire in his rhetoric of unity (*homonoia*) and rebellion (*stasis*) in the *ekklēsia*. In this chapter I will read orthodox Christian heresiology politically in two ways: in terms of its appeal to empire and as a product of empire. The early orthodox, motivated by apologetic concerns, tried to present their community as an ancient, non-transgressive social formation within the context of the traditional, Greco-Roman religion and culture. Positioning early orthodox Christianity *with* Rome also meant positioning themselves *against* other Christians. The discourse of Christian heresiology functioned politically against other Christians and for the Roman Empire. My approach foregrounds the ways in which early orthodox politics were entwined with Roman ideology. I read this discourse not within the traditional binary of "Christianity vs. Rome" (i.e., "Word against World"), but as a product of empire.[1]

Eschatological politics—that is, the problem of whether or when Christ might return—and the social position of the *ekklēsia* in the *oikoumenē*— that is, the political loyalties of Christians to the state—were the arenas for political self-definition in the orthodox project. Let us discuss first the problematic of Christianity and empire. Scholars of the New Testament and early Christianity have increasingly identified resistance and subversion as key themes. Early Christians are seen as agents of political dissent, from the revolutionary Jesus, to the subversive Paul, to anti-imperialist rhetoric in later Christian writings.[2] Yet these readings of early Christian texts interpret early orthodox politics via contemporary liberal political ideologies. The Roman Empire was tolerant of cults with ancient roots. While Christians were often suspect as part of a "new superstition," the connection with the tolerated religion of the Judeans helped Roman acceptance of Christians, although the elision of Jews and Christians brought anti-Jewish sentiment to bear on the new *ekklēsiai* as well.[3] Furthermore, Christians from Paul forward made explicit appeals to Roman power and administrators, even more so at the expense of the disgraced and defeated Judeans post-72 CE. These appeals to empire implicate early orthodox discourse with Roman ideology, even if the politics of orthodoxy were subversive in the attempt to create a Christian empire. Most significantly, the orthodox heresiological rhetoric appealed to empire to exclude and suppress alternative Christianities.

The eschatologies of the Deutero-Pauline letters and Revelation point to the second arena of ideological contest in the post-Pauline communities in Asia. The progression from persecuted cult to religion of the Empire required renegotiation of Christian eschatological expectations. The Apocalypse expresses eschatological politics most fully as it inscribes the destruction and re-formation of Roman society as a Christian theocracy.[4] In direct contrast, the Deutero-Pauline epistles and 1 Peter reformulate Paul's apology for Roman authority in Romans 13, laying the discursive foundations for a Christian society. While the redemptive trope of allegory would eventually reclaim Revelation for the orthodox canon, the apologetics of Luke-Acts (discussed ahead) and the Pastoral Epistles (in the previous chapter) re-position the early orthodox church to embrace Greco-Roman culture and society more heartily, in spite of—or after—the quest for martyrdom and apocalyptic eschatology fades.

SHADOWS OF EMPIRE

Every aspect of early Christianity, from the communities of James, Peter, and Paul in Jerusalem and Thessaloniki to the *ekklēsiai* of Ephesus in the second century, was situated in the Roman Empire. It is difficult to reconstruct how Roman power was conceived and negotiated by these different Christian communities. But there was clearly a spectrum of power, as well as a spectrum of acceptance or resistance to Rome. This power could be expressed in brutal executions and slavery; the ideology of the *mos maiorum*; in sacrifices to the Capitoline Triad of Gods, *Roma*, and the emperor himself; in taxes, tariffs, and bribes; in patronage and processions. Roman power was as multifarious as the Empire. In order to illustrate this diversity,

I have chosen three points on that spectrum in three structures that cast shadows of Roman power across different early Christian communities: the *Ara Pacis* in Rome; the Jerusalem Temple; and the Temple of the Sebastoi in Ephesus.

The Senate of Rome voted to build the *Ara Pacis* on July 4, 13 BCE.[5] Augustus described the actions this decree celebrated:

> When I returned from Spain and Gaul, in the consulship of Tiberius Nero and Publius Quintilius, after successful operations in those provinces, the Senate voted in honour of my return the consecration of an altar to Pax Augusta in the Campius Martius, and on this altar it ordered the magistrates and priests and Vestal virgins to make annual sacrifice. (*Res gestae* 12.2)[6]

He had spent three years in Lyons (Lugdunum) managing the campaigns of Drusus and Tiberius against the tribes north of the Alps; making diplomatic maneuvers to raise tribute from Gallia; and travelling through Iberia after Agrippa's fierce campaign. The official *dedicatio* was January 30, 9 BCE, some three and a half years later. It was erected on the northern Campus Martius, an open plateau where military and athletic exercises were carried out. The area included a sundial, the *Horologium Augusti*, with an obelisk Augustus acquired in Heliopolis, and his mausoleum to the north. A sacred grove stretched from the mausoleum and the *ustrinum*, where Augustus' remains were burnt. The entire complex would have been visible from the Tiber, perhaps to Christians making their way to Rome from Ostia in the first century.

The altar was about ten meters square. The four walls, decorated with two bands of reliefs, stood about six meters high on a large base of about two meters.[7] The design was the traditional *templum minus*, with a wooden fenced enclosure and decorated with cloths, garlands, and ox skulls (replicated in the interior frieze), with one opening leading to the *mensa*, the sacrificial altar. This traditional design of the *Ara Pacis* embodies the Roman ideologies of tradition, of the way of the ancestors or *mos maiorum*, and the emperor as father and priest. The west façade, which faced the Campius Martius, included two reliefs in the upper register depicting the sacred origins of the Romans.[8] On the right (south) stood the well-preserved, famous relief of Aeneas sacrificing to the *Penates*, the household gods and ancestors of his family. This relief clearly connects Augustus, who had been raised to *Pontifex Maximus* in 12 BCE, with Aeneas, the mythical ancestor of the *gens Iulia*; a small temple in the background might have suggested to Roman eyes the temple of the Penates on the Velian hill.[9] On the other side of the entrance to the *mensa*, also on the western side, stood a depiction of the Lupercal, the myth of Roman origins with Romulus and Remus. The eastern side held the relief of the mother goddess *Tellus* (*Terra Mater*), representing the bounty of the Empire and perhaps the *Pax Augusta*, and a panel of the goddess Roma, sitting on a pile of trophy weapons.[10] Connecting these reliefs, on the north and south walls of the altar, was a continuous procession of lictors, augurs, priests of the state religion or *flamines*, and the *Familia Augusta*. The south procession centers on Augustus himself, with veil and laurel wreath of a priest.[11]

Each of these decorative elements combines to express powerful Augustan ideologies: traditional, state-sponsored Roman religion presided over by the *flamines* and *Pontifex Maximus*; the emperor as *pater familias* of a family that honors the *mos maiorum* and is as well ordered as the Empire itself; and the benefits of the *Pax Romana*. The lost figure of *Roma* expresses best the contradictory nature of the *Pax Romana*, seated on a pile of weapons (also depicted on Neronian *sestertii* struck in 65 CE). This image recalls the famous line of the British chieftain Calcagus, recorded by Tacitus in the *Agricola* 30: "To ravage, to slaughter, to usurp under false titles, they call empire; and where they make a desert, they call it peace."[12] The *Ara Pacis* shows Roman power ideologically figured as peace.

The second structure is not Roman at all, the Second Temple in Jerusalem. But the arc of its construction and destruction tells a tale of Roman power and military might in the colonies. Herod the Great ruled effectively in Judea and represented Roman interests from 37 to 4 BCE.[13] His success corresponds to and complements the *Pax Augustana*, as Herod skillfully negotiated the shifting tides of the civil war after the death of Julius Caesar. He attached himself as a client to the victorious Octavius (Augustus) in 31 BCE after having supported his rival Marcus Antonius.[14] Around 19 BCE, just before Augustus' campaign in Gaul that resulted in the *Ara Pacis*, Herod launched an ambitious building project on the Temple that included tearing down the sixth-century BCE structure added on to by the Hasmoneans; filling in the southern end of the Temple Mount with gigantic quarried stones; constructing the massive new wall and colonnades; the courts of the Gentiles and of Women; and the Holy of Holies itself. Construction continued well into the 50s CE.

Herod ruled the kingdom of Israel and one of his sons, Herod Antipas, ruled as Roman client in Galilee during the time of Jesus. There was extensive social and political instability in Judea after his death that marked the problematic reign of his son Archelaus (4 BCE–6 CE); the story of the slaughter of the innocents in Matt 2:16 probably reflects the legendary memory of this period around Jesus' birth, as well as Herod's tendency to assassinate members of his own family. Judea was ruled directly by Roman procurators and prefects after Archelaus with the exception of Herod Agrippa I, who ruled Judea from 41 to 44, and his son Agrippa II, the last Herod who ruled from 48 to the 90s.

A relatively small number of regular and auxiliary Roman soldiers were stationed in Judea, perhaps three thousand, dispersed between the headquarters in Caesarea and various smaller garrisons such as the Antonia tower in Jerusalem.[15] A larger force came to Jerusalem during festivals at the Jerusalem Temple. While the passion stories in the Gospels have focused attention on the most famous crucifixion, and most infamous Roman ruler, of all time, Pontius Pilate's crucifixion of Jesus was typical of Pilate in particular and the official Roman response to disturbance or insurrection.[16] Josephus describes Pilate as ready to take swift military action in Judea against protests over Caesar's *eikones* (standards) in Jerusalem and construction of an aqueduct with Temple funds (*J.W.* 2.169–77). Pilate was, of course, neither the first nor the last Roman magistrate to exercise *imperium* via violence in Judea. Crucifixion was an instrument of Roman power well known throughout this period and area. Syrian legions under Varus crucified about two thousand Judeans after the death of Herod the Great (*J.W.* 2.66–57). The procurators Felix and Florus also crucified many Judeans regularly.

The Jewish civil war and revolt against Rome in 66–70 resulted in a massive military intervention, focusing ultimately on the Temple. The war itself was a product of sectarian and social unrest within Judea and Galilee during a time of political upheaval in Italy, all intersecting with the imperial ambitions of the Flavian family.[17] After Vespasian secured power in Rome, Titus returned to Judea and destroyed the Temple; I will examine Josephus' account of this ahead. The revolt and defeat of Judea, a victory celebrated on Vespasian's coins depicting *Judea captiva* and Titus' arch in Rome, foregrounded negotiation with Roman power as the central political task for the growing Christian communities. Constructed primarily during *Pax Augustana*, the destroyed Temple in Jerusalem represents the intersection of early Christianity and Roman military power.

Before turning to the aftermath of the Jewish War, however, let us consider the situation for Diaspora Jews and early Christians in the province of Asia Minor. There is no hint of future trouble with Rome in Paul's letters; rather, trouble with the Jewish authorities in the synagogues as well as the other Christians in Antioch and Jerusalem is in the forefront.[18] In Acts 19:35–41, the "town clerk" (*ho grammateus*) seems concerned with avoiding any disturbance that could result in Roman intervention. Asia Minor in the first century was a peaceful part of the Roman Empire with almost no military presence. Legions were needed in the *limes* (borders) and in strategic areas such as Egypt but not in Corinth, Ephesus, Smyrna, or Sardis. There was no legion stationed in Asia from Augustus until the invasions of the third century CE.[19] A Christian in Ephesus was unlikely to see a group of Roman soldiers larger than the contingent that took Ignatius to Rome for his hearing and execution.[20]

But power can be expressed in ways other than military might. In Asia the fabric of power in social and cultural life was intertwined with the phenomenon of "emperor worship," or the imperial cult. This brings us to our third structure, the Temple of the Sebastoi in Ephesus (popularly referred to as the Temple of Domitian). Set in a prominent spot near the Upper Agora, a spot that dominates the southeastern end of the city, the temple was placed on a monumental terrace over eighty meters long and almost sixty-five meters wide.[21] It was dedicated in 89/90 CE, during Domitian's reign. The dedication probably included Olympic games celebrating Domitian as Zeus Olympios. These games and cult continued through the second century, rededicated to Hadrian.

The imperial cult in Asian cities was part of a social ritual of gift giving and receiving, a negotiation of power and favor that is difficult to divide into our contemporary categories of religious or political.[22] This temple in Ephesus, the third imperial temple built in Asia in the first century, marks an important development in the cult, which Friesen has called "an evolving imperial discourse."[23] The two previous temples, in Pergamon to Augustus and Smyrna to Tiberius, both included *Roma*, the Senate, and, in Smyrna, Livia, the imperial mother. But the Temple of the Sebastoi celebrated only the Flavian family, including the revered Vespasian, the first emperor to have a son succeed him; Titus; and, until his *damnatio memoriae* by the Senate after his assassination, Domitian himself.[24] In Ephesus the Flavian imperial family stood alone for Roman power and authority in Asia. As Friesen and Price have shown, different cities in Asia used the imperial cult as a point of negotiation with each other as well as with Rome—for instance, the donated inscription from Aphrodisias in Ephesus that attempts to place Aphrodisias as the superior party in the relationship.[25] But here too, Rome's imperial power was at the center. The increasing frequency of the word *neōkoros*, "custodian of the temple," in second-century and later inscriptions reveals this as "the most coveted civic title" in Asia. While Palestinian and Syrian Christians faced Roman military power, for the developing Christian communities of Asia Minor, negotiation with Roman power meant negotiation with the imperial cult.

THE JEWISH WAR WITH ROME

Responses to the War

Jewish responses to the destruction of the Jerusalem Temple were shaped by the memory of the destruction of Solomon's Temple by the Babylonians in 586 BCE. Rome becomes encoded as "Babylon" in Jewish and Christian sources. But within Second Temple Judaism responses were by no means univocal. The messianic apocalypse 4 Ezra, written in or near Palestine at the end of the first century and preserved in the Christian literature as part of 2 Esdras, and the anti-messianic historian Flavius Josephus inscribe different ideological paths after 70 CE. These different Jewish responses recapitulate the different responses we saw in Chapter 2 to the desecration of the Temple by Antiochus IV and outline the ideological range for Christian negotiations with Roman power.[26]

4 Ezra

While the narrative is set in Babylon after the destruction of Solomon's Temple, 4 Ezra focuses on the destruction of the Second Temple by the Romans.[27] Theodicy or God's justice is the central problem in 4 Ezra: why do bad things happen to good people while the evil prosper? "I was troubled as I lay on my bed, and my thoughts welled up in my heart, because I saw the desolation of Zion and the wealth of those who lived in Babylon" (4 Ezra 3:1–2). Deuteronomic theodicy had developed during the Second Temple period to explain misfortunes on the sins of the people. As with Job and his "comforters," the seer of 4 Ezra rejects that standard solution, adopting instead a mystical, apocalyptic response. The first three of his seven visions focus on God's lack of justice and the evil of the Romans. Despite the prayers of his people, God has turned Israel over to nations that "abound in wealth" but are "unmindful of [God's] commandments" (3:33). In dialogue with the angel Uriel, Ezra refuses to accept an easy explanation for the plight of Israel but holds God responsible for the plight of Jerusalem and humanity.

The turning point of the book is the central fourth vision of a weeping woman (4 Ezra 9:23–10:4). Like Ezra himself, the woman refuses to be consoled for the death of her only son, born late in her life, on his wedding night. Ezra responds angrily that the woman mourns her own loss while all Zion mourns the loss of the holy city and Temple. He gives her a taste of what he himself refuses to accept: "For if you acknowledge the decree of God to be just, you will receive your son back in due time" (10:16). As he continues to console and berate her (10:19–24), the woman is suddenly transformed into a vision of the heavenly Jerusalem itself: "a city was being built, and a place of huge foundations showed itself." The transformation in this vision corresponds to a shift in theology from a rationalized struggle with theodicy to a political eschatology.[28] The fifth vision is of an eagle dominating the earth, overcoming rival "feathers" and "wings," before being destroyed by a lion. The interpreting angel equates the eagle with the fourth kingdom from Daniel 7, clearly here Rome, and the lion with the Messiah of the Most High. The sixth vision, which also reinterprets Daniel 7, is a vision of the Messiah and the Messianic kingdom. Finally, in the seventh vision, the angel surveys history in *vaticinium ex eventu* (prophecy after the event), "predicting" the rise and eventual fall of the Roman Empire.

In the aftermath of the Jewish War with Rome, apocalyptic eschatology would clearly have been a compelling worldview. This ideology allowed Jews to place hope in deliverance from God and to maintain political distance from, or indeed resistance to, the victorious Romans. Resistance was a course of action after 70 CE. Jews held out against the Romans until 73 at Masada and resistance to Roman rule in Judea continued for over fifty years. Subsequent Jewish apocalypses, such as *Second Baruch*, testify to the continuing apocalyptic hopes of Jews for divine intervention and restoration. Many Jews in Palestine, most notably the prominent sage Rabbi Akiba, followed the messianic movement led by Simon Bar-Kosiba, labeling him "Bar Kokhba," "Son of a Star" (cf. Num 24:17). This movement led to a second, even more disastrous revolt and defeat at the hands of the Romans in 132, a defeat that set the groundwork for the rejection of apocalyptic, messianic ideology by the Jewish rabbinic leaders.

Josephus and the Rehabilitation of Rome

While apocalyptic, messianic ideologies fueled continuing resistance to Roman rule and subsequent revolts by Jews, Josephus suggests a different political path via the ideology of accommodation.[29] Josephus' well-known pro-Roman stance was forged, remarkably, as he led Jewish forces in Galilee against the Roman army. The political future of the Empire was inscribed in his very biography. He was an apologist for Judaism to the Romans and for Rome to the Jews; his writings divide somewhat along these lines.[30] In the first work still extant, *The Jewish War*, composed between 75 and 79 CE, Josephus tried to explain himself and his Roman patrons to a Jewish audience that must have been skeptical, bitter, or militant.[31] The later works, the twenty-volume *Jewish Antiquities* and the polemical *Against Apion*, defend the antiquity and validity of Judaism to the Gentile Roman audience.[32] Finally, Josephus' *Life* is a defense of his actions as well as a view into aristocratic circles of the late Second Temple period. All these texts, of course, have multiple functions.

The *War*, a translation of a lost Aramaic work sent to the "barbarians in the interior," was addressed to "the subjects of the Romans" (*tois kata tēn Romaiōn hēgemonian*, 1.3) with the purpose of explaining "the truth in affairs" of the great upheavals that had engulfed Rome itself, with the year of four emperors in 69, and the war against the Jews during 66–72 CE. The audience was familiar with the social and religious complexities of Second Temple Judaism, as well as with the destruction of the Temple and Josephus' checkered career.[33]

The Jewish War represents Rome not as antagonistic victor but as God's chosen instrument. For Josephus, priest and prophetic reader of the Bible, God had ordained Roman rule.[34] Biblical prophetic historiography was an influence on Josephus, such as Daniel's visions of four successive empires (a schema used in Greek historiography from Hesiod).[35] Looking at the same passages from Daniel 2 and 7 as 4 Ezra 11:1 and 12:11, he sees the plan of God in the establishment of the fourth kingdom rather than the apocalyptic demise of Rome. This was not a messianic reading but a prophetic statement of Roman imperial ideology.[36] The role of fate and providence, *tychē* and *pronoia*, has been well documented in Josephus' account of the fall of Judea and the rise of Rome.[37] God shines on the Romans. They have demonstrated virtue, *aretē*—for instance, in the organization and training of their army—but they also have fortune. The rise of Rome was predicted by the prophets.

Josephus minimizes or ignores excessive Roman violence. In the *Antiquities*, he presents Pilate in a favorable light, explaining that his soldiers "inflicted much harder blows than Pilate had ordered" and that the crucifixion of Jesus was "on the accusation of men of the highest standing among us" (*Ant*. 18.3.3). Like the author of 4 Ezra, Josephus also considers God's justice in the destruction of the Temple in the *War*, but as an apologist for the Romans rather than apocalyptic prophet of Jewish redemption. His homage to Rome and minimization of its brutality against the Jews, particularly the destruction of the Temple itself by Titus, are part of a complex narrative of self-defense. At the moment of destruction, the gaze becomes blank in a well-known ellipsis. In Josephus' telling, Titus (called "Caesar" in *J.W.* 6) never planned to destroy the Temple itself and dispatched soldiers to extinguish the fire burning in the inner court as a result of the final battle. But the Zealot insurgents attacked one last desperate time, and the Romans put flame to the sanctuary itself (6.251–53). "Caesar, both by voice and hand, signaled to the combatants to extinguish the fire," but burn it did. Titus can only gaze on the massive edifice. "Thus, against Caesar's wishes, was the temple set on fire" (6.266). But Josephus' version was belied by the display of Temple treasures in the Triumph and recorded on the Arch of Titus in Rome.

Writing the *Jewish War* from his Jewish aristocratic context, Josephus blames the war on a minority of zealots and bandits within the Judeans. His distaste for lower-class agitators results in a highly developed "rhetoric of excoriation" for banditry.[38] Josephus blames the social unrest on zealot revolutionaries, bandits, and brigands in Judea rather than Roman policy itself.[39] While Josephus' idea of the causes of the war has been carefully studied and criticized, the point here is the elision of Judean and Roman aristocratic interests.[40] Josephus lives out his days in Rome supported not only by the Flavian pension but also by the proceeds from his Judean estates. The Judean elite would not naturally see an alliance of Jewish and Roman interests; the scribe in 4 Ezra is likely from the intellectual elite as well.[41] Josephus, the transplanted Judean *Flavius* Josephus, constructs a hybridized Jewish-Roman ideology that celebrates the colonizer from within the metropole, while 4 Ezra, forging a post-destruction identity as colonized subject in "Babylon," envisions a post-apocalyptic New Jerusalem completely unmoored from Roman historical realities.

CHRISTIANITY AND ROME

Christian patterns of resistance and accommodation followed these Jewish traditions. The messianic, apocalyptic roots of Christianity suggest the path of eschatological resistance rather than accommodation. Both John the Baptist and Jesus were executed as political agitators, by Herod Antipas in Galilee and by Pilate in Jerusalem, the later in collusion with the Jewish high priests. It is likely that many of Jesus' first followers were also executed; Church legend at least assigns martyrdom to most of the apostles. But early orthodox Christianity becomes less subversive and increasingly quietest in the late first and early second centuries due to the dampening effects of eschatological reservations and explicit appeals to shared Greco-Roman political values with Gentile converts. Good relations with Rome were politically expedient for social standing. This move to "bourgeois Christianity" in the second century, to use Hans Conzelmann's famous phrase for the Pastoral Epistles, is well known. But what has not been explored is the ways in which the rhetoric of heresiology mimics Roman ideology, implicating early orthodox Christianity in the rhetoric of empire in its demonization and exclusion of other Christianities.

JOHN AND JESUS

While Herod Antipas and Pontius Pilate certainly executed plenty of innocent victims, we have good evidence that both John the Baptist and Jesus provoked the authorities. According to the Gospels (Mark 6:17–29; par. Matt 14:3–12), John challenged Herod's marriage to Herodias, who was both his half-sister and his half-brother's wife. According to Josephus (*Ant.* 18.109–19), Herod feared that John would lead a popular revolt. As noted in Chapter 3, the two accounts can be reconciled and it is clear that John's prophetic and eschatological renewal movement had a strong political dimension.[42]

Jesus began his independent ministry in Galilee after John's arrest. Luke-Acts includes Simon the Zealot as one of Jesus' followers (Luke 6:15; Acts 1:13; called "Simon the Canaean" in Mark 3:18 and Matt 10:4). In Luke 23:2, the elders and chief priests accuse Jesus of sedition to Pilate.[43] Could Jesus have been associated with the Jewish "Zealots" who opposed Roman rule? While the Zealot party fueled resistance to Rome in the 60s, the existence of any such group during Jesus' time has been challenged.[44] Luke's perspective was influenced by the reputation of the Zealots during the Jewish War; they appear as a faction in the Temple after 66 CE (*J.W.* 4.161). Historians have conflated the various social revolutionary groups mentioned in the *Jewish War*—the Fourth Philosophy, the Zealots, and the Sicarii—as one continuous "Zealot" movement opposed to Rome during the first century CE.[45] As Horsley has argued, scholarly constructions of the Zealots during the time of Jesus allow a foil for a politically acceptable Jesus who found middle ground between the revolutionary Zealots and the accommodationist Sadducees and Herodians. The name itself is vague enough to include theological as well as political zeal; Luke uses the term to describe Paul in Acts 22:3.

While I would avoid elision of the wartime Zealots with all groups that opposed Rome or the Herodians, we should not underestimate the importance of the "Fourth Philosophy" of Judas of Galilee, developed in protest to the Roman census of 6 CE, as part of the ideological matrix of Jesus himself as well as his followers. Opposition to Herodian and Roman rule, drawing on Hebrew prophetic traditions, found multiple avenues in Second Temple Judaism.[46] Social banditry, prophetic opposition, and messianism were revolutionary political movements with deep biblical roots. That Luke, around the year 100 CE, would still associate Jesus and his followers with such revolutionary movements by naming one of them a Zealot suggests stronger opposition to Rome by Jesus than is often recognized.

Reading Jesus as an eschatological prophet foregrounds his actions of going to Jerusalem and "trashing" the Temple as gestures invoking or even forcing the arrival of the Kingdom of God.[47] While only symbolic (i.e., Jesus did not attack the Temple), this prophetic action had immediate consequences. Jesus was executed and his inner circle fled. If in fact one of this inner circle betrayed Jesus to the authorities, perhaps he intended to bring about the "Kingdom of God" during the festival of the Passover.

It is difficult to make claims for Jesus' political ideology separate from that of the Gospel writers and communities. Whether Jesus' actions during his final week in Jerusalem meant a symbolic, prophetic action disrupting Temple worship, a messianic revolt against Jewish and Roman authorities, or the eschatological kingdom of God on earth via the intervention of the Son of Man from Heaven is now very hard to decide. But clearly the eschatological theology of both John and Jesus quickly ran into opposition in Galilee and Jerusalem. They were not alone in first-century Palestine; numerous social and prophetic movements opposed the authorities in various ways.[48] Yet such movements did not survive long under the Romans, as the telling example of the Bar Kokhba revolt earlier shows. Passages such as the famous "Render unto Caesar what is Caesar's" (Mark 12:17; par. Matt 22:21; Luke 20:25) are redactional additions inscribing the increasing quietism of Christianity and ideology of accommodation, discussed ahead. The Gospels and other early Christian literature show increasing distance from the Jewish War and destruction of the Temple.[49] Christian orthodoxy developed a political theology for survival and eventual hegemony in the Roman world.

ENEMIES OF THE ROMAN ORDER

The politics of early Christianity formed within a larger context of dissent. Subversion, dissidents, and political rebellion have long been topics of study for scholars of Roman religions and early Christianity.[50] Stoic philosophers such as Dio Chrysostom were seen as subversive to the Empire and exiled under Nero and Domitian. Roman reactions to "new religious movements," such as Isis and Mithras, as well as dissident philosophers and nationalist groups in Egypt and Gaul could be xenophobic. "The Syrian Orontes has long since poured into the Tiber, bringing with it its lingo and its manners, its flutes and its slanting harp-strings" (Juv. *Sat.* III.61–63). But Juvenal's indictment of eastern mystery cults expressed traditional patrician values for the *mos maiorum* rather than the actual policies of the empire. In fact, the Romans were generally accepting of the religious customs of conquered peoples, often absorbing them into Roman religious life unless they perceived a political threat. The suppression of the Isis cult by Tiberius in 19 CE marks an exception to the standard practice of the Romans with religions from elsewhere in the Empire.

Where ethnic identities were strongly associated with traditional religious ideologies, conflict would arise. Expressions of such conflict, in addition to the Judeans, included the Druids in Gaul and some of the traditional expressions of Egyptian religion (e.g., *The Potter's Oracle*).[51] The frequent clashes between the Greek and Jewish communities in Alexandria, in which the emperors served as moderators (or in the case of Caligula, provocateurs), could be labeled as ethnic as much as religious conflict, although the Jewish community had been Hellenized for centuries. One of the first external accounts of Christians points to Jewish conflict within Rome. Claudius expelled the Jews from Rome because of disturbances instituted by "Chrestus" (Suet. *Claud.* 25; Acts 18:1–2).

ROMANS 13

The expulsion of the Jews from Rome by Claudius is also mentioned in Acts 18:2 to introduce Paul's coworkers Prisca and Aquila, who moved from Rome to Corinth at that time. Paul, our earliest Christian source, paradoxically planted the seeds of both apocalyptic revolution and political quietism in Christian discourse. Augustine and Luther mainstreamed Pauline theology and politics for the Western church, both Catholic and Protestant.[52] Only recently have scholars re-read Paul for views of alternative communities centered on a praxis of equality between genders and ethnicities.[53] Central passages such Gal 3:28 and the discussion of gender roles in 1 Corinthians (1 Cor 7:1–39; 11:2–16; 14:33–36) are the focus of Paul's sexual ethics. Slavery and class issues, mediated through Paul's basic Stoic ethics, are also central to the discussion of Pauline ethics. But the recovery of the "political Paul" remains tenuous.

In *Liberating Paul*, Neil Elliott has argued that Paul's theology of the cross evokes a strong political position against Rome.[54] He notes that crucifixion was reserved for the lower-class *humiliores*, arguing that Paul would have been aware of the social and political ramifications of Jesus' death at Roman hands. But Paul turns attention to the perpetrators only in the problematic 1 Thess 2:15–16, which Elliott labels a post-war interpolation, and in 1 Cor 2:8, "none of the rulers of this age understood [God's secret wisdom], for if they had, they would not have crucified the Lord of glory." This verse is thoroughly apocalyptic.[55] The death and resurrection of Jesus were, for Paul, the *krisis* points of cosmic history and the decisive point for human existence moving from the powers of sin and death to the powers of spirit and grace. But Elliott does not see the apocalyptic view of the crucifixion as apolitical; rather, Paul "internationalized" the significance of Jesus' death:

> He insists that the Roman colonists of Corinth, thousands of miles from Judea, must mold their lives into a constant remembrance of one particular crucifixion in Judea, because through the crucifixion God has revealed the imminent end of the Powers and has begun to bring "the scheme of this world" to an end (1 Cor. 7:31).[56]

Elliott tries to extend Paul's politics beyond his apocalyptic theology. While his exegesis of the eschatological tension in Paul's theology is on the mark, he cannot satisfactorily explain away the social quietism inherent in Paul's eschatological reservation.[57] To be sure, Paul does not celebrate triumph over the powers. They *will* be destroyed (1 Cor 2:6; 15:24); in the meantime, creation suffers and groans in anticipation (Rom 8:22–23). There is no doubt that, for Paul, God will ultimately and completely triumph. But in the meantime, "stay as you are" (1 Cor 7:17–24).[58] The cosmic and political victory is God's victory, through Christ. And while the Spirit lives *within* the *ekklēsia* and the Body of Christ, resulting in a life under Grace rather than Sin (Gal 5:22–26), the *ekklēsia* should treat the outside world with respect, quietly minding their own affairs (1 Thess 4:11–12; 1 Cor 6:1–6). The Pauline *ekklēsia* should not attempt to transform society. The triumph is in the *parousia* of Christ in the eschatological near-future. Paul's gospel is a gospel of cosmic and personal transformation (Rom 8:9–17; see *metamorphoō* 12:2), not social-political action.

This brings us to the *bête-noir* of Christian political ethics, Romans 13:1–7.[59] Despite some critics' efforts to mitigate the political ramifications of Paul's command to submit to authority, denying that this passage establishes a political theology, the Christian interpretive tradition elides the passive imperative of Paul's *hypotassesthō* in Romans 13:1 with a political imperative to be passively subject to rulers. Romans is a *general* letter introducing Paul's Gospel to the community, anticipating potential points of conflict and disagreement based on experiences in other communities, and generalizing, indeed *universalizing*, his theology. To this extent Elliott is correct with regard to Paul's theology of the cross. While critics of the political theology of Romans 13:1–7 have found comfort in limiting the significance of the passage to a particular situation, such as the avoidance of taxes or the treatment of the Jewish community in Rome, there is nothing particular about the passage.

Romans can be read as Paul's statement of universal theology in the light of particular problems. Just as Paul extends universally the significance of Christ's death and resurrection in Romans 4–8, he considers universally binding moral principles in Romans 12–15. (Romans 9:1–5 is hardly a theoretical concern but a troubling exception to Paul's universal Gospel, Romans 1:16). As part of the presentation of his universal gospel, Paul develops in Romans 1–3 what could be called a theory of religion and thus religious *difference*.[60] The Gospel of Christ is "the power of God for salvation to everyone who has faith (*tō pisteuonti*, NRSV "those who believe") and thus a new *typos* among religions. In arguing that the Gospel is the answer for both Jew and Greek, Paul develops a theory of religious difference that incorporates Greco-Roman religions as well as Judaism. The Gospel of Christ is a new species of the genus that relates humans to the divine, one that defeats the power of sin and death, the universal human condition, by means of the resurrection of Christ and the power of the Spirit. Such a universal notion of salvation inscribes its own imperialistic ideologies, as I showed with the *homonoia* trope in Chapter 4.

This modulation between universal claims and particular problems is the key for reading Romans 13. Scholars have interpreted the passage as part of the general moral *paraenesis* that begins in Romans 12:1.[61] The passage inscribes a general political theory because Paul could not conceive of a different political system or future for the *ekklēsia* beyond the impending *parousia*. But Paul was aware of potential problems between the *ekklēsia* and the authorities; anyone who had traveled the Empire as Paul had would have been aware of religious conflict. He himself had experienced punishments at the hands of the Romans as well as the Jews. While we should avoid mirror reading moral *paraenesis*, that does not mean that Paul and the recipients could not conceive of examples. For example, 1 Thess 4:3–4 does not necessarily imply that the Thessalonians were sexually profligate. But the exhortation there discursively constructs "Gentiles who do not know God." Romans 12–14 does not point to explicit problems in the Roman *ekklēsiai* over arguing within the community, subversion of the state, or eating meat purchased from the temple. But Paul and the Romans themselves could conceive of these problems with examples in mind. Both writer and audience would have been aware of groups who acted *against* these rules. Just as the Paul and the Thessalonians could conceive of giving way to lustful passions, perhaps with concrete examples in mind, so too the general exhortation in Romans 13:1–7 would evoke specific examples of social opposition and Roman oppression.[62] Paul therefore foregrounds the politics of the *ekklēsia* waiting for the *parousia*. Potential persecution of the *ekklēsia*, based on the treatment of Jews by the Romans, or persecution of Jews by the Christians, or concerns with taxes would all have been evoked by this passage. It is a "surprisingly unqualified call for submission to state authority."[63]

Romans develops a theory of religion, presents the Christian religion as a new and universal answer to sin and death, and probes the theological problem for Paul of the rejection of his gospel by the Jews. Without abandoning any eschatological reservation, Paul conceives of Christianity as a separate religion from Judaism that could be persecuted by the authorities. If Jews, and presumably some Greeks, reject the Gospel, then Christians become the "other" subject to the persecution of the state. Eschatological quietism is Paul's moral response, since these powers will be destroyed at the *parousia*. And yet this eschatological quietism masks a triumphant ideology of the universal power of Christ and grace against sin, death, and the ruling powers of the *kosmos*.[64] Paul cannot conceive of the Empire lasting beyond his lifetime. Therefore the power of Christ will replace the powers invoked in Romans 13. But in making this claim, he foreshadows the orthodox ideology of *ekklēsia* in Empire that is central to heresiological rhetoric against other Christian communities.

POST-PAULINE POLITICS

Romans 13 is not heresiological, although the rebellious other lurks here discursively in Paul's exhortation. What happens when the orthodox Christian tradition loses Paul's eschatological reservation but continues the *topos* of political quietism? I will trace this question in the Deutero-Pauline epistles, 1 Peter, and the politics of the Book of Revelation to show how orthodox politics acquires a heresiological function.

The Haustafel

The Deutero-Pauline epistles include the earliest examples of the Christian *Haustafel* or "household codes of duties," the classical text of patriarchal authority, as notorious in Christian traditions for submission of women and enslaved peoples as Romans 13 has been for enforcing submission to state authority.[65] While the role and function of the *Haustafel* in different letters continue to be debated, there is broad agreement on its origins in Greco-Roman moral philosophy and Hellenistic Judaism. The code invokes the ancient philosophical discussion of household management (e.g., Xen. *Oeconimicus*).[66] The *topos* appears in Hellenistic Jewish literature as well.[67] The code inscribes the ideological homology of *oikos* and *polis*; the power structures of a well-ordered household under the *paterfamilias* mimic the benevolent patriarchalism of the state under the emperor and, conversely, the well-ordered household consists of good citizens.[68] Contemporary critique of the code as oppressive has focused on gender and, to a lesser extent, class, in terms of the relation of master and slave. I will consider the *Haustafel* as political discourse. The code discursively negotiates a hybrid space between *ekklēsia* and *oikoumenē*, a political space in which the orthodox party constructs the ideology of patriarchal power construed as social stability while casting other Christians, *different* Christians, *heretical* Christians, as subversive to the Roman Empire.

Colossians and Ephesians

1 Peter is my primary *Haustafel*, but this is not the first Christian example. The sources set the political context for 1 Peter. I discussed the ideology of tradition and conflict with other Christians in Colossians in Chapter 6. The letter has little political rhetoric (Col 2:15) and only a few hints of concern with outsiders (4:5). This one reference to "those outside" in 4:5, significantly, follows close on the household code itself (Col 3:18–4:1). A command to prayer in 4:2–4 stands between the *Haustafel* and this short appeal to "conduct yourselves wisely" (*en sophia peripateite*) among outsiders. The letter thus links the image of stability in the *ekklēsia* presented by the *Haustafel* and the apologetic command with a gesture of community piety.

Ephesians presents a more complex, if also less specific, situation (note 2:20). The letter has an apologetic focus on outsiders. The "former life" of the implied Gentile audience functions metonymically to bring the "outsider" into the text (Eph 2:1–10; 4:17–19). The author uses political figures of moving from life "without Christ" to "in Christ Jesus": "remember that you were at that time without Christ, being aliens (*apēllotriōmenoi*) from the commonwealth (*politeias*) of Israel . . . So then you are no longer strangers and aliens (*paroikoi*), but you are citizens with the saints and also members of the household of God (*oikeioi tou theou*)" (Eph 2:12, 19; cf. *patria*, trans. "family," in 3:15). Strangers, aliens, and citizens were political categories expressing social status in the cities of the eastern Empire. In the discursive context of those political labels, the author elides *oikos* with *polis* and signals the political function of the *Haustafel* in Eph 5:21–6:9. Stable, well-ordered families and households make good citizens of the Empire.

The household codes in Colossians and Ephesians list the same actors: wives and husbands, children and fathers, masters and slaves. These codes emphasize submission to traditional authority (the husband, father, or master) along with reciprocity by the authoritative member for the state of the submissive one. The chain of benevolent patriarchalism in the ancient world extended from *polis* to *oikos*; the emperor was a benevolent *paterfamilias*. So too the Christian husband and father stands in the emperor's place within the family, representing the Christian *oikos* to the Empire and the Empire to the *oikos*. Both intertextually and ideologically, the codes renegotiate the social impact of Gal 3:28: "There is no longer Jew or Greek, there is no longer slave or free, there is no longer male and female, for all of you are one in Christ Jesus." There were most likely social disturbances within Christian communities acting out this baptismal ideal.[69] The codes in Colossians and Ephesians certainly suggest the possibility and include some intriguing hints. For instance, slaves receive longer instructions than masters and, in Ephesians, the exhortations to husbands are significantly longer than in Colossians. While the precise occasion for the inclusion of the *Haustafel* is debated, the very presence of the code in Colossians and Ephesians shows at the least an awareness of the problem of the appearance of social disturbance and, at the most, social disruption within the Church.[70]

1 Peter

Within the New Testament, the fullest expression of quietest politics and apologetic ideology is 1 Peter, a text that inscribes considerably more social stress in the *ekklēsia* than Colossians and Ephesians.[71] The authorship of 1 Peter has been a contentious issue because of both the ecclesial ideology of Petrine authority and the construct of the New Testament canon as "apostolic." The letter has been sourced variously to Pauline traditions, the Synoptic Gospels, Acts, and even James and Johannine traditions. Without eliminating the possibility of any literary dependence, particularly with the Deutero-Pauline traditions in Asia, it is more likely that the epistle contains a number of common Christian traditions.[72] In his analysis of authorship, Achtemeier concludes that 1 Peter contains a "linguistically stabilized [Christian] tradition" and "a fusion of Pauline and Synoptic elements," as well as an adaptation of Hebrew scripture reflecting Palestinian Jewish traditions, such as the Dead Sea Scrolls, more than Hellenistic religious thought.[73] This particular confluence of traditions in 1 Peter at the end of the first century is important. Achtemeier's formulation of "tradition" is fully enmeshed in the canonical frame of reference and the teleology of orthodoxy that demands critical interrogation.[74] At the end of the first century, "Christian traditions" were in no way monolithic. We have already examined different ideologies of difference in the non-canonical *Gospels of Thomas, Mary,* and *Judas* in Chapters 5 and 6. In formulating what Achtemeier labels "Christian tradition," we must remember that the author of 1 Peter chose some doctrines and rejected others. The particular constellation of traditions within the letter, then, marks it as the first fully orthodox Christian text. This intra-Christian polemical arena of contested Christian traditions signals a heresiological agenda as well. By choosing one constellation of Christian interests over others, the author re-inscribes the heresiological context of competing Christianities.

We find a number of early orthodox dogmatic positions in 1 Peter. In enumerating these positions, I am attempting to denaturalize this cluster rather than assume the teleology of orthodoxy. Christ's pre-existence is assumed in the letter and the eschatological events "at the end of the ages" are now complete. They are receiving "the salvation of your souls" (1:9). Christ was "destined before the foundation of the world, but revealed at the end of the ages for your sake" (1:20). God the Father and Christ are both fully divine, but the doctrine of the Trinity is not yet formulated; it is "the spirit of Christ" that speaks through the prophets in the scriptures (1:11). While the recipients are Greeks who have rejected their former life (1:14; 2:2) and now contrast their deeds to "the Gentiles" (2:12), the letter employs scriptural quotations as proof texts expressing the divine economy. God's saving act with Noah in the flood, for instance, prefigures (*antitypon*) the salvation of baptism (3:20–21). These are not the discursive formulations of a developing "Jesus movement" but an expression of the ideological foundations of orthodox Christian theology.

There are two important contrasts between the household codes in 1 Peter and the Deutero-Pauline letters. First, 1 Peter inscribes considerably more suffering within the community addressed than Colossians and Ephesians. The community is undergoing "tests," "trials," and "fiery ordeals," which the author theologizes as both redemptive and mimetic of Christ's sufferings (1:6–8; 3:14, 17; 4:12–13). Jewish apocalyptic traditions of redemptive, eschatological trials are part of the ideology of understanding this suffering (1:10–12; 4:12). Suffering means stress, rather than persecution. The clues in the letter suggest social ostracism or local persecutions rather than any organized imperial persecutions. They are accused of being Christians (4:16) as well as of being "a murderer, a thief, a criminal, or even a mischief maker [*allotriepiskopos*]" (4:15).[75] 1 Peter 3:15 could allude to actual trials: "Always be ready to make your defense [*apologian*] to anyone who demands from you an accounting for the hope that is in you." The author adds, "yet do it with gentleness and reverence [*phobou*]." Second, outsiders are much more in focus in 1 Peter, where apologetics are more integral to this letter to "aliens and exiles," than in Colossians or Ephesians: "Conduct yourselves honorably among the Gentiles, so that, though they malign you as evildoers, they may see your honorable deeds and glorify God when he comes to judge" (1 Peter 2:12; cf. 1 Thess 4:11–12; 1 Cor 14:16).

The household code follows this admonition with an explicitly political focus, reworking Paul's call to be subject to the authorities as part of its *Haustafel*. The dependence of 1 Peter on Romans is not literary as much as ideological in the call to be subordinate (*hypotassō*).[76] Several key phrases from Romans are repeated in 1 Peter. But whereas Paul makes an eschatological-political *argument* from his eschatological theology, as discussed earlier, 1 Peter takes a political position *theorized as central to orthodox identity*. Paul's political admonition functions as part of eschatological quietism. In 1 Peter, apologetics have replaced eschatology. "For it is by God's will that by doing right you should silence the ignorance of the foolish" (2:15). "To do right," (*agathopoiuntas*) is a technical term in 1 Peter for Christian action in an evil world. 1 Peter 2:11 and 3:13 frame the *Haustafel*; then the command to accept all governmental authority (i.e., human, *anthropinē*) is central to the ways in which Christians should "conduct yourselves honorably among the Gentiles" and do "what is good" (1 Peter 2:12, 3:13). By contextualizing the Pauline command to obey the authorities within the now-traditional *Haustafel*, which constructs a homology between *oikos* and *polis*, the letter links *ekklēsia* and *oikoumenē*. To be a Christian, an identity that 1 Peter fully embraces discursively, means to be a good citizen of the Empire, a project 1 Peter fully embraces ideologically.[77]

Outsiders, not other Christians, are the cause of stress on the recipients, the "fiery ordeal that is taking place among you," and the targets for the letter's apologetic focus. As the first orthodox Christian text, 1 Peter presents an interesting contrast and complement to 1 John (see Chapter 6). Unlike 1 John, which includes a doxography of heretical positions, only a few passages suggest heresiological rhetoric. There is a call for unity in 3:18 and the exhortation to obey the presbyters in 5:1ff. Finally, the author commends Silvanus as "a faithful brother," as well as the greetings from "your sister church in Babylon"—that is, Rome. The apologetic and aggressively pro-Roman stance of the Pauline tradition and 1 Peter suggests either extensive persecution of Christians in the Asian provinces or an alternative Christian politics opposed by the author. Scholars are in agreement that, while there was sporadic persecution and social ostracism of Christians in the late first and early second centuries (cf. Pliny *Ep.* 96), there was not extensive or empire-wide persecution until the third century. Since we can eliminate extensive persecution as the cause of the letter, we turn instead to an alternative Christian politics.

The Revelation of John

The code "Babylon" for Rome has a more notorious place in the New Testament than 1 Peter. Ranged against this quietist Pauline tradition is another eschatological politics that developed in Asia in the last quarter of the first century found in the Book of Revelation.[78] Even more than 1 Peter, Revelation seems to be crisis literature. John of Patmos' visions project a world in which Satan's forces wage fierce war against the saints of God. But the idea of an organized persecution of the Christian communities in Asia during Domitian's reign, when Revelation was completed, is unlikely.[79] Social stress and ostracism, as with 1 Peter, seem more likely. The Apocalypse does not reflect a crisis as much as it attempts to create one within the *ekklēsiai* of Asia.[80] Revelation also inscribes challenges to the Pauline politics of 1 Peter. The apocalyptic eschatology and political theology of Revelation challenged involvement with Greco-Roman society.

The prophet John's activity in the *ekklēsiai* of Asia Minor was contemporaneous to the composition of the Deutero-Pauline texts and almost certainly known to the authors of the later Pastoral Epistles. John and his circle of prophets, basing their power on apocalyptic visions, would have been destabilizing in the Pauline communities of the late first century, which were building creedal formulations based on received traditions. Specifically these include challenging the Pauline compromise on eating meat purchased from the temples, ideologically implicated in the Apocalypse as idolatry, as well as the authority of received tradition. And, as I showed in Chapter 6, of all late first-century New Testament texts, the Apocalypse is the most connected intertextually and rhetorically with other Christian leaders and groups: "false apostles" in Ephesus; the "Nicolaitans" in Ephesus and Pergamum; "Jezebel" and her disciples in Thyatira; "those who hold to the teaching of Balaam" in Pergamum; and "those who say they are Jews and are not" in Smyrna and Philadelphia (see Rev 2:2, 6, 9, 14, 20–23; 3:9).

Rome is polyphonically figured in Revelation. For the ancient auditor and modern reader alike, "Babylon" in Revelation is clearly marked as Rome in 17:9–18: "this calls for a mind that has wisdom (*sophian*): the seven heads are seven mountains on which the woman is seated . . . the woman you saw is the great city that rules over the kings of the earth." More "wisdom" is called for in the infamous *gematria* of Rev 13:18: "let anyone with understanding (*noun*) calculate the number of the beast, for it is the number of a person. Its number is six hundred sixty-six." While there are numerous potential referents for the "mark of the beast," most scholars see 13:18 as code for Nero Caesar, invoking the myth of *Nero Redivus*.[81] The "beast from the sea" suggests the emperor across the sea from Asia while the second beast, "from the land," signals the high priest of the imperial cult in Asia Minor.[82] Revelation 13 is a vision of these two beasts gaining complete social, political, religious, and economic control over "the whole earth" (*holē hē gē*).[83] Revelation 17–18 is an ecphrastic vision of Rome/Babylon, the Harlot and the City, disfigured, raped, and proleptically destroyed by the forces of heaven.[84]

While reading Revelation as vehemently opposed to aspects of Greco-Roman culture and Roman imperialism, I reject the methodology implied in traditional "Revelation against Rome" interpretations. Such a move essentializes Christianity against its context. Rome is, of course, not a "thing" opposed in the Apocalypse but the very fabric of social and cultural life for Christians in Asia Minor. Christopher Frilingos has shown recently how Revelation participates in the spectacle of Roman society. His work reveals Revelation as a product of the culture of the Roman Empire rather than objectifying the text (and the social world of its audience) as distinct and stable entities opposed to Rome. The rhetoric of the text fully implicates the Apocalypse in the "spectacles of empire" and Roman power itself.[85]

Significantly, just as the author is doubly implicated by mimicry of Roman power, fighting Rome with the master's tools, the Christian and Jewish teachers and philosophers who are vilified in the seven messages in Revelation 1–3 are carefully, rhetorically entwined with the demonic figures of Rome in the text. When the assembly marvels with John at the drunken "great whore" clothed in scarlet and pearls, fornicating the "kings of the earth" (*eporneusan hoi basileis tēs gēs*) and drinking the blood of the saints (Rev 17:1–6), would they see "Jezebel," the fornicating seductress who dares to call herself a prophet (2:19–24)? In the climactic speech by God from the throne in Rev 21:5–8, would the audience hear the condemnation to eternal death of "the cowardly, the faithless, the polluted, the murderers, the fornicators, the sorcerers, the idolaters, and all liars" as referring to their co-religionists in the *ekklēsiai* of the seven cities, condemned prophetically by the messages from Christ in similar terms?[86] By the end of the Apocalypse, which hegemonic imperialist discourse emerges triumphant, Rome's or Revelation's?

Eschatology as Heresiological Discourse

These metonymies forge ideological homologies among John's opposition. Revelation's rhetoric is explicitly heresiological: teachers are named; their positions are enumerated doxographically; their social authority and intellectual pedigrees are slandered; and they are genealogically unified in a demonized opposition. The rhetorical elision of John's inscribed enemies—Rome, Babylon, Satan, and other Christian teachers and prophets—turns our attention to heresiology and the politics of orthodoxy in Asia Minor. The stance vis-à-vis Greco-Roman culture and Roman imperialism is a salient moral-political issue in the Apocalypse.[87] The condemnation of Christians who take more accommodationist stances toward Roman authority and Greco-Roman culture entwines the Apocalypse intertextually with the developing Paulinist apologetic tradition. It is difficult to show that, in their original social contexts, the author of 1 Peter, with his quietest politics, actively opposed the apocalyptic politics of John of Patmos. But the imperial apologetics of 1 Peter and the apocalyptic politics of Revelation are conjoined discursively in the formation of orthodox Christianity. The rhetoric of empire in the Pauline tradition and 1 Peter discursively implies Christian opposition to Rome when inscribing a new Christian politics. And the Apocalypse clearly expresses that alternative Christian politics against Rome.

These discourses are both hybrid imperial discourses.[88] Heresiology functions politically in the Apocalypse in the double articulation of tropes of imperialistic power against other Christians. 1 Peter positions the *ekklēsia* with the emperor, adopting the power of the metropole from the periphery. The apparent clash of discourse in 1 Peter and Revelation can be read, via Bhabha, as "the work of hegemony . . . itself the process of iteration and differentiation. It depends on the production of alternative or antagonistic images that are always produced side by side and in competition with each other."[89] What Bhabha has called "the metonymy of antagonism" is the emerging politics of Christian orthodoxy. Eventually, and ironically, the imperial orthodox church legitimated the heresiology of Revelation via its adoption in the canon while at the same time systematically allegorizing and therefore subverting its apocalyptic politics.

LUKE-ACTS AND THE DELAY OF THE PAROUSIA

To conclude this chapter, I will interrogate the ideology of the "delay of the Parousia" in the Acts of the Apostles to uncover the heresiological functions of this discursive appeal to imperial power. I maintain that the notion of the "delay of the Parousia" has functioned as an apologetic trope for the teleology of Christian triumphalism in critical studies of the New Testament. The conventional theory follows a pattern such as this: the passage of time from the first to second generation resulted in a dulling of the original eschatological fervor of Christ's second coming (*parousia*) within the lifetime of the first Christians (see 1 Thess 4:17; 1 Cor 15:51; Mark 9:1). As later Christians accepted and theologized this shift in the eschatological horizon, the inevitable settling of the Church into the world, and the equally inevitable Christianization of the Empire, happened via "natural" social and historical forces. This theory presupposes the teleology of Christian triumph in the Roman world and is thus implicated in the privileging of orthodoxy as the original, Christian social formation. I argue instead that the *apologia* of Acts *pro imperium* and *pro ecclesiam*—that is, its defense of Rome to the Church and of the Church to Rome—reflects Christian divisions. Acts discursively forges a hegemonic position over the politics of Revelation and 1 Peter by means of the ideology of church unity. The historiography of Acts thus has a heresiological agenda to render other Christian politics invisible. The heresiology of Acts is a rhetoric of effacement.

Redaction criticism has highlighted the ways in which Luke modified Mark to delay eschatological expectations, reflecting a changed social situation for the community.[90] There are numerous examples. For instance, Luke changes Mark 9:1, "there are some standing here who will not taste death until they see that the kingdom of God has come with power," to "there are some standing here who will not taste death before they see the kingdom of God" (Luke 9:27). The kingdom becomes the establishment of the Church in the world rather than the eschatological kingdom of God. Luke adds an anti-eschatological introduction to the parable of the talents from Q (= Matt 25:14–30): "he went on to tell a parable, because he was near Jerusalem, and because they *supposed* (*kai dokein autous*) that the kingdom of God was to appear immediately (Luke 19:11, with my emphasis). The quotation of Dan 7:13 by Jesus in the trial scene, "you will see the Son of Man seated at the right hand of the 'Power,' and 'coming with the clouds of heaven,'" (Mark 14:62), becomes Christological rather than eschatological in Luke: "But from now on the Son of Man will be seated at the right hand of the power of God" (Luke 22:69). The redactional and theological changes extend beyond the idea of the kingdom of God (see also Luke 10:9; 11:20; 17:21). Conzelmann notes perceptible shifts in Markan eschatological terms such as *thlipsis* (oppression) and *metanoia* (repentance) due to "the alteration in eschatology on the one hand, and the psychology of faith on the other."[91]

The very existence of a second volume to an early Christian Gospel suggests a different view of the Church in the Roman world. Acts is widely considered to be an apologetic text. The meaning of that term is debated, as is whether Acts was written to explain and defend Christianity to the

Roman authorities; to defend the power of Rome and the actions of the Roman authorities to Christian communities; or some combination of the two positions.[92] Building on the shift in eschatological horizon in Luke, Acts develops the panel of salvation historiography. The themes of history, church, and world are foregrounded.[93] Continuity—continuity of Jesus and the Church with Israel, of the Church with Jesus, and the Church with Rome—is a major theme in Acts as well. Luke and Acts both begin in the Jerusalem Temple; only Luke has the disciples remain in Jerusalem after the crucifixion. Jesus, the universal savior, completes and continues the saving history of God for Israel and the Church carries forward the same mission. Acts extends the story of Jesus in Luke to the story of Peter, Paul, and the church, led by the Holy Spirit, in Acts. Acts inscribes both new theological *charisma* (the Holy Spirit, Acts 1–2) and new institutions (deacons, Acts 6; the Apostolic Council, Acts 15). Scripture, in the speeches of Peter in Acts 2 and Paul in Acts 13, maintains continuity between the Christian church— the name "Christian" first appears in Acts 11:26—and the ancient books of the Hebrews.[94]

While 1 Peter encourages the Christians to persevere as good citizens of the Empire, drawing on Jewish traditions of redemptive suffering and martyr-dom for a church under social stress, Acts presents the Christian *ekklēsia* as an institution at home in the Roman *oikoumenē*. It is important to denatu-ralize the view of Roman society in Acts, to again think with the help of Foucault's Chinese encyclopedia that ordered animals so differently. What has become "natural" in Christian historiography was a radically apologetic move, a *political* posture, by Luke. The ideologies of continuity and tradition were key rhetorical elements in presenting the Church to the Empire. Romans viewed new religions as threats only when they disturbed the social order; they formed illegal associations; or they lacked ancient standing and tradi-tion. While some charges might have led to arrest and death (Rev 2:12; Pliny *Ep.* 96), this third point underscores the degree to which Christians were subject to social ostracism and local persecution rather than official censure. Whether theorized ideologically as missionary apologetics or as mimicry of the metropole, the political posture of Acts was a realistic stance for a com-munity trying to avoid persecution and even execution. But reading this ideol-ogy as heresiological reveals another political agenda.

The heresiology of Acts is a submerged narrative.[95] Internal Christian divisions have been elliptically hidden in order to present a Christian church that belongs in the Roman Empire. Acts' theme of unity in the Church (*homothumadon*, "of one mind," eleven times in Acts) can be read as a heresiological response to the extensive divisions across the Christian landscape of the first and early second century. As with Paul's trope of *homonoia*, the ideology of unity in Acts is a political appeal to empire.[96] Luke's elision of difference eliminates other Christianities from the narra-tive, thereby constructing the nascent Church triumphant via the rhetoric of effacement.

I cite here two of the main instances of this rhetoric. Acts 6:1–7 narrates the appointment of deacons (*diakonoi*) to support distribution of food to widows of the church after "the Hellenists complained against the Hebrews" (Acts 6:1). This famous division between Jew and Greek became the thesis/antithesis within the Tübingen school to write early Christian history according to a Hegelian dialectic.[97] Luke transforms a story of deep cultural divisions into one of church unity. The incident begins with the complaint (*gongysmos*, 6:1) of the Hellenists, a complaint that the Twelve do not respond to directly. They focus instead on their own missionary task (6:2–4) and appoint seven Greek men to distribute the food. The Twelve please the "whole community" (*pantos tos plēthous*, 6:5) with their decision to elect. The result of this apparent division is further church growth and unity (6:7). Whatever cultural divisions existed between Palestinian and Hellenistic Christians have been completely erased. Luke employs the rhetorical effacement of the deep cultural divisions between the many different first-century Christian communities from Jewish or Greek backgrounds.

Acts also repackages the bitter dispute over circumcision in the early church. I analyzed in Chapter 4 Paul's heresiological responses to challenges to his authority in the churches of Galatia with the introduction of "another Gospel" that required circumcision. In Acts, Peter takes the lead against "some believers who belonged to the sect (*haireseōs*; see ahead) of the Pharisees" (15:5) who insisted on circumcision for Gentiles who joined the church. Peter himself universalizes Christianity for Gentiles by the power of the Holy Spirit (15:8), which eliminates any ethnic and social divisions (15:9). The testimony of Barnabas and Paul (15:12) suggests that Luke has redacted their original position to be Peter's rather than Paul's (cf. 15:1–4). James then links Peter's ideology of unity under the Holy Spirit to the Hebrew scriptures (15:16), now claimed as the Christian Old Testament. This adds the authority of tradition to the ideology of unity. While the actual underlying historicity of events in Acts 15 is still debated, the account is generally accepted as a whitewashing of an episode that roiled the Christian community long after Paul claimed that Peter "stood self-condemned" (Gal 2:15). As with the appointment of deacons, in Acts the retelling of this bitter dispute becomes a triumph of unity.

Significantly, this episode reveals the metonymy of heresiology in Acts. The narrative discursively places heretics in the group demanding particularity in the face of the Church's universality; that is, members of the sect or *hairesis* of the Pharisees. Six of the nine occurrences of *hairesis* in the New Testament are in Acts. In each case, Luke uses the term to describe a group that stands in the way of the universality of the Christian church guided by the Holy Spirit—in other words, a community opposing the ideology of unity. In the circumcision discussion at the so-called Jerusalem council, it is the believers who belong to this "sect" of the Pharisees who oppose the universalizing message of Peter. Earlier in Jerusalem, members of the *hairesis* of the Sadducees lead the arrest of the apostles (5:17). When Paul is taken to Felix in Caesarea, he is accused of being a "ringleader (*prōtostatēn*) of the sect (*haireseōs*) of the Nazarenes" (24:5), a negative characterization that he deflects in 24:14: "But this I admit to you, that according to the Way, which they *call* a sect (*hairesin*), I worship the God of our ancestors" (my emphasis). Here Paul co-opts the Hebrew God for the Christian church while dismissing the charge of *hairesis* against the Christians, reserving it for non-Christians (for instance, the Pharisees again in 26:5) and heretics, deviant or other Christians. Finally, the Jews of Rome portray Christians negatively as a *hairesis* (28:22). The word *hairesis* functions as a metonymy of Christian difference or heresy, a notion fully present in Acts despite its apparent silence on other Christian communities, by inscribing Jewish and other "particular" communities that oppose the universal Church. Even the Hebrew God and their scriptures have joined the Christians where the sects of the Pharisees and Sadducees have not.

Each of these themes—the delay of the *parousia*, the *apologia* to and for Rome, and the ideology of church unity that effaces difference—can be read heresiologically. The eschatological theology of Jewish messianism was foregrounded in the destruction of the Jerusalem Temple. Once Rome destroyed Jerusalem (and arguably well before), an apocalyptic stance was an anti-Roman stance. The ideology of the "delay of the parousia" in Luke-Acts thus opposes the politics of Revelation and other apocalyptic groups, such as the Jewish sages who wrote 4 Ezra. While to be sure the author portrays the moving and expanding Church as disturbing the social order in ways that might alarm a Roman official rather than alleviate concerns (the core of Walaskay's thesis), Acts also presents the Church as non-threatening to Roman authorities and outside of Roman legal concerns.[98] The apologetics of Luke-Acts are heresiological. In the context of competing Christianities, a pro-Roman position within the *ekklēsiai* challenges apocalyptic politics by reconfiguring Christian eschatology.

Most significantly for the heresiology of Acts, the ideology of unity was constructed as a rhetoric of effacement in response to divisions within Christianity. While Acts has been read as ignoring or passing by "heretics" in silence, in the second century this silence speaks volumes. Alternative Christianities are voiceless in this orthodox history of the Church guided by the Holy Spirit. Given the diversity of the social-discursive landscape of the late first and early second century, the silence of Acts with regard to these other Christians can only be seen as Christian imperialism under the ideology of church unity.

8 Conclusions

> Questions of heresy and orthodoxy in no way rise out of fanatical
> exaggeration of doctrinal mechanisms; they are a fundamental part
> of them.
>
> —Michel Foucault[1]

The political functions of Acts' submerged heresiological narrative brings us
full circle to Chapter 1 and Justin Martyr's appeal to the Romans that his
group of "right thinking" Christians is composed of good Romans. Justin's
apologia for Christianity follows discursively on Luke-Acts. The orthodox
Christian is constructed by Justin as a faithful Roman citizen in no small part
because the orthodox Christian party claimed the Roman world as its own.
This discursive move was also a political appeal by Justin to align his party of
Christians with the Romans and against the range of other Christians who,
he claims, do not deserve the name. For Justin, these other Christians are in
fact "heretics." As I outlined in Chapter 1, this was a technical term and the
"notion of heresy" was fully established in his writings.[2] As with Paul, the
Pastorals, and Luke-Acts, Justin's appeal to empire against these "heretics" is
a hybrid imperial discourse.[3] Paul's writings are absent from Justin's, perhaps
because of his opposition to Marcion's privileging of Paul, but he draws on
the "memoirs of the apostles" (apomnēmoneumata tōn apostolōn), primarily
the Synoptic Gospel traditions.[4] While scholars, following Le Boulluec, have
traditionally begun the history of heresiology with Justin and his "notion of
heresy" in the First Apology and Dialogue with Trypho, I have shown here
that Justin was part of a discursive tradition that developed in earlier Christian Gospels and post-Pauline literature. Justin's heresiology can thus be seen
as the end of a process of discursive formation of orthodox heresiology. The
Christian notion of heresy and the rhetoric of heresiology draw on these earlier Christian and Second Temple Jewish discursive formations, as shown in
Chapters 2–5. From the second century onwards, heresiology becomes the
primary rhetorical response to difference in orthodox Christian discourse.
    I have also analyzed the ways in which the politics of heresy policed
the boundaries of Christian communities (Chapter 6). Justin's heresiology performs this function as well, although the apologetic and dialogical
genres of his writings place the rhetorical focus more outside his community. The boundaries of tolerance for diversity of opinion within Justin's
"true Christians" can be more or less confining. For instance, in Dial. 80,
Justin defends the diversity of opinion within his Christian group on the
literal or allegorical interpretation of the millennium kingdom (Rev 20:4).

Irenaeus is the primary second-century heresiologist after Justin. Here we see more clearly the internal policing of the community as studied in Chapter 6. Irenaeus' five-volume *The Refutation and Overthrow of the Knowledge Falsely So-Called (Haer.)* can be read as a pastoral project.[5] From his perspective, the Christian churches in Lyon were infested with Christians who were not really Christians—the same problem Justin presented to the Romans. Part of his task is to define the other within doxographically in order to identify, demonize, and slander these "Gnostic" heretics. Irenaeus' doxography is notably tendentious but also detailed enough to provide recognizable descriptions of different Christian groups that, with the discovery of the Nag Hammadi and other early Christian texts, we can study on their own terms rather than through the lens of this heresiologist.[6]

More important here for my conclusions is how Irenaeus ideologically constructs orthodox Christianity within this range of alternative Christianities labeled as Gnostic. His main warrants are tradition, construed as apostolic tradition, and scripture. Irenaeus makes one of the earliest arguments for four and only four Gospels and maintains the continuity of what he and other orthodox bishops teach with the teaching of the apostles themselves (*Haer.* 1.10.1–12; 3.1–5). As I showed in Chapter 6, the ideological warrants of scripture and tradition were central in the rhetoric of first- and second-century texts such as Colossians, the Pastoral Epistles, and the letters of Polycarp and Ignatius. Irenaeus was a master heresiologist, but as with Justin, his discursive response to difference within Christianity builds from a developed tradition of heresiological rhetoric. The appeal to traditional authority, eventually vested in the office of the bishop, against prophetic or revelatory charisma and to scripture, construed as a metonym for tradition itself, has a long history in early Christian discourse, as I have shown in this book.

In tracing the origin of heresy in these early Christian texts, I highlighted a cluster of rhetorical features in the discursive responses to difference that become the notion of heresy. At least some of the earliest followers of Jesus— indeed the mentors of Jesus such as John the Baptist—were fully enmeshed in this developing heresiological discourse. I noted first the emergence of dogmatic definitions of community, from the Qumran community to the ideological proscriptions of salvation in the Apocalypse, Ignatius, and the Pastoral Epistles. Second, the notion of difference itself was theorized as both demonic and eschatological, a sign of the end times. The eschatological approach to difference runs from Qumran to 1 Timothy and, most significantly, drove the encounter with the enemies or heretics, whereas other strategies of avoidance, ellipsis, esoteric ideologies, and derision characterize the non-heresiological approaches explored in the final form of the *Gospel of Thomas* as well as the *Gospel of Mary* and *Judas*. Third, tradition becomes an ideological warrant of authority in the Christian communities that employ heresiological formations. Foundational to this ideology is the idea of difference as deviance from an original truth. The distinctive historiography of Hegesippus, I have shown, was fully inscribed in the post-Pauline literature including Colossians, Ignatius, and the Pastorals. Coupled with the ideology of tradition was the doxography of error, found as early as the *Halakhic Letter* (4QMMT) and in Matthew, Revelation, the Johannine epistles, and the Pastorals. Finally, coupled with the notion of the eschatological origins of difference was the construction of a unified web of opposition in which all Christians opposed to the orthodox were construed as the demonic other, the sons of Belial—as heretics, even when the word itself was not used.

This final rhetorical feature sources a powerful political move against other Christian communities in the colonial context in which early Christianity developed. In its earliest manifestations such as the Qumran texts and Revelation, all other religious groups and communities, whether Christian, Jewish, or Hellenistic, are elided with the *oikoumenē* as "other." Both the *Damascus Document* and the Apocalypse discursively define "us" against "them," other Jews and Christians, as well as against the Kittim and the Romans. And texts such as 1 Peter and Acts, followed by the writings of Justin, enmesh the heresiological politics of the Christian community with an appeal to empire. The other—the heretic—is constructed from the range of different Chrisitanities opposed to, and separate from, the orthodox. Heresiology then opposes these others against both the "true" Christians as well as Rome, aligning the orthodox community with empire.

Thus I repeat here as summary and conclusion, in modified form, the outlines of the rhetoric of heresiology presented in Chapter 1 and demonstrated in this book:

1   Membership (salvation) Depends on Belief or Ideas

The notion of heresy inscribes by implication an ontology of belief. While religious identity in the ancient world was shaped primarily through custom and practice, Christian orthodoxy centered on belief or dogma (*doxa*) as determinative for inclusion in the soteriological community.

2   The Eschatological Notion That Disagreement Was Satanic

The origins of religious difference must be theorized in the notion of heresy. The position on ideological difference that was systematized by the second-century heresiologists explained religious difference via eschatological and satanic tropes. This apocalyptic, eschatological worldview drives ideological confrontation with opponents, in contrast to other Christianities' responses to difference.

3   The Doxography of Opposing Beliefs

For philosophers, doxography functions to record and analyze different positions in order to transmit philosophical knowledge. Within early

Christian heresiology the function of heresiological doxography is ideological condemnation of different points of view by means of sarcasm,
reduction, or other figures diminishing the intellectual quality of the
opposing teachers.[7]

4 The Importance of Received Tradition

The ideology of orthodoxy relies on tradition as a warrant. As belief proper
becomes the ideological center of first-century Christian orthodoxy, tradition gains power. Late first-century texts construct "tradition" as a bulwark against opposing communities that embraced apocalyptic revelation
and philosophical speculation. Orthodox Christians claim an "original"
truth and label difference as deviance rather than innovation.

5 The Universalized Web of Opposition

The genealogy of heresy constructs a historiography of error, from its origins to contemporary opposing teachers or prophets, united against the true
church. Within orthodox Christian discourse, all other religious groups and
communities, whether Christian, Jewish, or Hellenistic, are elided within
and with the *oikoumenē* as "other."

The politics and theology of Christian orthodoxy are intricately connected;
the rhetoric of orthodoxy is its substance as well. It should be clear that I
have not written a history of early Christian theology. The Christian communities that became the orthodox and other Christian parties, however,
formed their identities in part around theological categories. And various
theological perspectives shaped the reception or rejection of difference and
the discourse of heresy. The problem of the existence of diverse theological
positions belongs more properly to the philosophy of religions than historical theology or the history of Christianity, although various Christian
traditions have dogmatized a philosophical position on religious difference
as a part of their theology.[8] While orthodox Christianity rejected ranges of
particular theological positions, such as Christologies now labeled either
"Gnostic" or "Jewish," orthodoxy also retained a wide set of theological
beliefs and practices. The recent scholarly and popular focus on texts and
beliefs that were excluded from the orthodoxy and the New Testament canon—the enormous popularity of *The Da Vinci Code* builds on this interest—has highlighted the degree to which orthodox theology was exclusive
of alternative points of view.[9] But orthodoxy was also inclusive of multiple
ideological positions. Paul's letter to the Romans, the Gospels of Matthew
and John, and the epistle to the Hebrews (to name four of the more systematic texts in the New Testament) are not obviously compatible—and the
Apocalypse of John or the epistle of James hardly fit with these four. The
eventual political success of orthodoxy surely stems in part from the range
of Christian theologies included. Again this is not a theological but a social

and political assessment of a movement that gained power in Rome and beyond. This formation of "Orthodoxy" proper depended on the development of ecclesial institutions and political shifts in the Roman empire of the third and fourth century that are beyond the scope of this book. I have shown here how the discursive framework for that development was in place by the second century.

Every religious group has to deal with difference within the community; group identity; and internal and external boundaries. But heresy is one particular strategy within a range of possible responses. This book has included a number of alternatives to heresiological rhetoric in each chapter to show that heresiology is a discursive choice, not an inevitable strategy. The discursive process of constructing heresy as a regime of power and knowledge becomes integral to the development of orthodox Christianity. The third-century bishop Cyprian echoes Paul's ideology of *homonoia* and Augustine, in the fourth century, develops a complex notion of *disciplina* that foregrounds the coercive power of *religio*.[10] Orthodox Christianity in the Byzantine Empire exhibited far more divisions, and polemical rhetoric against opponents, than the religion of the other great empire of its time, Zoroastrianism in Sasanian Persia.[11] The formation of Islam falls in this period; it inherits the notion of heresy as a response to difference within a religious tradition. The development of Islam and the medieval heresy trials, such as the Inquisition, are well beyond my scope here. But heresiological constructions and slandering opponents as evil and demonic become fundamental to Christianity itself. This rhetoric is foundational to our religious and political discourse to this day. We are immersed in a culture of diversity but seem at times to have forgotten alternative ways to respond to difference.

Whether we analyze the history of religious discourse in the Western tradition, or survey the state of religious dialogue in the world today, we see the fundamental preoccupation with truth and error, orthodoxy and heresy. Foucault suggests that such preoccupation is inherent in the nature of religious discourse. And in pursuing this critical genealogy of early Christian discourse, I acknowledge that genealogical criticism is implicated in the ideological and political situations of the author in his own contemporary setting as well as the objects of critique, here the ancient social religious contexts. We took away the lens of orthodoxy for reading the New Testament in the twentieth century and are still seeking new ways to look at these texts. This book has offered one way that paradoxically reuses the deconstructed terms "orthodoxy" and "heresy" to reevaluate the discursive origins of Christianity and orthodoxy in the political context of competing Christianities in the first and second century.

Notes

NOTES TO CHAPTER 1

1. The various examples cited in the first paragraph were all featured in recent news stories.
2. LSJ, *s.v.*; Heinrich Von Staden, "Hairesis and Heresy: The Case of the 'Haireseis Iatrikai,'" in *Jewish and Christian Self-Definition: Self-Definition in the Greco-Roman World*, ed. B. F. Meyer and E. P. Sanders (London: SCM, 1982).
3. See Jos. *Ant.* 13.5.9; 18.1.2; and *J.W.* 2.8.14 on the *haireseis* of the Pharisees, Sadducees, Essenes, and Zealots; and Acts 5:17; 15:5; 26:5; 24:5; 28:22. See Marcel Simon, "From Greek Hairesis to Christian Heresy," in *Early Christian Literature and the Classical Intellectual Tradition: In Honorem Robert M. Grant*, ed. William R. Schoedel and Robert L. Wilken (Paris: Editions Beauchesne, 1979); Michel Desjardins, "Bauer and Beyond: On Recent Scholarly Discussions of Hairesis in the Early Christian Era," *SecCent* 8, no. 2 (1991): 65–82.
4. I attribute the term "proto-orthodox" to Bart D. Ehrman, *The New Testament: A Historical Introduction to the Early Christian Writings* (New York: Oxford University Press, 1997).
5. Antoninus Pius was emperor from 138 to 161 and *1 Apol.* 1.46 suggests a date after 150. See Robert M. Grant, *Greek Apologists of the Second Century* (Philadelphia: Westminster, 1988), 52–53.
6. See the forthcoming textbook by Nicola Denzey Lewis, Oxford University Press.
7. See *Apol.* 4. For critical text see Justin Martyr et al., *Oeuvres Complètes: Grande Apologie, Dialogue Avec Le Juif Tryphon, Requête, Traité De La Résurrection* (Paris: Migne, 1994); also Charles Munier, *Saint Justin Apologie Pour Les Chrétiens: Édition Et Traduction* (Fribourg, Suisse: Éditions universitaires, 1995).
8. παραδεχθῆναι ἀξιοῦμεν ἀλλ' ὅτι τὸ ἀληθὲς λέγομεν; trans. Cyril Charles Richardson, *Early Christian Fathers* (New York: Macmillan, 1970).
9. See *1 Apol* 2.5; Elaine H. Pagels, "Christian Apologists and 'the Fall of the Angels': An Attack on Roman Imperial Power?," *HTR* 78, no. 3–4 (1985): 301–25; and Annette Yoshiko Reed, "The Trickery of the Fallen Angels and the Demonic Mimesis of the Divine: Aetiology, Demonology, and Polemics in the Writings of Justin Martyr," *JECS* 12, no. 2 (2004): 141–71.
10. See Jennifer Wright Knust, *Abandoned to Lust: Sexual Slander and Ancient Christianity* (New York: Columbia University Press, 2006).

11. The Sabine river god Semo Sancus misidentified; see Grant, *Greek Apologists*, 46–48, and Bart D. Ehrman, *Lost Christianities: The Battles for Scripture and the Faiths We Never Knew* (New York: Oxford University Press, 2003), 165.
12. See Eus. *E. H.* 4.18.
13. Miroslav Marcovich, ed., *Iustini Martyris Dialogus Cum Tryphone* (Berlin: Walter de Gruyter, 1997).
14. See Robert M. Royalty, "Justin's Conversion and the Rhetoric of Heresy," *StPatr* 40 (2006): 509–14.
15. See Daniel Boyarin, "Justin Martyr Invents Judaism," *CH* 70, no. 3 (2001): 427–61; *Border Lines: The Partition of Judaeo-Christianity* (Philadelphia: University of Pennsylvania Press, 2004).
16. See also *Dial.* 47.2.
17. See Alain Le Boulluec, *La Notion D'hérésie dans la Littérature Grecque IIe-IIIe Siècles. Tome I, De Justin à Irénée*, 2 vols. (Paris: Etudes Augustiniennes, 1985).
18. See Ehrman, *Lost Christianities*; and Elaine H. Pagels, "Irenaeus, the 'Canon of Truth,' and the Gospel of John: 'Making a Difference' through Hermeneutics and Ritual," *VC* 56, no. 4 (2002): 339–71.
19. See Virginia Burrus, *The Making of a Heretic: Gender, Authority, and the Priscillianist Controversy* (Berkeley: University of California Press, 1995); J. Rebecca Lyman, "The Making of a Heretic: The Life of Origen in Epiphanius *Panarion* 64," *StPatr* 31 (1997): 445–51; and Susanna Elm, Eric Rebillard, and Antonella Romano, *Orthodoxie, Christianisme, Histoire = Orthodoxy, Christianity, History* (Rome: Ecole française de Rome, 2000); Antti Marjanen and Petri Luomanen, *A Companion to Second-Century Christian "Heretics"* (Leiden: Brill, 2005).
20. Le Boulluec, *La Notion D'hérésie*. See Averil Cameron, "How to Read Heresiology," in *The Cultural Turn in Late Ancient Studies: Gender, Asceticism, and Historiography*, ed. Dale B. Martin and Patricia Cox Miller (Durham: Duke University Press, 2005).
21. See Michel Foucault, *The Archaeology of Knowledge*, trans. A. M. Sheridan Smith (New York: Pantheon Books, 1972), 21–30, 135–40, and "The Discourse on Language," 215–37; *The Order of Things: An Archaeology of the Human Sciences* (New York: Pantheon Books, 1971).
22. Judith Lieu, *Christian Identity in the Jewish and Graeco-Roman World* (Oxford: Oxford University Press, 2004); Boyarin, *Border Lines*; and Denise Kimber Buell, *Why This New Race: Ethnic Reasoning in Early Christianity* (New York: Columbia University Press, 2005).
23. For instance Knust, *Abandoned to Lust*.
24. Le Boulluec, *La Notion D'hérésie*, vol. 1; Boyarin, "Justin Martyr Invents Judaism"; J. Rebecca Lyman, "Hellenism and Heresy (2002 NAPS Presidential Address)," *JECS* 11, no. 2 (2003): 209–22; Pagels, "Canon of Truth."
25. Eusebius of Caesarea, *The Ecclesiastical History of Eusebius*, trans. Lake Kirsopp, John Ernest Leonard Oulton, and H. J. Lawlor, 2 vols. (London: Heinemann, 1926).
26. See Bruce Chilton and Craig A. Evans, *James the Just and Christian Origins* (Leiden: Brill, 1999).
27. See T. C. G. Thornton, "High-Priestly Succession in Jewish Apologetics and Episcopal Succession in Hegesippus," *JTS* 54 (2003): 160–63.
28. See Adolf Hilgenfeld, *Die Ketzergeschichte des Urchristentums* (Hildesheim: Georg Olms, 1966); Richard Adelbert Lipsius, *Die Quellen der ältesten Ketzergeschichte* (Leipzig: Johann Ambrosius Barth, 1975).
29. See Helmut Koester, "GNŌMAI DIAPHORAI: The Origin and Nature of Diversification in the History of Early Christianity," in *Trajectories through*

Early Christianity, ed. James M. Robinson and Helmut Koester (Philadelphia: Fortress, 1971).
30. See Knust, *Abandoned to Lust*.
31. Walter Bauer, *Rechtglaubigkeit und Ketzerei im ältesten Christentum*, 2nd. ed. (Tübingen: Mohr, 1934, 1961).
32. See Buell, *Why This New Race*, 173 n. 12.
33. See Walter Bauer, *Orthodoxy and Heresy in Earliest Christianity*, trans. Robert A. Kraft et al., 2nd. ed. (Philadelphia: Fortress 1971) and James M. Robinson, "Logoi Sophon: On the *Gattung* of Q," in *One Jesus and Four Primitive Gospels: Trajectories through Early Christianity*, ed. James M. Robinson and Helmut Koester (Philadelphia: Fortress, 1971).
34. Le Boulluec, *La Notion D'hérésie*.
35. See in particular Ehrman, *Lost Christianities*; Karen L. King, *The Gospel of Mary of Magdala: Jesus and the First Woman Apostle* (Santa Rosa, CA: Polebridge, 2003); and Elaine H. Pagels, *Beyond Belief: The Secret Gospel of Thomas* (New York: Random House, 2003).
36. See Pagels, *Beyond Belief*.
37. See Bauer, *Orthodoxy and Heresy*, xxv; noted by Arland J. Hultgren, *The Rise of Normative Christianity* (Minneapolis: Fortress, 1994), 9.
38. See the introduction to Dale B. Martin and Patricia Cox Miller, eds., *The Cultural Turn in Late Ancient Studies: Gender, Asceticism, and Historiography* (Durham: Duke University Press, 2005).
39. See Tina Pippin, *Death and Desire: The Rhetoric of Gender in the Apocalypse of John* (Louisville: Westminster/John Knox, 1992).
40. See in particular Hultgren, *The Rise of Normative Christianity*; Larry W. Hurtado, *Lord Jesus Christ: Devotion to Jesus in Earliest Christianity* (Grand Rapids: Eerdmans, 2003); and James D. G. Dunn, *Unity and Diversity in the New Testament: An Inquiry into the Character of Earliest Christianity*, 3rd ed. (London: SCM Press, 2006).
41. *Unity and Diversity*, 6 [2nd ed.], removing his original italics here.
42. Ibid., 31.
43. Ibid., 213.
44. Ibid., 29–32, 229.
45. See also Hurtado, *Lord Jesus Christ*.
46. On Q see Chapter 5.
47. See Burton L. Mack, *Who Wrote the New Testament?: The Making of the Christian Myth* (San Francisco: HarperSan Francisco, 1995), 43–44; *A Myth of Innocence: Mark and Christian Origins* (Philadelphia: Fortress, 1988).
48. *Who Wrote the New Testament?*, 75–96.
49. Ibid., 58; on miracles, 65–66.
50. E.g., Dunn, *Unity and Diversity*, 220; cf. 226.
51. See Hurtado, *Lord Jesus Christ*.
52. See also Shaye J. D. Cohen, *The Beginnings of Jewishness: Boundaries, Varieties, Uncertainties* (Berkeley: University of California Press, 1999); and Lawrence H. Schiffman, *Understanding Second Temple and Rabbinic Judaism* (Jersey City, NJ: Ktav, 2003).
53. Boyarin, *Border Lines*, 39–40.
54. Ibid., 43.
55. Ibid., 206–14.
56. Buell, *Why This New Race*, 1–28.
57. Ibid., 11, 45–46.
58. Ibid., 30–32; Chapter 1.
59. Boyarin, *Border Lines*.
60. Lieu, *Christian Identity*.

61. Ibid., 305.
62. Ibid., 27–61; quotations pp. 48, 53.
63. Ibid., 301.
64. See Robert M. Royalty, Jr. "Dwelling on Visions: On the Nature of the So-Called 'Colossians Heresy,'" *Bib* 83, no. 3 (2002): 329–57.
65. E.g., the "crisis" of Marcion; see also Boyarin, "Justin Martyr Invents Judaism," and Pagels, "Canon of Truth."
66. Le Boulluec refers to "sectarianism" before heresy was created by Justin.
67. As Lieu articulates the problem, I am reconsidering "early Catholicism."
68. See Jonathan Z. Smith, "What a Difference a Difference Makes," in *"To See Ourselves as Others See Us"*, ed. Jacob Neusner and Ernest S. Frerichs (Chico, CA: Scholars Press, 1985).
69. See Peter L. Berger, *The Sacred Canopy: Elements of a Sociological Theory of Religion* (Garden City, NY: Doubleday, 1967).
70. Peter Berger and Thomas Luckmann, *The Social Construction of Reality: A Treatise in the Sociology of Knowledge* (New York: Anchor Doubleday, 1966) and Clifford Geertz, "Religion as a Cultural System," in *The Interpretation of Cultures: Selected Essays* (New York: Basic Books, 1973), 87–125.
71. See Fredrik Barth, ed. *Ethnic Groups and Boundaries: The Social Organization of Culture Difference* (Prospect Heights, IL: Waveland 1998); and Richard Jenkins, *Social Identity* (London: Routledge, 1996).
72. Orthodoxy as a political project is teleological; see Talal Asad, *Genealogies of Religion: Discipline and Reasons of Power in Christianity and Islam* (Baltimore: Johns Hopkins University Press, 1993), 16.
73. This methodology is critiqued by Buell, *Why This New Race.*
74. Jacques Derrida, *Writing and Difference*, trans. Alan Bass (Chicago: University of Chicago Press, 1978).
75. See Hayden V. White, *Tropics of Discourse: Essays in Cultural Criticism* (Baltimore: Johns Hopkins University Press, 1985), "The Fictions of Factual Representation," 121–34.
76. The "myth of origins" in Smith, "What a Difference a Difference Makes."
77. See Homi K. Bhabha, *The Location of Culture* (London: Routledge, 1994); and R. S. Sugirtharajah, "Postcolonial Theory and Biblical Studies," in *Fair Play: Diversity and Conflicts in Early Christianity: Essays in Honour of Heikki Räisänen*, ed. Heikki Räisänen et al. (Leiden: Brill, 2002).
78. See Lyman, "Hellenism and Heresy"; "The Politics of Passing: Justin Martyr's Conversion as a Problem of Hellenization," in *Conversion in Late Antiquity and the Early Middle Ages: Seeing and Believing*, ed. Kenneth Mills and Anthony Grafton, *Studies in Comparative History* (Rochester: University of Rochester Press, 2003).
79. See Berger, *Sacred Canopy*, 68–71.
80. So Koester, "Gnomai Diaphorai"; see also Judith Lieu, "'The Parting of the Ways': Theological Construct or Historical Reality?," *JSNT* 56 (1994): 101–19; *Christian Identity.*
81. King, *Gospel of Mary*, 6, citing Christoph Markshies.
82. See Royalty, "Dwelling on Visions," 331–33.
83. See Richard Bauckham, "For Whom Were the Gospels Written?," in *The Gospels for All Christians: Rethinking the Gospel Audience*, ed. Richard Bauckham (Edinburgh: T&T Clark, 1998).
84. See Wendy Sproston North, "John for Readers of Mark? A Response to Richard Bauckham's Proposal," *JSNT* 25, no. 4 (2003): 449–68.
85. See Seth Schwartz, *Imperialism and Jewish Society, 200 B.C.E. To 640 C.E.* (Princeton: Princeton University Press, 2001), 89.

86. Michael B. Thompson, "The Holy Internet: Communication between Churches in the First Christian Generation," in *The Gospels for All Christians: Rethinking the Gospel Audience*, ed. Richard Bauckham (Edinburgh: T&T Clark, 1998).
87. See Averil Cameron, *Christianity and the Rhetoric of Empire: The Development of Christian Discourse* (Berkeley: University of California Press, 1991).
88. See Hurtado, *Lord Jesus Christ.*
89. See Karen L. King, *What Is Gnosticism?* (Cambridge, MA: Belknap Press of Harvard University Press, 2003).
90. See Pagels, *Beyond Belief*, on the "anti-Thomas" nature of John.
91. Wayne A. Meeks, "Breaking Away: Three New Testament Pictures of Christianity's Separation from the Jewish Communities," in *"To See Ourselves as Others See Us": Christians, Jews, and "Others" in Late Antiquity*, ed. Jacob Neusner and E. S. Frerichs (Chico, CA: Scholars Press, 1985).
92. Cf. Bentley A. Layton, "The Significance of Basilides in Ancient Christian Thought," *Representations* 28 (1989): 135–51.
93. "About the Beginning of the Hermeneutics of the Self," p. 169, in Michel Foucault and Jeremy R. Carrette (ed.), *Religion and Culture* (New York: Routledge, 1999).
94. So Layton, "Significance of Basilides"; see also the analysis of Justin's doxography in Le Boulluec, *La Notion D'hérésie*, 1.37–91.

NOTES TO CHAPTER 2

1. 1QM XV, 1; Géza Vermès, *The Complete Dead Sea Scrolls in English* (New York: Allen Lane/Penguin, 1997), 141.
2. See David E. Aune, *Prophecy in Early Christianity and the Ancient Mediterranean World* (Grand Rapids: Eerdmans, 1983).
3. A full study of Hebrew prophecy in its ancient near-eastern context is well beyond my scope. See *The Anchor Bible Dictionary*, s.v. "Prophecy," 5.477–95, for introduction and bibliography.
4. The compositional issues of DtrH and cousins (e.g., Dtr¹, Dtr², DtrG, DtrN,) are not central here. See S. L. McKenzie, "Deuteronomic History," *The Anchor Bible Dictionary*, 2.160–68; Albert de Pury and Thomas Römer, "Deuteronomistic Historiography (Dh): History of Research and Debated Issues," in *Israel Constructs Its History*, ed. Albert de Pury, Jean-Daniel Macchi, and Thomas Römer (Sheffield, England: Sheffield Academic Press, 2000).
5. See the 1951 essay of Albrecht Alt, "The Monarchy in the Kingdoms of Israel and Judah," in *Essays on Old Testament History and Religion*, The Biblical Seminar (Sheffield: JSOT, 1989).
6. See Marvin A. Sweeney, "The Critique of Solomon in the Josianic Edition of the Deuteronomistic History," *JBL* 114 (1995): 607–22.
7. On the "sin of Jeroboam" see Frank Moore Cross, *Canaanite Myth and Hebrew Epic: Essays in the History of the Religion of Israel* (Cambridge, MA: Harvard University Press, 1997), 278–85.
8. Biblical Hebrew from Karl Elliger, *Biblia Hebraica Stuttgartensia* (Stuttgart: Deutsche Bibelgesellschaft, 1983) in consultation with "Westminster Leningrad Codex," (Philadelphia: Westminster Theological Seminary and Bible-Works, v.9).
9. "Other gods" as constructed by the DtrH; see Mark S. Smith, *The Early History of God: Yahweh and the Other Deities in Ancient Israel*, 2nd ed.

(Grand Rapids: Eerdmans, 2002), 1–18, 65–107; Ziony Zevit, *The Religions of Ancient Israel: A Synthesis of Parallactic Approaches* (London: Continuum, 2001).

10. See Robert L. Cohn, "The Literary Logic of 1 Kings 17–19," *JBL* 101, no. 2 (1982): 333–50; Leah Bronner, *The Stories of Elijah and Elisha as Polemics against Baal Worship* (Leiden: Brill, 1968); Eckard Schwab, "Das Dürremotiv in I Regum 17:8–16," *ZAW* 99, no. 3 (1987): 329–39; and John A. Beck, "Geography as Irony: The Narrative-Geological Shaping of Elijah's Duel with the Prophets of Baal (1 Kings 18)," *SJOT* 17, no. 2 (2003): 291–302.

11. See Karl-Friedrich Pohlmann, *Studien zum Jeremiabuch: Ein Beitrage zur Frage nach der Entstehung des Jeremiabuches* (Göttingen: Vandenhoeck und Ruprecht, 1978); and Christopher R. Seitz, "The Crisis of Interpretation over the Meaning and Purpose of the Exile: A Redactional Study of Jeremiah 21–43," *VT* 35, no. 1 (1985): 78–97.

12. See the excursus in William Lee Holladay, *Jeremiah 1: A Commentary on the Book of the Prophet Jeremiah, Chapters 1–25* (Philadelphia: Fortress, 1986), 42–43.

13. See ibid., 62–68, Marvin A. Sweeney, "Structure and Redaction in Jeremiah 2–6," in *Troubling Jeremiah*, ed. A. R. Diamond, Kathleen M. O'Connor, and Louis Stulman (Sheffield: Sheffield Academic Press, 1999). On the rhetoric of gender here, see Renita J. Weems, *Battered Love: Marriage, Sex, and Violence in the Hebrew Prophets* (Minneapolis: Fortress, 1995); Angela Bauer-Levesque, "Jeremiah as Female Impersonator: Roles of Difference in Gender Perception and Gender Perceptivity," in *Escaping Eden*, ed. Harold C. Washington, Susan Lochrie Graham, and Pamela Lee Thimmes (Sheffield: Sheffield Academic Press, 1998).

14. Louis Stulman, "Insiders and Outsiders in the Book of Jeremiah: Shifts in Symbolic Arrangements," *JSOT* 66, no. 1 (1995): 65–85.

15. See Holladay, *Jeremiah 1, Chaps. 1–25*, 358–361; Louis Stulman, "The Prose Sermons as Hermeneutical Guide to Jeremiah 1–25: The Deconstruction of Judah's Symbolic World," in *Troubling Jeremiah*, ed. A. R. Diamond, Kathleen M. O'Connor, and Louis Stulman (Sheffield: Sheffield Academic Press, 1999).

16. See Holladay, *Jeremiah 1, Chaps. 1–25*, 528 and *s.v.*

17. Ibid., 528–29, reads this as against "the whole population."

18. See ibid., 236–240 and *Jeremiah 2: A Commentary on the Book of the Prophet Jeremiah, Chapters 26–52* (Minneapolis: Fortress, 1989), 101–3.

19. Jer 7:4 הֵיכַל (24:1; 50:28; 51:11); cf. בַּיִת (7:10, 11, 14; 23:11). See *Jeremiah 1, Chaps. 1–25*, 242; the "striking phrase" דִּבְרֵי הַשֶּׁקֶר occurs only here and 7:8 in the MT.

20. See Cross, *Canaanite Myth and Hebrew Epic*, 281–85.

21. See Gauri Viswanathan, *Outside the Fold: Conversion, Modernity, and Belief* (Princeton: Princeton University Press, 1998), 242.

22. So too Holladay, *Jeremiah 2, Chaps. 26–52*, 102.

23. With multiple terms for lying or emptiness (תַרְמוּת, אֱלִיל, שֶׁקֶר) and technical language for vision (חָזוֹן) and revelation (קֶסֶם); see *Jeremiah 1, Chaps. 1–25*, 435.

24. See Robert R. Wilson, *Prophecy and Society in Ancient Israel* (Philadelphia: Fortress, 1980), 135–295.

25. See Robert P. Carroll, *When Prophecy Failed: Cognitive Dissonance in the Prophetic Traditions of the Old Testament* (New York: Seabury Press, 1979), 184–96.

26. See Holladay, *Jeremiah 2, Chaps. 26–52*, 22–23 and 160–167 on compositional issues in Jeremiah 26–36.

27. See A. R. Pete Diamond, "Deceiving Hope: The Ironies of Metaphorical Beauty and Ideological Terror in Jeremiah," *SJOT* 17, no. 1 (2003): 34–48.

28. See Ezra 2:1–4:5; Zech 13:3, 7–9; Isa 56:9–12; 66:15–16; Mal 3:3; 4:1–3; Jill Anne Middlemas, *The Troubles of Templeless Judah* (Oxford: Oxford University Press, 2005); Schwartz, *Imperialism and Jewish Society*, 19–22.

29. See Stephen L. Cook, *Prophecy and Apocalypticism: The Postexilic Social Setting* (Minneapolis: Fortress, 1995); Paul D. Hanson, *The Dawn of Apocalyptic* (Philadelphia: Fortress, 1975); Michael E. Stone, "The Book of Enoch and Judaism in the Third Century, B.C.E," *CBQ* 40 (1978): 479–92.

30. See Albert I. Baumgarten, *The Flourishing of Jewish Sects in the Maccabean Era: An Interpretation* (Leiden: Brill, 1997), 26.

31. The identities of the parties are debated. See Elisha Qimron and John Strugnell, *Qumrân Cave 4. 5 V: Miqṣat Maʿaśē Ha-Torah* (Oxford: Clarendon Press 1994); Vermès, *Complete Dead Sea Scrolls*, 220; Gabriele Boccaccini, *Beyond the Essene Hypothesis: The Parting of the Ways between Qumran and Enochic Judaism* (Grand Rapids: Eerdmans, 1998); Lawrence H. Schiffman, "The New Halakhic Letter (4QMMT) and the Origins of the Dead Sea Sect," *BA* 53 (1990): 64–73; and *Reclaiming the Dead Sea Scrolls: The History of Judaism, the Background of Christianity, the Lost Library of Qumran* (Philadelphia: Jewish Publication Society, 1994), who sees the dispute as completely within the Sadducean Zadokite priesthood.

32. See Jodi Magness, *The Archaeology of Qumran and the Dead Sea Scrolls* (Grand Rapids: Eerdmans, 2002), 47–72. By "Qumran" here I mean the locus of religious practice and discourse typified by the central sectarian texts, not a coenobitic religious community.

33. See Albert I. Baumgarten, "The Pursuit of the Millennium in Early Judaism," in *Tolerance and Intolerance in Early Judaism and Christianity*, ed. Graham Stanton and Gedaliahu A. G. Stroumsa (Cambridge: Cambridge University Press, 1998); and Robert M. Royalty, Jr. *The Streets of Heaven: The Ideology of Wealth in the Apocalypse of John* (Macon, GA: Mercer University Press, 1998), 27–38.

34. See Joseph A. Fitzmyer, *The Dead Sea Scrolls and Christian Origins* (Grand Rapids: Eerdmans, 2000); and James H. Charlesworth, "Have the Dead Sea Scrolls Revolutionized Our Understanding of the New Testament?," in *Dead Sea Scrolls Fifty Years after Their Discovery: Proceedings of the Jerusalem Congress, July 20–25, 1997* (Jerusalem: Israel Exploration Society in collaboration with The Shrine of the Book Israel Museum, 2000).

35. See Michael E. Stone, "Categorization and Classification of the Apocrypha and Pseudepigrapha," *AbrN* 24 (1986): 167–77; and Boccaccini, *Beyond the Essene Hypothesis*, 5–67.

36. See Joseph A. Fitzmyer, *The Dead Sea Scrolls: Major Publications and Tools for Study*, rev. ed. (Atlanta: Scholars Press, 1990); Florentino García Martínez and Donald W. Parry, *A Bibliography of the Finds in the Desert of Judah 1970–1995: Arranged by Author with Citation and Subject Indexes* (Leiden: Brill, 1996); and the bibliography in each number of the *Revue de Qûmran*. For Hebrew text and translation see James H. Charlesworth and Frank Moore Cross, *The Dead Sea Scrolls: Hebrew, Aramaic, and Greek Texts with English Translations*, 6 vols. (Tübingen: Mohr (Siebeck), 1994).

37. See Vermès, *Complete Dead Sea Scrolls*, 46–48; challenged in Norman Golb, *Who Wrote the Dead Sea Scrolls?: The Search for the Secret of Qumran* (New York: Scribner, 1995). Boccaccini, *Beyond the Essene Hypothesis*, develops a pre-history for the Essenes in third-century "Enochic Judaism"; according to Magness, *Archaeology of Qumran*, revising de Vaux, the remains at Khirbet Qumran originated in the first rather than second century BCE.

38. 1QS, the most complete ms. of the *Community Rule*, is dated later than the Cave 4 fragments; Charlesworth and Cross, *Dead Sea Scrolls*, 1.2, 57.
39. Hebrew: Elisha Qimron and James H. Charlesworth et al., "Some Works of the Torah," in *The Dead Sea Scrolls: Hebrew, Aramaic, and Greek Texts with English Translations, Vol. 3*, ed. James H. Charlesworth and Frank Moore Cross (Tübingen: Mohr (Siebeck), 1993); Florentino García Martínez and Eibert J. C. Tigchelaar, eds., *The Dead Sea Scrolls Study Edition*, 2 vols. (Leiden: Brill, 2000); see the "composite text" of Qimron and Strugnell in Florentino García Martínez, *The Dead Sea Scrolls Translated: The Qumran Texts in English*, 2nd ed. (Leiden: Brill, 1996), 77–79, with reference to Vermès, *Complete Dead Sea Scrolls*, 220. Line numbers for 4QMMT refer to the "composite text."
40. See Schiffman, "The New Halakhic Letter"; and *Reclaiming the Dead Sea Scrolls*, 83–89. Florentino García Martínez, "4QMMT in a Qumran Context," in *Reading 4QMMT: New Perspectives on Qumran Law and History*, ed. John Kampen and Moshe J. Bernstein (Atlanta: Scholars Press, 1996); and Boccaccini, *Beyond the Essene Hypothesis*, 113–17.
41. See 1 Macc 10:1–21, 46–50; Jonathan A. Goldstein, *I Maccabees: A New Translation, with Introduction and Commentary* (Garden City, NY: Doubleday, 1976), 11.
42. See E. J. Bickerman, *The Jews in the Greek Age* (Cambridge, MA: Harvard University Press, 1988), 140–47.
43. See, however, Alison Schofield and James C. VanderKam, "Were the Hasmoneans Zadokites?," *JBL* 124, no. 1 (2005): 73–87.
44. Schiffman, *Reclaiming the Dead Sea Scrolls*, 86, describes the shifts between singular and plural "you" in the text as addressed to the Hasmonean ruler individually and the Saducees who have continued in Temple service under the Hasmonean priesthood.
45. See Boccaccini, *Beyond the Essene Hypothesis*; Cana Werman, "Genesis for Demarcation of Sect or Nation—the Case of *Jubilees*," presented at the European Association of Biblical Studies Annual Meeting (Lisbon 2008).
46. See Vermès, *Complete Dead Sea Scrolls*, 78–79.
47. See Magness, *Archaeology of Qumran*, 79–89. 4QMMT agrees with the Sadducees against the Pharisees in the Mishnah *Yadayim* 4:7; see Schiffman, *Reclaiming the Dead Sea Scrolls*, 87.
48. Yigael Yadin, *The Temple Scroll* (Jerusalem: Israel Exploration Society, 1983).
49. Schiffman, *Reclaiming the Dead Sea Scrolls*, 83–89.
50. Published by Solomon Schechter in 1910 as *Fragments of a Zadokite Work*. See Vermès, *Complete Dead Sea Scrolls*, 125; Joseph M. Baumgarten and with Michael T. Davis, "Cave IV, V, VI Fragments Related to the Damascus Document," in *The Dead Sea Scrolls: Hebrew, Aramaic, and Greek Texts with English Translations, Vol. 2*, ed. James H. Charlesworth and Frank Moore Cross (Tübingen: Mohr (Siebeck), 1994); and Joseph M. Baumgarten with James H. Charlesworth et al., "Damascus Document 4Q266–273 (4QDa-h)," in *The Dead Sea Scrolls: Hebrew, Aramaic, and Greek Texts with English Translations, Vol. 3*, ed. James H. Charlesworth and Frank Moore Cross (Tübingen: Mohr (Siebeck), 1993). The Cairo ms. A has been shown to be fairly reliable (ibid. 1) while about two-thirds of the text at Qumran was halakic material (Baumgarten and Davis, "Cave IV, V, VI Fragments," 59).
51. Solomon Zeitlin, *The Zadokite Fragments: Facsimile of the Manuscripts in the Cairo Genizah Collection in the Possession of the University Library, Cambridge, England* (Philadelphia: Dropsie College for Hebrew and Cognate

Learning, 1952); and Philip R. Davies, *The Damascus Covenant: An Interpretation of the "Damascus Document"* (Sheffield: University of Sheffield, 1983).

52. See *The Damascus Covenant*, and "The Judaism(s) of the Damascus Document," in *The Damascus Document: A Centennial of Discovery*, ed. Joseph M. Baumgarten, Esther G. Chazon, and Avital Pinnick, Studies on the Texts of the Desert of Judah (Leiden: Brill, 2000); Schiffman, *Reclaiming the Dead Sea Scrolls*, 90–95; Boccaccini, *Beyond the Essene Hypothesis*, 119–29; and Charlotte Hempel, "Community Origins in the *Damascus Document* in Light of Recent Scholarship," in *The Provo International Conference on the Dead Sea Scrolls: Technological Innovations, New Texts, and Reformulated Issues*, ed. Donald W. Parry and Eugene Charles Ulrich (Leiden: Brill, 1999).

53. "Community Origins in the *Damascus Document*" notes four historiographic sections in CD.

54. See Boccaccini, *Beyond the Essene Hypothesis*, 123, on the different construal of remnant here from "classic" Enochic Judaism. The notion of the remnant goes back to the eighth-century Hebrew prophets.

55. I have transcribed the pointed CD ms.

56. See Vermès, *Complete Dead Sea Scrolls*, 127, 144.

57. The Enochic literature was authoritative at Qumran. For Belial, Angel of Darkness and Prince of Lights see CD V, 18; 1QS III, 20–21 and *Melchizedeck*, 11Q13 (Joseph M. Baumgarten and Daniel R. Schwartz, "Damascus Document," in *The Dead Sea Scrolls: Hebrew, Aramaic, and Greek Texts with English Translations, Vol. 2*, ed. James H. Charlesworth and Frank Moore Cross (Tübingen: Mohr (Siebeck), 1994), p. 21 n. 51).

58. See 2 Tim 3:8; Babylonian Talmud *Menachot* 85a; *OTP* 2.427–42.

59. See Aharon Shemesh and Cana Werman, "Halakhah at Qumran: Genre and Authority," *DSD* 10, no. 1 (2003): 104–29, on the independent status of halakah in CD separate from its biblical sources; 108–9 on the "Well."

60. Cf. the "coming of the Messiah from Aaron and from Israel" in XX 1 (II.1); see John J. Collins, *The Scepter and the Star: The Messiahs of the Dead Sea Scrolls and Other Ancient Literature* (New York: Doubleday, 1995).

61. See Boccaccini, *Beyond the Essene Hypothesis*, 120.

62. See J. C. Greenfield, "The words of Levi son of Jacob in Damascus Document IV, 15–19," *Revue de Qûmran* 13 (1988), 319–22; and Robert A. Kugler, *From Patriarch to Priest: The Levi-Priestly Tradition from Aramaic Levi to Testament of Levi* (Atlanta: Scholars Press, 1996), 134–38.

63. Vermès, *Complete Dead Sea Scrolls*, 135, translates בית פלג in 2.22 as "House of Separation"; García Martínez, *Dead Sea Scrolls Translated*, 47 (= 20.22) and Baumgarten and Schwartz, "Damascus Document," 37 (= 20.22), choose "Peleg."

64. See Charlotte Hempel, "The Laws of the Damascus Document and 4QMMT," in *The Damascus Document: A Centennial of Discovery, Proceedings of the Third International Symposium of the Orion Center*, ed. Joseph M. Baumgarten, Esther G. Chazon, and Avital Pinnick (Leiden: Brill, 2000).

65. Worship at the Temple, however, is assumed at CD XI, 19–XII, 2 and XVI, 3.

66. B 19 in Baumgarten and Schwartz, "Damascus Document," and García Martínez, *Dead Sea Scrolls Translated*; BI and II in Vermès, *Complete Dead Sea Scrolls*.

67. See Baumgarten, *Flourishing of Jewish Sects*, 1–15.

68. Vermès, *Complete Dead Sea Scrolls*, 126, and Baumgarten and Schwartz, "Damascus Document," 5. Many of the statues in CD are repeated in 11QT.

69. See Sarianna Metso, "In Search of the *Sitz Im Leben* of the *Community Rule*," in *The Provo International Conference on the Dead Sea Scrolls: Technological Innovations, New Texts, and Reformulated Issues*, ed. Donald W. Parry and Eugene Charles Ulrich (Leiden Brill, 1999); and Davies, "Judaism(s) of the Damascus Document."

70. See Vermès, *Complete Dead Sea Scrolls*, 98; reading with 4QS^d (4Q258).

71. See John J. Collins, *Apocalypticism in the Dead Sea Scrolls* (London: Routledge, 1997), 47–51.

72. See Adela Yarbro Collins, "The Charge of Blasphemy in Mark 14.64," *JSNT* 26, no. 4 (2004): 379–401, who cites, on p. 393 n. 47, Yonder Gillihan, "The Community of Qumran in the Context of Greco-Roman Associations," (PhD dissertation, University of Chicago, 2007).

73. See also the "Register of Rebukes," 4Q477; Vermès, *Complete Dead Sea Scrolls*, 237–38.

74. Magness, *Archaeology of Qumran*, 74–75.

75. Ibid., 79–89.

76. Ibid., 81.

77. Ibid., 87.

78. Ibid., 113; see pp. 105–13.

79. See John C. Poirier, "Purity Beyond the Temple in the Second Temple Era," *JBL* 122, no. 2 (2003): 247–65.

80. See Baumgarten, *Flourishing of Jewish Sects*, 81–113, on Hellenism in Jewish sectarianism.

81. See Joseph Sievers, *The Hasmoneans and Their Supporters: From Mattathias to the Death of John Hyrcanus I* (Atlanta: Scholars Press, 1990); Vermès, *Complete Dead Sea Scrolls*, viii, 10; 54–57, on "Concealed References in the Scrolls."

82. See Maurya P. Horgan, *Pesharim: Qumran Interpretations of Biblical Books* (Washington: Catholic Biblical Association of America, 1979); Schiffman, *Reclaiming the Dead Sea Scrolls*, 223–41; and Vermès, *Complete Dead Sea Scrolls*, 429–30ff.

83. On references to rulers in 4Q471^a, see Esther Eshel and Menahem Kister, "A Polemical Qumran Fragment," *JJS* 43 (1992): 277–81; and Vermès, *Complete Dead Sea Scrolls*, 239.

84. CD and Josephus both describe two groups of Essenes, indicating possibly different approaches to Temple sacrifice (CD XI, 19–XII, 2; XVI, 3; on this see also Hempel, "Community Origins in the *Damascus Document*"). Complications include the sectarian status, or not, of 11QT; see Yadin, *The Temple Scroll*. For Vermès, *Complete Dead Sea Scrolls*, 191, 11QT is both sectarian and pre-Qumran while Boccaccini, *Beyond the Essene Hypothesis*, 99, claims that most specialists now see 11QT as presectarian, with *Jubilees*. See also Shemesh and Werman, "Halakhah at Qumran."

85. So Magness, *Archaeology of Qumran*, 113, 121.

86. See 4Q554–5, 5Q15; 1Q32; 2Q24; 4Q232; 11Q18; Vermès, *Complete Dead Sea Scrolls*, 568–70; and Royalty, *Streets of Heaven*, 71–78.

87. On the Hasmonean expansion of "Israel" see Doron Mendels, *The Land of Israel as a Political Concept in Hasmonean Literature: Recourse to History in Second Century B.C. Claims to the Holy Land* (Tübingen: Mohr, 1987), 47–50.

88. Magness, *Archaeology of Qumran*, 168–75.

89. See Andrea M. Berlin, "Power and Its Afterlife: Tombs in Hellenistic Palestine," *Near Eastern Archaeology* 65, no. 2 (2002): 138–48.

90. Ibid., 144.

91. See John J. Collins, "The Epic of Theodotus and the Hellenism of the Hasmoneans," *HTR* 73 (1980): 91–104.

92. Berlin, "Power and Its Afterlife: Tombs in Hellenistic Palestine," 145; and Sievers, *Hasmoneans and Their Supporters*, 92–103.
93. See Berlin, "Power and Its Afterlife: Tombs in Hellenistic Palestine," 142–43; L. Y. Rahmani, "Jason's Tomb," *IEJ* 17, no. 2 (1967): 61–100.
94. See Ehud Netzer, *The Palaces of the Hasmonean and Herod the Great* (Jerusalem: Israel Exploration Society, 2001), 13–39.
95. See Jos. *J.W.* 5.259, 304; Sievers, *Hasmoneans and Their Supporters*, 156.
96. See Goldstein, *I Maccabees*, 62–64.
97. See Seth Schwartz, "A Note on the Social Type and Political Ideology of the Hasmonean Family," *JBL* 112 (1993): 305–9; Schofield and VanderKam, "Were the Hasmoneans Zadokites?"
98. See Sievers, *Hasmoneans and Their Supporters*, 100–3.
99. Goldstein, *I Maccabees*, 4–12.
100. See Daniel R. Schwartz, "The Other in 1 and 2 Maccabees," in *Tolerance and Intolerance in Early Judaism and Christianity*, ed. Graham Stanton and Gedaliahu A. G. Stroumsa (Cambridge, UK: Cambridge University Press, 1998).
101. Ibid., 34.
102. Ibid., citing E. J. Bickerman, *The God of the Maccabees: Studies on the Meaning and Origin of the Maccabean Revolt* (Leiden: Brill, 1979), 17.
103. Sievers, *Hasmoneans and Their Supporters*, 103.
104. See Baumgarten, *Flourishing of Jewish Sects.*
105. Cf. 1 Macc 7:12–20; see John Kampen, *The Hasideans and the Origin of Pharisaism: A Study in 1 and 2 Maccabees* (Atlanta: Scholars Press, 1988).
106. The chronology of Magness, *Archaeology of Qumran.*
107. Against structuralist interpretations such as Baumgarten, "Pursuit of the Millennium."
108. See Royalty, *Streets of Heaven.*
109. Compare Wayne A. Meeks, "Social Functions of Apocalyptic Language in Pauline Christianity," in *Apocalypticism in the Mediterranean World and the near East*, ed. David Hellholm (Tübingen: Mohr (Siebeck), 1983).
110. See Royalty, *Streets of Heaven*, 27–38; and Baumgarten, "Pursuit of the Millennium."
111. See John J. Collins, *Daniel: A Commentary on the Book of Daniel* (Minneapolis: Fortress, 1993); 2–3 on Qumran attestation; and John J. Collins and Peter W. Flint, eds., *The Book of Daniel: Composition and Reception* (Leiden: Brill, 2001). Eight mss. of Daniel and a non-canonical Daniel cycle, 4Q242–6, were found at Qumran; Vermès, *Complete Dead Sea Scrolls*, 11, n. 28.
112. See Collins, *Daniel*, 24–38; Rainer Albertz, "The Social Setting of the Aramaic and Hebrew Book of Daniel," in *The Book of Daniel: Composition and Reception*, ed. John J. Collins and Peter W. Flint (Leiden: Brill, 2001).
113. The two visions, the first in Aramaic and second in Hebrew, present essentially the same political-apocalyptic scenario.
114. On the Human One or Son of Man in Daniel 7, 10–12 see the Excursus in Collins, *Daniel*, 304–11.
115. See ibid., 66–67.
116. See the options in Adela Yarbro Collins, "The Political Perspective of the Revelation to John," *JBL* 96 (1977): 241–56.
117. See Collins, *Daniel*, 67, 69. The Book of Dreams, which contains the so-called Animal Apocalypse (*1 Enoch* 85–91), and the Epistle, which includes the Apocalypse of Weeks (*1 Enoch* 93:1–10 + 91:11–17), can be dated roughly to the time of the Maccabean Revolt on internal and external grounds. On the redaction of *1 Enoch*, see Devorah Dimant, "The Biography of Enoch and the Books of Enoch," *VT* 33 (1983) 14–29; George Nickelsburg, *Jewish*

Literature between the Bible and the Mishnah: A Historical and Literary *Introduction* (Philadelphia: Fortress, 1981), 150–51.
118. So too Albertz, "Social Setting," 192–93, but with inscribed conflict among the *maśkîlîm*.

NOTES TO CHAPTER 3

1. See Martin Goodman, *The Ruling Class of Judaea: The Origins of the Jewish Revolt against Rome A.D. 66–70* (Cambridge: Cambridge University Press, 1987), 29–50.
2. See William E. Arnal and Michel R. Desjardins, *Whose Historical Jesus?* (Waterloo, Ont.: Wilfrid Laurier University Press, 1997); Bruce Chilton and Craig A. Evans, *Studying the Historical Jesus: Evaluation of the State of Current Research* (Leiden; New York: Brill, 1994); Craig A. Evans, ed. *The Historical Jesus*, 4 vols., Critical Concepts in Religious Studies (London: Routledge, 2004); and Marcus J. Borg and N. T. Wright, *The Meaning of Jesus: Two Visions* (San Francisco: HarperSanFrancisco, 1999).
3. Discounting the *Testimonium Flavium*, Jos. *Ant.* 18.3.3; see John P. Meier, *A Marginal Jew: Rethinking the Historical Jesus*, 4 vols. (New York: Doubleday, 1991), 1.58–69; 2.19–99, on John.
4. See Joan E. Taylor, *The Immerser: John the Baptist within Second Temple Judaism* (Grand Rapids: Eerdmans, 1997), 223–34. Cf. Rebecca Gray, *Prophetic Figures in Late Second Temple Jewish Palestine: The Evidence from Josephus* (Oxford: Oxford University Press, 1993), who excludes John.
5. See Richard A. Horsley, with John S. Hanson, *Bandits, Prophets, and Messiahs: Popular Movements in the Time of Jesus*, 2nd ed. (Harrisburg, PA: Trinity, 1999), 88–189; and Gray, *Prophetic Figures*, 112–44.
6. Horsley, *Bandits, Prophets, and Messiahs*. On Judas, see Jos *Ant.* 17.271–72; *J.W.* 2.56; Simon, *Ant.* 17.273–76; Athronges, *Ant.* 17.278–85; the "Samaritan," *Ant.* 18.85–87; Theudas, *Ant.* 20.97–98; and the "Egyptian," *Ant.* 20.169–71; *J.W.* 2.261–63; and Acts 21:38.
7. Cf. Mark 1:4; Luke 3:3; John 1:28; and Taylor, *The Immerser*, 42–48, 49–100. Meier, *A Marginal Jew*, vol. 2, 43–48, notes that John moved around and that the *erēmos* had literal as well as symbolic meanings.
8. See Taylor, *The Immerser*, 42–48 and 213–22.
9. See Goldstein, *I Maccabees*, 10, 381; 1 Macc 9:32–73.
10. See Meier, *A Marginal Jew*, 2.98–99 n. 188.
11. See Taylor, *The Immerser*, 105–6.
12. Meier, *A Marginal Jew*, 2.21.
13. Taylor, *The Immerser*, 101–2 and 132–49, downplays John's eschatological message; cf. Horsley, *Bandits, Prophets, and Messiahs*, 177, and Meier, *A Marginal Jew*, 2.28.
14. Following *A Marginal Jew*, 2.27–40. On the debatable Luke 3:10–14 see Taylor, *The Immerser*, 113–32.
15. See Isa 66:24; Joel 2:30; Mal. 4:1; Jdt 16:17; *1 Enoch* 10.6; 54:1–2; 90:24–25; 100:9; *Jub.* 9:15; 1QpHab 10:5, 13; *4 Macc.* 9:9; *Ps. Sol.* 15:4–5; W. D. Davies and Dale C. Allison, *A Critical and Exegetical Commentary on the Gospel According to Saint Matthew*, 3 vols. (Edinburgh: T. & T. Clark, 1988), 1.310.
16. So Taylor, *The Immerser*. Greek text Barbara and Kurt Aland et al., eds., *Nestle-Aland Novum Testamentum Graece*, 27 ed. (Stuttgart: Deutsche Bibelgesellschaft, 2001); Bibleworks (computer software) Ver. 9, Norfolk, VA.

17. See Horsley, *Bandits, Prophets, and Messiahs*, 178–79.
18. Translation Vermès, *Complete Dead Sea Scrolls*.
19. James M. Robinson, Paul Hoffmann, and John S. Kloppenborg, *The Critical Edition of Q: Synopsis Including the Gospels of Matthew and Luke, Mark and Thomas with English, German, and French Translations of Q and Thomas* (Philadelphia: Fortress, 2000), 6, strikes the Isaiah quotation in Q 3:4.
20. So Horsley, *Bandits, Prophets, and Messiahs*, 180–81, and Taylor, *The Immerser*, 221–22. See Meier, *A Marginal Jew*, 2.6.
21. Reading Matt 11:8; see Robinson, Hoffmann, and Kloppenborg, *Critical Edition of Q*, 128–32. See James A. Kelhoffer, *The Diet of John the Baptist: "Locusts and Wild Honey" in Synoptic and Patristic Interpretation* (Tübingen: Mohr (Siebeck), 2005).
22. See Taylor, *The Immerser*, 238–40; Paul W. Hollenbach, "John the Baptist," *ABD* 3.887–99.
23. See Collins, *Apocalypticism*, 92–93.
24. For dating see Yigael Yadin, *The Scroll of the War of the Sons of Light against the Sons of Darkness* (London: Oxford University Press, 1962).
25. See Collins, *Apocalypticism*, 107–9.
26. Translation Vermès, *Complete Dead Sea Scrolls*, 163, 179. See ibid., 161–63 and Collins, *Apocalypticism*, 94–95.
27. See Collins, *Scepter and Star*.
28. See ibid.
29. See ibid., 22–24; and Royalty, *Streets of Heaven*, 72 and n. 94. See Isa 2:2–4; 11:1–9; 25:6–10a; 27:12–13; 32:14–20; 33:20–22; 35:1–10; Jer 3:17; 31:1–14, 23–40; 33:9–11; Ezek 36:8–15; 37:1–14; 39:25–29.
30. See Collins, *Apocalypticism*, 77–90; and Martin G. Abegg, Craig A. Evans, and Gerbern S. Oegema, "Bibliography of Messianism and the Dead Sea Scrolls," in *Qumran-Messianism*, ed. James H. Charlesworth, Hermann Lichtenberger, and Gerbern S. Oegema (Tübingen: Mohr (Siebeck), 1998).
31. See George W. E. Nickelsburg, *Jewish Literature between the Bible and the Mishnah: A Historical and Literary Introduction* (Philadelphia: Fortress, 1981), 203–12, 229; and R. B. Wright, "Psalms of Solomon," in *Old Testament Pseudepigrapha*, ed. James H. Charlesworth (Garden City, NY: Doubleday, 1983). Kenneth Atkinson, "On the Herodian Origin of Militant Davidic Messianism at Qumran: New Light from Psalm of Solomon 17," *JBL* 118 (1999): 435–60, argues *Ps. Sol.* 17 was composed in 40 BCE.
32. Trans. Wright; see research review in Atkinson, "Herodian Origin of Militant Davidic Messianism," nn. 3–14.
33. Cited in Taylor, *The Immerser*, 220–21.
34. Following Schiffman, *Reclaiming the Dead Sea Scrolls*, 404. Taylor, *The Immerser*, 15–48, argues strongly against; so too Meier, *A Marginal Jew*, 2.25–27. Robert L. Webb, *John the Baptizer and Prophet: A Socio-Historical Study* (Sheffield: JSOT Press, 1991), associates John's baptism with Qumran. James H. Charlesworth, "John the Baptizer and Qumran Barriers in Light of the *Rule of the Community*," in *The Provo International Conference on the Dead Sea Scrolls: Technological Innovations, New Texts, and Reformulated Issues*, ed. Donald W. Parry and Eugene Charles Ulrich (Leiden: Brill, 1999), speculates John was expelled from Qumran.
35. See Vermès, *Complete Dead Sea Scrolls*, 46, and Géza Vermès and Martin D. Goodman, *The Essenes, According to the Classical Sources* (Sheffield: JSOT /Oxford Centre for Postgraduate Hebrew Studies, 1989).
36. Magness, *Archaeology of Qumran*, 163–87, on a minimal presence of women at Qumran.

37. See also the stronger case in Charlesworth, "John the Baptist and Qumran Barriers."

38. See E. P. Sanders, *Jesus and Judaism* (Philadelphia: Fortress, 1985), 11, 90–91; Meier, *A Marginal Jew*, 2. 100–5; and John Dominic Crossan, *The Historical Jesus: The Life of a Mediterranean Jewish Peasant* (San Francisco: HarperSanFrancisco, 1991), 225–64.

39. See E. P. Sanders, *The Historical Figure of Jesus* (London: Allen Lane, 1993), 94.

40. See Davies and Allison, *St. Matthew*, 2.234.

41. See Sanders, *Historical Figure of Jesus*, 123–27; cf. Mark 1:16–20; and John 1:40.

42. Ibid., 125, on 1 Cor 15:6 and Luke 10:1–16.

43. With ibid.; Paula Fredriksen, *Jesus of Nazareth, King of the Jews: A Jewish Life and the Emergence of Christianity* (New York: Knopf, 1999); Bart D. Ehrman, *Jesus, Apocalyptic Prophet of the New Millennium* (Oxford: Oxford University Press, 1999); and Albert Schweitzer, *The Quest of the Historical Jesus: A Critical Study of Its Progress from Reimarus to Wrede* (Baltimore, MD: Johns Hopkins University Press in association with the Albert Schweitzer Institute, 1998).

44. Sanders, *Historical Figure of Jesus*, 212–18.

45. Ibid.; Crossan, *Historical Jesus* and *Jesus: A Revolutionary Biography* (San Francisco: HarperSanFrancisco, 1994).

46. Sanders, *Historical Figure of Jesus*; and "Jesus and the Sinners," *JSNT* 19 (1983): 5–36.

47. See *Historical Figure of Jesus*, 254–61; Crossan, *Jesus: A Revolutionary Biography*, 130–32.

48. For instance, H. Gregory Snyder, *Teachers and Texts in the Ancient World: Philosophers, Jews, and Christians* (London: Routledge, 2000), on Jesus' scriptural interpretation.

NOTES TO CHAPTER 4

1. Albert Schweitzer and W. Montgomery, *The Mysticism of Paul the Apostle* (New York: Holt, 1931); Johan Christiaan Beker, *Paul the Apostle: The Triumph of God in Life and Thought* (Philadelphia: Fortress Press, 1980).

2. E. P. Sanders, *Paul and Palestinian Judaism: A Comparison of Patterns of Religion* (Philadelphia: Fortress, 1977); Heikki Räisänen, *Paul and the Law*, 2nd ed. (Tübingen: Mohr (Siebeck), 1987); Alan F. Segal, *Paul the Convert: The Apostolate and Apostasy of Saul the Pharisee* (New Haven: Yale University Press, 1990).

3. Rudolf Karl Bultmann, *Der Stil Der Paulinischen Predigt Und Die Kynisch-Stoische Diatribe* (Göttingen: Vandenhoeck & Ruprecht, 1910); Abraham J. Malherbe, *Paul and the Popular Philosophers* (Minneapolis: Fortress Press, 1989); Stanley Stowers, *The Diatribe and Paul's Letter to the Romans* (Chico, CA: Scholars Press, 1981); Troels Engberg-Pedersen, *Paul and the Stoics* (Edinburgh: T & T Clark, 2000).

4. John G. Gager, *Reinventing Paul* (Oxford: Oxford University Press, 2000); Stanley Stowers, *A Rereading of Romans: Justice, Jews, and Gentiles* (New Haven: Yale University Press, 1994).

5. Elisabeth Schüssler Fiorenza, *In Memory of Her: A Feminist Theological Reconstruction of Christian Origins* (New York: Crossroad, 1984); Antoinette Clark Wire, *The Corinthian Women Prophets: A Reconstruction through Paul's Rhetoric* (Minneapolis: Fortress Press, 1990).

6. Following Wayne A. Meeks, *The First Urban Christians: The Social World of the Apostle Paul* (New Haven: Yale University Press, 1983).
7. Note Troels Engberg-Pedersen, *Paul Beyond the Judaism/Hellenism Divide* (Louisville: Westminster John Knox, 2001).
8. So too Gordon D. Fee, *The First Epistle to the Corinthians* (Grand Rapids: Eerdmans, 1987), 16. See J. Murphy-O'Connor, *St. Paul's Corinth: Texts and Archaeology* (Wilmington, DE: Michael Glazier, 1983).
9. Margaret Mary Mitchell, *Paul and the Rhetoric of Reconciliation: An Exegetical Investigation of the Language and Composition of 1 Corinthians* (Tübingen: Mohr (Siebeck), 1991) makes a convincing case for unity.
10. See Paul Schubert, *Form and Function of the Pauline Thanksgivings* (Berlin: Alfred Töplemann, 1939).
11. See Dale B. Martin, *The Corinthian Body* (New Haven: Yale University Press, 1995) on the centrality of the ideology of the body; also Jorunn Økland, *Women in Their Place: Paul and the Corinthian Discourse of Gender and Sanctuary Space* (Edinburgh: T & T Clark, 2004).
12. See "The Parties," Hans Conzelmann, *1 Corinthians: A Commentary on the First Epistle to the Corinthians* (Philadelphia: Fortress, 1975), 33–34; Fee, *First Corinthians*.
13. See Werner Georg Kümmel, *The New Testament: The History of the Investigation of Its Problems* (Nashville: Abingdon, 1972), 127–43, for excerpts and analysis; Wayne A. Meeks, *The Writings of St. Paul*, 1st ed. (New York: Norton, 1972), 277–88.
14. John Howard Schütz, *Paul and the Anatomy of Apostolic Authority* (London: Cambridge University Press, 1975).
15. E.g., Walter Schmithals, *Gnosticism in Corinth: An Investigation of the Letters to the Corinthians*, trans. John E. Steely (Nashville: Abingdon, 1971).
16. Richard Reitzenstein, *Die hellenistischen Mysterienreligionen: Ihre Grundgedanken und Wirkungen* (Leipzig: Teubner, 1910).
17. See King, *What Is Gnosticism?*
18. Fee, *First Corinthians*, 5–6, citing other scholars in agreement.
19. For a dissenting view, see A. J. M. Wedderburn, *Baptism and Resurrection: Studies in Pauline Theology against Its Graeco-Roman Background* (Tübingen: Mohr (Siebeck), 1987).
20. Gerd Theissen, *The Social Setting of Pauline Christianity*, trans. and with an introduction by John Schütz (Philadelphia: Fortress, 1982).
21. Wire, *Corinthian Women Prophets*.
22. See ibid., 1–11.
23. Ibid., 55.
24. Økland, *Women in Their Place*.
25. Cf. Jerry L. Sumney, *'Servants of Satan', 'False Brothers' and Other Opponents of Paul* (Sheffield: Sheffield Academic Press, 1999), 14–32 on methodology and 33–78 on 1 Cor.
26. Note Daniel Boyarin, "One Church; One Voice: The Drive Towards Homonoia in Orthodoxy," *Religion & Literature* 33, no. 2 (2001): 1–22.
27. Mitchell, *Paul and the Rhetoric of Reconciliation*; Martin, *Corinthian Body*.
28. See Mitchell, *Paul and the Rhetoric of Reconciliation*, 63–64; quotation on p. 63; see also A. R. R. Sheppard, "'Homonoia' in the Greek Cities of the Roman Empire," *Ancient Society* 15 (1984), 229–52; Ursula Kampmann, "Homonoia Politics in Asia Minor: The Example of Pergamon," in *Pergamon, Citadel of the Gods*, ed. Helmut Koester (Harrisburg, PA: Trinity, 1998); S. R. F. Price, *Rituals and Power: The Roman Imperial Cult in Asia Minor* (Cambridge: Cambridge University Press, 1984), 126–32.

29. Mitchell, *Paul and the Rhetoric of Reconciliation*, 65–183 on *topoi* and 184–295 on rhetorical unity.
30. See Martin, *Corinthian Body*, 39–47, on the "Ideology of Concord"; cf. Dio Nicom.
31. See Elizabeth A. Castelli, *Imitating Paul: A Discourse of Power* (Louisville: Westminster/John Knox, 1991), 120.
32. Mitchell, *Paul and the Rhetoric of Reconciliation*, 81–111.
33. Ibid., 126–49.
34. See Theissen, *Social Setting of Pauline Christianity*, 121–43.
35. See Mitchell, *Paul and the Rhetoric of Reconciliation*, 142–47.
36. See ibid., 157–64; and Martin, *Corinthian Body*, 38–68.
37. See *Corinthian Body*, 87–103. Wire, *Corinthian Women Prophets*, 135–58, has complementary insights.
38. See Conzelmann, *1 Corinthians*, 96.
39. Adela Yarbro Collins, "The Function of 'Excommunication' in Paul," *HTR* 73 (1980): 251–63.
40. See ibid., 255, 257, 261; CD VIII, 1–5; 1QS II, 5–6, 15–17; VII, 17; VIII, 21–24; PGM 1.190–93 and 5.335–36. Of the five options for ἐν τῷ ὀνόματι τοῦ κυρίου in 5:4 I choose κέκρικα. See Conzelmann, *1 Corinthians*, 97–98.
41. On the destruction of the flesh here see Conzelmann, *1 Corinthians*, 97; Martin, *Corinthian Body*, 168–74.
42. See Conzelmann, *1 Corinthians*, 184–88; Økland, *Women in Their Place*; Wire, *Corinthian Women Prophets*.
43. See Conzelmann, *1 Corinthians* 249; also Schütz, *Paul and the Anatomy of Apostolic Authority*, 84–113.
44. See Conzelmann, *1 Corinthians*, 259–62.
45. Castelli, *Imitating Paul*. Martin, *Corinthian Body*, makes similar interpretive moves here.
46. See Castelli, *Imitating Paul*, 89–117, noting 1 Thess 1:6–6; 2:14; Phil 3:17; and Gal 4:12.
47. Ibid., 86 and 116.
48. Martin, *Corinthian Body*, 38–68.
49. Bhabha, *Location of Culture*, 122.
50. Ibid., 128; on metonymy of presence see 128–29.
51. Ibid., 28–56.
52. The dating of Gal relative to Acts 15 is not essential to the development from Gal to Rom and 2 Cor. See Hans Dieter Betz, *Galatians: A Commentary on Paul's Letter to the Churches in Galatia* (Philadelphia: Fortress, 1979), 9–12; and J. Louis Martyn, *Galatians: A New Translation with Introduction and Commentary* (New York: Doubleday, 1998), 19–20.
53. On Gal 3:27–28 as a pre-Pauline baptismal formula, see Martyn, *Galatians*, 378–83.
54. See Hans Dieter Betz, "Orthodoxy and Heresy in Primitive Christianity," *Int* 19 (1965): 299–311; and Bauer, *Rechtglaubigkeit und Ketzerei im ältesten Christentum*, 221–37.
55. See Lieu, *Christian Identity*, 54 on essentialist understandings of Jewish and Christian identity.
56. Cf. Betz, "Orthodoxy and Heresy," 309.
57. The Teachers could have had their own rhetoric of exclusion; see Martyn, *Galatians*, 117–26.
58. The theme of his commentary; see also Sanders, *Paul and Palestinian Judaism*, 430–508.

59. On the *correctio* see Betz, *Galatians*, 49, nn. 59 and 60; Heinrich Lausberg, *Handbook of Literary Rhetoric: A Foundation for Literary Study*, trans. Matthew T. Bliss, Annemiek Janswen, and David E. Orton (Leiden: Brill, 1998), §§ 784–86.
60. Betz, *Galatians*, 64 and 64–66; cf. Martyn, *Galatians*, 148–50.
61. Betz, *Galatians*, and Martyn, *Galatians*.
62. See *Galatians*, 112: a "180 degree turn."
63. So ibid., 159–61, comparing Ezra 7:1–9:5.
64. 2:14 continues to 2:16 although 2:15–16 are often separated as the start of a new topic. Betz, *Galatians*, 113–14, marks 2:15 as start of the *propositio* [Lausberg, *Handbook*, §346].
65. See Segal, *Paul the Convert*, 187–223.
66. See Martyn, *Galatians*, 240–45.
67. See ibid.; a party within the Jerusalem *ekklēsia*. Note that NRSV adds "faction" to ἐκ περιτομῆς in Gal 2:12.
68. The use of τις can be read as ironic or contemptuous; see BDB §302.
69. See Peter Marshall, *Enmity in Corinth: Social Conventions in Paul's Relations with the Corinthians* (Tübingen: Mohr (Siebeck), 1987), 341–48, on periphrasis.
70. Robert Jewett, "Agitators and the Galatian Congregation," *NTS* 17 (1971): 198–212.
71. Cf. Phil 3:2.
72. See Martyn, *Galatians*, 114; Paul's position is that his gospel is the "absolute norm."
73. See Betz, *Galatians*, 111 n. 483.
74. See Sanders, *Paul and Palestinian Judaism*, 511–15, on the ways Paul's religion can and cannot be described as "covenantal nomism," concluding, 543ff., that "Paul represents an *essentially different type of religiousness from any found in Palestinian Jewish literature*" (his italics). On Paul's polemics against Judaism, see 549–52.
75. See Chapter 2.
76. See J. Louis Martyn, "Apocalyptic Antinomies in Paul's Letter to the Galatians," *NTS* 31 (1985): 410–24.
77. See the reconstruction of the opponents on Abraham in *Galatians*, 302–6; Betz, *Galatians*, 137–53, categorizes Gal 3:6–14 as the second *probatio* with Abraham as *exemplum*.
78. See history of interpretation in Meeks, *Writings of St. Paul*.
79. See Sanders, *Paul and Palestinian Judaism*, 107–25; 543–52 (esp. 551–52 on circumcision and Judaism); John M. G. Barclay, "Who Was Considered an Apostate in the Jewish Diaspora?," in *Tolerance and Intolerance in Early Judaism and Christianity*, ed. Graham Stanton and Gedaliahu A. G. Stroumsa (Cambridge: Cambridge University Press, 1998), who suggests that the opponents considered Paul an apostate (92).
80. See Richard B. Hays, *Echoes of Scripture in the Letters of Paul* (New Haven: Yale University Press, 1989), for a different literary approach.
81. See Betz, *Galatians*, 253–55; 5:1–6:10 is a section of moral exhortation or *parenesis*.
82. See ibid., 281–83; Abraham J. Malherbe, *Moral Exhortation: A Greco-Roman Sourcebook* (Philadelphia: Westminster Press, 1986); Rom 1:29–31; 13:13; 1 Cor 5:10–11; 2 Cor 12:20.
83. See Betz, *Galatians*, 276.
84. Ibid. "Paul's concept of the Christian life," in terms of flesh and spirit.
85. See Paul Veyne, "La Famille Et L'amour Sous Le Haut-Empire Romain," *Annales (ESC)* 33 (1978): 35–63, cited in Foucault and Carrette (ed.),

Religion and Culture: "Pastoral Power and Political Reason," 135–52; and "About the Beginning of the Hermeneutics of the Self," 158–81.

86. See Sanders, *Paul and Palestinian Judaism*, 513. Wayne A. Meeks, *The Origins of Christian Morality: The First Two Centuries* (New Haven: Yale University Press, 1993), 68, writes that "Christian and Jewish lists [of vices] are interchangeable with those of other moralists of the time."

87. Betz, *Galatians*, 278.

88. See Chapter 2; Martyn, *Galatians*, 526, privileging Paul's theology, ascribes this dualism to "the Teachers."

89. In Gal 5:20–21 ἔχθραι, ἔρις, ζῆλος, θυμοί, ἐριθεῖαι, διχοστασίαι, αἱρέσεις.

90. Compare Martyn, *Galatians*, 532–33, to Meeks, *Origins of Christian Morality*, 66–71.

91. As Martyn, *Galatians*, notes, the Spirit here is the "Spirit of [God's] Son" (Gal 4:6).

92. Cf. Phil. 3:18, where Paul suggests that not "imitating me" makes one an "enemy of the cross"; see Castelli, *Imitating Paul*.

93. See ibid., 86, on difference as subversive of unity.

94. See the outline of possible sequences by John T. Fitzgerald in Wayne A. Meeks and Jouette M. Bassler, eds., *The Harpercollins Study Bible: New Revised Standard Version, with the Apocryphal/Deuterocanonical Books* (New York, NY: HarperCollins, 1993), 2164–65. On the history of scholarship, see Margaret E. Thrall, *A Critical and Exegetical Commentary on the Second Epistle to the Corinthians*, 2 vols. (Edinburgh: T&T Clark, 1994), 1:3–49. Victor Paul Furnish, *II Corinthians* (Garden City, NY: Doubleday, 1984), 35–48, holds to the "two-letter hypothesis" and that 2 Cor 10–13 is *not* the "letter of tears"; compare Francis Watson, "2 Cor 10–13 and Paul's Painful Letter to the Corinthians," *JTS* 35 (1984): 324–46; and Laurence L. Welborn, "The Identification of 2 Corinthians 10–13 with the 'Letter of Tears,'" *NovT* 37 (1995): 138–53. Cf. Hans Dieter Betz and George W. MacRae, *2 Corinthians 8 and 9: A Commentary on Two Administrative Letters of the Apostle Paul* (Philadelphia: Fortress, 1985).

95. See E. Randolph Richards, *The Secretary in the Letters of Paul* (Tübingen: Mohr (Siebeck), 1991).

96. Lloyd Bitzer, "The Rhetorical Situation," *Philosophy and Rhetoric* 1 (1968): 1–14.

97. See Thrall, *Second Corinthians*, 2:595–96; Hans-Georg Sundermann, *Der schwache Apostel und die Kraft der Rede: Eine rhetorische Analyse von 2 Kor 10–13* (Frankfurt am Main: P. Lang, 1996).

98. See Thrall, *Second Corinthians*, 2:928–40 and Sumney, *Opponents of Paul*, 79–80. On the critiqued concept of *theoi Andres* see Dieter Georgi, *The Opponents of Paul in Second Corinthians* (Philadelphia: Fortress, 1986). See Jaap Jan Flinterman, "The Ubiquitous 'Divine Man,'" *Numen* 43 (1996): 82–98.

99. Cf. Rev 2:2; the term was claimed by a number of Christian leaders for several generations in Asia and Achaia.

100. So Margaret E. Thrall, "Super-Apostles, Servants of Christ, and Servants of Satan," *JSNT* 6 (1980): 42–57; argued further in *Second Corinthians*, 2:926–65.

101. A central insight of Ernst Käsemann, "Die Legitimität des Apostels. Eine Untersuchung zu II Korinther 10–13," *ZNW* 41 (1942): 33–71.

102. The relationship of the opponents in 2 Cor 1–7 and 2 Cor 10–13 is tangential. Thrall, *Second Corinthians*, 926–45, prioritizes 2 Cor 10–13 and, speculatively, posits the group was from Jerusalem, aligned with the Petrine mission, and possibly associated with a proto-Matthean circle. Sumney, *Opponents of Paul*, 130–33, concludes that they are the same.

103. Thrall, *Second Corinthians*, 2:940–45.
104. See Donald Dale Walker, *Paul's Offer of Leniency (2 Cor 10:1): Populist Ideology and Rhetoric in a Pauline Letter Fragment* (Tübingen: Mohr (Siebeck), 2002).
105. See the list in Thrall, *Second Corinthians*, 2:605–6.
106. Ibid., 2:607; Georgi, *Opponents of Paul*.
107. See Abraham J. Malherbe, "Antisthenes and Odysseus, and Paul at War," *HTR* 76 (1983): 143–73. 2 Cor 10:1–11 is the *exordium* of the speech taking the form of *insinuatio*; see Sundermann, *Die Kraft der Rede*, 47; Thrall, *Second Corinthians*, 2:597–98; and Lausberg, *Handbook*, §§ 265, 280–81.
108. See Thrall, *Second Corinthians*, 2:654–57.
109. See ibid., 2:682–83; Marshall, *Enmity in Corinth*, 165–258. Negotiations here and in 1 Cor 8–10 indicate this was not part of the contention over the "other gospel."
110. See Lausberg, *Handbook*, §§ 280–81; Sundermann, *Die Kraft der Rede*, 45.
111. Collins, "Excommunication," notes the bridal language. Knust, *Abandoned to Lust*, 51–87, treats only 1 Cor. For Thrall, *Second Corinthians*, 2:661, this "belongs to a tradition of androcentric imagery" from the OT.
112. Furnish, *2nd Corinthians*, 499; Susan Treggiari, *Roman Marriage: Iusti Coniuges from the Time of Cicero to the Time of Ulpian* (Oxford: Clarendon, 1991).
113. On the notion that Satan seduced Eve, see Thrall, *Second Corinthians*, 2:662; Gary M. Anderson, "Celibacy or Consummation in the Garden: Reflections on Early Jewish and Christian Interpretations of the Garden of Eden," *HTR* 82 (1989): 121–48; *Wis. Sol.* 2.23–24 and *2 Enoch* 31.6.
114. For the longer reading ἀπὸ τῆς ἁπλότητος καὶ τῆς ἁγνότητος, see Thrall, *Second Corinthians*, 2:663.
115. There are thirteen occurrences of καυχάομαι in 2 Cor 10–13.
116. The closest analogy is Phil 3:2, which lacks this heresiological force.
117. See Thrall, *Second Corinthians*, 2:667–70, for summary of positions and her hypothesis of a connection with Matt 28:16–20.
118. See Lee A. Johnson, "Satan Talk in Corinth: The Rhetoric of Conflict," *BTB* 29 (1999): 145–55.
119. On the hardship catalogue see John T. Fitzgerald, *Cracks in an Earthen Vessel: An Examination of the Catalogues of Hardships in the Corinthian Correspondence* (Atlanta: Scholars Press, 1988); and Susan R. Garrett, "The God of This World and the Affliction of Paul: 2 Cor 4:1–12," in *Greeks, Romans, and Christians: Essays in Honor of Abraham J. Malherbe*, ed. Abraham J. Malherbe et al. (Minneapolis: Fortress, 1990). Laurence L. Welborn, "The Runaway Paul," *HTR* 92 (1999): 115–63; and Douglas A. Campbell, "An Anchor for Pauline Chronology: Paul's Flight from 'the Ethnarch of King Aretas' (2 Corinthians 11:32–33)," *JBL* 121, no. 2 (2002): 279–302.
120. The phrase is in Thrall, *Second Corinthians* 2:772 but see also Furnish, *2nd Corinthians*, 542–43 and the citations in both.
121. See Hans Dieter Betz, *Der Apostel Paulus und die sokratische Tradition: Eine exegetische Untersuchung zu seiner Apologie 2 Korinther 10–13* (Tübingen: Mohr, 1972), 89–90.
122. See Johnson, "Satan Talk," correctly identifying the references to Satan as rhetorical. Elaine H. Pagels, *The Origin of Satan* (New York: Random House, 1995), follows a similar method. See also Sanders, *Paul and Palestinian Judaism*, 1–12, who rejects facile assumptions about Paul's Jewish beliefs.
123. See Von Staden, "Hairesis and Heresy"; Luke Timothy Johnson, "The New Testament's Anti-Jewish Slander and the Conventions of Ancient Polemic," *JBL* 108 (1989): 419–41.

124. Gregory E. Sterling, "'Philo Has Not Been Used Half Enough': The Signifi-cance of Philo of Alexandria for the Study of the New Testament," *Perspectives in Religious Studies* 30, no. 3 (2003): 251–69; Samuel Sandmel, *The Genius of Paul: A Study in History* (Philadelphia: Fortress, 1979).
125. Philo of Alexandria, *Philo in Ten Volumes and Two Supplementary Volumes*, trans. F. H. Colson, G. H. Whitaker, and Ralph Marcus, 12 vols. (London: Heinemann, 1966). See Shaye J. D. Cohen, *From the Maccabees to the Mishnah* (Philadelphia: Westminster, 1987) on "covenantal nomism" in Sanders, *Paul and Palestinian Judaism* and Schwartz, *Imperialism and Jewish Society*, 66–68.
126. See David Dawson, *Allegorical Readers and Cultural Revision in Ancient Alexandria* (Berkeley: University of California Press, 1992); Ellen Birnbaum, "Allegorical Interpretation and Jewish Identity among Alexandrian Jewish Writers," in *Neotestamentica Et Philonica: Studies in Honor of Peder Borgen*, ed. David E. Aune, Torrey Seland, and Jarl Henning Ulrichsen, NovT-Sup (Leiden: Brill, 2003), 307–29.
127. Peder Borgen, Kåre Fuglseth, and Roald Skarsten, "The Philo Concordance Database in Greek," (BibleWorks software v.9, 2005).
128. The ms. is corrupt in this paragraph.
129. Three technical moral terms in Stoicism.
130. See Mary Ann Beavis, "Philo's Therapeutai: Philosopher's Dream or Utopian Construction?," *JSP* 14, no. 1 (2004): 30–42; Troels Engberg-Pedersen, "Philo's *De Vita Contemplativa* as a Philosopher's Dream," *JSJ* 30 (1999): 40–64.
131. On the *Testimonium Flavianum* see Alice Whealey, *Josephus on Jesus: The Testimonium Flavianum Controversy from Late Antiquity to Modern Times* (New York: Lang, 2003).
132. Flavius Josephus, *Works*, trans. H. St. J. Thackeray, 10 vols. (London: Heinemann, 1926). See *J.W.* 1.1–6, 16. On the *Antiquities* see Gregory E. Sterling, *Historiography and Self-Definition: Josephos, Luke-Acts, and Apologetic Historiography* (Leiden Brill, 1991).
133. Flavius Josephus, *Flavii Josephi Opera Edidit Et Apparatu Critico Instruxit Benedictus Niese* (Berlin: Weidmann (BibleWorks 9), 1887). See also Plat. *Apol.* 22a–e; Luc. *Dial. Mort.* 3; *Pisc.* 11–12; *Men.* 4–6; *Ps.-Clem.* I. 3–5; and Porphyry *Vita Plotini*, 3.

NOTES TO CHAPTER 5

1. Frederic R. Jameson, *The Political Unconscious: Narrative as a Socially Symbolic Act* (Ithaca, NY: Cornell University Press, 1982).
2. Sanders, *Historical Figure of Jesus*.
3. Willi Marxsen, *Mark the Evangelist: Studies on the Redaction History of the Gospel*, trans. James Boyce et al. (Nashville: Abingdon, 1969); Burton L. Mack, *A Myth of Innocence: Mark and Early Chrisian Origins* (Philadelphia: Fortress, 1988).
4. On the genre of Sayings Gospel see Robinson, "Logoi Sophon."
5. On the two-source hypothesis see H. J. Holtzmann, *Die synoptischen Evangelien: Ihr Ursprung und geschichtlicher Charakter* (Leipzig, 1863); and the four-source hypothesis B. H. Streeter, *The Four Gospels: A Study of Origins* (London: Macmillan, 1924).
6. See, however, William R. Farmer, *The Synoptic Problem, a Critical Analysis* (New York: Macmillan, 1964); and Mark S. Goodacre, *The Case against Q: Studies in Markan Priority and the Synoptic Problem* (Harrisburg, PA: Trinity, 2002).

7. See Dieter Lührmann, *Die Redaktion der Logienquelle* (Neukirchen-Vluyn: Neukirchener Verlag, 1969); and John S. Kloppenborg, *The Formation of Q: Trajectories in Ancient Wisdom Collections*, 2nd ed. (Harrisburg, PA: Trinity, 1999).

8. See Kloppenborg, *Formation of Q*, 41–80; Helmut Koester, *Ancient Christian Gospels: Their History and Development* (London: SCM Press, 1990), 133–35; and Robinson, Hoffmann, and Kloppenborg, *Critical Edition of Q*.

9. See Kloppenborg, *Formation of Q*, 80–88.

10. Ibid., 244–45.

11. Ibid.

12. Stone, "The Book of Enoch and Judaism in the Third Century, B.C.E."

13. See, for instance, Hultgren, *The Rise of Normative Christianity*, 31–41.

14. Crossan, *Historical Jesus*; Mack, *Myth of Innocence*.

15. See, e.g., Kloppenborg, *Formation of Q*, 132, 149–50.

16. See ibid., 152, 154, on Q 12:49, 51–53.

17. So Hultgren, *The Rise of Normative Christianity*, 37–39.

18. Crossan, *Historical Jesus*; Marcus J. Borg, *Conflict, Holiness & Politics in the Teachings of Jesus* (New York: E. Mellen Press, 1984).

19. See Mack, *Who Wrote the New Testament?*

20. See Hendrikus Boers, "The Formation of Q: Trajectories in Ancient Wisdom Collections," review of John S. Kloppenborg, *Formation of Q*, Philadelphia: Fortress, 1987, *Int* 43 (1989): 200–201; and John J. Collins, "Wisdom, Apocalypticism, and Generic Compatibility," in *In Search of Wisdom*, ed. L. G. Perdue, B. B. Scott, and W. J. Wiseman (Louisville: Westminster/John Knox, 1993).

21. Kloppenborg, *Formation of Q*, 171–245, 264–89, 317–22.

22. See Robinson, Hoffmann, and Kloppenborg, *Critical Edition of Q*, 154, 330.

23. See Kloppenborg, *Formation of Q*, 102–7 and Robinson, Hoffmann, and Kloppenborg, *Critical Edition of Q*, 6–17.

24. Kloppenborg, *Formation of Q*, 106, notes parallels with 1QS; see Chap. 2.

25. See ibid., 112.

26. Kloppenborg considers 11:16, 29–32 secondary.

27. Kloppenborg, *Formation of Q*, 126–27.

28. Ibid.

29. Ibid., 155–58, finds Matthean priority over Lucan order.

30. Ibid., 166.

31. See ibid., 139–47, on its tradition-history.

32. The order in Robinson, Hoffmann, and Kloppenborg, *Critical Edition of Q*, 264–73, is 11:39a, 42, 39b, 40 [excluded], 41.

33. Ibid., 284–89, omitting brackets and Abel and Zechariah.

34. See Kloppenborg, *Formation of Q*, 148; Lührmann, *Die Redaktion der Logienquelle*, 47–48.

35. A title of leadership; see Dale B. Martin, *Slavery as Salvation: The Metaphor of Slavery in Pauline Christianity* (New Haven: Yale University Press, 1990), 50–68. See, e.g., Matt 21:33–41; 22:1–14; 24:45–51; Luke 2:29; 12:41–46; 17:7–10; Acts 2:18; 4:29; 16:17; 20:19; 34–35; Rom 1:1; Gal 1:10; Phil 1:1; Col 4:12; 2 Tim 2:24; Tit 1:1; Jas 1:1; 2 Pet 1:1; Jude 1; and Rev 1:1; 6:11; 10:7; 11:18; 19:10; 22:9.

36. *Contra* Kloppenborg, *Formation of Q*, 150–51.

37. See James M. Robinson, ed. *The Nag Hammadi Library in English*, 3rd ed. (San Francisco: Harper & Row, 1988), 124–26; Francis T. Fallon and Ron Cameron, "The Gospel of Thomas: A *Forschungsbericht* and Analysis," in

ANRW (Berlin: Walter de Gruyter, 1988); Risto Uro, *Thomas at the Cross-roads: Essays on the Gospel of Thomas* (Edinburgh: T&T Clark, 1998); and Jon Ma Asgeirsson, April D. De Conick, and Risto Uro, eds., *Thomasine Traditions in Antiquity: The Social and Cultural World of the Gospel of Thomas*, Nag Hammadi and Manichaean Studies (Leiden: Brill, 2006).

38. Compare, for instance, Koester, *Ancient Christian Gospels* and Hultgren, *The Rise of Normative Christianity*. See also Gregory J. Riley, *The River of God: A New History of Christian Origins* (San Francisco: HarperSanFrancisco, 2001); and Richard Valantasis, *The Gospel of Thomas* (London: Routledge, 1997).

39. See Bentley A. Layton, *The Gnostic Scriptures: A New Translation with Annotations and Introductions* (New York: Doubleday, 1995) and King, *What Is Gnosticism?*; James M. Robinson and Helmut Koester, eds., *One Jesus and Four Primitive Gospels: Trajectories through Early Christian-ity* (Philadelphia: Fortress, 1971); Koester, *Ancient Christian Gospels*; and Robert Walter Funk and Roy W. Hoover, *The Five Gospels: The Search for the Authentic Words of Jesus: New Translation and Commentary* (San Francisco: HarperSanFrancisco, 1997).

40. April D. DeConick, *Recovering the Original Gospel of Thomas: A History of the Gospel and Its Growth* (London T&T Clark, 2005).

41. Ibid., 3–37.

42. Ibid., 55–63; see Vernon K. Robbins, "Rhetorical Composition and Sources in the Gospel of Thomas," *SBLSP* 36 (1997): 86–114.

43. DeConick, *Recovering the Original Gospel of Thomas*, 64–110.

44. Ibid., 5–8, 94–95, 123.

45. 16.1–3: Luke 12:51–52; 31: Matt 13:57; 39: Matt 10:16; Luke 11:52, Matt 23:23; 57: Matt 13:24–30; 61.1: Luke 17:34; Matt 24:40–41; 64: Luke 14:15–24; Matt 22:1–10; 65.1–7: Mark 12:1–12; 68.1: Matt 5:11; Luke 6:22; 71: Mark 14:58; Matt 26:61; 89: Matt 23:25; 93: Matt 7:6; 102: Luke 11:52; Matt 23:13. See B. H. Throckmorton, *Gospel Parallels: A Comparison of the Synoptic Gospels, with Alternative Readings from the Manuscripts and Non-canonical Parallels*, 5th ed. (Nashville: Nelson, 1992), xxx–xxxi; and ibid.; John S. Kloppenborg, *Q-Thomas Reader* (Sonoma, CA: Polebridge, 1990).

46. See DeConick, *Recovering the Original Gospel of Thomas*, 69–70.

47. See ibid., 131–55 on parallels.

48. See Cohen, *From the Maccabees to the Mishnah*; Jacob Neusner, *From Politics to Piety: The Emergence of Pharasaic Judaism* (Englewood, NJ: Prentice-Hall, 1973); and Schiffman, *Understanding Second Temple and Rabbinic Judaism*.

49. See Pagels, *Beyond Belief*; challenged by Ismo Dunderberg, *The Beloved Disciple in Conflict?: Revisiting the Gospels of John and Thomas* (Oxford: Oxford University Press, 2006).

50. See DeConick, *Recovering the Original Gospel of Thomas*, 92.

51. See Boyarin, *Border Lines*.

52. See DeConick, *Recovering the Original Gospel of Thomas*, 90.

53. See Pagels, *Beyond Belief*, 46–57.

54. See Davies and Allison, *St. Matthew*, 1.138–47. Jerusalem, Palestine, and Alexandria are also proposed.

55. See the table and bibliography, ibid., 1.10.

56. See J. Andrew Overman, *Matthew's Gospel and Formative Judaism: The Social World of the Matthean Community* (Minneapolis: Fortress, 1990); and Anthony J. Saldarini, *Matthew's Christian-Jewish Community* (Chicago: University of Chicago Press, 1994).

57. So David C. Sim, *The Gospel of Matthew and Christian Judaism: The His-tory and Social Setting of the Matthean Community* (Edinburgh: T&T

Clark, 1998). See also Thrall, *Second Corinthians*, on a connection between Paul's opponents in Corinth and the Gospel of Matthew.

58. See Douglas R. A. Hare, "How Jewish Is the Gospel of Matthew?," *CBQ* 62, no. 2 (2000): 264–77; and Donald A. Hagner, "Matthew: Apostate, Reformer, Revolutionary?," *NTS* 49, no. 2 (2003): 193–209.

59. Hagner, "Matthew . . . ?," 197–98.

60. See Boyarin, "Justin Martyr Invents Judaism," n. 19, p. 432.

61. J. Louis Martyn, *History & Theology in the Fourth Gospel*, 2nd ed. (Nashville: Abingdon, 1979).

62. Steven T. Katz, "Issues in the Separation of Judaism and Christianity after 70 CE: A Reconsideration," *JBL* 103 (1984): 43–76.

63. See, for instance, Reuven Kimelman, "*Birkat Ha-Minim* and the Lack of Evidence for an Anti-Christian Prayer in Late Antiquity," in *Jewish and Christian Self-Definition, Vol. 2*, ed. E. P. Sanders, Albert I. Baumgarten, and Alan Mendelson (London: SCM Press, 1981); and Meeks, "Breaking Away."

64. With Kimelman, "*Birkat Ha-Minim*." See Lieu, "The Parting of the Ways."

65. Stephen Motyer, *Your Father the Devil?: A New Approach to John and 'the Jews'* (Carlisle, UK: Paternoster, 1997), 93.

66. Boyarin, "Justin Martyr Invents Judaism."

67. See ibid.; *Border Lines*; and Lieu, *Christian Identity*.

68. Boyarin, "Justin Martyr Invents Judaism," and *Border Lines*.

69. Lieu, "The Parting of the Ways," 116–17.

70. With Sim, *Gospel of Matthew and Christian Judaism*, 113–15. See Overman, *Matthew's Gospel*; Neusner, *From Politics to Piety: The Emergence of Pharasaic Judaism*; Sanders, *Jesus and Judaism*.

71. See Lieu, "The Parting of the Ways," 108–9.

72. See Overman, *Matthew's Gospel*.

73. See Foucault, *Archaeology of Knowledge*, 40–49, quotation on p. 47.

74. Ibid., 48.

75. See Petri Luomanen, "The 'Sociology of Sectarianism' in Matthew: Modeling the Genesis of Early Jewish and Christian Communities," in *Fair Play: Diversity and Conflicts in Early Christianity: Essays in Honour of Heikki Räisänen*, ed. Heikki Räisänen et al. (Leiden: Brill, 2002); Gerd Theissen, *The Gospels in Context: Social and Political History in the Synoptic Tradition* (Minneapolis: Fortress, 1991), 269.

76. Meeks, "Breaking Away."

77. See also Luomanen, "Sociology of Sectarianism."

78. So Hagner, "Matthew . . . ?"; see also Hare, "How Jewish Is the Gospel of Matthew?."

79. See Barth, *Ethnic Groups and Boundaries*; and Jenkins, *Social Identity*.

80. On Matthew and Mark, see Davies and Allison, *St. Matthew*, 1.98–115.

81. See Hans Dieter Betz, *The Sermon on the Mount: A Commentary on the Sermon on the Mount, Including the Sermon on the Plain (Matthew 5:3–7:27 and Luke 6:20–49)* (Minneapolis: Fortress, 1995).

82. Ibid., 330.

83. Ibid., 142–46.

84. See Davies and Allison, *St. Matthew*, 1.461–62; Betz, *Sermon on the Mount*.

85. Davies and Allison, *St. Matthew*, 1.462 n. 51.

86. So also Sim, *Gospel of Matthew and Christian Judaism*, 5, 123–27; Overman, *Matthew's Gospel*, 78–90; Saldarini, *Matthew's Christian-Jewish Community*, 124–64; Betz, *Sermon on the Mount*, 166–97; and Davies and Allison, *St. Matthew*, 1.481–503.

87. Suggesting Paulinist opponents; see Sim, *Gospel of Matthew and Christian Judaism*; and Thrall, *Second Corinthians*.
88. On multiple opposition in Matthew, see Jean Zumstein, *La Condition du Croyant dans L'évangile selon Matthieu* (Göttingen: Vandenhoeck & Ruprecht, 1977), 171–200; and Davies and Allison, *St. Matthew*, 1.501 n. 54.
89. See David C. Sim, "Matthew 7.21–23: Further Evidence of Its Anti-Pauline Perspective," *NTS* 53 (2007): 325–43.
90. See Barth, *Ethnic Groups and Boundaries*, 9–38.
91. On this confession, see Sim, "Matthew 7.21–23," 329–30.
92. See Davies and Allison, *St. Matthew*, 2.160–2, 750–1.
93. See ibid., 1.58–62 on the "five books of Matthew" as a new Pentateuch.
94. Ibid., 169.
95. Cf. William G. Thompson, *Matthew's Advice to a Divided Community* (Rome: Biblical Institute Press, 1970), 27–68.
96. Davies and Allison, *St. Matthew*, 2.754, maintain that 18:1–5 refers to actual children while 18:6–14 to believers.
97. See Gerd Theissen, *Sociology of Early Palestinian Christianity* (Philadelphia: Fortress, 1978).
98. Cf. Thompson, *Matthew's Advice*, 152–74.
99. See Davies and Allison, *St. Matthew*, 2.784–86; Lev 19:15–18; Deut 19:15; Prov 3:12; 10:18; 25:9–10; 26:24–5; 27:5–6; Sir. 19:13–20:2; CD IX, 2–8; 1QS V, 24–VI, 1; *T. Gad* 4, 6; *y. Yoma* 45c. See Thompson, *Matthew's Advice*, 175–202, esp. 186.
100. Davies and Allison, *St. Matthew*, 2.635–39.
101. Ibid., 2.791.
102. Possibly original to Jesus; ibid., 2.794.
103. So Joachim Jeremias, *The Parables of Jesus*, rev. ed. (New York: Scribner, 1963), 109; and Martinus C. de Boer, "Ten Thousand Talents: Matthew's Interpretation and Redaction of the Parable of the Unforgiving Servant (Matt 18:23–35)," *CBQ* 50 (1988): 214–32.
104. See Eta Linnemann, *Jesus of the Parables; Introduction and Exposition* (New York: Harper & Row, 1967), 109; and J. Duncan M. Derrett, *Law in the New Testament* (London: Darton Longman & Todd, 1970), 34–35.
105. Jeremias, *Parables*, 30, on Jesus' "shock tactics," but Derrett, *Law in the New Testament*, an actual amount. Cf. Jos., *Ant.* 12.175–76; Boer, "Ten Thousand Talents," on 10,000 denarii changed to talents; cf. Matt 25:16–28 and Luke 19:11–27.
106. See Bernard Brandon Scott, "The King's Accounting: Matthew 18:23–34," *JBL* 104, no. 3 (1985): 429–42; and Warren Carter, "Resisting and Imitating the Empire: Imperial Paradigms in Two Matthean Parables," *Int* 56, no. 3 (2002): 260–72.
107. On Mark 13 and Vespasian propaganda, see Theissen, *Gospels in Context*, 265–66.
108. Sim, *Gospel of Matthew and Christian Judaism*, 117.
109. Thompson, *Matthew's Advice*.
110. See Günther Bornkamm, *Tradition and Interpretation in Matthew* (London: SCM Press, 1963), 15–24.
111. See Eduard Schweizer, *Church Order in the New Testament* (London: SCM, 1961), 56.
112. See Davies and Allison, *St. Matthew*, 3.67–68.
113. Ibid., 3.68–69; cf. 15:11–32.
114. See ibid., 3.67–68.
115. Rudolf Karl Bultmann, *The History of the Synoptic Tradition* (New York: Harper & Row, 1963), 190.

116. See Barth, *Ethnic Groups and Boundaries*, 9–10; Jenkins, *Social Identity*, 96.
117. See Davies and Allison, *St. Matthew*, 3.60, on Matt 19:30, Matt 20:16 (cf. Luke 13:30; *Gos. Thom.* 4); Richard Bauckham, "The Rich Man and Lazarus: The Parable and the Parallels," *NTS* 37 (1991): 225–46.
118. See "The Parable of the Royal Wedding Feast (Matthew 22:1–14) and the Parable of the Lame Man and the Blind Man (Apocryphon of Ezekial)," *JBL* 115 (1996): 471–88.
119. See Davies and Allison, *St. Matthew*, 3.193–98.
120. Ibid., 1.555 on Matt 5:45.
121. See Wolfgang Trilling, *Das wahre Israel; Studien zur Theologie des Matthäusevangeliums*, 2nd ed. (Leipzig: St. Benno-Verlag, 1961), 117.
122. See Neusner, *From Politics to Piety: The Emergence of Pharasaic Judaism*; and Anthony J. Saldarini, *Pharisees, Scribes and Sadducees in Palestinian Society: A Sociological Approach* (Wilmington, DE: Michael Glazier, 1988).
123. Meeks, "Breaking Away," 109; Overman, *Matthew's Gospel*, 142; Sim, *Gospel of Matthew and Christian Judaism*, 119.
124. See Davies and Allison, *St. Matthew*, 3.257–63; Anthony J. Saldarini, "Delegitimation of Leaders in Matthew 23," *CBQ* 54 (1992): 659–80, also *Matthew's Christian-Jewish Community*; Overman, *Matthew's Gospel*; and Sim, *Gospel of Matthew and Christian Judaism*.
125. *Gospel of Matthew and Christian Judaism*, 119–20.
126. Ibid., 117, 120.
127. Mostly from Mark; 12:1–8 (Mark 2:23–28), 9–14 (Mark 3:1–6); 15:1–20 (Mark 7:1–23); 19:3–9 (Mark 10:2–9); 22:34–40 (Mark 12:31–36, changing scribe to Pharisee lawyer); and Matt 22:41–46 (Mark 12:35–37, changing scribe to Pharisee). See ibid., 119.
128. See Johnson, "The New Testament's Anti-Jewish Slander and the Conventions of Ancient Polemic"; and Davies and Allison, *St. Matthew*, 3.259–60.
129. Cited in nn. 56–58.
130. See David Nirenberg, *Communities of Violence: Persecution of Minorities in the Middle Ages* (Princeton: Princeton University Press, 1996).
131. Saldarini, "Delegitimation of Leaders"; Graham Stanton, *A Gospel for a New People: Studies in Matthew* (Louisville: Westminster/John Knox, 1993), 109. See also Overman, *Matthew's Gospel*, 142–43; and Sim, *Gospel of Matthew and Christian Judaism*, 121–22.
132. Saldarini, "Delegitimation of Leaders," notes the structural parallels between the eight beatitudes and the seven woes.
133. See Davies and Allison, *St. Matthew*, 3.294.
134. On the warnings 23:1–12 and woes in 23:13–33, see ibid., 3.264–6, 282–84.
135. See Kurt Niederwimmer, *The Didache: A Commentary* (Minneapolis: Fortress, 1998); and Bart D. Ehrman, *The Apostolic Fathers* (Cambridge, MA: Harvard University Press, 2003), 1.405–11.
136. See Niederwimmer, *Didache*, 171–88.
137. Trans. Ehrman, *Apostolic Fathers*; cf. Niederwimmer, *Didache*, "using Christ to make a living."

NOTES TO CHAPTER 6

1. See Asad, *Genealogies of Religion*, 68.
2. Barth, *Ethnic Groups and Boundaries*; Lewis A. Coser, *The Functions of Social Conflict* (New York: Free Press of Glencoe, 1964); Jenkins, *Social Identity*.

3. See Berger and Luckmann, *The Social Construction of Reality: A Treatise in the Sociology of Knowledge.*

4. See Max Weber, Guenther Roth, and Claus Wittich, *Economy and Society: An Outline of Interpretive Sociology,* 2 vols. (Berkeley: University of California Press, 1978), 1.63–312 (215); and Max Weber and Talcott Parsons, *Max Weber: The Theory of Social and Economic Organization* (New York: Free Press, 1964), 363–69.

5. Willi Marxsen, *Mark the Evangelist: Studies on the Redaction History of the Gospel,* trans. James Boyce et al. (Nashville: Abingdon, 1969). See, however, Helmut Koester, *Synoptische Überlieferung bei den apostolischen Vätern* (Berlin: Akademie-Verlag, 1957).

6. See Royalty, "Dwelling on Visions."

7. See James D. G. Dunn, *The Epistles to the Colossians and to Philemon: A Commentary on the Greek Text* (Grand Rapids: Eerdmans, 1996), 83–85.

8. See Schweizer, *Colossians,* 123.

9. See Dunn, *Colossians,* 138.

10. In Revelation, John claims such authority.

11. See 1 Tim 3:1–13, 5:17–22; Tit 1:5–9; Ign. *Magn.* 3–4; *Trall.* 2; *Smyrn.* 8.

12. See David E. Aune, *Revelation 1–5,* 3 vols., vol. 1 (Waco, TX: Word, 1997), 108–12.

13. See Roman Heiligenthal, "Wer waren die 'Nikolaiten'? Ein Beitrag zur Theologiegeschichte des frühen Christentums," *ZNW* 82 (1991): 133–37.

14. See David Frankfurter, "Jews or Not? Reconstructing the 'Other' in Rev 2:9 and 3:9," *HTR* 94, no. 4 (2001): 403–25; and Elaine H. Pagels, "The Social History of Satan Part Three, John of Patmos and Ignatius of Antioch: Contrasting Visions of 'God's People,'" *HTR* 99, no. 4 (2006): 487–505.

15. See Paul Brooks Duff, *Who Rides the Beast?: Prophetic Rivalry and the Rhetoric of Crisis in the Churches of the Apocalypse* (Oxford: Oxford University Press, 2001).

16. Knust, *Abandoned to Lust.*

17. See C. K. Barrett, "Gnosis and the Apocalypse of John," in *The New Testament and Gnosis. Essays in Honour of Robert McL. Wilson,* ed. A. H. B. Logan and A. J. M Wedderburn (Edinburgh: T & T Clark, 1983), 128.

18. See Royalty, *Streets of Heaven,* 27–34.

19. See Mary Rose D'Angelo, "Eusebeia: Roman Imperial Family Values and the Sexual Politics of 4 Maccabees and the Pastorals," *BibInt* 11, no. 2 (2003): 139–65.

20. Martin Dibelius and Hans Conzelmann, *The Pastoral Epistles,* trans. P. Buttolph and A. Yarbro (Philadelphia: Fortress, 1972), 39–41.

21. Bhabha, *Location of Culture,* 122–23.

22. Using the longer *BG* 8502 ms. trans. King, *Gospel of Mary.*

23. See Christopher M. Tuckett, "Synoptic Tradition in Some Nag Hammadi and Related Texts," *VC* 36, no. 2 (1982): 173–90.

24. Dibelius and Conzelmann, *Pastoral Epistles,* 108.

25. Likely, although the text ends with "I will receive rest in silence" (9:29).

26. See King, *Gospel of Mary,* 63–67.

27. Thomas, Judas, and Peter exhibit similar bravery in other gospels.

28. The unnamed "Beloved Disciple" was the likely founder of the Johannine community; see John 13:23; 19:26–27; 20:8–10; 21:7.

29. William Schoedel, *Ignatius of Antioch* (Philadelphia: Fortress, 1985), 10, notes a common theme in *Eph.* 14.2 with 1 John, but considers a shared source the likely cause.

30. See Martyn, *History & Theology in the Fourth Gospel.*

31. See μένω in John 6:56; 14:20; 15:4–7; 17:23 and ζωὴν αἰώνιον in John 3:16–36; 5:24; 6:40, 47; 10:10, 28; 11:25ff; 20:31.
32. Cf. *1 Clem.* 5.5; 47.1
33. *Eph.* 9.2, 12.1, 20.1, 21.1; *Magn.* 15.1, *Trall.* 3.3, *Rom.* 4.1, 7.2, 10.1; *Phil.* 11.2, 12.1; *Pol.* 3.1; see Schoedel, *Ignatius*, 175.
34. Trans. Ehrman, *Apostolic Fathers*.
35. See Schoedel, *Ignatius*, 7, 9–10, 137.
36. On Ignatius' knowledge of Pauline epistles vs. traditional imagery, see ibid., 9–10.
37. On the two-source theory, see Ehrman, *Apostolic Fathers*, 1.328.
38. 1 Cor 15:28; Phil 2:10; 3:21; 2 Cor 4:14; Col 2:8–10; 3:2; 1 Tim 1:6; 1 Pet 1:21; 3:9.
39. Koester, *Synoptische Überlieferung*.
40. On ἐπιστρέφω to describe conversion in Acts: 3:19; 14:15; 15:19; 26:18, 20; 28:27; also Matt 13:15; Mark 4:12; Luke 1:16, 17; 17:4; 22:32; 2 Cor 3:16; Gal 4:9; James 5:19, 20.
41. Latin mss only.
42. See Schoedel, *Ignatius*, 12 n. 56; 12–13; Chapter 1.
43. Ibid., 220, labels "truly" (ἀληθῶς) here an "anti-docetic" marker.
44. See ibid. 225 n. 1; par. in John 2:19 and 10:18. Ignatius usually states that God raised Jesus.
45. Ibid. 226–27 nn. 5–7 on the source of the quotation in 3.2.
46. A collection of traditions, not a written gospel; ibid., 234.
47. See ibid., 235–36.
48. So too ibid., 240.
49. See also *Trall.* 6.2; 7.2; 11.1.
50. On prophets see ahead and Pagels, "John of Patmos and Ignatius of Antioch."
51. See Schoedel, *Ignatius*, 69; see, however, *Smyrn.* 4.1.
52. See ibid., 119.
53. *Eph.* 4.1–2, 13.1; *Magn.* 6.1, 15.1; *Trall.* 2.2; *Phil.* 1.1, 11.2.
54. See Christine Trevett, "Prophecy and Anti-Episcopal Activity: A Third Error Combated by Ignatius?" *JEH* 34, no. 1 (1983): 1–18; Pagels, "John of Patmos and Ignatius of Antioch."
55. See King, *What Is Gnosticism?*, 44–45.
56. On "Jewish Christians" see Chapter 5.
57. See Trevett, "Prophecy and Anti-Episcopal Activity."
58. See also Pagels, "John of Patmos and Ignatius of Antioch."
59. See Layton, "Significance of Basilides."
60. *Eph.* 6.1; *Magn.* 2–3.2, 6.1, 7.1, 13.1; *Trall.* 2.1–3.2, 12.2, 13.2; *Phld.* 3.1, 4.1, 7.2; *Smyr.* 8.1–9.1; *Poly.* 6.1l.
61. There was no one "Roman" church; see Peter Lampe, *From Paul to Valentinus: Christians at Rome in the First Two Centuries*, trans. Michael Steinhauser (Minneapolis: Fortress, 2003); Schoedel, *Ignatius*, 14–15.
62. Rodolphe Kasser, Marvin W. Meyer, and Gregor Wurst, *The Gospel of Judas: From Codex Tchacos* (Washington: National Geographic, 2006).
63. With *Ap. John*; *Allogenes*; *Eugnostos*; and *Soph. Jes. Chr*; see ibid., 137–69.
64. See Robert Graves, *King Jesus* (New York: Farrar, Straus & Cudahy, 1946); Meyer, Kasser, Meyer, and Wurst, *Gospel of Judas*, 2–3; Elaine H. Pagels and Karen L. King, *Reading Judas: The Gospel of Judas and the Shaping of Christianity* (New York: Viking, 2007), 3–31.
65. Contra *Reading Judas*.

66. See Ehrman in Kasser, Meyer, and Wurst, *Gospel of Judas*, 90; Meyer, ibid., 138.
67. On "generations," see *Gos. Jud.* 36, 53; and ibid., 24 n. 30.
68. Agreeing here with Pagels and King, *Reading Judas*.

NOTES TO CHAPTER 7

1. Cf. H. Richard Niebuhr, *Christ and Culture* (San Francisco: HarperSan-Francisco, 2001); and Bhabha, *Location of Culture*.
2. See Horsley, *Bandits, Prophets, and Messiahs*; Richard A. Horsley, ed. *Paul and Empire: Religion and Power in Roman Imperial Society* (Harrisburg, PA: Trinity, 1997); and "Religion and Other Products of Empire," *JAAR* 71, no. 1 (2003): 13–44.
3. See Dale B. Martin, *Inventing Superstition: From the Hippocratics to the Christians* (Cambridge, MA: Harvard University Press, 2004). Lucian and Galen elided the groups in the second century.
4. See Royalty, *Streets of Heaven*, 244–46.
5. Orietta Rossini, *Ara Pacis* (Milan: Electa, 2007), 6.
6. Ibid.
7. Ibid., 22.
8. Paul Zanker, *The Power of Images in the Age of Augustus* (Ann Arbor: University of Michigan Press, 1988).
9. Rossini, *Ara Pacis*, 30.
10. On the *Tellus* as *Pax Augusta* see Zanker, *Power of Images*. See also Rossini, *Ara Pacis*, 36, 46.
11. *Ara Pacis*, 48.
12. Oxford Revised Translation: auferre trucidare rapere falsis nominibus imperium, atque ubi solitudinem faciunt, pacem appellant.
13. See Sanders, *Historical Figure of Jesus*, 18–20.
14. See Jos. *Ant.* 15.183–98.
15. See Sanders, *Historical Figure of Jesus*, 5–6.
16. See Martin Hengel, *Crucifixion in the Ancient World and the Folly of the Message of the Cross* (Philadelphia: Fortress, 1977).
17. See Horsley, *Bandits, Prophets, and Messiahs* and Goodman, *Ruling Class of Judea*.
18. See, however, Davina C. Lopez, *Apostle to the Conquered: Reimagining Paul's Mission* (Minneapolis: Fortress, 2008); and Neil Elliott, *The Arrogance of Nations: Reading Romans in the Shadow of Empire* (Minneapolis: Fortress 2008).
19. Price, *Rituals and Power*, 54.
20. David Magie, *Roman Rule in Asia Minor: To the End of the Third Century after Christ*, 2 vols. (Princeton: Princeton University Press, 1950).
21. Steven J. Friesen, *Imperial Cults and the Apocalypse of John: Reading Revelation in the Ruins* (Oxford: Oxford University Press, 2001), 50.
22. See Price, *Rituals and Power*.
23. Friesen, *Imperial Cults and the Apocalypse*, 53.
24. Ibid., 46. His wife Domitia and other women might have been included.
25. Ibid., 47; Price, *Rituals and Power*, 126–32.
26. On transmission see Stone, "Categorization and Classification of the Apocrypha and Pseudepigrapha."
27. See "Reactions to Destructions of the Second Temple: Theology, Perception and Conversion," *JSJ* 12 (1981): 195–204; *Fourth Ezra: A Commentary on the Book of Fourth Ezra* (Minneapolis: Augsburg Fortress, 1990).

28. For Stone a religious conversion.
29. See H. W. Attridge, "Josephus and His Works," in *Jewish Writings of the Second Temple Period*, ed. Michael E. Stone (Assen, Netherlands: Van Gorcum, 1984).
30. See M. J. Edwards et al., *Apologetics in the Roman Empire: Pagans, Jews, and Christians* (Oxford: Oxford University Press, 1999), 1–13.
31. See *J.W.* 1.1–6, 16; Gregory E. Sterling, "Explaining Defeat: Polybius and Josephus on the Wars with Rome," in *Internationales Josephus-Kolloquium: Aarhus 1999*, ed. Jürgen U. Kalms (Münster: Lit, 1999), 144–45.
32. See *Historiography and Self-Definition*; Martin Goodman, "Josephus' Treatise *Against Apion*," in *Apologetics in the Roman Empire: Pagans, Jews, and Christians*, ed. M. J. Edwards, S. R. F. Price, and Christopher Rowland (Oxford: Oxford University Press, 1999); and John M. G. Barclay, "The Politics of Contempt: Judaeans and Egyptians in Josephus's *Against Apion*," in *Negotiating Diaspora: Jewish Strategies in the Roman Empire*, ed. John M. G. Barclay (London: T & T Clark, 2004).
33. See Chapter 3.
34. See Sterling, "Explaining Defeat," and Paul Spilsbury, "Flavius Josephus on the Rise and Fall of the Roman Empire," *JTS* 54, no. 1 (2003): 1–24.
35. See "Flavius Josephus."
36. See ibid.
37. See Sterling, "Explaining Defeat"; Spilsbury, "Flavius Josephus"; on God's hand in Rome's rise (and fall?) see also Barclay, "Politics of Contempt."
38. See Sterling, "Explaining Defeat," 147.
39. Even more so in *Ant.* 18.60–64, cited by Neil Elliott, *Liberating Paul: The Justice of God and the Politics of the Apostle* (Maryknoll, NY: Orbis Books, 1994), 175.
40. See Goodman, *Ruling Class of Judea*; and Per Bilde, "The Causes of the Jewish War According to Josephus," *JSJ* 10 (1979): 179–202.
41. See Ernest Gellner, *Nations and Nationalism* (Ithaca: Cornell University Press, 1983), 8–18 and the horizontally stratified elite in Gellner's diagram, 9.
42. Compare Sanders, *Historical Figure of Jesus*, 22, and Horsley, *Bandits, Prophets, and Messiahs*, 175–81.
43. See Richard J. Cassidy, *Christians and Roman Rule in the New Testament: New Perspectives* (New York: Crossroad, 2001), 20.
44. See Morton Smith, "Zealots and Sicarii, Their Origins and Relation," *HTR* 64, no. 1 (1971): 1–19; and Horsley, *Bandits, Prophets, and Messiahs*.
45. See also Goodman, *Ruling Class of Judea*, 93–97, 219–20.
46. The thesis of Horsley, *Bandits, Prophets, and Messiahs*.
47. Fredriksen, *Jesus of Nazareth, King of the Jews: A Jewish Life and the Emergence of Christianity*, argues for more than one climactic journey to Jerusalem.
48. See Horsley, *Bandits, Prophets, and Messiahs*, 260–61.
49. See Theissen, *Gospels in Context*, 258–81; Pagels, *The Origin of Satan*, 3–34.
50. See H. Fuchs, *Der geistige Widerstand gegen Rom in der antiken Welt* (Berlin: Walter de Gruyter, 1938); Ramsay MacMullen, *Enemies of the Roman Order: Treason, Unrest, and Alienation in the Empire* (Cambridge, MA: Harvard University Press, 1966).
51. See John J. Collins, "The Sibyl and the Potter: Political Propaganda in Ptolemaic Egypt," in *Religious Propaganda and Missionary Competition in the New Testament World*, ed. Lukas Bormann, Kelly Del Tredici, and Angela Standhartinger (Leiden: Brill, 1994).
52. See Meeks, *Writings of St. Paul*.

53. See Elliott, *Liberating Paul*; Schüssler Fiorenza, *In Memory of Her.*
54. See Elliott, *Liberating Paul*, 93–139, "Paul and the Violence of the Cross," repr. in Horsley, *Paul and Empire*, 167–83 as "The Anti-Imperial Message of the Cross."
55. Following Beker, *Paul the Apostle: The Triumph of God in Life and Thought.*
56. Elliott, *Liberating Paul*, 113–114.
57. See Elliott, *Arrogance of Nations*, 143–61.
58. See James Albert Harrill, *The Manumission of Slaves in Early Christianity* (Tübingen: Mohr (Siebeck), 1995).
59. So-called by Ben Witherington, "Liberating Paul: The Justice of God and the Politics of the Apostle," review of *Liberating Paul*, by Neil Elliott, *JBL* 115, no. 3 (1996): 554–57.
60. See Hans Dieter Betz, "Christianity as Religion: Paul's Attempt at Definition in Romans," *JR* 71, no. 3 (1991): 315–44.
61. See David Horrell, "The Peaceable, Tolerant Community and the Legitimate Role of the State: Ethics and Ethical Dilemmas in Romans 12:1–15:13," *RevExp* 100, no. 1 (2003): 81–99.
62. See Elliott, *Arrogance of Nations*, 154.
63. Horrell, "Tolerant Community and the Legitimate Role of the State," 94.
64. See the reading against universalism in Lopez, *Apostle to the Conquered.*
65. The term was coined by Martin Luther. Colossians could date from the 70s while 1 Peter could not plausibly date before the 80s. See D. L. Balch, *ABD*, III, p. 319, for 1 Peter, and rebuttal in Andrew T. Lincoln, "The Household Code and Wisdom Mode of Colossians," *JSNT*, no. 74 (1999): 93–112, p. 93 n. 1.
66. See Angela Standhartinger, "The Origin and Intention of the Household Code in the Letter to the Colossians," *JSNT* 79 (2000): 117–30, 117–118; David L. Balch, *Let Wives Be Submissive: The Domestic Code in 1 Peter* (Chico, CA: Scholars Press, 1981), 21–62; and Dieter Lührmann, "Neutestamentliche Haustafeln und antike Ökonomie," *NTS* 27 (1980): 83–97.
67. See Balch, *Let Wives Be Submissive*, 52–56; and Lincoln, "The Household Code and Wisdom Mode of Colossians," 102–8.
68. See Chapter 3.
69. See Wire, *Corinthian Women Prophets.*
70. See Balch, *Let Wives Be Submissive*, 65–80.
71. On 1 Peter see ibid.; and John Hall Elliott, *A Home for the Homeless: A Sociological Exegesis of 1 Peter, Its Situation and Strategy* (Philadelphia: Fortress, 1981).
72. See Paul J. Achtemeier, *1 Peter: A Commentary on First Peter* (Minneapolis: Fortress, 1996), 12–23.
73. Ibid., 23. See Norbert Brox, "Der erste Petrusbrief in der literarischen Tradition des Urchristentums," *Kairos* NF 20, no. 3 (1978): 182–92, 182 on "sprachlich verfestigte Traditionen."
74. See Bhabha, *Location of Culture*, 52–56.
75. G. E. M. de Ste Croix, "Why Were the Early Christians Persecuted?," *Past & Present*, no. 26 (1963): 6–38; "Why Were the Early Christians Persecuted?—a Rejoinder," *Past & Present*, no. 27 (1964): 28–33; A. N. Sherwin-White, "Why Were the Early Christians Persecuted?—an Amendment," *Past & Present*, no. 27 (1964): 23–27.
76. See Achtemeier, *1 Peter*, 180–82.
77. 1 Peter is "making Christians" and has been interpreted as a baptismal homily.
78. See Royalty, "Dwelling on Visions."
79. See Leonard L. Thompson, *The Book of Revelation: Apocalypse and Empire* (Oxford: Oxford University Press, 1990).

80. See Royalty, *Streets of Heaven*, 1–38.
81. See David E. Aune, *Revelation 6–16*, 3 vols., vol. 2 (Nashville: Thomas Nelson, 1998). *Gematria* also appears in the *Sibylline Oracles*.
82. See Price, *Rituals and Power*; and Friesen, *Imperial Cults and the Apocalypse*.
83. See Royalty, *Streets of Heaven*, 183–87.
84. See ibid., 177–210; Pippin, *Death and Desire*; and Barbara R. Rossing, *The Choice between Two Cities: Whore, Bride, and Empire in the Apocalypse* (Harrisburg, PA: Trinity, 1999).
85. See Christopher A. Frilingos, *Spectacles of Empire: Monsters, Martyrs, and the Book of Revelation* (Philadelphia: University of Pennsylvania Press, 2004); Royalty, *Streets of Heaven*, 243–46.
86. See Royalty, *Streets of Heaven*, 163–64, 209–10, and 223–25.
87. See Collins, "The Political Perspective of the Revelation to John."
88. See Bhabha, *Location of Culture*, "The Commitment to Theory," 28–56.
89. Ibid., 42–23.
90. See Hans Conzelmann, *The Theology of St. Luke* (London: Faber and Faber, 1960), 95–136.
91. Ibid., 99; see 98–113.
92. See Loveday Alexander, "The Acts of the Apostles as an Apologetic Text," in *Apologetics in the Roman Empire: Pagans, Jews, and Christians*, ed. M. J. Edwards et al. (Oxford: Oxford University Press, 1999); cf. the complicating Paul W. Walaskay, *"And So We Came to Rome": The Political Perspective of St. Luke* (Cambridge: Cambridge University Press, 1983). See also Richard J. Cassidy, *Society and Politics in the Acts of the Apostles* (Maryknoll, NY: Orbis Books, 1987).
93. See Hans Conzelmann, Eldon Jay Epp, and Christopher R. Matthews, *Acts of the Apostles: A Commentary on the Acts of the Apostles* (Philadelphia: Fortress, 1987), xlv–xlviii.
94. See Chapter 6.
95. Jameson, *Political Unconscious*, 17–103.
96. See Chapter 4 and Castelli, *Imitating Paul*.
97. See Craig C. Hill, *Hellenists and Hebrews: Reappraising Division within the Earliest Church* (Minneapolis: Fortress, 1992).
98. So Conzelmann, *Acts of the Apostles*. Alexander, "Acts of the Apostles," imagines Agrippa II (Acts 25–26) as the "ideal" and "idealized" ancient reader.

NOTES TO CHAPTER 8

1. See "The Discourse on Language," trans. Rupert Swyer, in Foucault, *Archaeology of Knowledge*.
2. Le Boulluec, *La Notion D'hérésie*.
3. Lyman, "Hellenism and Heresy"; "Politics of Passing."
4. See Charles H. Cosgrove, "Justin Martyr and the Emerging Christian Canon: Observations on the Purpose and Destination of the Dialogue with Trypho," *VC* 36, no. 3 (1982): 209–32.
5. See Pagels, *Beyond Belief*, 74–142.
6. See King, *What Is Gnosticism?*; and David Brakke, *The Gnostics: Myth, Ritual, and Diversity in Early Christianity* (Cambridge, MA: Harvard University Press, 2010).
7. So Layton, "Significance of Basilides"; see also the analysis of Justin's doxography in Le Boulluec, *La Notion D'hérésie*, 1.37–91.
8. See Paul J. Griffiths, *Problems of Religious Diversity* (Malden, MA: Blackwell, 2001).

9. See Bart D. Ehrman, *Truth and Fiction in the Da Vinci Code: A Historian Reveals What We Really Know About Jesus, Mary Magdalene, and Constantine* (Oxford: Oxford University Press, 2004).
10. Asad, *Genealogies of Religion*, 38.
11. See Fred McGraw Donner, *Muhammad and the Believers: At the Origins of Islam* (Cambridge, MA: The Belknap Press of Harvard University Press, 2010), Chapter 1.

Bibliography

Abegg, Martin G., Craig A. Evans, and Gerbern S. Oegema. "Bibliography of Messianism and the Dead Sea Scrolls." In *Qumran-Messianism*, edited by James H. Charlesworth, Hermann Lichtenberger and Gerbern S. Oegema, 204–14. Tübingen: Mohr (Siebeck), 1998.

Achtemeier, Paul J. *1 Peter: A Commentary on First Peter*. Hermeneia. Minneapolis: Fortress, 1996.

Aland, Barbara, Kurt Aland, Johannes Karavidopoulos, Carlo M. Martini, and Bruce Metzger, eds. *Nestle-Aland Novum Testamentum Graece*. 27th ed. Stuttgart: Deutsche Bibelgesellschaft, 2001.

Albertz, Rainer. "The Social Setting of the Aramaic and Hebrew Book of Daniel." In *The Book of Daniel: Composition and Reception*, edited by John J. Collins and Peter W. Flint, 171–204. Leiden: Brill, 2001.

Alexander, Loveday. "The Acts of the Apostles as an Apologetic Text." In *Apologetics in the Roman Empire: Pagans, Jews, and Christians*, edited by M. J. Edwards, Martin Goodman, S. R. F. Price, and Christopher Rowland, 15–44. Oxford: Oxford University Press, 1999.

Alt, Albrecht. "The Monarchy in the Kingdoms of Israel and Judah." In *Essays on Old Testament History and Religion*, 311–35. The Biblical Seminar. Sheffield: JSOT, 1989.

Anderson, Gary M. "Celibacy or Consummation in the Garden: Reflections on Early Jewish and Christian Interpretations of the Garden of Eden." *HTR* 82 (1989): 121–48.

Arnal, William E., and Michel R. Desjardins. *Whose Historical Jesus?* Waterloo, Ont.: Wilfrid Laurier University Press, 1997.

Asad, Talal. *Genealogies of Religion: Discipline and Reasons of Power in Christianity and Islam*. Baltimore: Johns Hopkins University Press, 1993.

Asgeirsson, Jon Ma, April D. De Conick, and Risto Uro, eds. *Thomasine Traditions in Antiquity: The Social and Cultural World of the Gospel of Thomas*. Nag Hammadi and Manichaean Studies, vol. 59. Leiden: Brill, 2006.

Atkinson, Kenneth. "On the Herodian Origin of Militant Davidic Messianism at Qumran: New Light from Psalm of Solomon 17." *JBL* 118 (1999): 435–60.

Attridge, H. W. "Josephus and His Works." In *Jewish Writings of the Second Temple Period*, edited by Michael E. Stone, 185–232. Assen, Netherlands: Van Gorcum, 1984.

Aune, David E. *Prophecy in Early Christianity and the Ancient Mediterranean World*. Grand Rapids: Eerdmans, 1983.

———. *Revelation 1–5*. WBC 52a. 3 vols. Vol. 1, Waco, TX: Word 1997.

———. *Revelation 6–16*. WBC 52b. 3 vols. Vol. 2, Nashville: Thomas Nelson, 1998.

Balch, David L. *Let Wives Be Submissive: The Domestic Code in 1 Peter*. Society of Biblical Literature Monograph Series 26. Chico, CA: Scholars Press, 1981.

Barclay, John M. G. "The Politics of Contempt: Judaeans and Egyptians in Josephus's *Against Apion*." In *Negotiating Diaspora: Jewish Strategies in the Roman Empire*, edited by John M. G. Barclay, 109–27. London: T & T Clark, 2004.
———. "Who Was Considered an Apostate in the Jewish Diaspora?" In *Tolerance and Intolerance in Early Judaism and Christianity*, edited by Graham Stanton and Gedaliahu A. G. Stroumsa, 80–98. Cambridge: Cambridge University Press, 1998.
Barth, Fredrik, ed. *Ethnic Groups and Boundaries: The Social Organization of Culture Difference*. Prospect Heights, IL: Waveland, 1998.
Bauckham, Richard. "For Whom Were the Gospels Written?" In *The Gospels for All Christians: Rethinking the Gospel Audience*, edited by Richard Bauckham, 9–48. Edinburgh: T&T Clark, 1998.
———. "The Parable of the Royal Wedding Feast (Matthew 22:1–14) and the Parable of the Lame Man and the Blind Man (Apocryphon of Ezekial)." *JBL* 115 (1996): 471–88.
———. "The Rich Man and Lazarus: The Parable and the Parallels." *NTS* 37 (1991): 225–46.
Bauer, Walter. *Orthodoxy and Heresy in Earliest Christianity*. Translated by Robert A. Kraft et al. 2nd ed. Philadelphia: Fortress, 1971.
———. *Rechtglaubigkeit und Ketzerei im ältesten Christentum*. 2nd ed. Tübingen: Mohr, 1934, 1961.
Bauer-Levesque, Angela. "Jeremiah as Female Impersonator: Roles of Difference in Gender Perception and Gender Perceptivity." In *Escaping Eden*, edited by Harold C. Washington, Susan Lochrie Graham, and Pamela Lee Thimmes, 199–207. Sheffield: Sheffield Academic Press, 1998.
Baumgarten, Albert I. *The Flourishing of Jewish Sects in the Maccabean Era: An Interpretation*. Leiden: Brill, 1997.
———. "The Pursuit of the Millennium in Early Judaism." In *Tolerance and Intolerance in Early Judaism and Christianity*, edited by Graham Stanton and Gedaliahu A. G. Stroumsa, 38–60. Cambridge: Cambridge University Press, 1998.
Baumgarten, Joseph M., with James H. Charlesworth et al. "Damascus Document 4Q266–273 (4QD^a–h)." In *The Dead Sea Scrolls: Hebrew, Aramaic, and Greek Texts with English Translations, Vol. 3*, edited by James H. Charlesworth and Frank Moore Cross, 1–185. Tübingen: Mohr (Siebeck), 1993.
Baumgarten, Joseph M., with Michael T. Davis. "Cave IV, V, VI Fragments Related to the Damascus Document." In *The Dead Sea Scrolls: Hebrew, Aramaic, and Greek Texts with English Translations, Vol. 2*, edited by James H. Charlesworth and Frank Moore Cross, 59–79. Tübingen: Mohr (Siebeck), 1994.
Baumgarten, Joseph M., and Daniel R. Schwartz. "Damascus Document." In *The Dead Sea Scrolls: Hebrew, Aramaic, and Greek Texts with English Translations, Vol. 2*, edited by James H. Charlesworth and Frank Moore Cross, 4–57. Tübingen: Mohr (Siebeck), 1994.
Beavis, Mary Ann. "Philo's Therapeutai: Philosopher's Dream or Utopian Construction?" *JSP* 14, no. 1 (2004): 30–42.
Beck, John A. "Geography as Irony: The Narrative-Geological Shaping of Elijah's Duel with the Prophets of Baal (1 Kings 18)." *SJOT* 17, no. 2 (2003): 291–302.
Beker, Johan Christiaan. *Paul the Apostle: The Triumph of God in Life and Thought*. Philadelphia: Fortress Press, 1980.
Berger, Peter L. *The Sacred Canopy: Elements of a Sociological Theory of Religion*. Garden City, NY: Doubleday, 1967.
Berger, Peter, and Thomas Luckmann. *The Social Construction of Reality: A Treatise in the Sociology of Knowledge*. New York: Anchor Doubleday, 1966.
Berlin, Andrea M. "Power and Its Afterlife: Tombs in Hellenistic Palestine." *Near Eastern Archaeology* 65, no. 2 (2002): 138–48.

Betz, Hans Dieter. "Christianity as Religion: Paul's Attempt at Definition in Romans." *JR* 71, no. 3 (1991): 315–44.

———. *Der Apostel Paulus und die sokratische Tradition; eine exegetische Untersuchung zu seiner Apologie 2 Korinther 10–13.* Tübingen: Mohr, 1972.

———. *Galatians: A Commentary on Paul's Letter to the Churches in Galatia.* Hermeneia. Philadelphia: Fortress, 1979.

———. "Orthodoxy and Heresy in Primitive Christianity." *Int* 19 (1965): 299–311.

———. *The Sermon on the Mount: A Commentary on the Sermon on the Mount, Including the Sermon on the Plain (Matthew 5:3–7:27 and Luke 6:20–49).* Minneapolis: Fortress, 1995.

Betz, Hans Dieter, and George W. MacRae. *2 Corinthians 8 and 9: A Commentary on Two Administrative Letters of the Apostle Paul.* Philadelphia: Fortress, 1985.

Bhabha, Homi K. *The Location of Culture.* London: Routledge, 1994.

Bibleworks Software, Version 9, Norfolk, VA.

Bickerman, E. J. *The God of the Maccabees: Studies on the Meaning and Origin of the Maccabean Revolt.* Leiden: Brill, 1979.

———. *The Jews in the Greek Age.* Cambridge, MA: Harvard University Press, 1988.

Bilde, Per. "The Causes of the Jewish War According to Josephus." *JSJ* 10 (1979): 179–202.

Birnbaum, Ellen. "Allegorical Interpretation and Jewish Identity among Alexandrian Jewish Writers." In *Neotestamentica Et Philonica: Studies in Honor of Peder Borgen,* edited by David E. Aune, Torrey Seland, and Jarl Henning Ulrichsen, 307–29. Supplements to Novum Testamentum. Leiden: Brill, 2003.

Bitzer, Lloyd. "The Rhetorical Situation." *Philosophy and Rhetoric* 1 (1968): 1–14.

Boccaccini, Gabriele. *Beyond the Essene Hypothesis: The Parting of the Ways between Qumran and Enochic Judaism.* Grand Rapids: Eerdmans, 1998.

Boer, Martinus C. de. "Ten Thousand Talents: Matthew's Interpretation and Redaction of the Parable of the Unforgiving Servant (Matt 18:23–35)." *CBQ* 50 (1988): 214–32.

Boers, Hendrikus. "The Formation of Q: Trajectories in Ancient Wisdom Collections." Review of *Formation of Q,* by John S. Kloppenborg. *Int* 43 (1989): 200–201.

Borg, Marcus J. *Conflict, Holiness & Politics in the Teachings of Jesus.* Studies in the Bible and Early Christianity. New York: E. Mellen Press, 1984.

Borg, Marcus J., and N. T. Wright. *The Meaning of Jesus: Two Visions.* San Francisco: HarperSanFrancisco, 1999.

Borgen, Peder, Kåre Fuglseth, and Roald Skarsten. "The Philo Concordance Database in Greek." BibleWorks v.9, 2005.

Bornkamm, Günther. *Tradition and Interpretation in Matthew.* New Testament Library. London: SCM Press, 1963.

Boyarin, Daniel. *Border Lines: The Partition of Judaeo-Christianity.* Philadelphia: University of Pennsylvania Press, 2004.

———. "Justin Martyr Invents Judaism." *CH* 70, no. 3 (2001): 427–61.

———. "One Church; One Voice: The Drive Towards Homonoia in Orthodoxy." *Religion & Literature* 33, no. 2 (2001): 1–22.

Brakke, David. *The Gnostics: Myth, Ritual, and Diversity in Early Christianity.* Cambridge, MA: Harvard University Press, 2010.

Bronner, Leah. *The Stories of Elijah and Elisha as Polemics against Baal Worship.* Pretoria Oriental Series. Leiden: Brill, 1968.

Brox, Norbert. "Der erste Petrusbrief in der literarischen Tradition des Urchristentums." *Kairos* NF 20, no. 3 (1978): 182–92.

Buell, Denise Kimber. *Why This New Race: Ethnic Reasoning in Early Christianity.* New York: Columbia University Press, 2005.

Bultmann, Rudolf Karl. *Der Stil der paulinischen Predigt und die kynisch-stoische Diatribe.* Göttingen: Vandenhoeck & Ruprecht, 1910.

———. *The History of the Synoptic Tradition.* New York: Harper & Row, 1963.

Burrus, Virginia. *The Making of a Heretic: Gender, Authority, and the Priscillianist Controversy.* Berkeley: University of California Press, 1995.

Cameron, Averil. *Christianity and the Rhetoric of Empire: The Development of Christian Discourse.* Sather Classical Lectures, vol. 55. Berkeley: University of California Press, 1991.

———. "How to Read Heresiology." In *The Cultural Turn in Late Ancient Studies: Gender, Asceticism, and Historiography,* edited by Dale B. Martin and Patricia Cox Miller, 193–212. Durham: Duke University Press, 2005.

Campbell, Douglas A. "An Anchor for Pauline Chronology: Paul's Flight from 'the Ethnarch of King Aretas' (2 Corinthians 11:32–33)." *JBL* 121, no. 2 (2002): 279–302.

Carroll, Robert P. *When Prophecy Failed: Cognitive Dissonance in the Prophetic Traditions of the Old Testament.* New York: Seabury Press, 1979.

Carter, Warren. "Resisting and Imitating the Empire: Imperial Paradigms in Two Matthean Parables." *Int* 56, no. 3 (2002): 260–72.

Cassidy, Richard J. *Christians and Roman Rule in the New Testament: New Perspectives.* New York: Crossroad, 2001.

———. *Society and Politics in the Acts of the Apostles.* Maryknoll, NY: Orbis Books, 1987.

Castelli, Elizabeth A. *Imitating Paul: A Discourse of Power.* Louisville: Westminster/John Knox, 1991.

Charlesworth, James H. "Have the Dead Sea Scrolls Revolutionized Our Understanding of the New Testament?" In *Dead Sea Scrolls Fifty Years after Their Discovery: Proceedings of the Jerusalem Congress, July 20–25, 1997,* 116–32. Jerusalem: Israel Exploration Society with The Shrine of the Book Israel Museum, 2000.

———. "John the Baptizer and Qumran Barriers in Light of the *Rule of the Community.*" In *The Provo International Conference on the Dead Sea Scrolls: Technological Innovations, New Texts, and Reformulated Issues,* edited by Donald W. Parry and Eugene Charles Ulrich, 353–75. Leiden: Brill, 1999.

———. *The Old Testament Pseudepigrapha.* 2 vols. New York: Doubleday, 1983, 1985.

Charlesworth, James H., and Frank Moore Cross. *The Dead Sea Scrolls: Hebrew, Aramaic, and Greek Texts with English Translations.* Princeton Theological Seminary Dead Sea Scrolls Project. 6 vols. Tübingen: Mohr (Siebeck), 1994.

Chilton, Bruce, and Craig A. Evans. *James the Just and Christian Origins.* Leiden: Brill, 1999.

———. *Studying the Historical Jesus: Evaluation of the State of Current Research.* Leiden: Brill, 1994.

Cohen, Shaye J. D. *The Beginnings of Jewishness: Boundaries, Varieties, Uncertainties.* Hellenistic Culture and Society. Berkeley: University of California Press, 1999.

———. *From the Maccabees to the Mishnah.* Library of Early Christianity. Philadelphia: Westminster, 1987.

Cohn, Robert L. "The Literary Logic of 1 Kings 17–19." *JBL* 101, no. 2 (1982): 333–50.

Collins, Adela Yarbro. "The Charge of Blasphemy in Mark 14.64." *JSNT* 26, no. 4 (2004): 379–401.

———. "The Function of 'Excommunication' in Paul." *HTR* 73 (1980): 251–63.

———. "The Political Perspective of the Revelation to John." *JBL* 96 (1977): 241–56.

Collins, John J. *Apocalypticism in the Dead Sea Scrolls.* London: Routledge, 1997.

———. *Daniel: A Commentary on the Book of Daniel.* Hermeneia. Minneapolis: Fortress, 1993.

———. "The Epic of Theodotus and the Hellenism of the Hasmoneans." *HTR* 73 (1980): 91–104.

———. *The Scepter and the Star: The Messiahs of the Dead Sea Scrolls and Other Ancient Literature.* New York: Doubleday, 1995.

———. "The Sibyl and the Potter: Political Propaganda in Ptolemaic Egypt." In *Religious Propaganda and Missionary Competition in the New Testament World,* edited by Lukas Bormann, Kelly Del Tredici, and Angela Standhartinger, 57–69. Leiden: Brill, 1994.

———. "Wisdom, Apocalypticism, and Generic Compatibility." In *In Search of Wisdom,* edited by L. G. Perdue, B. B. Scott, and W. J. Wiseman, 165–85. Louisville: Westminster/John Knox, 1993.

Collins, John J., and Peter W. Flint, eds. *The Book of Daniel: Composition and Reception.* Leiden: Brill, 2001.

Conzelmann, Hans. *1 Corinthians: A Commentary on the First Epistle to the Corinthians.* Hermeneia. Philadelphia: Fortress, 1975.

———. *The Theology of St. Luke.* London: Faber and Faber, 1960.

Conzelmann, Hans, Eldon Jay Epp, and Christopher R. Matthews. *Acts of the Apostles: A Commentary on the Acts of the Apostles.* Hermeneia. Philadelphia: Fortress, 1987.

Cook, Stephen L. *Prophecy and Apocalypticism: The Postexilic Social Setting.* Minneapolis: Fortress, 1995.

Coser, Lewis A. *The Functions of Social Conflict.* New York: Free Press of Glencoe, 1964.

Cosgrove, Charles H. "Justin Martyr and the Emerging Christian Canon: Observations on the Purpose and Destination of the Dialogue with Trypho." *VC* 36, no. 3 (1982): 209–32.

Croix, G. E. M. de Ste. "Why Were the Early Christians Persecuted?" *Past & Present,* no. 26 (1963): 6–38.

———. "Why Were the Early Christians Persecuted?—a Rejoinder." *Past & Present,* no. 27 (1964): 28–33.

Cross, Frank Moore. *Canaanite Myth and Hebrew Epic: Essays in the History of the Religion of Israel.* Cambridge, MA: Harvard University Press, 1997.

Crossan, John Dominic. *The Historical Jesus: The Life of a Mediterranean Jewish Peasant.* San Francisco: HarperSanFrancisco, 1991.

———. *Jesus: A Revolutionary Biography.* San Francisco: HarperSanFrancisco, 1994.

D'Angelo, Mary Rose. "Eusebeia: Roman Imperial Family Values and the Sexual Politics of 4 Maccabees and the Pastorals." *BibInt* 11, no. 2 (2003): 139–65.

Davies, Philip R. *The Damascus Covenant: An Interpretation of the "Damascus Document".* Journal for the Study of the Old Testament Supplement. Sheffield: University of Sheffield, 1983.

———. "The Judaism(s) of the Damascus Document." In *The Damascus Document: A Centennial of Discovery,* edited by Joseph M. Baumgarten, Esther G. Chazon, and Avital Pinnick, 27–43. Studies of the Texts of the Desert of Judah. Leiden: Brill, 2000.

Davies, W. D., and Dale C. Allison. *A Critical and Exegetical Commentary on the Gospel According to Saint Matthew.* 3 vols. Edinburgh: T. & T. Clark, 1988.

Dawson, David. *Allegorical Readers and Cultural Revision in Ancient Alexandria.* Berkeley: University of California Press, 1992.

DeConick, April D. *Recovering the Original Gospel of Thomas: A History of the Gospel and Its Growth.* Early Christianity in Context. London: T&T Clark, 2005.

Derrett, J. Duncan M. *Law in the New Testament.* London: Darton Longman & Todd, 1970.

Derrida, Jacques. *Writing and Difference.* Translated by Alan Bass. Chicago: University of Chicago Press, 1978.

Desjardins, Michel. "Bauer and Beyond: On Recent Scholarly Discussions of Hairesis in the Early Christian Era." *SecCent* 8, no. 2 (1991): 65–82.

Diamond, A. R. Pete. "Deceiving Hope: The Ironies of Metaphorical Beauty and Ideological Terror in Jeremiah." *SJOT* 17, no. 1 (2003): 34–48.

Dibelius, Martin, and Hans Conzelmann. *The Pastoral Epistles.* Translated by P. Buttolph and A. Yarbro. Hermeneia. Philadelphia: Fortress, 1972.

Donner, Fred McGraw. *Muhammad and the Believers: At the Origins of Islam.* Cambridge, MA: The Belknap Press of Harvard University Press, 2010.

Duff, Paul Brooks. *Who Rides the Beast?: Prophetic Rivalry and the Rhetoric of Crisis in the Churches of the Apocalypse.* Oxford: Oxford University Press, 2001.

Dunderberg, Ismo. *The Beloved Disciple in Conflict?: Revisiting the Gospels of John and Thomas.* Oxford: Oxford University Press, 2006.

Dunn, James D. G. *The Epistles to the Colossians and to Philemon: A Commentary on the Greek Text.* New International Greek Testament Commentary. Grand Rapids: Eerdmans, 1996.

———. *Unity and Diversity in the New Testament: An Inquiry into the Character of Earliest Christianity.* 3rd ed. London: SCM Press, 2006.

Edwards, M. J., Martin Goodman, S. R. F. Price, and Christopher Rowland. *Apologetics in the Roman Empire: Pagans, Jews, and Christians.* Oxford: Oxford University Press, 1999.

Ehrman, Bart D. *The Apostolic Fathers.* 2 vols. Loeb Classical Library. Cambridge, MA: Harvard University Press, 2003.

———. *Jesus, Apocalyptic Prophet of the New Millennium.* Oxford: Oxford University Press, 1999.

———. *Lost Christianities: The Battles for Scripture and the Faiths We Never Knew.* New York: Oxford University Press, 2003.

———. *The New Testament: A Historical Introduction to the Early Christian Writings.* New York: Oxford University Press, 1997.

———. *Truth and Fiction in the Da Vinci Code: A Historian Reveals What We Really Know About Jesus, Mary Magdalene, and Constantine.* Oxford: Oxford University Press, 2004.

Elliger, Karl. *Biblica Hebraica Stuttgartensia.* Stuttgart: Deutsche Bibelgesellschaft, 1983.

Elliott, John Hall. *A Home for the Homeless: A Sociological Exegesis of 1 Peter, Its Situation and Strategy.* Philadelphia: Fortress, 1981.

Elliott, Neil. *The Arrogance of Nations: Reading Romans in the Shadow of Empire.* Paul in Critical Contexts. Minneapolis: Fortress, 2008.

———. *Liberating Paul: The Justice of God and the Politics of the Apostle.* Maryknoll, NY: Orbis Books, 1994.

Elm, Susanna, Eric Rebillard, and Antonella Romano. *Orthodoxie, Christianisme, Histoire = Orthodoxy, Christianity, History.* Rome: Ecole française de Rome, 2000.

Engberg-Pedersen, Troels. *Paul and the Stoics.* Edinburgh: T & T Clark, 2000.

———. *Paul Beyond the Judaism/Hellenism Divide.* Louisville: Westminster John Knox, 2001.

———. "Philo's *De Vita Contemplativa* as a Philosopher's Dream." *JSJ* 30 (1999): 40–64.

Eshel, Esther, and Menahem Kister. "A Polemical Qumran Fragment." *JJS* 43 (1992): 277–81.

Eusebius of Caesarea. *The Ecclesiastical History of Eusebius*. Translated by Lake Kirsopp, John Ernest Leonard Oulton, and H. J. Lawlor. Loeb Classical Library. 2 vols. London: Heinemann, 1926.

Evans, Craig A., ed. *The Historical Jesus*. 4 vols. Critical Concepts in Religious Studies. London: Routledge, 2004.

Fallon, Francis T., and Ron Cameron. "The Gospel of Thomas: A *Forschungsbericht* and Analysis." In *Aufstieg und Niedergang der Römischen Welt*, Principat 25,6, 4195–251. Berlin: Walter de Gruyter, 1988.

Farmer, William R. *The Synoptic Problem, a Critical Analysis*. New York: Macmillan, 1964.

Fee, Gordon D. *The First Epistle to the Corinthians*. Grand Rapids: Eerdmans, 1987.

Fitzgerald, John T. *Cracks in an Earthen Vessel: An Examination of the Catalogues of Hardships in the Corinthian Correspondence*. Society of Biblical Literature Dissertation Series. Atlanta: Scholars Press, 1988.

Fitzmyer, Joseph A. *The Dead Sea Scrolls: Major Publications and Tools for Study*. Rev. ed. Atlanta: Scholars Press, 1990.

———. *The Dead Sea Scrolls and Christian Origins*. Grand Rapids: Eerdmans, 2000.

Flinterman, Jaap Jan. "The Ubiquitous 'Divine Man.'" *Numen* 43 (1996): 82–98.

Foucault, Michel. *The Archaeology of Knowledge*. Translated by A. M. Sheridan Smith. New York: Pantheon Books, 1972.

———. *The Order of Things: An Archaeology of the Human Sciences*. New York: Pantheon Books, 1971.

Foucault, Michel. *Religion and Culture*. Edited by Jeremy R. Carrette. New York: Routledge, 1999.

Frankfurter, David. "Jews or Not? Reconstructing the 'Other' in Rev 2:9 and 3:9." *HTR* 94, no. 4 (2001): 403–25.

Fredriksen, Paula. *Jesus of Nazareth, King of the Jews: A Jewish Life and the Emergence of Christianity*. New York: Knopf, 1999.

Friesen, Steven J. *Imperial Cults and the Apocalypse of John: Reading Revelation in the Ruins*. Oxford: Oxford University Press, 2001.

Frilingos, Christopher A. *Spectacles of Empire: Monsters, Martyrs, and the Book of Revelation*. Philadelphia: University of Pennsylvania Press, 2004.

Fuchs, H. *Der geistige Widerstand gegen Rom in der antiken Welt*. Berlin: Walter de Gruyter, 1938.

Funk, Robert Walter, and Roy W. Hoover. *The Five Gospels: The Search for the Authentic Words of Jesus: New Translation and Commentary*. San Francisco: HarperSanFrancisco, 1997.

Furnish, Victor Paul. *II Corinthians*. The Anchor Bible. Garden City, NY: Doubleday, 1984.

Gager, John G. *Reinventing Paul*. Oxford: Oxford University Press, 2000.

García Martínez, Florentino. "4QMMT in a Qumran Context." In *Reading 4QMMT: New Perspectives on Qumran Law and History*, edited by John Kampen and Moshe J. Bernstein, 15–27. Atlanta: Scholars Press, 1996.

———. *The Dead Sea Scrolls Translated: The Qumran Texts in English*. 2nd ed. Leiden: Brill, 1996.

García Martínez, Florentino, and Donald W. Parry. *A Bibliography of the Finds in the Desert of Judah 1970–1995: Arranged by Author with Citation and Subject Indexes*. Leiden: Brill, 1996.

García Martínez, Florentino, and Eibert J. C. Tigchelaar, eds. *The Dead Sea Scrolls Study Edition*. 2 vols. Leiden: Brill, 2000.

Garrett, Susan R. "The God of This World and the Affliction of Paul: 2 Cor 4:1–12." In *Greeks, Romans, and Christians: Essays in Honor of Abraham J. Malherbe*, edited by Abraham J. Malherbe, David L. Balch, Everett Ferguson, and Wayne A. Meeks, 99–117. Minneapolis: Fortress, 1990.

Geertz, Clifford. "Religion as a Cultural System." In *The Interpretation of Cultures: Selected Essays*, 87–125. New York: Basic Books, 1973.

Gellner, Ernest. *Nations and Nationalism.* Ithaca: Cornell University Press, 1983.

Georgi, Dieter. *The Opponents of Paul in Second Corinthians.* Philadelphia: Fortress, 1986.

Golb, Norman. *Who Wrote the Dead Sea Scrolls?: The Search for the Secret of Qumran.* New York: Scribner, 1995.

Goldstein, Jonathan A. *I Maccabees: A New Translation, with Introduction and Commentary.* The Anchor Bible. Garden City, NY: Doubleday, 1976.

Goodacre, Mark S. *The Case against Q: Studies in Markan Priority and the Synoptic Problem.* Harrisburg, PA: Trinity, 2002.

Goodman, Martin. "Josephus' Treatise *Against Apion*." In *Apologetics in the Roman Empire: Pagans, Jews, and Christians*, edited by M. J. Edwards, S. R. F. Price, and Christopher Rowland, 45–58. Oxford: Oxford University Press, 1999.

———. *The Ruling Class of Judaea: The Origins of the Jewish Revolt against Rome A.D. 66–70.* Cambridge: Cambridge University Press, 1987.

Grant, Robert M. *Greek Apologists of the Second Century.* Philadelphia: Westminster, 1988.

Graves, Robert. *King Jesus.* New York: Farrar, Straus & Cudahy, 1946.

Gray, Rebecca. *Prophetic Figures in Late Second Temple Jewish Palestine: The Evidence from Josephus.* Oxford: Oxford University Press, 1993.

Greenfield, Jonas C. "The Words of Levi Son of Jacob in Damascus Document IV, 15–19." *Revue de Qûmran* 13 (1988): 319–22.

Griffiths, Paul J. *Problems of Religious Diversity.* Malden, MA: Blackwell, 2001.

Hagner, Donald A. "Matthew: Apostate, Reformer, Revolutionary?" *NTS* 49, no. 2 (2003): 193–209.

Hanson, Paul D. *The Dawn of Apocalyptic.* Philadelphia: Fortress, 1975.

Hare, Douglas R. A. "How Jewish Is the Gospel of Matthew?" *CBQ* 62, no. 2 (2000): 264–77.

Harrill, James Albert. *The Manumission of Slaves in Early Christianity.* Hermeneutische Untersuchungen zur Theologie. Tübingen: Mohr (Siebeck), 1995.

Hays, Richard B. *Echoes of Scripture in the Letters of Paul.* New Haven: Yale University Press, 1989.

Hempel, Charlotte. "Community Origins in the *Damascus Document* in Light of Recent Scholarship." In *The Provo International Conference on the Dead Sea Scrolls: Technological Innovations, New Texts, and Reformulated Issues*, edited by Donald W. Parry and Eugene Charles Ulrich, 316–29. Leiden: Brill, 1999.

———. "The Laws of the Damascus Document and 4QMMT." In *The Damascus Document: A Centennial of Discovery*, edited by Joseph M. Baumgarten, Esther G. Chazon, and Avital Pinnick, 69–84. Studies of the Texts of the Desert of Judah. Leiden: Brill, 2000.

Hengel, Martin. *Crucifixion in the Ancient World and the Folly of the Message of the Cross.* Philadelphia: Fortress, 1977.

Hilgenfeld, Adolf. *Die Ketzergeschichte des Urchristentums.* Hildesheim: Georg Olms, 1966. Leipzig, 1884.

Hill, Craig C. *Hellenists and Hebrews: Reappraising Division within the Earliest Church.* Minneapolis: Fortress, 1992.

Holladay, William Lee. *Jeremiah 1: A Commentary on the Book of the Prophet Jeremiah, Chapters 1–25.* Hermeneia. Philadelphia: Fortress, 1986.

————. *Jeremiah 2: A Commentary on the Book of the Prophet Jeremiah, Chapters 26–52.* Hermeneia. Minneapolis: Fortress, 1989.

Hollenbach, Paul W. "John the Baptist." In *The Anchor Bible Dictionary,* edited by David N. Freedman, 3.887–99. 6 vols. New York: Doubleday, 1992.

Holtzmann, H. J. *Die synoptischen Evangelien: ihr Ursprung und geschichtlicher Charakter.* Leipzig, 1863.

Horgan, Maurya P. *Pesharim: Qumran Interpretations of Biblical Books.* Washington: Catholic Biblical Association of America, 1979.

Horrell, David. "The Peaceable, Tolerant Community and the Legitimate Role of the State: Ethics and Ethical Dilemmas in Romans 12:1–15:13." *RevExp* 100, no. 1 (2003): 81–99.

Horsley, Richard A., ed. *Paul and Empire: Religion and Power in Roman Imperial Society.* Harrisburg, PA: Trinity, 1997.

————. "Religion and Other Products of Empire." *JAAR* 71, no. 1 (2003): 13–44.

Horsley, Richard A., with John S. Hanson. *Bandits, Prophets, and Messiahs: Popular Movements in the Time of Jesus.* 2nd ed. Harrisburg, PA: Trinity, 1999.

Hultgren, Arland J. *The Rise of Normative Christianity.* Minneapolis: Fortress, 1994.

Hurtado, Larry W. *Lord Jesus Christ: Devotion to Jesus in Earliest Christianity.* Grand Rapids: Eerdmans, 2003.

Jameson, Frederic R. *The Political Unconscious: Narrative as a Socially Symbolic Act.* Ithaca, NY: Cornell University Press, 1982.

Jenkins, Richard. *Social Identity.* London: Routledge, 1996.

Jeremias, Joachim. *The Parables of Jesus.* Rev. ed. New York: Scribner, 1963.

Jewett, Robert. "Agitators and the Galatian Congregation." *NTS* 17 (1971): 198–212.

Johnson, Lee A. "Satan Talk in Corinth: The Rhetoric of Conflict." *BTB* 29 (1999): 145–55.

Johnson, Luke Timothy. "The New Testament's Anti-Jewish Slander and the Conventions of Ancient Polemic." *JBL* 108 (1989): 419–41.

Josephus, Flavius. *Flavii Iosephi Opera Edidit Et Apparatu Critico Instruxit Benedictus Niese.* Berlin: Weidmann (BibleWorks 9), 1887.

————. *Works.* Translated by H. St. J. Thackeray. 10 vols. Loeb Classical Library. London: Heinemann, 1926.

Justin Martyr. *Oeuvres Complètes: Grande Apologie, Dialogue avec le Juif Tryphon, Requête, Traité de la Résurrection.* Edited by Adalbert G. Hamman, Georges Archambault, Louis Pautigny, and Élisabeth Gauché. Paris: Migne, 1994.

Juvenal and Persius. Translated by G. G. Ramsay. Loeb Classical Library. Cambridge, MA: Heinemann, 1918.

Kampen, John. *The Hasideans and the Origin of Pharisaism: A Study in 1 and 2 Maccabees.* Atlanta: Scholars Press, 1988.

Kampmann, Ursula. "Homonoia Politics in Asia Minor: The Example of Pergamon." In *Pergamon, Citadel of the Gods,* edited by Helmut Koester, 373–93. Harrisburg, PA: Trinity, 1998.

Käsemann, Ernst. "Die Legitimität des Apostels. Eine Untersuchung zu II Korinther 10–13." *ZNW* 41 (1942): 33–71.

Kasser, Rodolphe, Marvin W. Meyer, and Gregor Wurst. *The Gospel of Judas: From Codex Tchacos.* Washington: National Geographic, 2006.

Katz, Steven T. "Issues in the Separation of Judaism and Christianity after 70 CE: A Reconsideration." *JBL* 103 (1984): 43–76.

Kelhoffer, James A. *The Diet of John the Baptist: "Locusts and Wild Honey" in Synoptic and Patristic Interpretation.* Tübingen: Mohr (Siebeck), 2005.

Kimelman, Reuven. "*Birkat Ha-Minim* and the Lack of Evidence for an Anti-Christian Prayer in Late Antiquity." In *Jewish and Christian Self-Definition*, Vol. 2, edited by E. P. Sanders, Albert I. Baumgarten, and Alan Mendelson, 226–44. London: SCM Press, 1981.

King, Karen L. *The Gospel of Mary of Magdala: Jesus and the First Woman Apostle.* Santa Rosa, CA: Polebridge, 2003.

———. *What Is Gnosticism?* Cambridge, MA: Belknap Press of Harvard University Press, 2003.

Kloppenborg, John S. *The Formation of Q: Trajectories in Ancient Wisdom Collections.* 2nd ed. Harrisburg, PA: Trinity, 1999.

———. *Q-Thomas Reader.* Sonoma, CA: Polebridge, 1990.

Knust, Jennifer Wright. *Abandoned to Lust: Sexual Slander and Ancient Christianity.* New York: Columbia University Press, 2006.

Koester, Helmut. *Ancient Christian Gospels: Their History and Development.* London: SCM Press, 1990.

———. "GNŌMAI DIAPHORAI: The Origin and Nature of Diversification in the History of Early Christianity." In *Trajectories through Early Christianity*, edited by James M. Robinson and Helmut Koester, 114–57. Philadelphia: Fortress, 1971.

———. *Synoptische Überlieferung bei den apostolischen Vätern.* Berlin: Akademie-Verlag, 1957.

Kugler, Robert A. *From Patriarch to Priest: The Levi-Priestly Tradition from Aramaic Levi to Testament of Levi.* Atlanta: Scholars Press, 1996.

Kümmel, Werner Georg. *The New Testament: The History of the Investigation of Its Problems.* Nashville: Abingdon, 1972.

Lampe, Peter. *From Paul to Valentinus: Christians at Rome in the First Two Centuries.* Translated by Michael Steinhauser. Minneapolis: Fortress, 2003.

Lausberg, Heinrich. *Handbook of Literary Rhetoric: A Foundation for Literary Study.* Translated by Matthew T. Bliss, Annemiek Janswen, and David E. Orton. Leiden: Brill, 1998.

Layton, Bentley A. *The Gnostic Scriptures: A New Translation with Annotations and Introductions.* Anchor Yale Bible Reference Library. New York: Doubleday, 1995.

———. "The Significance of Basilides in Ancient Christian Thought." *Representations* 28 (1989): 135–51.

Le Boulluec, Alain. *La Notion D'hérésie dans la Littérature Grecque IIe-IIIe Siècles. Tome I, De Justin À Irénée.* 2 vols. Paris: Etudes Augustiniennes, 1985.

Liddell, H. G. R., H. S. Scott, and A. Jones. *A Greek-English Lexicon.* 9th ed. with revised supplement. Oxford: Oxford University Press, 1996.

Lieu, Judith. *Christian Identity in the Jewish and Graeco-Roman World.* Oxford: Oxford University Press, 2004.

———. "'The Parting of the Ways': Theological Construct or Historical Reality?" *JSNT* 56 (1994): 101–19.

Lincoln, Andrew T. "The Household Code and Wisdom Mode of Colossians." *JSNT*, no. 74 (1999): 93–112.

Linnemann, Eta. *Jesus of the Parables: Introduction and Exposition.* New York: Harper & Row, 1967.

Lipsius, Richard Adelbert. *Die Quellen der ältesten Ketzergeschichte.* Leipzig: Johann Ambrosius Barth, 1875.

Lopez, Davina C. *Apostle to the Conquered: Reimagining Paul's Mission.* Paul in Critical Contexts. Minneapolis: Fortress, 2008.

Lührmann, Dieter. *Die Redaktion der Logienquelle.* Wissenschaftliche Monographien zum Alten und Neuen Testament 33. Neukirchen-Vluyn: Neukirchener Verlag, 1969.

———. "Neutestamentliche Haustafeln und antike Ökonomie." *NTS* 27 (1980): 83–97.

Luomanen, Petri. "The 'Sociology of Sectarianism' in Matthew: Modeling the Genesis of Early Jewish and Christian Communities." In *Fair Play: Diversity and Conflicts in Early Christianity: Essays in Honour of Heikki Räisänen*, edited by Heikki Räisänen, Ismo Dunderberg, C. M. Tuckett, and Kari Syreeni, 107–30. Leiden: Brill, 2002.

Lyman, J. Rebecca. "Hellenism and Heresy (2002 NAPS Presidential Address)." *JECS* 11, no. 2 (2003): 209–22.

———. "The Making of a Heretic: The Life of Origen in Epiphanius *Panarion* 64." *StPatr* 31 (1997): 445–51.

———. "The Politics of Passing: Justin Martyr's Conversion as a Problem of Hellenization." In *Conversion in Late Antiquity and the Early Middle Ages: Seeing and Believing*, edited by Kenneth Mills and Anthony Grafton, 36–60. Studies in Comparative History. Rochester: University of Rochester Press, 2003.

Mack, Burton L. *A Myth of Innocence: Mark and Christian Origins*. Philadelphia: Fortress, 1988.

———. *Who Wrote the New Testament?: The Making of the Christian Myth*. San Francisco: HarperSan Francisco, 1995.

MacMullen, Ramsay. *Enemies of the Roman Order: Treason, Unrest, and Alienation in the Empire*. Cambridge, MA: Harvard University Press, 1966.

Magie, David. *Roman Rule in Asia Minor: To the End of the Third Century after Christ*. 2 vols. Princeton: Princeton University Press, 1950.

Magness, Jodi. *The Archaeology of Qumran and the Dead Sea Scrolls*. Studies in the Dead Sea Scrolls and Related Literature. Grand Rapids: Eerdmans, 2002.

Malherbe, Abraham J. "Antisthenes and Odysseus, and Paul at War." *HTR* 76 (1983): 143–73.

———. *Moral Exhortation: A Greco-Roman Sourcebook*. Philadelphia: Westminster Press, 1986.

———. *Paul and the Popular Philosophers*. Minneapolis: Fortress Press, 1989.

Marcovich, Miroslav, ed. *Iustini Martyris Dialogus cum Tryphone*. Berlin: Walter de Gruyter, 1997.

Marjanen, Antti, and Petri Luomanen. *A Companion to Second-Century Christian "Heretics"*. Leiden: Brill, 2005.

Marshall, Peter. *Enmity in Corinth: Social Conventions in Paul's Relations with the Corinthians*. Wissenschaftliche Untersuchungen zum Neuen Testament. Tübingen: Mohr (Siebeck), 1987.

Martin, Dale B. *The Corinthian Body*. New Haven: Yale University Press, 1995.

———. *Inventing Superstition: From the Hippocratics to the Christians*. Cambridge, MA: Harvard University Press, 2004.

———. *Slavery as Salvation: The Metaphor of Slavery in Pauline Christianity*. New Haven: Yale University Press, 1990.

Martin, Dale B., and Patricia Cox Miller, eds. *The Cultural Turn in Late Ancient Studies: Gender, Asceticism, and Historiography*. Durham: Duke University Press, 2005.

Martyn, J. Louis. "Apocalyptic Antinomies in Paul's Letter to the Galatians." *NTS* 31 (1985): 410–24.

———. *Galatians: A New Translation with Introduction and Commentary*. Anchor Bible. New York: Doubleday, 1998.

———. *History & Theology in the Fourth Gospel*. 2nd ed. Nashville: Abingdon, 1979.

Marxsen, Willi. *Mark the Evangelist: Studies on the Redaction History of the Gospel*. Translated by James Boyce et al. Nashville: Abingdon, 1969.

McKenzie, S. L. "Deuteronomic History." In *The Anchor Bible Dictionary*, edited by David N. Freedman, 2.160–68. 6 vols. New York: Doubleday, 1992.

Meeks, Wayne A. "Breaking Away: Three New Testament Pictures of Christianity's Separation from the Jewish Communities." In *To See Ourselves as Others See Us*: *Christians, Jews, and "Others" in Late Antiquity*, edited by Jacob Neusner and E. S. Frerichs, 93–115. Chico, CA: Scholars Press, 1985.

———. *The First Urban Christians: The Social World of the Apostle Paul*. New Haven: Yale University Press, 1983.

———. *The Origins of Christian Morality: The First Two Centuries*. New Haven: Yale University Press, 1993.

———. "Social Functions of Apocalyptic Language in Pauline Christianity." In *Apocalypticism in the Mediterranean World and the near East*, edited by David Hellholm, 687–705. Tübingen: Mohr (Siebeck), 1983.

———. *The Writings of St. Paul*. New York: Norton, 1972.

Meeks, Wayne A., and Jouette M. Bassler, eds. *The HarperCollins Study Bible: New Revised Standard Version, with the Apocryphal/Deuterocanonical Books*. New York: HarperCollins, 1993.

Meier, John P. *A Marginal Jew: Rethinking the Historical Jesus*. Anchor Yale Bible Reference Library. 4 vols. New York: Doubleday, 1991.

Mendels, Doron. *The Land of Israel as a Political Concept in Hasmonean Literature: Recourse to History in Second Century B.C. Claims to the Holy Land*. Tübingen: Mohr, 1987.

Metso, Sarianna. "In Search of the *Sitz im Leben* of the Community Rule." In *The Provo International Conference on the Dead Sea Scrolls: Technological Innovations, New Texts, and Reformulated Issues*, edited by Donald W. Parry and Eugene Charles Ulrich, 306–15. Leiden: Brill, 1999.

Middlemas, Jill Anne. *The Troubles of Templeless Judah*. Oxford: Oxford University Press, 2005.

Mitchell, Margaret Mary. *Paul and the Rhetoric of Reconciliation: An Exegetical Investigation of the Language and Composition of 1 Corinthians*. Hermeneutische Untersuchungen zur Theologie. Tübingen: Mohr (Siebeck), 1991.

Motyer, Stephen. *Your Father the Devil?: A New Approach to John and 'the Jews'*. Carlisle, UK: Paternoster, 1997.

Munier, Charles. *Saint Justin Apologie pour les Chrétiens: Édition et Traduction*. Paradosis. Fribourg, Switzerland: Éditions universitaires, 1995.

Murphy-O'Connor, J. *St. Paul's Corinth: Texts and Archaeology*. Wilmington, DE: Michael Glazier, 1983.

Netzer, Ehud. *The Palaces of the Hasmonean and Herod the Great*. Jerusalem: Israel Exploration Society, 2001.

Neusner, Jacob. *From Politics to Piety: The Emergence of Pharasaic Judaism*. Englewood, NJ: Prentice-Hall, 1973.

———. *Judaism and Christianity in the Age of Constantine: History, Messiah, Israel, and the Initial Confrontation*. Chicago: University of Chicago Press, 1987.

Nickelsburg, George W. E. *Jewish Literature between the Bible and the Mishnah: A Historical and Literary Introduction*. Philadelphia: Fortress, 1981.

Niebuhr, H. Richard. *Christ and Culture*. San Francisco: HarperSanFrancisco, 2001.

Niederwimmer, Kurt. *The Didache: A Commentary*. Hermeneia. Minneapolis: Fortress, 1998.

Nirenberg, David. *Communities of Violence: Persecution of Minorities in the Middle Ages*. Princeton: Princeton University Press, 1996.

North, Wendy Sproston. "John for Readers of Mark? A Response to Richard Bauckham's Proposal." *JSNT* 25, no. 4 (2003): 449–68.

Økland, Jorunn. *Women in Their Place: Paul and the Corinthian Discourse of Gender and Sanctuary Space*. Journal for the Study of the Old Testament Supplement. Edinburgh: T & T Clark, 2004.

Overman, J. Andrew. *Matthew's Gospel and Formative Judaism: The Social World of the Matthean Community*. Minneapolis: Fortress, 1990.

Pagels, Elaine H. *Beyond Belief: The Secret Gospel of Thomas*. New York: Random House, 2003.

———. "Christian Apologists and 'the Fall of the Angels': An Attack on Roman Imperial Power?" *HTR* 78, no. 3–4 (1985): 301–25.

———. "Irenaeus, the 'Canon of Truth,' and the Gospel of John: 'Making a Difference' through Hermeneutics and Ritual." *VC* 56, no. 4 (2002): 339–71.

———. *The Origin of Satan*. New York: Random House, 1995.

———. "The Social History of Satan Part Three, John of Patmos and Ignatius of Antioch: Contrasting Visions of 'God's People.'" *HTR* 99, no. 4 (2006): 487–505.

Pagels, Elaine H., and Karen L. King. *Reading Judas: The Gospel of Judas and the Shaping of Christianity*. New York: Viking, 2007.

Philo of Alexandria. *Philo in Ten Volumes and Two Supplementary Volumes*. Translated by F. H. Colson, G. H. Whitaker, and Ralph Marcus. 12 vols. Loeb Classical Library. London: Heinemann, 1966.

Pippin, Tina. *Death and Desire: The Rhetoric of Gender in the Apocalypse of John*. Louisville: Westminster/John Knox, 1992.

Pliny the Elder. *Natural History*. Translated by H. Rackham. 10 vols. Loeb Classical Library. Cambridge: Harvard University Press, 1958.

Pliny the Younger. *Letters, and Panegyricus*. Translated by Betty Radice. 2 vols. Loeb Classical Library. Cambridge: Harvard University Press, 1969.

Pohlmann, Karl-Friedrich. *Studien zum Jeremiabuch: Ein Beitrage zur Frage nach der Entstehung des Jeremiabuches*. Göttingen: Vandenhoeck und Ruprecht, 1978.

Poirier, John C. "Purity Beyond the Temple in the Second Temple Era." *JBL* 122, no. 2 (2003): 247–65.

Price, S. R. F. *Rituals and Power: The Roman Imperial Cult in Asia Minor*. Cambridge: Cambridge University Press, 1984.

Pury, Albert de, and Thomas Römer. "Deuteronomistic Historiography (Dh): History of Research and Debated Issues." In *Israel Constructs Its History*, edited by Albert de Pury, Thomas Römer, and Jean-Daniel Macchi, 24–141. Sheffield: Sheffield Academic Press, 2000.

Qimron, Elisha, and James H. Charlesworth et al. "Some Works of the Torah." In *The Dead Sea Scrolls: Hebrew, Aramaic, and Greek Texts with English Translations, Vol. 3*, edited by James H. Charlesworth and Frank Moore Cross, 187–251. Tübingen: Mohr (Siebeck), 1993.

Qimron, Elisha, and John Strugnell. *Qumrân Cave 4. 5 V: Miqṣat Ma'aśē Ha-Torah*. Oxford: Clarendon Press 1994.

Rahmani, L. Y. "Jason's Tomb." *IEJ* 17, no. 2 (1967): 61–100.

Räisänen, Heikki. *Paul and the Law*. 2nd ed. Tübingen: Mohr (Siebeck), 1987.

Reed, Annette Yoshiko. "The Trickery of the Fallen Angels and the Demonic Mimesis of the Divine: Aetiology, Demonology, and Polemics in the Writings of Justin Martyr." *JECS* 12, no. 2 (2004): 141–71.

Reitzenstein, Richard. *Die hellenistischen Mysterienreligionen: Ihre Grundgedanken und Wirkungen*. Leipzig: Teubner, 1910.

Richards, E. Randolph. *The Secretary in the Letters of Paul*. Wissenschaftliche Untersuchungen zum Neuen Testament. Tübingen: Mohr (Siebeck), 1991.

Richardson, Cyril Charles. *Early Christian Fathers*. New York: Macmillan, 1970.

Riley, Gregory J. *The River of God: A New History of Christian Origins*. San Francisco: HarperSanFrancisco, 2001.

Robbins, Vernon K. "Rhetorical Composition and Sources in the Gospel of Thomas." *SBLSP* 36 (1997): 86–114.

Robinson, James M. "Logoi Sophon: On the *Gattung* of Q." In *One Jesus and Four Primitive Gospels: Trajectories through Early Christianity*, edited by James M. Robinson and Helmut Koester, 71–113. Philadelphia: Fortress, 1971.

———, ed. *The Nag Hammadi Library in English*. 3rd ed. San Francisco: Harper & Row, 1988.

Robinson, James M., Paul Hoffmann, and John S. Kloppenborg. *The Critical Edition of Q: Synopsis Including the Gospels of Matthew and Luke, Mark and Thomas with English, German, and French Translations of Q and Thomas*. Philadelphia: Fortress, 2000.

Robinson, James M., and Helmut Koester, eds. *One Jesus and Four Primitive Gospels: Trajectories through Early Christianity*. Philadelphia: Fortress, 1971.

Rossing, Barbara R. *The Choice between Two Cities: Whore, Bride, and Empire in the Apocalypse*. Harrisburg, PA: Trinity, 1999.

Rossini, Orietta. *Ara Pacis*. Milan: Electa, 2007.

Royalty, Robert M. Jr. "Dwelling on Visions: On the Nature of the So-Called 'Colossians Heresy.'" *Bib* 83, no. 3 (2002): 329–57.

———. "Justin's Conversion and the Rhetoric of Heresy." *StPatr* 40 (2006): 509–14.

———. *The Streets of Heaven: The Ideology of Wealth in the Apocalypse of John*. Macon, GA: Mercer University Press, 1998.

Saldarini, Anthony J. "Delegitimation of Leaders in Matthew 23." *CBQ* 54 (1992): 659–80.

———. *Matthew's Christian-Jewish Community*. Chicago: University of Chicago Press, 1994.

———. *Pharisees, Scribes and Sadducees in Palestinian Society: A Sociological Approach*. Wilmington, DE: Michael Glazier, 1988.

Sanders, E. P. *The Historical Figure of Jesus*. London: Allen Lane, 1993.

———. *Jesus and Judaism*. Philadelphia: Fortress, 1985.

———. "Jesus and the Sinners." *JSNT* 19 (1983): 5–36.

———. *Paul and Palestinian Judaism: A Comparison of Patterns of Religion*. Philadelphia: Fortress, 1977.

Sandmel, Samuel. *The Genius of Paul: A Study in History*. Philadelphia: Fortress, 1979.

Schiffman, Lawrence H. "The New Halakhic Letter (4QMMT) and the Origins of the Dead Sea Sect." *BA* 53 (1990): 64–73.

———. *Reclaiming the Dead Sea Scrolls: The History of Judaism, the Background of Christianity, the Lost Library of Qumran*. Philadelphia: Jewish Publication Society, 1994.

———. *Understanding Second Temple and Rabbinic Judaism*. Jersey City, NJ: Ktav, 2003.

Schmithals, Walter. *Gnosticism in Corinth: An Investigation of the Letters to the Corinthians*. Translated by John E. Steely. Nashville: Abingdon, 1971.

Schoedel, William. *Ignatius of Antioch*. Hermeneia. Philadelphia: Fortress, 1985.

Schofield, Alison, and James C. VanderKam. "Were the Hasmoneans Zadokites?" *JBL* 124, no. 1 (2005): 73–87.

Schubert, Paul. *Form and Function of the Pauline Thanksgivings*. Berlin: Alfred Töplemann, 1939.

Schüssler Fiorenza, Elisabeth. *In Memory of Her: A Feminist Theological Reconstruction of Christian Origins*. New York: Crossroad, 1984.

Schütz, John Howard. *Paul and the Anatomy of Apostolic Authority*. London: Cambridge University Press, 1975.

Schwab, Eckard. "Das Dürremotiv in I Regum 17:8–16." *ZAW* 99, no. 3 (1987): 329–39.

Schwartz, Daniel R. "The Other in 1 and 2 Maccabees." In *Tolerance and Intolerance in Early Judaism and Christianity*, edited by Graham Stanton and

Gedaliahu A. G. Stroumsa, 30–37. Cambridge: Cambridge University Press, 1998.

Schwartz, Seth. *Imperialism and Jewish Society, 200 B.C.E. To 640 C.E.* Princeton: Princeton University Press, 2001.

———. "A Note on the Social Type and Political Ideology of the Hasmonean Family." *JBL* 112 (1993): 305–9.

Schweitzer, Albert. *The Quest of the Historical Jesus: A Critical Study of Its Progress from Reimarus to Wrede.* Baltimore, MD: Johns Hopkins University Press with the Albert Schweitzer Institute, 1998.

Schweitzer, Albert, and W. Montgomery. *The Mysticism of Paul the Apostle.* New York: Holt, 1931.

Schweizer, Eduard. *Church Order in the New Testament.* London: SCM, 1961.

Scott, Bernard Brandon. "The King's Accounting: Matthew 18:23–34." *JBL* 104, no. 3 (1985): 429–42.

Segal, Alan F. *Paul the Convert: The Apostolate and Apostasy of Saul the Pharisee.* New Haven: Yale University Press, 1990.

Seitz, Christopher R. "The Crisis of Interpretation over the Meaning and Purpose of the Exile: A Redactional Study of Jeremiah 21–43." *VT* 35, no. 1 (1985): 78–97.

Shemesh, Aharon, and Cana Werman. "Halakhah at Qumran: Genre and Authority." *DSD* 10, no. 1 (2003): 104–29.

Sheppard, A. R. R. "'Homonoia' in the Greek Cities of the Roman Empire." *Ancient Society* 15 (1984): 229–52.

Sherwin-White, A. N. "Why Were the Early Christians Persecuted?—an Amendment." *Past & Present*, no. 27 (1964): 23–27.

Sievers, Joseph. *The Hasmoneans and Their Supporters: From Mattathias to the Death of John Hyrcanus I.* Atlanta: Scholars Press, 1990.

Sim, David C. *The Gospel of Matthew and Christian Judaism: The History and Social Setting of the Matthean Community.* Edinburgh: T&T Clark, 1998.

———. "Matthew 7.21–23: Further Evidence of Its Anti-Pauline Perspective." *NTS* 53 (2007): 325–43.

Simon, Marcel. "From Greek Hairesis to Christian Heresy." In *Early Christian Literature and the Classical Intellectual Tradition: In Honorem Robert M. Grant*, edited by William R. Schoedel and Robert L. Wilken, 101–16. Paris: Editions Beauchesne, 1979.

Smith, Jonathan Z. "What a Difference a Difference Makes." In *"To See Ourselves as Others See Us"*, edited by Jacob Neusner and Ernest S. Frerichs, 3–48. Chico, CA: Scholars Press, 1985.

Smith, Mark S. *The Early History of God: Yahweh and the Other Deities in Ancient Israel.* 2nd ed. Grand Rapids: Eerdmans, 2002.

Smith, Morton. "Zealots and Sicarii, Their Origins and Relation." *HTR* 64, no. 1 (1971): 1–19.

Snyder, H. Gregory. *Teachers and Texts in the Ancient World: Philosophers, Jews, and Christians.* London: Routledge, 2000.

Spilsbury, Paul. "Flavius Josephus on the Rise and Fall of the Roman Empire." *JTS* 54, no. 1 (2003): 1–24.

Standhartinger, Angela. "The Origin and Intention of the Household Code in the Letter to the Colossians." *JSNT* 79 (2000): 117–30.

Stanton, Graham. *A Gospel for a New People: Studies in Matthew.* Louisville: Westminster/John Knox, 1993.

Sterling, Gregory E. "Explaining Defeat: Polybius and Josephus on the Wars with Rome." In *Internationales Josephus-Kolloquium: Aarhus 1999*, edited by Jürgen U. Kalms, 135–51. Münster: Lit, 1999.

———. *Historiography and Self-Definition: Josephos, Luke-Acts, and Apologetic Historiography.* Supplements to Novum Testamentum. Leiden: Brill, 1991.

224   Bibliography

———. "'Philo Has Not Been Used Half Enough': The Significance of Philo of Alexandria for the Study of the New Testament." *Perspectives in Religious Studies* 30, no. 3 (Fall 2003): 251–69.

Stone, Michael E. "The Book of Enoch and Judaism in the Third Century, B.C.E." *CBQ* 40 (1978): 479–92.

———. "Categorization and Classification of the Apocrypha and Pseudepigrapha." *AbrN* 24 (1986): 167–77.

———. *Fourth Ezra: A Commentary on the Book of Fourth Ezra.* Hermeneia. Minneapolis: Augsburg Fortress, 1990.

———. "Reactions to Destructions of the Second Temple: Theology, Perception and Conversion." *JSJ* 12 (1981): 195–204.

Stowers, Stanley. *The Diatribe and Paul's Letter to the Romans.* Society of Biblical Literature Dissertation Series. Chico, CA: Scholars Press, 1981.

———. *A Rereading of Romans: Justice, Jews, and Gentiles.* New Haven: Yale University Press, 1994.

Streeter, B. H. *The Four Gospels: A Study of Origins.* London: Macmillan 1924.

Stulman, Louis. "Insiders and Outsiders in the Book of Jeremiah: Shifts in Symbolic Arrangements." *JSOT* 66, no. 1 (1995): 65–85.

———. "The Prose Sermons as Hermeneutical Guide to Jeremiah 1–25: The Deconstruction of Judah's Symbolic World." In *Troubling Jeremiah*, edited by A. R. Diamond, Kathleen M. O'Connor, and Louis Stulman, 34–63. Sheffield: Sheffield Academic Press, 1999.

Sugirtharajah, R. S. "Postcolonial Theory and Biblical Studies." In *Fair Play: Diversity and Conflicts in Early Christianity: Essays in Honour of Heikki Räisänen*, edited by Heikki Räisänen, Ismo Dunderberg, C. M. Tuckett, and Kari Syreeni, 541–52. Leiden: Brill, 2002.

Sumney, Jerry L. *'Servants of Satan', 'False Brothers' and Other Opponents of Paul.* Sheffield: Sheffield Academic Press, 1999.

Sundermann, Hans-Georg. *Der schwache Apostel und die Kraft der Rede: Eine rhetorische Analyse von 2 Kor 10–13.* Frankfurt am Main: P. Lang, 1996.

Sweeney, Marvin A. "The Critique of Solomon in the Josianic Edition of the Deuteronomistic History." *JBL* 114 (1995): 607–22.

———. "Structure and Redaction in Jeremiah 2–6." In *Troubling Jeremiah*, edited by A. R. Diamond, Kathleen M. O'Connor, and Louis Stulman, 200–218. Sheffield, England: Sheffield Academic Press, 1999.

Taylor, Joan E. *The Immerser: John the Baptist within Second Temple Judaism.* Grand Rapids: Eerdmans, 1997.

Theissen, Gerd. *The Gospels in Context: Social and Political History in the Synoptic Tradition.* Minneapolis: Fortress, 1991.

———. *The Social Setting of Pauline Christianity.* Translated by and with an introduction by John Schütz. Philadelphia: Fortress, 1982.

———. *Sociology of Early Palestinian Christianity.* Philadelphia: Fortress, 1978.

Thompson, Leonard L. *The Book of Revelation: Apocalypse and Empire.* Oxford: Oxford University Press, 1990.

Thompson, Michael B. "The Holy Internet: Communication between Churches in the First Christian Generation." In *The Gospels for All Christians: Rethinking the Gospel Audience*, edited by Richard Bauckham, 49–70. Edinburgh: T&T Clark, 1998.

Thompson, William G. *Matthew's Advice to a Divided Community.* Rome: Biblical Institute Press, 1970.

Thornton, T. C. G. "High-Priestly Succession in Jewish Apologetics and Episcopal Succession in Hegesippus." *JTS* 54 (2003): 160–63.

Thrall, Margaret E. *A Critical and Exegetical Commentary on the Second Epistle to the Corinthians.* 2 vols. International Critical Commentary. Edinburgh: T&T Clark, 1994.

————. "Super-Apostles, Servants of Christ, and Servants of Satan." *JSNT* 6 (1980): 42–57.

Throckmorton, B. H. *Gospel Parallels: A Comparison of the Synoptic Gospels, with Alternative Readings from the Manuscripts and Noncanonical Parallels.* 5th ed. Nashville: Nelson, 1992.

Treggiari, Susan. *Roman Marriage: Iusti Coniuges from the Time of Cicero to the Time of Ulpian.* Oxford: Clarendon, 1991.

Trevett, Christine. "Prophecy and Anti-Episcopal Activity: A Third Error Combated by Ignatius?" *JEH* 34, no. 1 (1983): 1–18.

Trilling, Wolfgang. *Das wahre Israel: Studien zur Theologie des Matthäusevangeliums.* 2nd. ed. Leipzig: St. Benno-Verlag, 1961.

Tuckett, Christopher M. "Synoptic Tradition in Some Nag Hammadi and Related Texts." *VC* 36, no. 2 (1982): 173–90.

Uro, Risto. *Thomas at the Crossroads: Essays on the Gospel of Thomas.* Edinburgh: T&T Clark, 1998.

Valantasis, Richard. *The Gospel of Thomas.* London: Routledge, 1997.

Vermès, Géza. *The Complete Dead Sea Scrolls in English.* New York: Allen Lane/Penguin, 1997.

Vermès, Géza, and Martin D. Goodman. *The Essenes, According to the Classical Sources.* Sheffield: JSOT/Oxford Centre for Postgraduate Hebrew Studies, 1989.

Veyne, Paul. "La Famille et L'amour sous le Haut-Empire Romain." *Annales (ESC)* 33 (1978): 35–63.

Viswanathan, Gauri. *Outside the Fold: Conversion, Modernity, and Belief.* Princeton: Princeton University Press, 1998.

Von Staden, Heinrich. "Hairesis and Heresy: The Case of the 'Haireseis Iatrikai'." In *Jewish and Christian Self-Definition: Self-Definition in the Greco-Roman World,* edited by B. F. Meyer and E. P Sanders. London: SCM, 1982.

Walaskay, Paul W. *"And So We Came to Rome": The Political Perspective of St. Luke.* Cambridge: Cambridge University Press, 1983.

Walker, Donald Dale. *Paul's Offer of Leniency (2 Cor 10:1): Populist Ideology and Rhetoric in a Pauline Letter Fragment.* Tübingen: Mohr (Siebeck), 2002.

Watson, Francis. "2 Cor 10–13 and Paul's Painful Letter to the Corinthians." *JTS* 35 (1984): 324–46.

Webb, Robert L. *John the Baptizer and Prophet: A Socio-Historical Study.* Journal for the Study of the Old Testament Supplement. Sheffield: JSOT Press, 1991.

Weber, Max, and Talcott Parsons. *Max Weber: The Theory of Social and Economic Organization.* New York: Free Press, 1964.

Weber, Max, Guenther Roth, and Claus Wittich. *Economy and Society: An Outline of Interpretive Sociology.* 2 vols. Berkeley: University of California Press, 1978.

Wedderburn, A. J. M. *Baptism and Resurrection: Studies in Pauline Theology against Its Graeco-Roman Background.* Tübingen: Mohr (Siebeck), 1987.

Weems, Renita J. *Battered Love: Marriage, Sex, and Violence in the Hebrew Prophets.* Minneapolis: Fortress, 1995.

Welborn, Laurence L. "The Identification of 2 Corinthians 10–13 with the 'Letter of Tears.'" *NovT* 37 (1995): 138–53.

————. "The Runaway Paul." *HTR* 92 (1999): 115–63.

Werman, Cana. "Genesis for Demarcation of Sect or Nation—the Case of *Jubilees.*" Presented at the European Association of Biblical Studies Annual Meeting, Lisbon, 2008.

Westminster Leningrad Codex of the Hebrew Bible. Philadelphia: Westminster Theological Seminary and BibleWorks Software, v.9.

Whealey, Alice. *Josephus on Jesus: The Testimonium Flavianum Controversy from Late Antiquity to Modern Times.* New York: Lang, 2003.

White, Hayden V. *Tropics of Discourse: Essays in Cultural Criticism.* Baltimore: Johns Hopkins University Press, 1985.

Wilson, Robert R. *Prophecy and Society in Ancient Israel.* Philadelphia: Fortress, 1980.

Wire, Antoinette Clark. *The Corinthian Women Prophets: A Reconstruction through Paul's Rhetoric.* Minneapolis: Fortress Press, 1990.

Witherington, Ben. "Liberating Paul: The Justice of God and the Politics of the Apostle." Review of *Liberating Paul,* by Neil Elliott. *JBL* 115, no. 3 (1996): 554–57.

Wright, R. B. "Psalms of Solomon." In *Old Testament Pseudepigrapha,* edited by James H. Charlesworth, 2.639–49. Garden City, NY: Doubleday, 1983.

Xenophon. Translated by C. L. Brownson et al. 5 vols. Loeb Classical Library. London: Heinemann, 1932.

Yadin, Yigael. *The Scroll of the War of the Sons of Light against the Sons of Darkness.* London: Oxford University Press, 1962.

———. *The Temple Scroll.* Jerusalem: Israel Exploration Society, 1983.

Zanker, Paul. *The Power of Images in the Age of Augustus.* Jerome Lectures. Ann Arbor: University of Michigan Press, 1988.

Zeitlin, Solomon. *The Zadokite Fragments: Facsimile of the Manuscripts in the Cairo Genizah Collection in the Possession of the University Library, Cambridge, England.* Philadelphia: Dropsie College for Hebrew and Cognate Learning, 1952.

Zevit, Ziony. *The Religions of Ancient Israel: A Synthesis of Parallactic Approaches.* London: Continuum, 2001.

Zumstein, Jean. *La Condition du Croyant dans L'évangile selon Matthieu.* Göttingen: Vandenhoeck & Ruprecht, 1977.

Index